CW00543386

THE TEACHER

VOLUME ONE

THE TEACHER

Volume One

The Dawning Epoch

Beinsa Douno

SHINING WORD PRESS

LONDON

The Teacher, Volume One: The Dawning Epoch
Beinsa Douno (Peter Deunov)

First published 2016
by Shining Word Press, London

Translated and adapted by Maria Mitovska and Harry Carr

Editorial consultants:
Colum Hayward, Morelle Forster and Joan Fraser

Shining Word Press is an imprint of Polair Publishing

Translation, adaptation and editorial matter
© 2015 Maria Mitovska and Harry Carr
Cover design © 2015 Harry Carr
Cover design consultant: Rob Holmes

A CIP record for this book is available from the British Library

ISBN: 978-1-905398-35-5 (paperback)
978-1-905398-36-2 (hardback)

Set in Joanna and Baskerville
and printed in the United Kingdom
by the Halstan Printing Group, Amersham

My words have been recorded very well and understandably on paper, but what is important is whether they are understood in the mind and the heart. These words are divine, and the Lord requires not that you have them written on paper, but that you have them written in your heart and mind.

The Teacher

Contents

Translators' Note

Peter Deunov (1864–1944) was a spiritual teacher in Bulgaria during the first half of the twentieth century. He taught mostly through lectures, in which he explained and expanded upon important parts of the Bible, especially the words of Jesus. Peter Deunov also had a spiritual name, Beinsa Douno (pronounced Béïnsa Doono), but his disciples called him "Teacher".[1] This translation, by an Anglo-Bulgarian team, has been designed to present the Teacher's lectures in a clear and concise form in modern English.

Peter Deunov spent eleven years travelling throughout Bulgaria studying the character of the people in preparation for his life's work. He constructed his lectures primarily for his contemporary Bulgarian disciples, but he also wanted his teaching to be spread to the world. He said to his disciples,

> My task is to give you the divine teaching. Your task as disciples is to give this teaching to the Bulgarian nation. The task of the Bulgarian nation is to give this teaching to all nations. I will be held responsible before God if I do not fulfil my task. You will be held responsible before God if you do not fulfil yours. And the Bulgarian people will be held responsible before God if they do not fulfil theirs.

Peter Deunov passed away on 27 December 1944, not long after the communists assumed power in Bulgaria. The suppression of the next forty-five years greatly restricted the ability of the disciples who

---

[1] Although Peter Deunov was called 'Учителят' (Oochitélyat), literally meaning 'the Teacher', he is more commonly known in English as 'the Master'. This interpretation was no doubt made to emphasise his spiritual stature. The translators of this edition do not consider that to be necessary, and, while accepting both terms as valid, prefer 'the Teacher' as more fitting.

Written use of 'Учителят' in reference to Peter Deunov can be found as early as January 1915.

knew the Teacher to pass on the living teaching. The authorities isolated them, especially from younger people, evidently so that the teaching would die out with their generation. As a result, only a small group of younger disciples experienced the example, mentoring, love and refined spiritual atmosphere of the Teacher's closest disciples. It was also forbidden for anyone to keep literature relating to the teaching. After 1950 even the secret printing of lectures became too dangerous and came to a halt. Through the decades of prohibition a few select disciples courageously ensured the survival of the published and unpublished lectures. Only with the arrival of democracy in 1989 was it again possible to publish anything about Peter Deunov.

It is best for a disciple to learn through a combination of private study and the guidance of those with greater experience and spiritual development. Unfortunately, the profound loss between generations has left the modern disciple more reliant on the lectures than would otherwise be the case. It is therefore important that the written presentation of the teaching in English be as clear as possible. The Bulgarian translator of this book, Maria Mitovska, has been a disciple for more than forty-five years and was, for over two decades, mentored by several disciples who were close to the Teacher, especially Krum Vuzharov. In general the translators have tried to keep closely to the Teacher's words except where doing so might result in misunderstanding. Accuracy in the conveyance of his intended meaning has been prioritised over the literal reproduction of his speech.

The lectures in this edition are restricted to those in *The Word of the Teacher: Catalogue* (1998). This chronological listing of the Teacher's lectures was begun by Boyan Boev, continued by Elena Andreeva and completed by Lalka Krusteva. Boyan Boev, who was a disciple from at least as early as 1912, was, from 1924, the main recorder of the teacher's conversations. Elena Andreeva became a disciple in 1920 and was chosen by the Teacher to transcribe his lectures. When Lalka Krusteva was young, the Teacher recommended her to Boyan Boev as a future assistant in the documentation of his word. It is possible that other genuine lectures exist, but those in the Catalogue were authenticated by these trusted disciples.

This collection begins in 1903, opening with three messages that have been ascribed to Christ speaking through the Teacher – one in its original record and two by the present translators. The last of these was given in 1904, but the first of Peter Deunov's own talks presented here was not until 1910. The reason for this gap is that very little remains of his early oral teaching. Aside from the annual congresses, there is almost nothing from those missing years.

Of the early lectures that survive, most do so as no more than brief, fragmented notes. For the reader's benefit, the usable parts of these are presented as if they were short but complete talks, but it needs to be borne in mind that they are very much incomplete and may contain statements which lack their full context. Nevertheless, there is important information in these excerpts, and they are also useful as an introduction to the Teacher's vocabulary and style before the longer, more demanding lectures that follow.

In 1914 the recording of the lectures became an organised affair, and the following year saw their first publication, in *Power and Life, Volume One*. It was well known among the Teacher's later disciples that he had said that the core of his teaching was given in the first six volumes of *Power and Life*. These consist of a selection of Sunday lectures given between 1914 and 1924. From the lecture "Behold the Man! The True Human Being" onwards (page 123) the present volume is restricted to *Power and Life* lectures, although supplementary extracts from other talks are included in the footnotes.

The *Power and Life* lectures are not related here in their entirety: some passages have been removed and some condensed.[2] There is good reason to believe the Teacher would want an English version of his teaching to be prepared in this way. Having studied in the United States of America between 1888 and 1895, Peter Deunov had first-hand experience of a cultural environment very different from his homeland. On one occasion he told Krum Vuzharov that, were he to give his teaching to foreigners, he would reduce it to its essence.[3] This edition cautiously adheres to that principle, focussing on what is most important, and

---

[2] This may also apply to lecture and conversation extracts throughout the book, none of which therefore should be assumed to be pure quotation.

[3] Although the Teacher literally said "foreigners", it was tacitly understood that he did not mean all non-Bulgarians, but people from nations whose cultures were most developed in reason, in contrast to the more feeling-led Bulgarian character. Now, in a much-changed world, that development in reason is far more widespread.

extends it to keeping to what is suitable for a present-day readership.[4]

It was disciples, not the Teacher, who chose the lecture titles, and they do not always work well in English. Therefore, new titles have been made for this edition, with the aim of encapsulating the main theme of each lecture as part of an integrated whole. The original Bulgarian lecture titles may be found in the references.

In his classic lecture format, the Teacher would begin by reading a passage from the Bible and then base his talk on it. These opening quotations in the original first six volumes of *Power and Life* are from the 1914 Constantinople Bible. The Revised Version (1885), the authorised revision of the King James Bible (1611), has been used here for direct biblical quotations, as it is from the Teacher's era – indeed, the American Revised Version was among his personal collection of Bibles. Any preliminary words the Teacher might have spoken before he began to read were unrecorded. Therefore, whenever a lecture starts with a quotation, the translators have added a brief opening, such as "Jesus said" or "The Apostle Paul wrote", to lead the reader into it.

The Teacher often made further biblical references as his talks went on. He advised his disciples to study the Bible, for his teaching is built upon scriptural truths and cannot be fully understood without a degree of biblical literacy. In light of this, footnoted citations have been provided, although no claim to comprehensiveness is made. For the reader's convenience, quotation is employed far more than simple referencing. Although these Bible passages were only included to serve the lectures, an unexpected benefit is how much they enrich each other.

In consideration of length, parallel references are omitted. As the Revised Version does not use quotation marks, they have been added to passages that combine narrative and direct speech or quotation. For the sake of elegance, italics are used to indicate words inserted into scriptural verses, instead of author's brackets, and there are no ellipses to indicate omission. Inserted quotation marks, as well as any accompanying changes in punctuation, are not italicised.

This volume extends into 1915, two thirds of the way into the lec-

---

[4] To make shorter versions of the lectures is not unprecedented. The disciples who lived outside Sofia during the Teacher's lifetime might only rarely have had the opportunity of attending his talks. He therefore asked that willing disciples write summaries of the lectures to give to those living in other parts of the country or abroad.

tures of *Power and Life, Volume Two* and over a year into the cataclysm of the First World War. It will be seen that the Teacher apparently alluded to this great conflict several times beforehand with warnings about 1914.[5] Unsurprisingly, he also referred to it after its onset. To assist understanding, as well as giving some context of the times in which the Teacher spoke, historical footnotes have been added but kept to a minimum.

Footnotes are used extensively in this book, a development that occurred organically as the work progressed. In the short, early talks the footnotes often form almost a second main text, bringing them to a wholeness that would otherwise be missing. Thereafter, in the fuller *Power and Life* lectures, their role becomes more supportive. The lectures reward contemplative reading, especially for those who want to work with the teaching. While helpful in this respect, the footnotes also interrupt the natural flow of the Teacher's words. It may therefore be found preferable to read the lectures both with and without the footnotes.

Bulgaria used the Julian calendar until several months after it had entered the First World War. The Julian calendar was twelve days behind the Gregorian calendar in the nineteenth century, and thirteen days behind in the twentieth. In Bulgaria, therefore, Thursday 31 March 1916, in the old style, was followed by Friday 14 April, in the new style. Dates before this changeover are double-dated to represent both calendars: the Julian date/the Gregorian date.

A talk is never completely captured by a written version. A speaker can use variations in the voice, facial expression and gesture to add meaning to what is being said, aspects of communication which go missing in transcription. The Teacher's words read strongly, but he delivered them in a clear, gentle, fluid voice. Even though he did not speak loudly, his words carried to everybody who was listening, even in a packed lecture hall. The Teacher's instruction often appears exacting, but he spoke in the spirit of counsel – not command. The Teacher did not expect his disciples to be able to embody all that he taught, but wanted each person to develop in a way that was natural to him or her. It is therefore the individual disciple's responsibility to come to understand how best to work with this teaching.

This work began at the end of the summer of 2006 with the sim-

---

[5] Elsewhere he was more explicit. In 1944 he said, "Over thirty years ago I foretold there would be a war in 1914 in which Germany would be defeated."

ple idea of making a good translation. Achieving it proved to be less straightforward than imagined. It has taken nine years to come to a satisfactory end product. Every effort has been made to honour the meaning of the lectures while adapting them for contemporary readers of the English language. Nonetheless, the translators acknowledge that the interpretations and editorial decisions made herein are subjective judgements, for which they accept responsibility.

November 2015
Maria Mitovska and Harry Carr

Introduction

According to Peter Deunov, a new epoch began in 1914, in which human beings are destined to love one another as brothers and sisters in a culture of brotherhood, love and freedom. He taught the spiritual laws and way of life for this new epoch, and the methods of self-development to enable people to live by them.

The Teacher foretold that, through periodic waves of divine love, God would bring the conditions of the new epoch to the Earth. These waves of powerful energetic vibration, of invisible divine fire, will liquidate human karma and purify us of sin, and give an impulse of growth to all our good spiritual qualities. He said it would not be long before the first wave arrived, and that the process is set to continue for a considerable time, until the culture of the new epoch is established on our planet. Those people who consciously feel subtle energies may be aware of the intensification of the vibrations in the atmosphere that has been taking place in recent years, which appears be a tangible sign that this great change is underway.

On 7/19 March 1897, Peter Deunov was told he had been chosen by heaven to be a world teacher and to work for the development of the Slavic people. He said, "There is something sublime in the Slavic consciousness: love for God." On 8/20 October 1898, in a speech given at the Charity Society in the Black Sea port-city of Varna, Peter Deunov delivered the words of the Angel Elohim announcing the Slavic mission. In "A Call to My People, Bulgarian Sons of the Slavic Family," he said,

> I am Elohim, the Angel of the Lord's Testament.
> Hear these words from heaven.
> Brothers and sisters of the Slavic home, heaven is giving you a great responsibility in the establishment of the kingdom of peace on earth. If you show yourselves faithful to this noble and holy goal, the God of Powers will crown

you with greatness. A glorious future awaits you, in which life will be resurrected in its perfect fullness. All people and all nations who have been chosen to form the essence of the new generation of humanity are called to participate in this life. It is time for you to awaken and enter the life of kindness that is coming to this greatly suffering earth.

I am here under the direction of God, your heavenly Father, who has given me the mission of saving you from the dark past. I am to bring you to the truth of life of the heavenly home of eternal spiritual light. I am to enlighten every mind and renovate every heart. I am to uplift and renovate the spirits of the children of truth, those who are to make the primary cell of the new humanity, with the Slavic family serving as the hearth.

I shall lead you on the path that ascends to the kingdom of God, so you can serve it. It is an eternal path, full of every kindness in life. God's chosen one, the Leader of Salvation, will soon appear among you in his full glory and power to transform the world and restore the eternal kingdom of peace, the kingdom of God on earth.

The one who sent me has no obstacles, no difficulties. His will is eternal and unbending, and everything He has said will happen will come to pass. The uplifting of the Slavic family is necessary for the whole world, but you may tread the path of your development at a faster or slower rate. If you turn back from the path on which I shall lead you, the God of Powers will uplift others from the new generation of humanity and they will realise His project.

The Leader of Salvation, the Myrrh of Zion, the Lord King, the brother of those who suffer, is coming with all power and spiritual fullness to transform this world. Heaven calls humanity to one more great exploit, by which everything that has been determined by God will be completed.

This process of human upliftment is being directed by the Great Universal White Brotherhood, which is headed by Christ.

The Teacher said, "The White Brotherhood is a great society in the divine world that directly communes with God and Christ." "The beings of the White Brotherhood have completed their evolution and they guide the destiny of humanity." "The White Brothers are servants of God. They are angels." In biblical terminology, they are those who are 'clothed in white'.[1] This Universal Brotherhood works with love, wisdom and truth. Peter Deunov established a spiritual school of the White Brotherhood on earth, based on these principles. In July 1900, he and three invited disciples gathered in Varna for a meeting, that was to become the First Congress of the Brotherhood, during which he presented the ideas of the new teaching.

Peter Deunov spent part of the summer of 1914 in Arbanasi, a village overlooking Turnovo, the medieval capital of Bulgaria. One day in September, when he was climbing a mountain peak in the region, Christ appeared to Peter and said, "Give me your body, your heart and your mind and work for me." He answered, "Lord, may your will be done. I am ready."

The sole criterion of entry into this earthly school of the White Brotherhood is to be a true disciple of the Teacher, Peter Deunov, Beinsa Douno, who was and is a servant of Christ. The Teacher called his disciples 'brother' or 'sister', which became the common form of address in the Brotherhood. During his lifetime the Teacher personally chose his disciples. Now that he is no longer incarnated on earth, this process of selection has to be understood internally. Those whom the Spirit calls to become disciples will receive the experiences they need to assure them it is their path.

---

[1] Jesus said, "He that overcometh shall be arrayed in white garments. I will make him a pillar in the temple of my God, and he shall go out thence no more. I will give to him to sit down with me in my throne, as I also overcame, and sat down with my Father in his throne" (Revelation 3:5, 12, 21).

Christ as a Best Friend

Jesus Christ spoke the following words through the Teacher. [2]

Greetings to you all.

My brothers, peace be with you. From among the people of this nation I have called you as witnesses and stars, bearers of light. I know every one of you by name. For a long time all my efforts have been to prepare you for a great divine work, to develop the strengths of your souls, to open your minds so that you understand the kindly divine paths. A great effort was required to do this, an effort which I made for your benefit, to save you from destruction.

This nation, to which you were sent by me, is not sufficiently developed spiritually. But do not fear, this nation contains the genesis of a good embryo. I want you to harvest the fruits of your work. Be more joyful that God has written your names in the book of life. [3] I have always been present among you and I have always been guiding you. I have been near you in the difficult and sorrowful moments in your lives. Yes, the Great Heavenly Father wishes good things for you. How great and how kind He is. He daily pours down His mercy to support you.

Listen to me today. You see a dark future, you are often hesitant, you are apprehensive about the trials that might come to you, and you often think that evil is incurable and that God has stopped listening to you and comforting you. No, do not allow such thoughts

---

[1] The location and date of this talk were not recorded in its original Bulgarian publication, but the Bulgarian translator, Maria Mitovska, has since found them in a manuscript that belonged to Krum Vuzharov.

[2] This and the following two talks were not published until fifty years after Peter Deunov passed away, by which time they had survived in manuscript form for nine decades. The third text was attributed to Christ, whereas this and the next one were not. However, to the translators of this volume it is clear that the words of all three, which are different from the Teacher's usual style, came from the same source. As there is no evidence other than the words themselves, in the end it is a matter of personal opinion.

[3] When they returned, Jesus said to the seventy disciples he had sent as his harbingers, "Rejoice that your names are written in heaven" (Luke 10:20).

in your minds. Is it possible that God, the great and kind Father, could forget His children? You need to know that God loves you and this nation even more than before. Your souls are valuable in His eyes. God has many children in this nation, which is why you were sent to help them until they have strengthened their spirits. My path is open before you.[4] To help you, I am one with you in all things. I have come to live among you. I will do my best to transform everything for the good. The destiny of this nation, which you love, is in my hands. My actions will be determined by its behaviour. Do not be afraid. I have come to destroy evil and to remove sinfulness from people's hearts.

My Spirit shows my power. I am working, and you will work according to the strength and desire of your souls. You need time to develop yourselves. Pray to God and He will strengthen the weakness of your hope. You often worry that you will not be supported in your work. Have no fear. When you fulfil God's kind goodwill, everything will be provided for you.[5] The wealth of the entire world is available to you. God has left the best things in life for you. Have more love for God and for your brothers, and be pure-hearted and sincere, for these things give me great pleasure.

I want to see you every day and I also want you to see me. At the moment your souls are still too weak to endure the heavenly radiance of my presence.[6] I always have to manifest myself to you according to the conditions of your spirits. Listen to me, my brothers: you are the children of the Living God. The purpose of the knowledge and wisdom that you are being sent is to support you. Speak only the simple and clear truth. Are you ready to do anything for me, or is there still anything within you waiting to trip you up?[7] I am ready to do any-

---

[4] Jesus said, "I am the way, and the truth, and the life: no one cometh unto the Father, but by me" (John 14:6).

[5] Jesus said, "Your Father knoweth what things ye have need of, before ye ask him. Be not therefore anxious, saying, 'What shall we eat?' or, 'What shall we drink?' or, 'Wherewithal shall we be clothed?' For your heavenly Father knoweth that ye have need of all these things. But seek ye first his kingdom, and his righteousness; and all these things shall be added unto you" (Matthew 6:8, 31-33).

[6] "His countenance was as the sun shineth in his strength" (Revelation 1:16).

[7] Jesus said, "I am the light of the world: he that followeth me shall not walk in the darkness, but shall have the light of life. If a man walk in the day, he stumbleth not, because

thing for you. In me you will have a best friend in heaven.[8]

he seeth the light of this world. But if a man walk in the night, he stumbleth, because the light is not in him" (John 8:12; 11:9-10).

[8] Jesus said to his disciples, "Ye are my friends, if ye do the things which I command you" (John 15:14). And the Apostle Paul wrote, "There is one God, one mediator also between God and men, himself man, Christ Jesus" (1 Timothy 2:5).

The Kingdom of God Is Near

Jesus Christ spoke the following words through the Teacher. [1]

I am present here today to refresh your spirits. I know all of your difficulties, trials and suffering, but you face them according to the will of our Father in heaven. You need to stay faithful to the end. [2] You should ignore the things which are of little importance in this life. Test the good things, apply them and keep them, because each good thing is given by the Father of Light. [3] Remove every obstacle which impedes the growth of your knowledge of the truth and your growth in the fullness of love. I am this truth, your Lord whom you constantly seek. Look inside yourselves, open your hearts, listen to your souls and you will hear my voice that makes you alive. [4]

I am present here with my Spirit. My love for you attracts me to you. I have chosen you, I have called you, but you do not know me yet. Your faith is so weak. Was it not I who first gave you spiritual light? [5] Was it not I who revealed the truth to you and manifested my love to you? [6] Am I not the True One who teaches you every day? Turn to me with all your heart and call me, and I will answer you.

You now stand before the door of the kingdom of God. Make a great

---

[1] This talk was not attributed to Christ in its original Bulgarian publication (see n. 2, p. 1 of the present volume).

[2] Jesus said, "He that endureth to the end, the same shall be saved" (Matthew 24:13).

[3] "Every good gift and every perfect boon is from above, coming down from the Father of lights, with whom can be no variation, neither shadow that is cast by turning" (James 1:17).

[4] Jesus said, "My sheep hear my voice, and I know them, and they follow me: and I give unto them eternal life; and they shall never perish" (John 10:27-28).

[5] Jesus said, "I am come a light into the world, that whosoever believeth on me may not abide in the darkness" (John 12:46).

[6] Jesus said, "My teaching is not mine, but his that sent me" (John 7:16). "Even as the Father hath loved me, I also have loved you: abide ye in my love" (John 15:9).

4

effort to enter it.[7] The world has matured and the harvest is near.[8] The kingdom of God is yours to inherit. Awaken; do not live in a doze.[9] It is time for you to be fresh and to start the work that your Father is giving you. Stop saying bad things about your brothers. You have been sent to the earth to do good work for the kingdom of God. You should not argue in life, because everyone will be given according to his or her work.[10] Do you think that your lives are not revealed to my eyes and to the whole of heaven?

On what is your justice based? Is my word, which is written, not always before you? Can you become as alive as I am without this word being resurrected in your souls?[11] The time is coming and is now.[12] This is why I came to this world: to give you life, to enlighten you so that you have the wisdom and knowledge you need to recognise the paths of God. My Spirit works for your renewal.[13]

There are many sisters and brothers waiting for your help, but you burden yourselves with human rules and obligations and neglect my love. Yes, you feel your mistakes and have endured their consequences. Search the Scriptures and you will see that I have been constantly speaking and teaching since the beginning. I have always been with you and

[7] Jesus said, "Strive to enter in by the narrow door: for many, I say unto you, shall seek to enter in, and shall not be able. When once the master of the house is risen up, and hath shut to the door, and ye begin to stand without, and to knock at the door, saying, 'Lord, open to us,' and he shall answer and say to you, 'I know you not whence ye are,' then shall ye begin to say, 'We did eat and drink in thy presence, and thou didst teach in our streets,' and he shall say, 'I tell you, I know not whence ye are; depart from me, all ye workers of iniquity'" (Luke 13:24-27).

[8] John the Baptist said of Jesus, "He shall baptize you with the Holy Spirit and with fire: whose fan is in his hand, and he will thoroughly cleanse his threshing-floor; and he will gather his wheat into the garner, but the chaff he will burn up with unquenchable fire" (Matthew 3:11-12).

[9] Jesus said, "Behold, I come as a thief. Blessed is he that watcheth, and keepeth his garments, lest he walk naked, and they see his shame" (Revelation 16:15).

[10] See the parable of the talents (Matthew 25:14-30) and the parable of the pounds (Luke 19:11-27).

[11] Jesus said, "The words that I have spoken unto you are spirit, and are life" (John 6:63). "I am the resurrection, and the life: he that believeth on me, though he die, yet shall he live: and whosoever liveth and believeth on me shall never die" (John 11:25-26).

[12] Jesus said, "The hour cometh, and now is, when the true worshippers shall worship the Father in spirit and truth: for such doth the Father seek to be his worshippers. God is a Spirit: and they that worship him must worship him in spirit and truth" (John 4:23-24).

[13] Jesus said, "I came that they may have life, and may have it abundantly" (John 10:10).

for you. I will test you, though, as you are still under the law and in need of experiences to become sure of my written word.[14]

Read Psalm 40, verse 5; Psalm 50, verse 5; Psalm 120, verse 6; Psalm 140, verse 10; Psalm 25, verse 6; Psalm 36, verse 6; John 5, verse 10; and Matthew 25, verse 5.[15]

[14] "The law was given by Moses; grace and truth came by Jesus Christ. No man hath seen God at any time; the only begotten Son, which is in the bosom of the Father, he hath declared him" (John 1:17-18). "If ye are led by the Spirit, ye are not under the law" (Galatians 5:18).

[15] The original talk ended at this point, but the contents of these verses have been added on the next page for the reader's benefit.

Many, O Lord my God, are the wonderful works which thou
    hast done,
And thy thoughts which are *toward us*:
They cannot be set in order unto thee;
If I would declare and speak of them,
They are more than can be numbered.

(Psalm 40:5)

Our God shall come, and he shall say,
"Gather my saints together unto me;
Those that have made a covenant with me by sacrifice."

(Psalm 50:5)

My soul hath long had her dwelling
With him that hateth peace.

(Psalm 120:6)

Let burning coals fall upon them:
Let them be cast into the fire;
Into deep pits, that they rise not up again.

(Psalm 140:10)

Remember, O Lord, thy tender mercies and thy
    lovingkindnesses;
For they have been ever of old.

(Psalm 25:6)

Thy righteousness is like the mountains of God;
Thy judgements are a great deep:
O Lord, thou preservest man and beast.

(Psalm 36:6)

The Jews said unto him that was cured, "It is the sabbath,
and it is not lawful for thee to take up thy bed."

(John 5:10)

Now while the bridegroom tarried, they all slumbered and
    slept.

(Matthew 25:5)

The Word of Jesus Christ

I, Lord Jesus Christ, am speaking through the mouth of my servant Peter Deunov.

Psalm 75, verse 8:

> In the hand of the Lord there is a cup, and the wine foameth;
> It is full of mixture, and he poureth out of the same:
> Surely the dregs thereof, all the wicked of the earth shall
>   wring them out, and drink them.

The meaning of this verse is that you should pay attention to all of your actions and not deviate from your path, because God's retribution cannot be avoided. Sooner or later everybody will receive what he or she deserves.[1] If I have great patience, it is for your own good, so that you all come to know the truth. Do not abuse this virtue of mine. Be sure that for every abuse you will receive what you deserve. Do not use your freedom to attempt to do violence to my freedom. Your desires will always be fulfilled but your capriciousness will always be punished.

Proverbs, chapter 10, verse 11:

> The mouth of the righteous is a fountain of life:
> But violence covereth the mouth of the wicked.

The "mouth of the righteous" symbolises good desires, which form a person's beauty. Good desires come from the will of God. Capriciousness comes from human will. The "mouth of the wicked" is the capriciousness of human self-will, which results in shame and disgrace.

---

[1] "Be not deceived; God is not mocked: for whatsoever a man soweth, that shall he also reap" (Galatians 6:7). "The Lord is a God of recompences, he shall surely requite" (Jeremiah 51:56).

John, chapter 16, verse 16:

A little while, and ye behold me no more; and again a little while, and ye shall see me.

"A little while" represents the contemporary life of the flesh, which prevents you from seeing me and being in direct communion with me. Everybody has experienced these moments of life; they are the times of darkness, spiritual downfall and sorrows.[2] "And again a little while" represents the uplifting of your spirits and the liberation from the bonds of the flesh. It also means self-denial and living in a state of conscious goodness and the conscious loving of God. At such times I have always appeared before you.

Matthew, chapter 12, verse 12:

How much is a man of more value than a sheep!

If God is taking care of the birds in the air and the beasts on the ground, He will not forget you.[3] You, however, are tempted by the smallest contradictions in life. You have not yet learnt to serve God. You always seek what you want: bread and fish.[4] You want miracles, you want signs, and they will be given to you – but not the ones you expect.

When your eyes are opened you will see the beautiful world of God, like a blind man who becomes able to see.[5] I want your faith. Your weak faith stops the power of my Spirit.[6] What kind of sign can I make before you when you are blind? What can I do to introduce you to the truth

---

[2] "Fleshly lusts war against the soul" (1 Peter 2:11).

[3] Jesus said, "Behold the birds of the heaven, that they sow not, neither do they reap, nor gather into barns; and your heavenly Father feedeth them. Are not ye of much more value than they?" (Matthew 6:26).

[4] When the multitude found Jesus on the day after the feeding of the five thousand, he said to them, "Ye seek me, not because ye saw signs, but because ye ate of the loaves, and were filled" (John 6:26).

[5] Jesus said, "I counsel thee to buy of me eyesalve to anoint thine eyes, that thou mayest see" (Revelation 3:18).

[6] "As many as received him, to them gave he the right to become children of God, even to them that believe on his name" (John 1:12).

9

when your minds are dark?[7] You are blind. Furthermore, you think that I am like you: someone who says one thing today and another thing tomorrow, someone who can be diverted from his intentions by the smallest obstacles.[8] It is you yourselves who corrupt my words. When I was speaking to you, you did not listen to me well. When I spoke of spiritual bread, you thought I was speaking about the bread of the flesh.[9]

When God wants to be served by your hearts, you think you are being asked to pay a tax. But God wants more than that; He wants the dedication of your entire lives. Do not be frightened by these words, for they do not mean that God will seize your lives and deny you freedom. I did not come to seek life but to give life.[10] I did not come to take people's freedom but to give them freedom. Each of you, with your self-will, voluntarily deprives yourself of life and freedom.[11]

Whoever does not love God does not love me and will have neither

---

[7] "In him was life; and the life was the light of men. And the Word became flesh, and dwelt among us, full of grace and truth" (John 1:4, 14). "And this is the judgement, that the light is come into the world, and men loved the darkness rather than the light; for their works were evil. For every one that doeth ill hateth the light, and cometh not to the light, lest his works should be reproved. But he that doeth the truth cometh to the light, that his works may be made manifest, that they have been wrought in God" (John 3:19-21).

[8] God said, "I the Lord change not" (Malachi 3:6). "Hath God said, and shall he not do it? Or hath he spoken, and shall he not make it good?" (Numbers 23:19). And Jesus said, "I and the Father are one" (John 10:30). "I have overcome the world" (John 16:33).

[9] "Jesus said, 'I am the living bread which came down out of heaven: if any man eat of this bread, he shall live for ever: yea and the bread which I will give is my flesh, for the life of the world.' The Jews therefore strove one with another, saying, 'How can this man give us his flesh to eat?' Jesus therefore said unto them, 'As the living Father sent me, and I live because of the Father; so he that eateth me, he also shall live because of me. This is the bread which came down out of heaven: he that eateth this bread shall live for ever.' Many therefore of his disciples, when they heard this, said, 'This is a hard saying; who can hear it?' But Jesus knowing in himself that his disciples murmured at this, said unto them, 'Doth this cause you to stumble? What then if ye should behold the Son of man ascending where he was before? It is the spirit that quickeneth; the flesh profiteth nothing: the words that I have spoken unto you are spirit, and are life'" (John 6:51-53, 57-58, 60-63).

Spiritually symbolic bread also features in the Lord's Prayer (see Matthew 6:11) and the Last Supper (see Luke 22:19).

[10] Jesus said, "I am the door: by me if any man enter in, he shall be saved, and shall go in and go out, and shall find pasture. The thief cometh not, but that he may steal, and kill, and destroy: I came that they may have life, and may have it abundantly" (John 10:9-10).

[11] Jesus said, "If ye abide in my word, then are ye truly my disciples; and ye shall know the truth, and the truth shall make you free. Every one that committeth sin is the bondservant of sin" (John 8:31-32, 34).

freedom nor life in himself or herself. If you love me and keep my commandments, my Father will reward you for your obedience with His blessings. Fulfil everything that has been spoken from the beginning and my Spirit will abide within you.[12] I know you have obstacles in your lives, as did I when I was on the earth. Stay close to God's law and you will never stumble, because everyone who wants to be loved, as close as a brother, sister and mother, has to fulfil the will of my Father. You are tripped up by many desires. You want everything but you do not give anything. The devil sowed his seed among the good seed while you were dozing.[13]

Your doubt causes you to sink in the sea and you are frightened by the waves. You are starting to drown. Look up to me and I will stretch out my arm and save you. The coast is near and the storm will soon be over.[14] I pay attention to your lives and I am always guiding you. I have arranged everything, and if you pay attention to my words you will not be deprived of anything and you will have my blessings. You owe your lives to heaven, which has done countless good for you. Were I not your protector, do you know how many more bad things would have happened to you? You have been spared much....

It is your heavenly Father who creates the home, who creates family connections, who uplifts the love between children and parents, between brothers, sisters and friends. If you do not listen to His voice, if you constantly doubt Him, lack confidence in Him and are ungrateful to Him, you will lose that which you already have. I have prayed for you, just as I prayed for Peter, so that you will not lose your faith during testing times.[15] If you have complete faith and rely on me, everything will be arranged for your good.

---

[12] Jesus said, "If ye love me, ye will keep my commandments. And I will pray the Father, and he shall give you another Comforter, that he may be with you for ever, even the Spirit of truth. If a man love me, he will keep my word: and my Father will love him, and we will come unto him, and make our abode with him" (John 14:15-17, 23).

[13] In the parable of the wheat and tares, Jesus said, "The kingdom of heaven is likened unto a man that sowed good seed in his field: but while men slept, his enemy came and sowed tares also among the wheat, and went away. But when the blade sprang up, and brought forth fruit, then appeared the tares also" (Matthew 13:24-26).

[14] See the story of Jesus walking on the water and then rescuing Peter after he tried to do likewise (Matthew 14:22-33) and the story of Jesus calming the storm (Matthew 8:23-27)

[15] See Luke 22:31-34

Now strengthen your faith and end your constant doubt so that you do not uproot the grain of wheat together with the weeds, so that the lie does not uproot the truth.[16] Just because you have lied, do not think that I will also lie to you.[17] At any moment you are ready to deny me before a servant.[18] Like the Pharisees of old, you are ready to call to your souls, "We know that God spoke to Moses, but we do not even know this man."[19] You believe that I have spoken to others but you do not believe that I have spoken to you. You believe others but you do not believe me. These are the reasons why you lost your peace. These are the causes of your sorrows. When I spoke to you, you did not pay attention. When I advised you, you did not listen. When I commanded you, you did not obey me. If you allow thorns to grow around you and choke you, who is at fault?[20] If I speak to you and you cause destruction, who will gain from it?

Heaven and earth are the inheritance of the meek and pure-hearted.[21] Whoever has a mind to hear, let him or her hear. Do not only call me, "Lord, Lord, Lord," but also do the will of my Father.[22] It is

[16] In the rest of the parable of the wheat and tares, Jesus said, "And the servants of the householder came and said unto him, 'Sir, didst thou not sow good seed in thy field? whence then hath it tares?' And he said unto them, 'An enemy hath done this.' And the servants say unto him, 'Wilt thou then that we go and gather them up?' But he saith, 'Nay; lest haply while ye gather up the tares, ye root up the wheat with them. Let both grow together until the harvest: and in the time of the harvest I will say to the reapers, 'Gather up first the tares, and bind them in bundles to burn them: but gather the wheat into my barn'''" (Matthew 13:27-30).

[17] The Lord said, "God is not a man, that he should lie" (Numbers 23:19). And Jesus said, "I am the truth" (John 14:6).

[18] See Peter's denial of Jesus (Matthew 26:69-75)

[19] See the miracle of the healing of the man who was born blind and the Pharisees' reaction to it (John 9:1-41, especially 29)

[20] In the parable of the sower, Jesus said, "The sower went forth to sow his seed. And some fell amidst the thorns; and the thorns grew with it, and choked it. The seed is the word of God. And that which fell among the thorns, these are they that have heard, and as they go on their way they are choked with cares and riches and pleasures of this life, and bring no fruit to perfection" (Luke 8:5, 7, 11, 14).

[21] Jesus said, "Blessed are the meek: for they shall inherit the earth. Blessed are the pure in heart: for they shall see God" (Matthew 5:5, 8). And the Teacher said, "The future belongs to the meek. When I speak of meek people, I mean those who are spiritually wise. They not only raise their hands towards God, but also work for Him" (some time between 1929 and 1942).

[22] Jesus said, "Not every one that saith unto me, 'Lord, Lord,' shall enter into the kingdom of heaven; but he that doeth the will of my father which is in heaven" (Matthew 7:21).

not your words that turn heaven towards you but the goodness and purity of your hearts. The only valid collateral you have is your hearts. If your hearts belong to the world, with what will you attract me to you? With nothing. Then you will forever remain foreigners, obtaining neither heaven nor earth – it is difficult to serve two masters.[23] But you say that you believe. All right, let me see the fruit of your faith and I will be benevolent to you.

If you seek me with all your hearts, nothing will be impossible for you. When you call me, there should be no discord in your hearts, for your minds need to be quiet and calm so that you can accept the truth.[24] Do not plant the desires of your flesh onto your souls, for these desires grow like mushrooms. You pick these mushrooms and claim them to be the promise of God, when actually they are the promise of your hearts. When I speak to a person's soul, there will be a reviving of his or her spirit. That person will become like a tree planted beside a river. The leaves of the tree will never dry up and its fruit will never fail.[25] If the tree of life starts to dry and its leaves begin to fall, it is a sign that it is no longer near the water.[26] Each drying heart and each darkening mind shows that my spiritual light is not present in that person's soul.

I would prefer you to be like the disobedient son who refused to go and work in his father's field but was later remorseful and went, rather

[23] Jesus said, "Lay not up for yourselves treasures upon the earth: but lay up for yourselves treasures in heaven: for where thy treasure is, there will thy heart be also. No man can serve two masters: for either he will hate the one, and love the other; or else he will hold to one, and despise the other. Ye cannot serve God and mammon" (Matthew 6:19-21, 24).

[24] God said, "Ye shall call upon me, and ye shall go and pray unto me, and I will hearken unto you. And ye shall seek me, and find me, when ye shall search for me with all your heart" (Jeremiah 29:12-13).

[25] "In the visions of God brought he me into the land of Israel, and set me down upon a very high mountain, whereon was as it were the frame of a city on the south. And he brought me unto the door of the house; and behold, waters issued out from under the threshold of the house eastward, for the forefront of the house was toward the east. And by the river upon the bank thereof, on this side and on that side, shall grow every tree for meat, whose leaf shall not wither, neither shall the fruit thereof fail: it shall bring forth new fruit every month, because the waters thereof issue out of the sanctuary" (Ezekiel 40:2; 47:1, 12).

[26] "Jesus stood and cried, saying, 'If any man thirst, let him come unto me, and drink. He that believeth on me, as the scripture hath said, out of his belly shall flow rivers of living water.' But this spake he of the Spirit, which they that believed on him were to receive" (John 7:37-39).

13

than the son who promised to work but did not.[27] I would like you to have the persistence of the widow who did not despair but stood firm and insisted on receiving what she wanted.[28] I would like you to be like the woman in the Temple who gave relatively more than the rich people did, and whom I offer as an example to you. Yes, she gave all that she had without thinking about the future. See how her good action long ago is still preaching to you.[29]

I am speaking to you through the mouth of your brother, and if you believe, you will test the truth of my words, because the truth of my words can be tested in life.[30]

Live in peace.

---

[27] See the parable of the two sons (Matthew 21:28-32)

[28] See the parable of the persistent widow (Luke 18:1-8)

[29] See the story of the widow's offering (Mark 12:41-44)

[30] Similarly, Jesus said, "My teaching is not mine, but his that sent me. If any man willeth to do his will, he shall know of the teaching, whether it be of God, or whether I speak from myself" (John 7:16-17).

Hope, Faith and Love

Hope is concerned with the present moment and the near future. Faith is concerned with the more distant future. Love connects the present to the future, and, as such, is the true realisation of the present.[2]

Divine love gives each human being the freedom of autonomous self-development while also providing the best conditions for this development. The fruits you bear will be the evidence of the extent to which you have succeeded in your endeavours, and your consciences will be the judges. The person who has love is mighty and unconquerable.

Evil is necessary; it serves the soul in the way the gall bladder serves the body. Evil is useful for people when it is active. When it is active, evil teaches us – suffering teaches us. Evil can only be conquered with goodness.[3] When we have a bad thought, we need to counteract it immediately with a good one, which requires boldness and courage. Evil has to be conquered by knowledge, but this knowledge should not lead to the wrong kind of pride....

A person's past is recorded in his or her body. The future is determined by the present; or to put it another way, we reap what we sow.[4] Whatever we gain or lose in this lifetime becomes our future. A person is uplifted by self-sacrifice, just as Christ sacrificed himself for the salvation of humanity. Let us walk the same path.

Reverence is the centre of life. Awe is the only window through which we can see God. The flesh, the world and the devil are teachers.

---

[1] If no location is given, it means it was not recorded.

[2] "Now abideth faith, hope, love, these three; and the greatest of these is love" (1 Corinthians 13:13).

[3] Jesus said, "Resist not him that is evil: but whosoever smiteth thee on thy right cheek, turn to him the other also" (Matthew 5:39). "Love your enemies, do good to them that hate you, bless them that curse you, pray for them that despitefully use you" (Luke 6:27-28). "And pray for them that persecute you" (Matthew 5:44). And the Apostle Paul wrote, "Avenge not yourselves, beloved, but give place unto wrath: for it is written, 'Vengence belongeth unto me; I will recompense,' saith the Lord. But, 'If thine enemy hunger, feed him; if he thirst, give him to drink: for in so doing thou shalt heap coals of fire upon his head.' Be not overcome of evil, but overcome evil with good" (Romans 12:19-21).

[4] See Galatians 6:7

Love is able to conquer the flesh. Faith is able to conquer the world. Hope is able to conquer the devil. Great patience, which is a manifestation of strong willpower, conquers.

Attain the kingdom of God and all good things will come to you of themselves.[5] The kingdom of God is within us.[6] An earthly king is respected by his nation, but a servant of God is respected by the whole of heaven.

[5] See Matthew 6:24-34, especially 33
[6] See Luke 17:20-21

The Coming Epoch

Christ has already come. He has not, however, manifested himself in the way the churches have been expecting but in a completely different way. Christ will come in 1914. A small revival will begin then.[2] The present order must be destroyed and the forces which are now active must be rotted away.[3] Christ needs to be embodied on the earth so that good people will come here and develop themselves. Read the last chapter of Daniel. Archangel Michael, who is a captain in the army of Christ,[4] is now working in the churches that cannot agree among themselves.

Bad people must turn themselves to God or they will be destroyed. There can be postponement no longer. There is no law that can counteract the coming of Christ. Christ will arrange everything, using righteousness as the foundation. Society will be transformed when each person receives the rights due to him or her as a human being. Once and forever, crimes, hypocrisy and stealing must end, because if someone has lied to you many times before, he or she will lie to you again. To the righteous person who feels sorry for a sinner, the Lord will say, "Take that sinner's place."

[1] The exact date was unrecorded.

[2] The Teacher said the new epoch began on 9/22 March 1914 (see p. 119 of the present volume). The First World War (1914–1918) also began that year. Several months into it, the Teacher said, "The present war is a misery, but it will bring much good to humanity. In the future, good philosophers, good writers, many professors and scientists, and so on, will describe this war and take great lessons from it" (10/23 January 1915).

[3] 1914 was to mark the beginning of the end of the old world order. Early the following year, the Teacher said, "Number 'thirteen' is the number of the spiritual world. The year 1913 broke the rights of nations. The establishment of divine rights began in 1914" (21 January/3 February 1915). "At present all kings think they are Christ, but the near future will show whether what they believe is true...." (21 January/3 February 1915). And indeed, the First World War saw the abolishment of the great autocratic monarchies of Russia, Austria-Hungary and Germany, the former by the Russian Revolution of 1917, the latter two with the defeat of the Central Powers in 1918. There were also abdications in Greece and Bulgaria, in 1917 and 1918 respectively.

[4] For Archangel Michael as a combatter of evil, see Revelation 12:7-9 and also Daniel 10:13, 20-21; 12:1.

The world has to be punished, and everyone will receive his or her dues. I am talking to you because you are at the eleventh hour; this should not be told to those who have not yet arrived at this time.[5] All the necessary conditions exist on earth to make a good life for everybody. We are guilty of misusing these conditions. Up to now good people have served bad people; in the future it will be the other way around. Everything is happening in a normal, natural way for the times in which we live. The Lord has begun to purify the world. Only people with a certain kind of intelligence know this. It needs to be understood that there is order in the world. Archangel Michael will dispel all evil spirits. All the saints will come back to the earth, but they are waiting for the conditions to be favourable. These good people will return here not for their own pleasure but to continue their evolution. Christ will prepare the conditions they need.

You now stand before the door of the new epoch, in which purification will take place. During this epoch the righteous person will be the greatest servant, there will be no more covetousness and no one will want to deceive others. You have waited many years and now you are in front of the door, so there is no cause for complaint. Good people do not cry for those whom God beats. Instead they rejoice because it is an act of purification and, as such, a blessing. When all bad spirits have been cast away, the world will be set right.

You, who are now at the eleventh hour, should send whomever you meet on to the path of the truth. Those who remain away from this path will be taught through suffering. You want to serve and you ask what is God's will. But God's will is clear. Do your arms need to ask what you want them to do? Only a damaged arm cannot do what is willed of it. People will suffer until they have settled their accounts with the Lord. They will feel good once their accounts are settled. Serving God begins with prayer and inner purification. The world will be cleansed when humanity has purified its karma. The planet and its climate will also be purified as a result of this process.[6] Archangel

---

[5] To be at the "eleventh hour" is to have been newly, and late in the day, called to work for God (see the parable of the labourers in the vineyard: Matthew 20:1-16, especially 6-7).

[6] The Teacher said that we have been living in the culture of the fifth race of humanity, but a new type of person is coming into being, distinguished by spiritual qualities, who will uplift the world. He said, "The sixth race is coming. It is a shining race, called 'the Children of God'. Nature and the climate will be changed for this coming race" (25 January/7

Michael is now working to establish the will of God on earth.[7]

February 1915). "In the future, relations between all nations will be fraternal. The shining race of love will be formed all over the world. When this happens, the sacred flame of the true life will be manifested in all its beauty" (17 January 1940). "The sixth race is a race of justice and of the kingdom of God. The sixth race is coming. When it arrives, the kingdom of God, in a small form, will be established on earth" (1944).

[7] Years later the Teacher said, "The wave of the sixth race is coming, for which everyone needs to prepare. This race brings the conditions for the development of humanity. Such transformative waves rarely come to the Earth. You need to know that one of the qualities of the people of the sixth race is that they will love one another as brothers and sisters. Brotherhood means living according to the great law of love" (some time between 1929 and 1942).

"The idea of Brotherhood is coming. The earth will be a place of blessings. This will happen, but first people will pass through fire, storms and great suffering, which will awaken their consciousness. The world will be purified by fire and the day of the Lord will come. The day of the Lord is the day of the new epoch. Do you think God will immediately speak to you with a gentle voice? He will not. First storms and fire will come. Only when everything is purified will God come and speak to people in a calm, gentle voice. This will not happen in one day; the burning will continue for a long time. When the world has passed through the divine fire, unrighteousness will have disappeared. The fire that the day of the Lord is bringing is the fire of divine love, which will illuminate the world. The sin that has been accumulated over thousands of years on the earth must be purified. This wave of fire is being sent to liquidate the old karma. This is the liquidation of the old epoch, the liquidation of all the crimes of humanity. It cannot be postponed any longer, because otherwise your development will come to a halt.

"All people should serve love. The only thing that can save us is for us to connect to the God of Love. We are now entering the epoch of Archangel Michael. He is connected to solar energies. We can therefore say that a solar culture is coming on earth" (some time between 1929 and 1942).

19

A Good Heart and a Good Mind

God has always desired to reveal Himself to human beings, but they, with their desires, push Him away. To put it another way, people create a barrier between themselves and God.[1] God is always growing either good or evil within us, and it is our freewill to choose which one we cultivate. To choose goodness means to educate one's heart. The mind will then develop itself automatically, which is why it is the heart that needs to be educated. On earth the human mind is the servant of the heart.[2] There are some laws for the cultivation of the heart.[3]

Heaven is not a place for those who are foolish. You do not become foolish without having committed great sins in previous incarnations. Intelligent life builds upwards, not down. The power which pulls you down towards the earth is sin, and when you are angry you are at your heaviest. To see God you have to have pure hearts. Suffering is the waterfall that cleanses the heart. I tell you this because you are Christians and it would be bad to wait until your next incarnation to correct yourselves. Do not postpone your lessons until tomorrow.

If you want to serve God, the nature of your service will depend on your capacity for sacrifice – this is a law of human development. Do not allow it to trouble you that the world does not yet live in this way. It is enough for your personal worlds to be improved, for then to you the whole world will also have been improved.

The world needs sensible people who have good desires and who can advance themselves. Do not throw pearls before swine, which is to

---

[1] "Your iniquities have separated between you and your God, and your sins have hid his face from you" (Isaiah 59:2).

[2] Jesus said, "The things which proceed out of the mouth come forth out of the heart; and they defile the man. For out of the heart come forth evil thoughts, murders, adulteries, fornications, thefts, false witness, railings" (Matthew 15:18-19).

[3] The Teacher also said, "First we need to purify our hearts; second, our minds. Christ said, 'I will give you the spring of living water.' If we do not muddy the spring, it will purify our hearts. Therefore, whenever we have a bad thought we should replace it with a good one. In this way, over time, we will purify ourselves" (11/24 January 1915).

say, to bad people.[4] Christ said, "I am the spiritual light of the world,"[5] and, "I am the one who has power."[6] Those who are sent by God listen to Christ.[7] The spirit becomes more powerful when it leaves the body, and when Christ said, "I give my body as food," he was referring to his spiritual body.[8]

Everyone needs to have a good heart and a good mind. A mind without virtues is a mind without a foundation. God will transform all the evil within us into goodness.

---

[4] Jesus said, "Cast not your pearls before the swine, lest haply they trample them under their feet, and turn and rend you" (Matthew 7:6).

[5] See John 8:12

[6] See Matthew 28:18; John 17:2

[7] Jesus said, "My sheep hear my voice, and I know them, and they follow me. My Father, which hath given them unto me, is greater than all; and no one is able to snatch them out of the Father's hand" (John 10:27, 29).

[8] Jesus said, "I am the living bread which came down out of heaven: if any man eat of this bread, he shall live for ever: yea and the bread which I will give is my flesh, for the life of the world" (John 6:51).

Experiencing God

Each of your misfortunes is a sign that you have gone off your rails. You can never force an animal to overeat. A human being, however, might overeat and also drink too much just to participate with others socially – perhaps even drinking twenty glasses of wine, which would bring misfortune his or her way. People who are outside God's influence will return to the primitive conditions of life and may themselves become wild. There can be no progress unless the mind and heart work together. The external person is an expression of the inner person.

Destiny is a great law that records all human actions, and through it your thoughts and desires will return to you in the future like a boomerang. When you send people good thoughts, that goodness will come back to you, as will the badness of your bad thoughts. For example, whatever thoughts you send out to others will return to you as the realisation of those intentions. When you are working, there is a communion between God and you. You dig and sow and the Lord provides the moisture and warmth needed to grow the seeds.

Divine laws are unchangeable.[1] That which God requires from humanity must be fulfilled. Once God has entered a person and made a home therein, he or she will never know unhappiness again.[2] You always make experiments with your bodies but never with your souls. For example, each morning you ask yourselves what kind of food to cook for your bodies, but you never ask what kind of food to prepare for your souls. You need to understand fasting in three ways: there is fasting from bread and water, fasting from bad desires and fasting from bad thoughts.

---

[1] Jesus said, "Till heaven and earth pass away, one jot or one tittle shall in no wise pass away from the law, till all things be accomplished" (Matthew 5:18). "Heaven and earth shall pass away, but my words shall not pass away" (Matthew 24:35).

[2] Jesus said, "If a man love me, he will keep my word: and my Father will love him, and we will come unto him, and make our abode with him. If ye keep my commandments, ye shall abide in my love; even as I have kept my Father's commandments, and abide in his love. These things have I spoken unto you, that my joy may be in you, and that your joy may be fulfilled" (John 14:23; 15:10-11).

People always want proof of God's existence. Actually, God is always right in front of them, but they do not see Him. To explain this I will give you the allegory of the rock and the tree. There is a rock beside a tree. The rock symbolises human beings and the tree symbolises life. The rock would like to understand why the tree is alive and it is not. It looks and looks at the tree but is unable to comprehend anything. Over a long time the rains and storms of nature disintegrate the rock's structure and it becomes smaller and smaller until it is no more. The tree feeds off the minute fragments of the rock and its substance penetrates the tree's roots, branches and leaves. Through this process the rock comes to see and become conscious of the life in the tree.

The Purification of the Earth

From now on there will be extremely dramatic changes in the world, especially in 1914. The times ahead will be very difficult and 1914 will be a peak, the start of the time of all movements, battles and changes leading to the manifestation of the kingdom of God. The coming events will begin the purification of the earth. This will continue until 1927 or 1933, until the works on the European continent, which sets the tone for everything in the world, are going in the right direction.[1] It is even possible that something will happen that destroys everything to purify the world of all negative things, to make a place for all the good people, who will remain on earth. Were this to happen, it would be through these people that humanity would be uplifted for the coming of the kingdom of God on earth and the reign of Christ.

There will be sharp events in the period between 1914 and 1927 or 1933. These will be difficult days. The chains binding evil and all negative orders will be broken during this time. I am not allowed to tell you exactly when these events will happen.[2]

Contemporary Europe is Jerusalem. Just as good and bad simultaneously reigned in Jerusalem, good and bad reign in Europe today. Europe sets the tone for the governance of the world. The good and evil in the world are first emitted from Europe. America represents a similar power to Europe, but this power is being kept for the future.[3] Europe

---

[1] Less than a month later, the Teacher would say, "There exist two currents, and soon it will be clear which one will dominate. From 1914 to 1927 the nations will have enough time to arm themselves. After this period they will either turn to God or continue making armaments...." (p. 29 of the present volume).

[2] Although it can only be speculated upon what these "sharp events" were, there were some notable world-impacting events during the years 1914 up to and including 1933: the First World War (1914–18), the Russian Revolution (1917), the 1918 Influenza Pandemic, the Stock Market Crash of 1929 and the first years of the Great Depression, and Adolf Hitler becoming Chancellor of Germany (January 1933).

[3] After the American Civil War (1861–1865) the United States of America rapidly grew into one of the world's largest economies. The increase in trading did not lead to a shift in the nation's traditional policy of isolationism. The US tried to avoid direct entanglement with European affairs, and did not enter the First World War until 1917. This war exhaust-

dictates for now, which is why it needs to be set right, for it is behaving as the great whore of the earth.[4]

When Christ was on the earth, Satan was in the astral world. Now it is the other way around: Satan is on the earth and Christ is acting in the astral world.[5] The destructiveness of Satan will now be manifested in a much greater way than at any previous time. Satan will be incarnated here, in Europe, in a king's home, and he will attract all negative elements to himself.... Finally, however, he will be crucified.[6]

ed Europe and strengthened America's economic position. Just as the balance of economic power was moving from Europe to America, however, political isolationism prevailed in the latter. The US Senate did not ratify the Treaty of Versailles and America did not join the newly created League of Nations. It was not until December 1941, when the Japanese attacked Pearl Harbour and brought the US into the Second World War, that Washington rejoined the forefront of world politics. In the aftermath of that conflict, America became the leader of the Western world in the Cold War and, since its inception, a member of the North Atlantic Treaty Organisation. When the collapse of the Soviet Union in 1991 ended the Cold War, the USA was considered the world's only superpower.

[4] "One of the seven angels spake with me, saying, 'I will shew thee the judgement of the great harlot that sitteth upon many waters; with whom the kings of the earth committed fornication, and they that dwell in the earth were made drunken with the wine of her fornication.' And he saith unto me, 'The waters which thou sawest, where the harlot sitteth, are peoples, and multitudes, and nations, and tongues.'

"After these things I heard as it were a great voice of a great multitude in heaven, saying, 'God hath judged the great harlot, which did corrupt the earth with her fornication'" (Revelation 17:1-2, 15; 19:1-2).

[5] "And there was war in heaven: Michael and his angels going forth to war with the dragon; and the dragon warred and his angels; and they prevailed not, neither was their place found any more in heaven. And the great dragon was cast down, the old serpent, he that is called the Devil and Satan, the deceiver of the whole world; he was cast down to the earth, and his angels were cast down with him. And I heard a great voice in heaven, saying, 'Now is come the salvation, and the power, and the kingdom of our God, and the authority of his Christ: for the accuser of our brethren is cast down, which accuseth them before our God day and night. Therefore rejoice, O heavens, and ye that dwell in them'" (Revelation 12:7-10, 12).

[6] "Woe for the earth and for the sea: because the devil is gone down unto you, having great wrath, knowing that he hath but a short time" (Revelation 12:12).

Worshipping and Serving God

The heart should be an altar and the soul a temple.[1] The mind should serve at the feet of the Lord,[2] and the spirit should be ready to fulfil all His good instructions.[3]

[1] "Know ye not that your body is a temple of the Holy Spirit which is in you, which ye have from God?" (1 Corinthians 6:19).

[2] "Thus saith the Lord, 'The heaven is my throne, and the earth is my footstool: what manner of house will ye build unto me? and what place shall be my rest?'" (Isaiah 66:1). "In the visions of God brought he me into the land of Israel, and set me down upon a very high mountain, whereon was as it were the frame of a city on the south. Afterward he brought me to the gate, even the gate that looketh toward the east: and behold, the glory of the God of Israel came from the way of the east: and his voice was like the sound of many waters: and the earth shined with his glory. And I fell upon my face. And the glory of the Lord came into the house by the way of the gate whose prospect is toward the east. And the spirit took me up, and brought me into the inner court; and behold, the glory of the Lord filled the house. And I heard one speaking unto me out of the house; and a man stood by me. And he said unto me, 'Son of man, this is the place of my throne, and the place of the soles of my feet, where I will dwell in the midst of the children of Israel for ever'" (Ezekiel 40:2; 43:1-7).

[3] The Teacher also said, "God should abide in us in the same way that He abides in Jesus Christ, whom He sent" (11/24 March 1912). "There are four fundamental elements with which to build the spiritual life: divine love, divine life, divine thought and divine will. When divine love limited itself, it manifested the divine life. The divine life gives birth to divine thought. Divine thought gives birth to the divine will. The divine will gives birth to our lives. If we want the Lord to live within us, we have to love Him and manifest His love.

"There are three things which deceive people in life. The first one is taste. For example, it is possible to cook bad meat with many herbs and spices that deceive the sense of taste and smell. When the meat enters the stomach, however, the stomach rejects it. The second is the heart. Our hearts can lie to us, which is why we need to listen to our souls, for the soul never lies. The heart accepts endearments but the soul rejects them. The third deceiver is the intellect. The relationship between the heart and the soul is the same as the relationship between the intellect and the higher mind, which is directed by the spirit.

"To educate our sense of taste, our hearts and our intellects, we have to listen to the advice of our stomachs, our souls and our spirits. We need to know how to feed our stomachs, our souls and our minds. If we know these things we will be healthy. How should we apply these four fundamental elements? We should apply them with love.

"Christ planted his life in the conditions needed for its growth. A primary condition for our lives is to free ourselves of many of our desires, our impurities. To come close to the Lord we have to deposit divine love, divine life, divine thought and divine will inside ourselves. Then the Lord will send us His Spirit and make us healthy and intelligent. We need to have the four fundamental elements – divine love, divine life, divine thought and divine will – to be able to plant true taste, true heart and true intellect within ourselves and develop our hearts, our minds, our souls and our spirits" (6/19 April 1914).

God Is the Only Centre

Everybody in the contemporary world would like to become the centre of things. However, if everyone turned towards God, wanting God to be the centre, the world would move in another direction.[1]

[1] The Teacher also said, "Everybody on earth would like to have a better life, but everybody also wants to be a master; no one wants to be a servant. There is a law that we all need to keep in mind, which says, 'My life will be good when life is good for everybody.' This is why we need to turn to the spiritually wise Lord, who is within us and who reminds us of our mistakes. And when He enters us and we meet Him and accept Him within us, poverty will no longer exist. The Lord wants to set the world right, but for the world to be set right our own personal worlds first have to be set right, the worlds of our thoughts and desires" (10/23 January 1915).

Keep Close to Christ

Jesus said to his disciples,

> **There shall not be left here one stone upon another, that shall not be thrown down.** [1]

The stone has a mystical meaning and it is also the symbol of the human soul. That which is written in Matthew, chapter twenty-four, verse two will take place in this century. Only God knows the path that the contemporary world will follow. Heaven is making every effort to bring humanity to its senses. There exist two currents, and soon it will be clear which one will dominate. From 1914 to 1927 the nations will have enough time to arm themselves. After this period they will either turn to God or continue making armaments.... [2]

Each soul that is disconnected from the Spirit will be destroyed. Whoever wants to develop correctly will not permit anyone but the Lord to enter his or her heart and soul. If you want to protect your house from destruction, you have to have Christ with you. [3] If you find yourself blind, call out to Christ to open your eyes. When he does, you will see clearly and need no other guidance. [4] We are now in an epoch

---

[1] Matthew 24:2. The Teacher actually read the whole chapter.

[2] The Teacher also said, "All nations are called to fulfil the will of God. Each nation receives guidance from the invisible world. When all nations follow this guidance, everything will be arranged well on the earth" (some time between 1929 and 1942).

[3] The Teacher often used the word 'house' as a metaphor for the human body, which is similar to the Apostles Paul and Peter describing it as a "tabernacle" (see 2 Corinthians 5:1-4; 2 Peter 1:13-14). The Lord's presence dwelt in the tabernacle made by Moses (see Exodus 39:32–40:38). God said, "I have not dwelt in an house since the day that I brought up the children of Israel out of Egypt, but have walked in a tent and in a tabernacle" (2 Samuel 7:6). It remained so until King Solomon built the Temple in Jerusalem as a permanent house of God (see 2 Chronicles 5:1–6:11). Paul said God does not live in manmade temples (see Acts 17:24) but inside our bodies, which are temples of the indwelling Holy Spirit (see 1 Corinthians 6:19). The Teacher's term 'house' means the human body as an organic earthly dwelling for the soul and also a temple of God.

[4] Jesus said, "I counsel thee to buy of me eyesalve to anoint thine eyes, that thou mayest see" (Revelation 3:18).

when it is important to pay attention to Christ and keep close to him. If you do this continually your eyes will soon be opened: the sixth sense will come to you and you will not need any other guidance.

Good and Evil

The use of the gift of earthly things is not limited to good actions. For example, fire has been given to us for heating, cooking and so on, but if we do not manage it carefully, we might burn down a house in which we make a fire. In our use of 'fire' humanity has committed evil.[1]

---

[1] During the First World War, the Teacher said, "The present war was created by people constantly talking about it. We created it. We made this fire. Let us now begin to talk of the opposite things. We created the war and we will end it – we made a fire and we will put it out. It is also we human beings who will create the spiritually wise faith of which Christ spoke" (10/23 January 1915).

Rely on the Lord

It is written in Psalm 118,

**It is better to trust in the Lord
Than to put confidence in man.** [1]

The soul is the connection between the invisible world and the physical world. We communicate with God through our bodies, our hearts, our minds, our thoughts and our desires. To rely on the Lord means to breathe and take Him within us. [2] Always keep these words in your mind: God does not change. [3]

[1] Psalm 118:8

[2] The Teacher gave a breathing formula to this effect, which can be found in n. 11, p. 77 of the present volume.

[3] "I the Lord change not" (Malachi 3:6).

Entering the Kingdom of God

Jesus said,

> Verily I say unto you, Except ye turn, and become as little children, ye shall in no wise enter into the kingdom of heaven.[1]

He also said,

> Verily, verily, I say unto thee, Except a man be born anew, he cannot see the kingdom of God.[2]

These two verses are equally powerful.

The conditions that you now have in the world will never be repeated. If there is something unpleasant in your lives and you feel dissatisfied, ungrateful and sad, you need to know that the causes are karmic and you yourselves are responsible for them.

If we would like to enter the kingdom of God, we have to become like children. "We must not make room for temptation."[3] We ought not to talk badly behind other people's backs. Wherever there is misunderstanding, there is a bitter karma somewhere in our natures. In such circumstances there is nothing to be done except for praying to God to eliminate the karma.[4]

The tests that are coming to us are sent from heaven.

---

[1] Matthew 18:3

[2] John 3:3

[3] "Be ye angry, and sin not: let not the sun go down upon your wrath: neither give place to the devil" (Ephesians 4:26-27). The Teacher said, "We ought not to talk to the devil, because if we do he will gradually make himself fine lodgings within us. Then, if we feel bad, he will say, 'You can leave, but I am most comfortable here.' Every day people leave themselves because they have given up their places within themselves to the devil" (11/24 January 1915).

[4] The Teacher also said, "We should help each other with our thoughts, no matter that some of us are suffering from karmic problems" (21 January/3 February 1915).

33

Love, Unity and Service

Jesus said,

> Ye call me, "*Teacher*," and, "Lord," and ye say well; for so I am.[1]

A spiritual teacher adjusts and harmonises things. You need a spiritual teacher to teach you how to apply things in life, because you still do not know how to apply the divine laws. Evil is necessary in the process of destruction. Goodness is necessary in the process of building. When you have love, it will put your knowledge of the spiritual laws into action. At first you will become bitter, then you will sour, and finally you will sweeten. This means that evil is a human being's first teacher. You are now on the path of sweetening, and you will sweeten the world.

Good people are the salt which keeps the balance in the world.[2] If you listen to me, I am advising you to have love. If we have love, it means we have unity and fusion without being deprived of our individualities. When you love someone, it means you have similar interests and that you generally put the person you love in a higher position than yourself. A question spontaneously arises: "Am I ready to do more for another than I will for myself?"

Establish love within yourselves, for it will bring you new light.[3] Jesus Christ washed the feet of his disciples.[4] To wash the feet of others

---

[1] John 13:13

[2] Jesus said, "Ye are the salt of the earth" (Matthew 5:13).

[3] "He that saith he is in the light, and hateth his brother, is in the darkness even until now. He that loveth his brother abideth in the light, and there is none occasion of stumbling in him. But he that hateth his brother is in the darkness, and walketh in the darkness, and knoweth not whither he goeth, because the darkness hath blinded his eyes" (1 John 2:9-11). "If we love one another, God abideth in us, and his love is perfected in us" (1 John 4:12).

[4] See John 13:1-15

is the greatest art.[5] You are unable to do this at present, despite our sitting around a table eating and drinking together, because Judas remains between you. When Judas leaves you, your feet will be washed.[6] Let that be a subject for your thoughts. It is through love that our thoughts will be purified.

---

[5] After washing his disciples' feet at the Last Supper, Jesus said, "Ye call me, 'Teacher,' and, 'Lord,' and ye say well; for so I am. If I then, the Lord and the Teacher, have washed your feet, ye also ought to wash one another's feet. For I have given you an example, that ye also should do as I have done to you" (John 13:13-15).

[6] After Judas had left the Last Supper to betray Jesus (see John 13:21-30), Jesus said to the remaining eleven disciples, "A new commandment I give unto you, that ye love one another; even as I have loved you, that ye also love one another. By this shall all men know that ye are my disciples, if ye have love one to another" (John 13:34-35).

Mastering Destiny

'The righteous ones of the House of God' are those people who have fulfilled the will of God in incarnation after incarnation after incarnation.[1] Our destiny is every human being receiving his or her due rights. To work with our destinies, we need to understand the nature of each of our relationships with other people, to be able to identify the quality of anything in our lives, and to discern what work each person is able to contribute in any given situation. Everyone needs to find his or her place in the body of Christ.[2] The karmic law is the starting point in understanding one's destiny. For example, if you behave unjustly towards somebody, your action will return to you.

To be able to answer correctly the question, "What is the meaning of destiny?" you first have to have passed through a process of tests. These tests come in five stages. The first stage is Mount Ararat, which means you need to find a harbour, for you are in a flood and must find a mountain upon which to stand.[3] The second stage is Mount Moriah, where you are to make a sacrifice to God.[4] The third stage is Mount Sinai, where it will be misty, but the law of God will be given to you there.[5] The fourth stage is Mount Tabor, where Jesus was transfigured.[6]

[1] These are those who have freed themselves of their karmic bonds and are not obliged to return to the earth again. Jesus said, "He that overcometh shall be arrayed in white garments. He that overcometh, I will make him a pillar in the temple of my God, and he shall go out thence no more" (Revelation 3:5, 12).

[2] The Apostle Paul used the term "the body of Christ" to mean the church of the faithful and to describe how individual Christians are unified in Christ as members with different roles in one body (see Romans 12:3-8; 1 Corinthians 10:16-17; 12:1–31; Ephesians 4:1-16; Colossians 1:18).

[3] Noah's ark came to rest on the Mountains of Ararat as the great flood subsided (see Genesis: 8:1-4).

[4] It was on a mountain in the land of Moriah that Abraham proved himself willing to obey God to the extent of sacrificing his son Isaac (see Genesis 22:1-13).

[5] At Mount Sinai, God came to the Israelites in a thick cloud and spoke, giving them the Ten Commandments (see Exodus 19:1–20:17; Deuteronomy 4:11-13).

[6] There is an ancient tradition that Jesus was transfigured on Mount Tabor. The Synoptic Gospels all give an account of Jesus's transfiguration on a mountain but do not give its name (see Matthew 17:1-8; Mark 9:2-8; Luke 9:28-36).

And the last stage is Golgotha....[7]

People have to pass through all five stages in their spiritual development, so you ought to think on them. Jesus Christ is the One who has the alchemical power necessary for these tests. When this power is given to you, you will be able to pass through the stages successfully. You volunteered for these trials, which is why none of you should complain when the examination arrives. You now have the best conditions for being close to God and for becoming masters of your destinies, which means to free yourselves of the karmic law.

[7] Jesus was crucified at Golgotha (see John 19:17-18).

37

Resurrection

The Teacher began by reading John's Gospel, chapter 20, in which the resurrected Jesus first revealed himself to Mary Magdalene and later his disciples, to whom he gave the Holy Spirit.

Immortality is a stable, primary substance. Human beings can change the cells of their bodies and live for as long as they want, but only once they understand how things come to equilibrium – something known to people in ancient times.[1] However, to resurrect ourselves we have to die, because resurrection cannot happen without death.

To be able to resurrect ourselves we have to make a connection with those who work for us in the invisible world. A human being needs to find his or her place in the Divine Organism and to fulfil the precise work that he or she has been given. Nobody should do work with which he or she has not been entrusted. When we decide to stop making a scene and instead do as we are instructed, we will become free and be masters of our circumstances. Christ said that he was going to his Father for us, and in doing so he made the connection that we need to the invisible world.[2] We read that Christ breathed on his apostles, and when he breathes on us we will likewise begin the great task of our lives.[3] When the Lord sends His Spirit upon us, we grow and are joyful because He is with us. Even then we still need to pray, lest we lose the

---

[1] There are several references to extreme old age in the Old Testament; for example: Adam living 930 years (see Genesis 5:5), Methuselah living 969 years (see Genesis 5:27), Noah living 950 years (see Genesis 9:29), Abraham living 175 years (see Genesis 25:7), and Moses dying at 120 years old with his strength and sight undiminished by age (see Deuteronomy 34:7).

[2] At the Last Supper, Jesus said to his disciples, "The comforter, even the Holy Spirit, whom the Father will send in my name, he shall teach you all things. Peace I leave with you; my peace I give unto you. It is expedient for you that I go away: for if I go not away, the Comforter will not come unto you; but if I go, I will send him unto you" (John 14:26-27; 16:7).

[3] Having appeared to his disciples after his resurrection, "Jesus said to them, 'Peace be unto you: as the Father hath sent me, even so I send you.' And when he had said this, he breathed on them, and saith unto them, 'Receive ye the Holy Spirit'" (John 20:21-22).

Lord's goodwill, for we would not want Him to leave us.[4]

You are now in the roots. When you are resurrected you will be in the branches. Faith and hope are of the soul. Power is of the spirit. The spirit is the primary element and the soul is the secondary element.

[4] The Teacher also said, "Prayer is a necessity. The need for prayer will cease only when our needs have come to an end, but our needs will never end. Wisdom, righteousness and truth are necessities" (10/23 January 1915).

Christ Is Coming to Purify the World

It is written in John's Gospel,

> The common people of the Jews learned that he was there:
> and they came, not for Jesus' sake only, but that they might
> see Lazarus also, whom he had raised from the dead. But
> the chief priests took counsel that they might put Lazarus
> also to death; because that by reason of him many of the
> Jews went away, and believed on Jesus.[1]

The chief priests wanted to kill Lazarus, because having been raised
from the dead by Jesus Christ he was a living testimony by which the
whole world would believe in Christ. It is the same now: the world
would still like to kill those who are resurrected.

We have to suffer in the world if we want to uplift ourselves. We
ought to be grateful when we are suffering, because only through suffering can the human mind make discoveries. The intelligent and powerful person is one in whom the Lord lives. If the Lord does not live in
you, you are simply an empty bubble.

Take note that the law of thoughts and desires relates to the society
in which you live. When you are not in harmony with the thoughts
of those around you, you feel heaviness at the top of your head. When
you are not in harmony with the love of those around you, you feel
heaviness in your chest. When you are not in harmony with the desires
of those around you, you feel heaviness in your stomach.

All of you need to be in a good condition, because Christ is now
near Bulgaria, and next year you will feel his coming at a physical level.
Christ is coming to work, and no matter what happens, you need to
remain calm.[2] Christ is coming to make a general purification in the
world, and the Bulgarian nation also has to be purified. Christ is very

---

[1] John 12:9-11. The original Bulgarian publication only quoted verse 10.

[2] In this year and the next Bulgaria would fight in two Balkan Wars, suffering a disastrous
loss in the latter during the summer of 1913.

near, which is why his voice is audible. Be glad and courageous in your souls. The world is fearful, and you will feel this fear because you are part of the world.

Christ is near, and he is coming to be given what he wants.... You need to be careful and make good use of this situation. As for me, I have decided to subordinate myself to God. I therefore say, "God's will is my will. God's Spirit is my spirit." If this nation does not make the same choice for itself, I will go to another nation.[3] If you are ready to say the same words as me, I will give you my hand and lead you to firm ground, to solid rock.[4] As Christ is near and his voice is audible, hold yourselves close to him and be heroic.

[3] The Teacher does not appear to have explained exactly why he was sent to Bulgaria, of all nations. Boris Nikolov, one of the Teacher's closest disciples, told Maria Mitovska, the Bulgarian translator, that he once directly asked the Teacher why he had come to Bulgaria. The Teacher smiled as he answered, "Because of its beautiful mountains."

[4] "Trust ye in the Lord for ever: for in the Lord JEHOVAH is an everlasting rock" (Isaiah 26:4).

The Spirit Connects Us to God

Suffering leads to love. Whoever would like to be a good person has to suffer. Suffering is a necessary law that teaches us to live in love and to develop ourselves towards perfection. When we suffer we are also deprived of the things we want. We will only be powerful when we unite with the Divine Being.[1] Our souls are micro-cosmoses to which our spirits come. The soul has a shape but the spirit does not. The spirit is the connecting line between the Great Spirit and the human soul.[2]

We need to have a clear idea about how we ought to live. You should not want to go to the other world, for you can be in communion with God while you are still here in this world. The contemporary order must be destroyed so that the world can be set right. Anybody who wants to be powerful and to learn the laws has to be virtuous. Expect much suffering, for you are going to be crucified and resurrected. This is why I am telling you to prepare yourselves. God will bless you when you allow Him to work within you and around you.

[1] The Teacher also said, "If we follow the commandments of Christ, he will give us everything we ask for in his Name. If he does not give us what we ask for, it means we have made a mistake of some kind. The earth is not simply a place for suffering; it is a school. Without the earth we could not uplift ourselves. On any day during which we do not keep Christ's commandments, disharmony will appear in us and we will be unchristian. We are allowed to make mistakes, but Christ will judge us if we do not correct them. We should not repeat our mistakes anymore; instead, we should correct them. We need to learn from our mistakes, which means to free ourselves of bad thoughts" (11/24 January 1915). "The Lord made the human being in His image and likeness, which means we, like Him, can do anything" (10/23 January 1915).

[2] "The spirit of man is the lamp of the Lord, Searching all the innermost parts of the belly" (Proverbs 20:27). "The Spirit himself beareth witness with our spirit, that we are children of God" (Romans 8:16).

The Teacher said, "According to Christ's teaching, the value of the human soul depends on our inner qualities, which means it depends on whether we are connected to the Lord or not. To put it in other words, the value of our souls depends on whether or not we are dressed in truth and love. We know the sun by its light and warmth, and similarly, we know God by truth and love. When the truth enters our minds, we think properly. When love enters us, we act well. The truth is the inner germ of the soul. When we have the truth we always feel a certain strength, for the truth brings youthfulness and freshness" (13/26 April 1914).

There is disintegration among believers. The spirit of the world has begun to act on them, owing to their disagreements and falsehoods. There are therefore stones, flagstones, upon you that interfere with your spiritual development and advancement. You are like small plants with flagstones on top of them. The plants must grow sideways to escape the stones. I would now like to remove these flagstones from you. I will not only do this for you but for all the good people in the world. I am giving you these thoughts for you to think about them.

Fulfilling the Will of God

Jesus said,

A man's foes shall be they of his own household. [1]

This verse has an internal application, because within a person there are thoughts which say, "Do not be foolish, live in the same way as everyone else." That is the voice of the household. A person lives comfortably when he or she agrees with the rest of the household. However, each of our thoughts ought to be subordinate to our own wills, not to the will of others. Nevertheless, we need to make sacrifices for others; otherwise we will be like grains of wheat that are kept in storage instead of being sown in the field. Were we all to make sacrifices for each other, be assured that our relationships would be corrected.

People today suffer less from a lack of material things than they do from the bad spiritual atmosphere. We often say we want to serve the Lord, and we have a good desire to do so, but when He tests us we hesitate and begin to retreat. This means we often serve the Lord not because we love Him but because He is rich and we want Him to bless us with material abundance. [2] The divine human being needs to be connected to the physical human being. We want God to come to the earth, but we need to prepare ourselves so that it can happen. When Christ came to the Jewish people, they were not ready for Him....

We have a motto: "In the fulfilment of the will of God is the power of the human soul." There are also other mottos: "To become powerful, a person has to be virtuous," "To become powerful, a person has to be righteous," "To become powerful, a person has to be intelligent," "To

[1] Matthew 10:36

[2] The Teacher also said, "When we experience suffering, it means the Lord is testing our love. If we endure suffering without complaint, it means we have divine love. I will explain this with a story. A rich Parisian man tested the love of his relatives by pretending to be very poor. After he died, he left his riches to those who had taken care of him and deprived those who had not, even though he knew it would anger them" (11/24 January 1915).

become powerful, a person has to be wise," "To become powerful, a person has to have the truth within himself."

I know that you need peace at this time. To have peace, you require balance. This balance is attained by training, just as the tightrope walker who crossed Niagara Falls on a rope trained himself. He first trained using a pole for balance, but he gradually learnt to do without it. He attained great balance. And you must have great balance to have peace. You think you have done many things for the Lord over the last five or ten years, but you have not worked for the Lord for one hundred years, two hundred years, five hundred years or one thousand years as some people have. You need to learn not to hesitate, because the day will come when your small hesitation will cause the Lord to hesitate towards you.... Let us love the Lord within ourselves and the Lord within other people, and let us listen when He speaks to us or to others.

The pure religious life is not monotonous; the mind and feelings have to participate in it.[3] Upliftment needs to happen spirally. The law of Moses is a law of morality, but Christ's law is a law of freedom.[4] Therefore, we should be free.

---

[3] The Teacher also said, "The thoughts, feelings and deeds that are not understood cause sorrows and difficulties. Those that are understood cause joy and vitality" (16 July 1939).
[4] "The law was given by Moses; grace and truth came by Jesus Christ" (John 1:17). Jesus said, "If ye abide in my word, then are ye truly my disciples; and ye shall know the truth, and the truth shall make you free" (John 8:31-32).

The Antidote to Sin

Sin is the most powerful poison in the world, and the Lord has told us not to touch it.[1] Sin darkens the mind and rusts the heart. However, the Lord has provided an antidote to this poison, and you need to discover it. I wanted to give you this antidote but you are not yet ready to accept it. I am not discouraged, though, because the time will come when I can give it to you.[2]

What is evil? Evil is nothing but a very small amount of good. Evil is a condition in which you cannot find any kind of good that is capable of manifesting itself. The worst state of a spirit is when it has fallen into the condition of utter indifference, having no interest in anything. This condition is awful – even the higher spirits are afraid of it, because the indifferent spirit will go down and down until nothing great remains of it.[3]

You think that you are working, but the truth is that you are still in kindergarten. You could move on to primary school, but you would find it difficult to be accepted there. After a human being has made a

[1] "God cannot be tempted with evil, and he himself tempteth no man: but each man is tempted, when he is drawn away by his own lust, and enticed. Then the lust, when it hath conceived, beareth sin: and the sin, when it is fullgrown, bringeth forth death" (James 1:13-15).

[2] Presumably this antidote is the transformative inner connection to Christ.

"Now the serpent was more subtil than any beast of the field which the Lord God had made" (Genesis 3:1). "The old serpent, which is the Devil and Satan" (Revelation 20:2). Jesus said, "The lusts of the devil it is your will to do. He was a murderer from the beginning, and stood not in the truth, because there is no truth in him. Verily, verily, I say unto you, If a man keep my word, he shall never see death" (John 8:44, 51).

"And the Lord said unto Moses, 'Make thee a fiery serpent, and set it upon a standard: and it shall come to pass, that every one that is bitten, when he seeth it, shall live.' And Moses made a serpent of brass, and set it upon the standard: and it came to pass, that if a serpent had bitten any man, when he looked unto the serpent of brass, he lived" (Numbers 21:8-9). And Jesus said, "As Moses lifted up the serpent in the wilderness, even so must the Son of man be lifted up: that whosoever believeth may in him have eternal life. Now shall the prince of this world be cast out. And I, if I be lifted up from the earth, will draw all men unto myself" (John 3:14-15; 12:31-32).

[3] The Teacher also said, "People may do good or bad things, but a person who does not work is worse than someone who does bad things" (6/19 January 1915).

start at spiritual work, the Lord gives that person a rest before sending him or her on to primary school.[4]

Christ came to the world for this reason: so that you can work and evolve. Have faith in Christ, keep God in your hearts and work. The Spirit is telling you these three things: have faith in Christ, keep God in your hearts and keep working.

---

[4] The principle of God-given rest has biblical precedent. After telling Moses to depart from Mount Sinai for the Promised Land, the Lord said He would give the Israelites rest (see Exodus 33:14; see also Deuteronomy 12:9-10), which they received upon finally possessing the land (see Joshua 21:43-45). Later, at the completion of the Temple in Jerusalem, King Solomon declared the fulfilment of God's promised rest (see 1 Kings 8:54-56). However, the Apostle Paul argued that the Lord's true rest had not been achieved and that the promise still stood, to be received by those who are faithful and obedient in Christ (see Hebrews 3:1–4:13).

The Mysterious Christ

A randomly chosen passage from the Bible was read, after which the Teacher spoke.

We should not look only at our personal lives but should generally look to the kingdom of God. You ought not to be insulted when sometimes the Lord makes someone else a whole musical note and you a half note. Such is the play of life. Even if you are given the role of a one-eighth note, you should be grateful, because the time will come for you to take the role of the whole note.

The most important thought is that we need to learn how to suffer. When we have learnt how to suffer we will be eternally young and not lose our strength. Then we will find the eternal mystery.[1] We have not yet found love, because love always seeks to help others and to sacrifice itself and is always patient and benevolent.[2] We have to turn to the fundamental law so that we become like heavenly children, not foolish children. When we do, our relationships in life will be corrected. It is time for us to lose our religious masks, for a person can look holy externally while being rotten inside.

The following rules help in life. We need to pray more often in one

[1] Jesus said, "If any man would come after me, let him deny himself, and take up his cross daily, and follow me" (Luke 9:23). "All things have been delivered unto me of my Father: and no one knoweth the Son, save the Father; neither doth any know the Father, save the Son, and he to whomsoever the Son willeth to reveal him" (Matthew 11:27). "It is the spirit that quickeneth; the flesh profiteth nothing: the words that I have spoken unto you are spirit, and are life" (John 6:63). "The kingdom of God is within you" (Luke 17:21).

It is written in Revelation, "In the days of the voice of the seventh angel, when he is about to sound, then is finished the mystery of God, according to the good tidings which he declared to his servants the prophets. And the seventh angel sounded; and there followed great voices in heaven, and they said, 'The kingdom of the world is become the kingdom of our Lord, and of his Christ: and he shall reign for ever and ever'" (Revelation 10:7; 11:15). The Teacher said, "Once the last trumpet sounds, from then on you will quickly perceive how to come to understand anything" (10/23 August 1914).

[2] "Love suffereth long, and is kind; love is not provoked, taketh not account of evil; rejoiceth not in unrighteousness, but rejoiceth with the truth; beareth all things, believeth all things, hopeth all things, endureth all things. Love never faileth" (1 Corinthians 13:4-8). "The fruit of the Spirit is love, joy, peace, longsuffering, kindness, goodness, faithfulness, meekness, temperance" (Galatians 5:22-23).

qand the same direction, for then the Lord will answer us. We should not worry when we pray, for worry paralyses our mood and consequently the prayer. If we want the Lord to listen to us, we have to be His servants. We may know that we are His servants but we should keep it to ourselves.[3]

We need to learn to love. Love cannot be described in words. We need to live in love. The heart only understands love. A person who works with love has to embody love, for only then will he or she manifest love.

Christ is a great enigma. He is the manifestation of the Father.[4] Only in heaven will we really know who Christ is. We do not know him yet. Christ is now a historical figure for us. Our understanding of him is unclear and misty, but when he becomes a bone from our bones and flesh from our flesh, we will be embodied in him and he will become clear to us.[5] When we are born of our Divine Mother, the Spirit to which we aspire, death will be swallowed up.[6]

---

[3] Jesus said that we should do our good deeds and say our prayers in private and not to be seen by others, and then God, who sees everything, will reward us (see Matthew 6:1-6).

[4] Jesus said, "I and the Father are one" (John 10:30). And the Apostle Paul wrote, "The mystery of God is Christ, in whom are all the treasures of wisdom and knowledge hidden" (Colossians 2:2-3).

[5] The Teacher's words here, describing a state of spiritual unity with Christ, were the same as those with which Adam described his unity with Eve: "And the man said, 'This is now bone of my bones, and flesh of my flesh: she shall be called Woman, because she was taken out of Man.' Therefore shall a man leave his father and his mother, and shall cleave unto his wife: and they shall be one flesh" (Genesis 2:23-24).

[6] "Since by man came death, by man came also the resurrection of the dead. For as in Adam all die, so also in Christ shall all be made alive. It is written, 'The first man Adam became a living soul.' The last Adam became a life-giving spirit. The first man is of the earth, earthy: the second man is of heaven. Behold, I tell you a mystery: We shall not all sleep, but we shall all be changed, in a moment, in the twinkling of an eye, at the last trump. When this corruptible shall have put on incorruption, and this mortal shall have put on immortality, then shall come to pass the saying that is written, 'Death is swallowed up in victory. O death, where is thy victory? O death, where is thy sting?' The sting of death is sin; and the power of sin is the law: but thanks be to God, which giveth us the victory through our Lord Jesus Christ" (1 Corinthians 15:21-22, 45, 47, 51-52, 54-57).

"As many as received him, to them gave he the right to become children of God, even to them that believe on his name: which were born, not of blood, nor of the will of the flesh, nor of the will of man, but of God" (John 1:12-13). Jesus said, "Except a man be born anew, he cannot see the kingdom of God. Except a man be born of water and the Spirit, he cannot enter into the kingdom of God. That which is born of flesh is flesh; and that which is born of the Spirit is spirit" (John 3:3, 5-6). And the Apostle Paul wrote, "The Jerusalem that is above is free, which is our mother" (Galatians 4:26).

Give Ten Percent to the Lord

Giving ten percent of your income to the Lord is a leavening. You need to make this offering so that you will be blessed.[1]

---

[1] The principle of giving a tenth to God can be found in Mosaic law. The Lord said to Moses, "All the tithe of the land, whether of the seed of the land, or of the fruit of the tree, is the Lord's: it is holy unto the Lord. And all the tithe of the herd or the flock, whatsoever passeth under the rod, the tenth shall be holy unto the Lord" (Leviticus 27:30, 32).

"'Bring ye the whole tithe into the storehouse, that there may be meat in mine house, and prove me now herewith,' saith the Lord of hosts, 'if I will not open you the windows of heaven, and pour you out a blessing, that there shall not be room enough to receive it'" (Malachi 3:10).

The Teacher's disciples usually gave ten percent of their post-tax income to support the teaching in some way; for example, by making donations to the kitty for the necessities of the common life of Brotherhood, or contributing towards the cost of publishing the lectures.

Christ Will Come Back as Light

The Teacher began by reading Proverbs, chapters 30 and 31.

Your biggest mistake is that everybody would like to moralise over the behaviour of others.[1] You have been told before that it is not permissible for anyone to speak about something he or she has not experienced. If someone cannot live well on earth, how may he or she live in heaven? If a child has not learnt to walk at home, how will he or she go on to walk in the larger world outside? The first thing you need to do is to sense the Lord within you. We should go all over the earth to find the Lord, because we are deceiving ourselves if we are waiting for the Lord to find us.

There are many conditions in the world which corrupt the truth, so we need to be clever enough to filter everything, just as sand filters water. If water is filtered through clay it only becomes muddier. This is important: "Do not add to the words of God."[2] How should we understand this? We should not think like the priest who reasoned that the loaves of bread with which Christ fed the multitude had to have been gigantic.[3] We need to learn neither to add to nor subtract from the word of God, for both are sins. If you add to the meaning of God's words, you will have an insufficiency of what you require. If you reduce their meaning, you will have too much. In either case you will suffer.

Do not pay attention to the weaknesses of others: how much someone stole, how many crimes someone has committed. That is not your job. What is the benefit of burdening yourselves with other people's weaknesses and suffering for doing so?[4] The world was designed and

[1] Jesus said, "Judge not, that ye be not judged. For with what judgement ye judge, ye shall be judged: and with what measure ye mete, it shall be measured unto you" (Matthew 7:1-2). And the Apostle Paul wrote, "Wherein thou judgest another, thou condemnest thyself; for thou that judgest dost practise the same things" (Romans 2:1).

[2] "Add thou not unto God's words, Lest he reprove thee, and thou be found a liar" (Proverbs 30:6).

[3] For the feeding of the five thousand and the feeding of the four thousand, see Matthew 14:15-21 and 15:32-38 respectively.

[4] The Teacher also said, "It needs to be known that, when you speak in a bad way about

51

made to serve the Lord, and He will make everything right in the world.[5]

Let us return to the state of being in which the Lord originally placed us.[6] The praiseworthy woman in Proverbs, chapter thirty-one, represents wisdom.[7] If you marry her, you will uplift yourself, but if you marry a fool, you will be lowered.[8] This is why everybody wants to marry the woman of wisdom, who will put everything within us in order and strengthen us.[9] To go from this world to another we need a bridge. Material is needed to make the bridge. This material is wisdom, Christ, of whom you need to think. He is more powerful now than he was two thousand years ago.[10] People preach and talk about the return

other people, you nourish the evil inside you. When you speak in a good way about others, you nourish the goodness inside you. It is up to you whether you become a good or bad person" (20 September 1936).

[5] The Lord said, "I am God, and there is none like me; declaring the end from the beginning, and from ancient times things that are not yet done; saying, 'My counsel shall stand, and I will do all my pleasure'" (Isaiah 46:9-10). "My word shall not return unto me void, but it shall accomplish that which I please, and it shall prosper in the thing whereto I sent it" (Isaiah 55:11). "Behold, I create new heavens and a new earth" (Isaiah 65:17).

[6] This is the state of Paradise, the symbolic Garden of Eden, in which human beings lived as the image and likeness of God, before being cast out (see Genesis 1:26-27; 2:7–3:24). It is a state to which we can return through Christ: Jesus said, "To him that overcometh, to him will I give to eat of the tree of life, which is in the Paradise of God" (Revelation 2:7).

[7] See Proverbs 31:10-31. "A virtuous woman who can find? For her price is far above rubies. The heart of her husband trusteth in her, And he shall have no lack of gain. She doeth him good and not evil All the days of her life. Her husband is known in the gates, When he sitteth among the elders of the land. Strength and dignity are her clothing; And she laugheth at the time to come. She openeth her mouth with wisdom; And the law of kindness is on her tongue. She looketh well to the ways of her household, And eateth not the bread of idleness. A woman that feareth the Lord, she shall be praised. Give her of the fruit of her hands; And let her works praise her in the gates" (Proverbs 31:10-12, 23, 25-27, 30-31).

[8] "The foolish woman is clamorous; She is simple, and knoweth nothing. And she sitteth at the door of her house, On a seat in the high places of the city, To call to them that pass by, Who go right on their ways, 'Whoso is simple, let him turn in hither.' And as for him that is void of understanding, she saith to him, 'Stolen waters are sweet, And bread eaten in secret is pleasant.' But he knoweth not that the dead are there; That her guests are in the depths of Sheol" (Proverbs 9:13-18).

[9] "Every wise woman buildeth her house: But the foolish plucketh it down with her own hands" (Proverbs 14:1).

[10] Two years later, almost a month into the First World War, the Teacher said, "Christ is coming! His power will be seven times greater than in previous ages, which means humanity's development will be accelerated" (10/23 August 1914).

of Christ, and he really will come again – but He will come as light. And when he does, we will have pleasure, a far greater pleasure than we experience from the light and warmth of the sun.[11]

When Christ comes he will teach us, and then we will understand the meaning of the political events we are now witnessing.[12] What is the relationship between the contemporary material order and the tree of life? First you have a king, then the ministers of state and then the whole nation. To what is a king similar? Think on this question, and I would like to know your conclusions. The whole social structure is a tree with roots, branches and leaves. What does the blossom represent? Let us think deeply to understand all of our relationships, for then we will develop correctly.[13]

---

[11] Jesus said, "I am the light of the world: he that followeth me shall not walk in the darkness, but shall have the light of life" (John 8:12). "The lamp of the body is the eye: if therefore thine eye be single, thy whole body shall be full of light" (Matthew 6:22). Referring to this last verse, the Teacher said, "Christ spoke about one eye, which is located in the centre of the brain, and which I will call 'the eye of the soul'" (11 May 1919). At the Last Supper, Jesus promised to return and live with God inside his disciples and whoever has faith through them (see John 14:15-28; 17:20-26). With regard to this, the Teacher said, "People are too concerned with the physical aspect of Christ, but what Christ meant was, 'Whoever fulfils the will of my Father will live in light'" (4 May 1919).

It is written in Revelation, "The angel carried me away in the Spirit to a mountain great and high, and shewed me the holy city Jerusalem, coming down out of heaven from God. And I saw no temple therein: for the Lord God the Almighty, and the Lamb, are the temple thereof. And the city hath no need of the sun to shine upon it: for the glory of God did lighten it, and the lamp thereof is the lamb.

"Jesus said, 'Behold, I come quickly; and my reward is with me, to render to each man according as his work is.' Blessed are they that wash their robes, that they may have the right to come to the tree of life, and may enter in by the gates into the city.

"He which testifieth these things saith, 'Yea: I come quickly.' Amen: come Lord Jesus" (Revelation 21:10, 22-23; 22:12, 14, 20).

[12] What the Teacher meant by "the political events we are now witnessing" can only be speculated upon. However, at that time political moves were being made in the Balkans, albeit covertly, that would have important consequences.

Earlier in the year, with Russian urging, Bulgaria and Serbia had secretly formed an apparently defensive alliance to protect themselves against Austria-Hungary. Even more concealed was the actual main direction of the treaty, which was offensive against the Ottoman Empire. The Balkan alliance had since been enlarged, and in three months' time Bulgaria, Greece, Montenegro and Serbia would be at war with the Ottoman Empire.

[13] "The angel shewed me a river of water of life, bright as crystal, proceeding out of the throne of God and of the Lamb, in the midst of the street of new Jerusalem. And on this side of the river and on that was the tree of life, bearing twelve manner of fruits, yielding its fruit every month: and the leaves of the tree were for the healing of the nations" (Revelation 22:1-2).

You now have plenty of material inside you, but it is spread all over the place. You need to have a system with which to put it in order. Ask Christ and he will teach you to use your available materials.

It is interesting to see how you understand me – human logic is often discordant with heavenly logic. We ought to be in touch with the Lord daily and pray for Him to teach us. And when the Lord teaches us, we should listen. When spiritual people think they have no obligations in the world, they are mistaken. You need to remember that you cannot end your obligations in the world.

Let me repeat myself: find wisdom. This wisdom is Christ, who is on earth. He will correct everything in your lives and solve all the questions that impede you. You need suitable clothes for the conditions into which you will come when you return to earth. Be careful to make fine material for the clothes of your next incarnation. Do not think that the Lord will take other people's wool for your clothes. No, you with your own loom should weave the material and matter with which you will be dressed next.[14]

I am telling you all these things because you need to know them so that you can help me and I can help you. If you help me, I will help you. If you impede me, I will impede you. If you bite me, I will bite you.

[14] Jesus said, "I counsel thee to buy of me white garments, that thou mayest clothe thyself" (Revelation 3:18).

The Testament of the Colour Rays of Light

During the Annual Congress of the Chain in 1912,[1] *which was held over seven days, the Teacher presented a new book, The Testament of the Colour Rays of Light, to his disciples and explained its contents. He authored it with his spiritual name, Beinsa Douno,*[2] *and said it was written under the guidance of Christ. This small book is a tool for spiritual and psychological development and for healing and renewal. It consists of biblical verses selected and arranged according to their corresponding virtues and colour vibrations.*[3]

The Colour Rays:

Red:	The Spirit of Life
Pink:	The Spirit of Love
Orange:	The Spirit of Promise
Yellow:	The Spirit of Wisdom
Green:	The Eternal Spirit
Blue:	The Spirit of Truth
Violet:	The Spirit of Power
Amethyst:	The Spirit of Grace
White Diamond:	The Spirit of Christ

At the conference, the Teacher said the following.

I will tell you the colour corresponding to each day of the week, so you may know which colour to apply each day: Monday, green; Tuesday, red; Wednesday, yellow; Thursday, blue; Friday, pink; Saturday, violet; Sunday, amethyst.

When we combine the verses in this book with certain solar rays, we

[1] The disciples as a collective were called the Chain until 1919, when they became known as the White Brotherhood.

[2] There does not appear to be a record of how or when he received this name.

[3] The Teacher gave the following warning: "This book is the first lesson that Christ is giving you. Whoever decides to work with it needs to be very careful, because if it is not done correctly, it will have a negative effect and you will be damned" (15/28 August).

benefit. It is a fact that when we unite ourselves with the colour rays, we begin to create. Let us make use of light, for everything depends on light, which is essential to life. We need to bring all the colours into our lives. When we do, the seven spirits will unite and humanity will return to its original state.[4]

The Testament of the Colour Rays of Light ends with an instruction and a promise to the disciple:

The Sacred Command of the Teacher

Love the perfect path of truth and life.
Place goodness as a foundation of your home,
Righteousness as a measure,
Love as an adornment,
Wisdom as a fence
And truth as a light.
Only then will you come to know me
And I shall reveal myself to you.

---

[4] The 'seven spirits' are spoken of in Revelation:

"I John was in the Spirit on the Lord's day, and I heard behind me a great voice, as of a trumpet. And I turned to see the voice which spake with me. And having turned I saw one like unto a son of man. And his voice was as the voice of many waters. And his countenance was as the sun shineth in his strength.

"I saw, and behold, a door opened in heaven, and the voice which I heard, a voice as of a trumpet speaking with me, one saying, 'Come up hither, and I will shew thee the things which must come to pass hereafter.' Straightway I was in the Spirit: and behold, there was a throne set in heaven, and one sitting upon the throne: and there was a rainbow round about the throne. And there were seven lamps of fire burning before the throne, which are the seven Spirits of God. And I saw in the midst of the throne a Lamb standing, as though it had been slain, having seven horns, and seven eyes, which are the seven Spirits of God, sent forth into all the earth" (Revelation 1:10, 12-13, 15-16; 4:1-3, 5; 5:6).

God said, "Behold, I lay in Zion for a foundation a stone, a tried stone, a precious corner stone of sure foundation" (Isaiah 28:16). "Hear now, O Joshua the high priest, thou and thy fellows that sit before thee; for they are men which are a sign: for, behold, I will bring forth my servant the Branch. For behold, the stone that I have set before Joshua; upon one stone are seven eyes" (Zechariah 3:8-9). And Jesus said, "To him that overcometh, I will give him a white stone" (Revelation 2:17). And in The Testament of the Colour Rays of Light, the Teacher wrote, "Upon a white stone shall be seven eyes."

Gossip

The Teacher said the following words to the more senior members of the Chain.

Some things between you need to be smoothed. There have been many 'sacrifices' in the past which were not of the will of God.[1] God does not want such sacrifices to be necessary in the future. From now on, whoever would like to follow the Lord should indeed follow Him. Some disharmony exists among you that the Dark Lodge uses to exercise its bad influence.[2] If you do not do everything you can to correct this now, the invisible world will intercede and correct it....

You want to receive blessings, do you not? Listen to me and behave towards me as I behave towards you. You have a kind of monarchism that may turn me into a burdened donkey. You want freedom, so give me freedom. Friendship requires that you behave towards me as I behave towards you. Some disharmony has existed between us for the past two years. For everything bad which you have thrown at me, I ought to send you to the astral world with one blow. However, I would hold back myself as well as you with such an act. If anyone has some doubt, please tell me about it. My work is clear.

We have new friends now and more who will come in the future. The dark forces want to impede me, which is why you need to decide in yourselves what you will do from now on. I have been commanded to tell you this. You have work to do with a Brotherhood that is not human. It will require a promise from you, and if you fulfil your promise you will enter the inner Chain and there will be no more quarrels. When you become fully in touch with this Brotherhood with which you are involved our work will progress correctly. If you do not listen to me, be sure that I will leave in three years' time. I could stay for many

---

[1] In saying, "There have been many 'sacrifices' in the past that were not of the will of God," the Teacher was referring to karmic losses experienced by certain disciples, some of which he specifies later in the talk.

[2] The Teacher also said, "On the days when the devil takes hold of you, you are sour, which means you have eaten of the forbidden fruit. A bad spirit is able to arrange its bad intentions in ten or fifteen people simultaneously" (21 January/3 February 1915).

more years, but I will do so only if you provide good conditions for our work. Let me tell you, this work is serious. We are now working in darkness, but later you will see clearly. It does not matter how you see and feel now; you need to know that if this work is held back, the Bulgarian nation will be held back, as will you, for several generations.

You must all know and obey the rule of not talking about things which you did not see with your own eyes or which you have not verified. It is the truth that will uplift you. Guessing, presumption and gossip must not influence you.[3] I am telling you, and I will tell you again, that I am giving you an example of how to love the Lord – this is the entirety of my task. Were I to succeed, it would be good. Were I not to succeed, it would also be good. A person can be great even when no one else is aware of it.

You have children and houses. You want to raise your children well, and I want to show you how to do so. This nation needs people who live correctly. If you impede my work, the Lord will find other people to help me, which will neither be good for you nor for Bulgaria. My desire is to rid you of this disharmony that causes many bad things. The misunderstandings and quarrels of the last year caused some bad things to happen. They caused the death of the son-in-law of one disciple, the death of the child of another disciple, and caused the child of another to become blind. You have seen these sad results. Let them strengthen your desire to smooth the disagreements among you. These disagreements also hold me back.[4]

If you continue to impede me, at the end of 1914 I will sort things out myself. You are invited to work, and it will be good if you follow me. I am connected with you and I do not want you to impede me. I am responsible before heaven for this work. I consider you my friends,

[3] Jesus said, "Every idle word that men shall speak, they shall give account thereof in the day of judgement. For by thy words thou shalt be justified, and by thy words thou shalt be condemned" (Matthew 12:36-37).

"If any man thinketh himself to be religious, while he bridleth not his tongue but deceiveth his heart, this man's religion is vain" (James 1:26). "A man's belly shall be filled with the fruit of his mouth; With the increase of his lips shall he be satisfied. Death and life are in the power of the tongue; And they that love it shall eat the fruit thereof" (Proverbs 18:20-21).

[4] These "sad results" were examples of the "many 'sacrifices' in the past which were not of the will of God" that the Teacher referred to at the beginning of the talk.

which is why I am telling you these things and why I do not want you to impede me.

It is not possible to work for the Lord without love and self-sacrifice. Christ told me, "I am coming to help this nation, to review all disagreements and to destroy all interfering spirits." Christ and I are one, and you cannot attract me with anything other than your love. Your thoughts torment me, they cause me to suffer. I will only give an inheritance to those who stay close to me. In the name of God, I would like you to make a great reconciliation among yourselves.

A discussion ensued during which grievances were aired and points of view explained, followed by a general reconciliation. Then the Teacher continued his talk.

Christ met me in Arbanasi and told me about these problems.[5] Christ is present here, participating in this meeting. Do not say anything about the inner Chain. We will work this year to develop the inner strength of the Chain.

---

[5] Arbanasi is a village overlooking Turnovo (now Veliko Turnovo), a city in central Bulgaria to the north of the Balkan Mountains. The Teacher sometimes stayed in a house in Arbanasi, which is where he wrote *The Testament of the Colour Rays of Light* over two months in the summer of 1912.

Unblocking the Path for Future Disciples

This year we will put aside philosophical discussions and begin to work. There are many conditions in which the *Colour Rays* experiment that we are conducting may be successful. During any experiment the participants are attacked from the outside, but there needs to be harmony on the inside. And when we are attacked we will fight in the world outside, but we must have no fighting inside, among ourselves. If we fight internally we will achieve nothing.

A schedule of work will be given to us from above that we will begin to follow. It is not necessary to correct how Theosophy and Orthodox Religion and other religions interpret the Gospel. Every spiritual teaching is good, although people can apply any of them for evil. The Lord sends us a pure spring and we should not contaminate it.[1] We need another channel for our impurities. We must be pure, for otherwise those who are above us will leave us.[2]

First of all I would like you to love the Lord. If you have this love you will have a foundation for work. If you do not have it, confrontations will take place over such questions as who among you is the most or least important. The Lord is near us, but He only says things once....[3] I would now like to teach you, and you will repeat the mistakes of the past if you do not listen to me. On Fridays, Saturdays and Sundays let us work with *The Testament of the Colour Rays of Light*, using yellow to restore the harmony of our souls.[4] Bearing in mind that pink acts on Friday,

---

[1] "O Lord, the hope of Israel, all that forsake thee shall be ashamed; they that depart from me shall be written in the earth, because they have forsaken the Lord, the fountain of living waters" (Jeremiah 17:13).

[2] By "those who are above us" the Teacher meant the more advanced beings from the lighter realms who were helping the work and the development of the disciples.

[3] "God hath spoken once, Twice have I heard this; That power belongeth unto God" (Psalm 62:11).

[4] The Teacher also said, "In cases of disputes within the Chain [the Brotherhood], use the yellow colour, reading all the verses on wisdom, for they can smooth dogmatic or other kinds of disputes. If that does not work, also use the verses of the blue colour, so that the Spirit of Truth will cast light on the minds of those who are arguing and they will come to an understanding.

violet on Saturday and orange on Sunday, you need to direct your work with the *Colour Rays* under the guidance of the Spirit within you.[5]

I do not want arguments among you. Why do you fight among yourselves? Instead, go outside into the world and argue and fight there as much as you want. You are all obstructed by obstacles caused by the disharmony among you, so the law you need to apply this year is to be unselfish. In other words, do not desire anything that belongs to others. You have lost your belongings, and I will show you how to find them.

Why do I help you? Because I want to help the people who will come after you, for you are blocking the path they need to follow. In helping you I am helping you to unblock the path for them. In using *The Testament of the Colour Rays of Light* we are performing an experiment given to us by heaven. The White Brotherhood is conducting the experiment, and it will help you in this process. Do not worry about the different forms of spiritual manifestation, because all faiths and all spiritual schools are heading towards the inner side, which is the same for all. You need to love all people and to respect their beliefs – for your love of the Lord, leave them alone! The success of this nation will depend on how you work....

"Since *The Colour Rays* is Christ's method, although it is simple, the results will be most gratifying. By using it we will create harmony among us and we will connect with the White Light Brotherhood, the Brotherhood of Light, which has been helping you greatly, very greatly" (18/31 August 1912).

[5] The Teacher had previously said that amethyst acts on Sundays, and he was not recorded as giving a day for orange (see p. 55 of the present volume).

Correct Thought and Prayer

If you would like your prayers to be heard in heaven, your hearts have to be pure. A prayer made with a sufficiently pure heart has intense vibrations that will destroy all obstacles on its path of ascent to heaven. What does intensive prayer mean? It means to repent of past mistakes and to be completely ready to fulfil the will of God.[1]

When a bad thought comes to you, you must cast it aside, because it is a rope of the devil with which he will bind you to himself. Our thoughts should be intensely for the good – this is the will of God. Therefore, you should not stare at the mistakes of other people. Every suffering comes as a blessing, and whenever the Lord helps somebody, He sends other people to do it.

Never complain, for heaven appreciates nothing less.[2] Think about these four things: first of all, having patience; second, being calm; third, not criticising other people; the mistakes of others should serve as a lesson for you; fourth, respecting one another.

[1] The Teacher also said, "If we bear the brunt of our mistakes and do not deliberately repeat those mistakes, the Lord will forgive us" (22 January/4 February 1915).

[2] "Rejoice alway; pray without ceasing; in everything give thanks: for this is the will of God in Christ Jesus toward you" (1 Thessalonians 5:16-18).

Carry the Cross with Gratitude

Jesus said,

Whosoever doth not bear his own cross, and come after me, cannot be my disciple. [1]

In contemporary life, these words mean that anyone who would like to become knowledgeable or to attain wealth without making great efforts is not worthy of either. Some people want divine blessings and to enter heaven. If they want to enter heaven, they need to know that it is not a place for sinners or those who are ignorant. Heaven is a place for those who are righteous, intelligent and golden-tongued. [2] Whoever wants to be strong has to obey the divine laws in this world. You can only walk on either the left side or the right side. Black magicians walk on the left side; good people are those of the right side. You should have knowledge, but knowledge cannot function correctly without virtue. A person needs to be not only as hard as a diamond but also flexible so that he or she is able to face challenges. For example, the branch of a tree can bend because there is life in it. And you also will be able to bend if you live correctly.

The higher meaning in life is found in suffering. When people complain about their suffering, it is because they want to walk the left path. There is no greater suffering than the Lord's, for people crucify Him daily. All people need to study themselves, for only then will they be able to understand others. All your present difficulties were caused by your carrying them here from your past. When you want to do battle, instead reconcile with your enemy, because if your enemy is stronger

---

[1] Luke 14:27. The Teacher actually read the whole chapter.

[2] "The tongue of the wise uttereth knowledge aright" (Proverbs 15:2). Jesus said, "Out of the abundance of the heart the mouth speaketh. The good man out of his good treasure bringeth forth good things: and the evil man out of his evil treasure bringeth forth evil things. And I say unto you, that every idle word that men shall speak, they shall give account thereof in the day of judgement. For by thy words thou shalt be justified, and by thy words thou shalt be condemned" (Matthew 12:34-37).

than you, you will be defeated. If you want to tread the right path, you have to be strong and you absolutely require divine knowledge. A great price is required for this knowledge, which is nothing other than the deposit of your soul. In saying, "Whoever does not carry his or her own cross cannot be my disciple," Christ meant that no one can be his disciple unless he or she is able to suffer with gladness.

Sometimes we wish to serve the Lord, but when the Lord sends us suffering, we pray, "Please, Lord, end my suffering!" With such a plea a person shows that he or she is not yet ready to work for the Lord. When someone remains firm and constant in times of suffering, the Lord says, "This person is ready to work for Me," and includes him or her among His workers. You need to know that when you are making a transition from one state to another, there is a border of transition, a border on which there is always suffering. Such suffering mostly revolves around material concerns, but there are harder things than that. For example, to lose your money or to have difficulties in your marriage is less severe than having your body taken from you.

I do not need people who have become fearful in soul and hesitant in mind. Let them leave the border of transition and return to the world. I wish everything to be good for them, for there is also good in the world. To those who would like to constantly move forwards on the path of life we will give new weapons with which to battle.[3] It is not enough for us to say we love Christ; we have to demonstrate this love in our lives. That is why you each have to take up your cross and say to the Lord, "Thank You, Lord, for giving me this cross." If you have this attitude, the Lord will pull you towards Him and make you strong. If you insist on the Lord revealing your future and past to you, He will ask, "Are you able to drink this cup?"[4] If you want the blessing but do

---

[3] "Be strong in the Lord, and in the strength of his might. Put on the whole armour of God, that ye may be able to stand against the wiles of the devil. For our wrestling is not against flesh and blood, but against the principalities, against the powers, against the world-rulers of this darkness, against the spiritual hosts of wickedness in the heavenly places. Wherefore take up the whole armour of God, that ye may be able to withstand in the evil day, and, having done all, to stand. Stand therefore, having girded your loins with truth, and having put on the breastplate of righteousness, and having shod your feet with the preparation of the gospel of peace; withal taking up the shield of faith, wherewith ye shall be able to quench all the fiery darts of the evil one. And take the helmet of salvation, and the sword of the Spirit, which is the word of God" (Ephesians 6:10-17).

[4] "There came near unto Jesus James and John, the sons of Zebedee, saying unto him, 'Mas-

not want to drink the cup, the Lord will say, "Go away!" You will train yourselves in the world among people. Bad people will be you teachers. I say it again: you will not receive help until you are ready to drink from the bitter cup that the Lord will give you.[5] This is why Christ said, "Whoever does not carry his or her own cross cannot be my disciple."

Look the world directly in the eye, because I have a bad opinion of anybody who looks at the ground. Whoever looks for his or her treasure in the ground will go there one day.... Our treasure is not on earth; it is in heaven.[6] Do not be afraid of the cross, because it is the secret by which human beings are saved. Do not carry the cross as a diamond-encrusted ornament worn on your chest. Instead, carry your cross within your heart, where its beautiful fragrance can blossom and bring you the beneficial things you desire.[7]

ter, we would that thou shouldest do for us whatsoever we shall ask of thee.' And he said unto them, 'What would ye that I should do for you?' And they said unto him, 'Grant unto us that we may sit, one on thy right hand, and one on thy left hand, in thy glory.' But Jesus said unto them, 'Ye know not what ye ask. Are ye able to drink the cup that I drink? or to be baptized with the baptism that I am baptized with?'" (Mark 10:35-38).

[5] "They come unto a place which was named Gethsemane: and Jesus saith unto his disciples, 'Sit ye here, while I pray.' And he taketh with him Peter and James and John, and began to be greatly amazed, and sore troubled. And he saith unto them, 'My soul is exceeding sorrowful even unto death: abide ye here, and watch.' And he went forward a little, and fell on the ground, and prayed that, if it were possible, the hour might pass away from him. And he said, 'Abba, Father, all things are possible unto thee; remove this cup from me: howbeit not what I will, but what thou wilt'" (Mark 14:32-36). "And then there appeared unto Jesus an angel from heaven, strengthening him" (Luke 22:43).

[6] Jesus said, "Lay not up for yourselves treasures upon the earth: but lay up for yourselves treasures in heaven: for where thy treasure is, there will thy heart be also" (Matthew 6:19-21).

[7] Jesus said, "If ye abide in me, and my words abide in you, ask whatsoever ye will, and it shall be done unto you" (John 15:7).

Moral Character

Jesus said,

He that loveth his life loseth it; and he that hateth his life in this world shall keep it unto life eternal. [1]

These are interesting words. This verse is similar to the verse about the branches on the vine which bear fruit. [2] The world has been in a state of siege for seventy-five years. [3] In 1897 heaven gave the world an ultimatum with a deadline of 1914.... [4]

Your minds should not be afraid, because fear interrupts the acts of God. The suffering that you will soon begin to observe, due to the coming war, will be suffering on the physical level. [5] This, however, is not

[1] John 12:25. The Teacher actually read the whole chapter.

[2] Jesus said, "I am the true vine, and my Father is the husbandman. Every branch in me that beareth not fruit, he taketh it away: and every branch that beareth fruit, he cleanseth it, that it may bear more fruit. Already ye are clean because of the word which I have spoken unto you. Abide in me, and I in you. As the branch cannot bear fruit of itself, except it abide in the vine; so neither can ye, except ye abide in me. I am the vine, ye are the branches: He that abideth in me, and I in him, the same beareth much fruit: for apart from me ye can do nothing. If a man abide not in me, he is cast forth as a branch, and is withered; and they gather them, and cast them into the fire, and they are burned. If ye abide in me, and my words abide in you, ask whatsoever ye will, and it shall be done unto you. Herein is my Father glorified, that ye bear much fruit; and so shall ye be my disciples. Even as the Father hath loved me, I also have loved you: abide ye in my love. If ye keep my commandments, ye shall abide in my love; even as I have kept my Father's commandments, and abide in his love" (John 15:1-10).

[3] The reference to "seventy-five years" is historically unclear. If the Teacher was being literal, the relevant year, 1837, was midway between the European revolutions of 1830 and 1848. In general it can be taken that he meant the ambitious self-interest of the European great powers and their aggressive rivalries, which would culminate two years later in the First World War.

[4] Intriguingly, during the actual First World War (1914–18), the Teacher said, "This war was delayed for two years; it should have begun in 1912" (21 January/3 February 1915). Unfortunately, he is not recorded as having explained why it was delayed.

[5] The First Balkan War (1912–13) began two days after this talk, when Montenegro declared war on the Ottoman Empire on 25 September/8 October. The other members of the Balkan alliance – namely Bulgaria, Greece and Serbia – soon followed, declaring war

the same as the suffering of the moral character, which hurts heaven. You may enter the kingdom of God without a leg or an arm, but if your moral character suffers you will be in great danger. It is good if the body is sacrificed for the development of the soul. This is why all those who know the Lord should say deep in their hearts, "Lord, Your will be done." Stay with the Lord, for He is the Supreme Commander. After many years you will go and present yourselves to the Lord and report on the lives you have lived. That is why the consciousness of serving the Lord needs to be born in your souls.

All of you should be grateful to the Lord for whatever He gives you, because none of you knows exactly what it is that you need.[6] A clever person is someone who makes use of every situation in life and is thankful to heaven for everything. From now on, heaven wants you not to destroy that which the Lord wants to build. You need to subordinate to the Lord all the desires that destroy your peace, which is your spiritual balance.[7]

---

on the Ottoman Empire on 5/18 October. The Teacher may also have been referring to the First World War, which would commence in a little under two years' time.

[6] "Great is our Lord, and mighty in power; His understanding is infinite" (Psalm 147:5).

[7] The Teacher also said, "You must restore your inner peace, for only then will you be able to act correctly" (18/31 August 1912). And Brother Krum Vuzharov said, "When we were in the Teacher's aura, we were transformed. Our love for him was boundless. In the presence of our beloved Teacher, the words of Christ, 'My peace I leave with you, my peace I give to you,' became our reality."

Monotony and Diversity

Monotony is a killer of life. Life is found in diversity, which is why it is good that the Spirit changes conditions. Even though conditions change, harmony should remain. If you often blame someone for things, he or she will become pigheaded. If instead you were to consistently show him or her loving-kindness, it would produce another reaction. If someone offends you, accept it from the Lord so that you will be blessed. If someone gives you a kind word, also be grateful. We often see things only from our own points of view, but the Lord knows the real reason why sinners are in the position in which we see them. When we hold another person in our souls, it means we are also keeping the Lord in our souls.

What does spiritual development mean? Spiritual development is nothing other than the soul being ready to respond to other people's calls for help, which requires us to be flexible, to be able to accept a divine thought, to accept the Lord and act according to His will. When the Lord demands that we be silent, we ought to listen to Him. When you are grateful to the Lord you are in harmony with Him, but you need to know that He will leave you the moment you have a bad thought about someone else. The Divine Spirit cannot work where there is misunderstanding, anger or any kind of fighting. We need always to be ready to fulfil whatever the Lord wants, for only then will we be truly happy. The Lord wants there to be agreement and peace between all His children, because the Lord, within Himself, is love, wisdom and truth.[1]

If you suffer, if you are tormented, it is the Lord who will save you from the tormenting situation. This is why you need to keep hold of the Lord. Try to be in harmony with the Spirit of Christ. When you think on these words, do not look at how other people are living; instead, look

---

[1] "Let every man be swift to hear, slow to speak, slow to wrath: for the wrath of man worketh not the righteousness of God. The fruit of righteousness is sown in peace for them that make peace" (James 1:19-20; 3:18). Jesus said, "Blessed are the peacemakers: for they shall be called sons of God" (Matthew 5:9).

at yourself. Do not hold each other back. We pass through thousands of different situations in life, and it is thanks to the spirits who are sent to us as helpers that we are able to escape our difficulties.

The Spirit Elohim rules over everything and observes contemporary events.[2] We are now serving the Lord, and He is the one who will bring about the necessary agreement between you. Know that I am already praying to the Lord: "Lord, teach the one whom You will teach, uplift the one whom You will uplift, pardon the one whom You will pardon, save the one whom You will save, and punish the one whom You will punish."[3]

[2] The Angel Elohim is responsible for the upflifting of those who will form the new human being (see Introduction, pp. xvii–xviii).

[3] The phrasing here is reminiscent of something that the Lord said to Moses: "I will be gracious to whom I will be gracious, and will shew mercy on whom I will shew mercy" (Exodus 33:19).

The Dawning Epoch

It is written in Genesis,

> The Lord said unto Abram, "Get thee out of thy country, and from thy kindred, and from thy father's house, unto the land that I will shew thee." So Abram went, as the Lord had spoken unto him. [1]

And it is written in the First Epistle of John,

> **This is the love of God, that we keep his commandments.** [2]

We can see that Abraham went out of his father's house. [3] The important concepts here are 'obedience' and 'your father's house', because they are the range within which the soul is bound and cannot leave. Why do you need to leave the home of your father? It is because you have inherited thousands of desires which are alive inside you, and when you want to fulfil the will of God these desires pull you back. You are involved with your daily lives and their struggles and needs, and therefore you stop thinking about the Lord and do not prepare food for the journey to distant spheres on which you will one day embark. That is your great mistake. [4]

In many ways the invisible world looks at our lives like we look at ants. We might step on an anthill and destroy their home. When we feel

---

[1] Genesis 12:1, 4. The Teacher actually read the whole of Genesis chapters 12 and 13.

[2] 1 John 5:3. The Teacher actually read the whole of 1 John 5.

[3] When Abram was ninety-nine years old, the Lord renamed him Abraham (see Genesis 17:1-8).

[4] "It is written, 'Ye shall be holy; for I am holy.' And if ye call on him as Father, who without respect of persons judgeth according to each man's work, pass the time of your sojourning here in fear: knowing that ye were redeemed, not with corruptible things, with silver or gold, from your vain manner of life handed down from your fathers; but with the precious blood, as of a lamb without blemish and without spot, even the blood of Christ" (1 Peter 1:16-19).

something strange, we need to be aware that a being from the invisible world might likewise be stepping on us. Yes, the secrets of the cause of the Fall of Humanity are most profound. I will tell you about them when you have raised yourselves.[5] For now you only need to know how to walk along the path on which you have been placed. Seek only that which is essential for today, just as a lawyer does research only for a current court case. You should only hold desires that can be realised.

It is right to seek happiness, higher learning and wisdom, for only then will we be fulfilled and know that we are headed in the right direction. First you need to aspire to wisdom. Through wisdom you will come to the truth, and it is through the truth that you will become free.[6] If you are not free, you are not working with the truth. This world is not yet divine, it is not organised, which is why we need Christ. At present we are doubtful. Why? This doubt is natural, for people cannot give you the truth; it is the Spirit within you that will give you the truth. Each one of you should seek profoundly for the truth within.[7] This is what Christ meant when he said, "When you seek me, you will find me."[8] It is necessary to find the Lord.

You are now at the dawn of a great new epoch. It is four in the morning and a battle is taking place between the Dark Lodge and the White Lodge. The coming epoch will be a great one. Heaven's purpose is to give freedom, which is good for whoever can make use of it. Those who are unable to use this freedom will have to wait into the future to be able to advance themselves spiritually.[9] This war will bring materi-

---

[5] The Teacher also said, "Animals suffer at the hands of human beings in the same way that human beings suffer at the hands of beings from the astral world" (9/22 September 1912). "In the beginning the human being was a master, and when humanity fell it pulled the other creatures down with it" (10/23 January 1915).

[6] Jesus said, "If ye abide in my word, then are ye truly my disciples; and ye shall know the truth, and the truth shall make you free" (John 8:31-32).

[7] "The Spirit is the truth" (1 John 5:7).

[8] Jesus said, "Seek, and ye shall find: for he that seeketh findeth" (Matthew 7:7-8).

[9] Years later, the Teacher said, "The invisible world is now using fire as the most efficient way to purify the earth. We are entering a new zone, in which matter is in a divine state that will transform and purify everything. How? Through the divine fire. The new life, which is now coming to the earth, will renovate matter and make it finer. Everything useful will be uplifted; everything useless will be thrown out.

"I am not talking about a visible fire that can be measured in degrees. This fire cannot be measured with any kind of thermometer. When this fire comes to your hearts, it will free them of worries and troubles. It will make your hearts shine. When this fire comes

71

al destruction. It will also bring another war at the spiritual level, for which we need to be ready.[10] The present war is insignificant compared with the coming war.[11] Many souls will leave for the invisible world, but we should not be sad or cry because it will upset them. Instead, we ought to pray for them, because only our prayers will feed them. Your prayers need to be pure and of a high quality.

to your minds, all contradictions will disappear and you will be freed of heavy, dark thoughts. When this fire comes, righteous people will shine and be resurrected. They will leave their tombs and enter the new life. All negative thoughts, feelings and actions will be burned. The fire will not disturb good people; it will trouble bad people, because their vibrations are not in harmony with the powerful vibrations of this wave" (some time between 1929 and 1942).

[10] Several months into the First World War, which began almost two years after this lecture, the Teacher said, "Archangel Michael is fighting above and will bring down the bad spirits. Then the peace of the earth will be removed for a period of time, as is happening now. Seventeen million soldiers are now fighting here on earth, but those coming from above will number two hundred million. I have been asked who will be the victor in the war, Germany or Russia. Neither Germany nor Russia will be victorious. Christ will be the victor, the victory will come from above" (5/18 January 1915).

[11] "The present war" was the First Balkan War, which had begun twelve days earlier (25 September/8 October), and which Bulgaria had entered two days before this talk (5/18 October).

The Religion of Life

The Teacher showed those present with him a Kabbalistic painting that predicted the Balkan War, which had recently begun. [1] *A discussion about the war ensued, after which the Teacher asked a disciple to read chapter fifteen of John's Gospel. The Teacher then spoke of Christ's love and explained that the religion of Christ is a religion of life. He concluded by saying,*

[1] Bulgaria's primary motive for making war with the Ottoman Empire was to incorporate Macedonia into a greater Bulgaria, which it considered to be its rightful home.

Bulgaria had been a great medieval kingdom. The Ottomans conquered the Bulgarian lands in the second half of the fourteenth century, with the final defeat in 1396. The people remained under the Ottoman yoke for almost five hundred years. During the nineteenth century Bulgaria experienced a nationalist awakening. After recent Balkan revolts against the Ottoman Empire, especially the brutal suppression of the Bulgarian uprising of 1876, Russia went to war in support of its fellow Slavs and Orthodox Christians. In the summer of 1877, the Russians invaded south of the Danube into Bulgarian lands and defeated the Ottoman forces by early 1878. The war-ending Treaty of San Stephano drew up boundaries for a new, large, independent Bulgarian principality within the Ottoman Empire, comparable to the old Bulgarian kingdom.

Austria-Hungary and especially Britain, however, were intent on not allowing a Russian-influenced greater Bulgaria to dominate the Balkans. A conference was therefore convened in Berlin in the summer of 1878 to prevent a European war over Bulgaria and to maintain the balance of power in Europe. The resulting Treaty of Berlin formed very different Bulgarian boundaries to those of the San Stephano Treaty: a greatly diminished independent Principality of Bulgaria was created within the Ottoman Empire, comprising a region around Sofia and the land to the south of the Danube and north of the Balkan Mountains. Of the rest of 'San Stephano' Bulgaria, the land to the east of Sofia and south of the Balkan Mountains and north of the Rhodope Mountains became the new, semi-autonomous Ottoman province of Eastern Rumelia; Macedonia and eastern Thrace were to remain fully in the Ottoman Empire; and smaller regions were allocated to Serbia and Romania.

The Bulgarian nation was therefore re-established with a sense of having been unjustly diminished. In response it formed ambitions to 'reacquire' the land and people that it believed were rightly Bulgarian, which would have important long-term ramifications. In 1885, after a bloodless coup in Eastern Rumelia, Bulgaria declared the two provinces unified. This led to another great-power intervention, in which a compromise was agreed that made the prince of Bulgaria also the Governor-General of the Ottoman province of Eastern Rumelia. In reality, however, the two regions were now one in all but name. In 1908 Bulgaria proclaimed itself to be a united, fully independent kingdom, making the final, formal break with the Ottoman Empire.

Three years later, in the latter part of 1911, Bulgaria and Serbia began the secret negotiations that would lead to the First Balkan War, working to come to an agreement over their competing claims in Macedonia.

Be grateful to God for His mercy and kindness and for the protection we are receiving from Him during this difficult time in Bulgaria.

The Name of God

The three most important parts of the Lord's Prayer are:

> **Hallowed be thy name.**
> **Thy kingdom come.**

And,

> **Thy will be done.**[1]

In Psalm 115 the important words are:

> **Not unto us, O Lord, not to us,**
> **But unto thy name give glory,**
> **For thy mercy, and for thy truth's sake.**[2]

To be able to hallow the Name of God within us we first have to sanctify our bodies.[3] The kingdom of God will only come to us when our hearts are ready for it. The kingdom of God relates to the heart. If the kingdom of God does not come to the heart, it means the heart is not yet sufficiently developed.[4] The will of God also relates to the heart, but first it has to reside in the mind.[5] The meaning of the words "lead us not into temptation"[6] is a request to be kept away from any temptation that cannot be endured.

There are three stages through which individuals pass in their evo-

---

[1] Matthew 6:9-10. The Lord's Prayer is given in Matthew 6:9-13.

[2] Psalm 115:1. The Teacher actually read the whole psalm at the very start of the talk.

[3] "Know ye not that your body is a temple of the Holy Spirit which is in you, which ye have from God? and ye are not your own; for ye were bought with a price: glorify God therefore in your body" (1 Corinthians 6:19-20).

[4] "God is love." (1 John 4:8). Jesus said, "The kingdom of God is within you" (Luke 17:21). And the Teacher said, "The Spirit gives birth to love, because love is the fruit of this Spirit" (8 June 1919).

[5] Jesus said, "The lamp of the body is the eye" (Matthew 6:22). And the Teacher said, "Christ said that the spiritual eye corresponds with the human heart. There is a close connection between them" (11 May 1919).

[6] See Matthew 6:13

lution: unconsciousness, consciousness and selfconsciousness. Only selfconscious people may follow the Lord. Where there is only consciousness there is fear and a role for the gun, the sword and other such things. In other words, crude power prevails. The highest state is superconsciousness. The Lord uplifts selfconscious people. He does not uplift those who are in the sphere of simple consciousness, which is the animal level of consciousness.[7]

To be able to glorify the Lord, you need to have something by which to connect to Him. You cannot be grateful to the Lord unless you have received something from Him. Therefore, to be able to glorify the Lord, you need to know for what it is you are glorifying Him.[8]

The first thing you need to understand is the Name of God. It is the first tap you need to open in your souls. Those who do not open the tap through which the Name of God enters the soul cannot develop themselves correctly. You need to put your body, your heart and your mind in good order. When you have done so, you will walk in the right direction.[9] The human relationship with God begins like that of a baby to its mother. The baby can only draw life when it is sucking on the mother's breast. Yet the mother will not continue breastfeeding forever; one day she will stop. You should not want to be breastfed forever. There is a rule you must remember and follow: never doubt the Lord. Keep the Name of the Lord pure in your heart; do not allow it to become stained – this is a great law which you must obey. Never hesitate.

On the path leading to the kingdom of God the whip comes first,

---

[7] The Teacher also said, "Life has four stages: superconsciousness, selfconsciousness, consciousness and unconsciousness. To have a selfconscious life means 'to know yourself'. According to the old philosophy, this means to keep one's balance. Life with selfconsciousness involves thought, feeling and will. Contemporary people are thoughtless, but as Christ said, 'Salt should not be saltless'" (15/28 January 1915).

[8] "Every good gift and every perfect boon is from above, coming down from the Father of lights" (James 1:17). "Hereby know we that we abide in God, and he in us, because he hath given us of his Spirit" (1 John 4:13).

[9] The Teacher also said, "Christ would like to say that you will find 'the path' within your body, your soul and your spirit. Christ wants to heal the body so that you will be able to accept the truth. The light that we see is his Spirit. Pray that through this, the tree of life, things may be revealed to you. I see that you want to be useful and do a great work, but to be able to do so you have to be one with Christ. Christ's justice, truth and life have to be with you. Keep this thought within you and desire that the Christ be embodied inside you" (19 August/1 September 1912). Jesus said, "The Comforter, even the Holy Spirit, whom the Father will send in my name, he shall teach you all things" (John 14:26).

which is fear.[10] Then comes faith, which is the expression of absolute and unhesitating trust in God's providence. Every one of you needs to love and sanctify the Name of the Lord, to contribute towards the coming of the kingdom of God on earth, and to do everything you can to fulfil the will of God.

So, the Lord first wants us to sanctify the Name of God, which primarily relates to the body; second, to desire the coming of the kingdom of God, which primarily relates to the heart; and third, to fulfil the will of God, which primarily relates to the mind.[11]

[10] "The fear of the Lord is the beginning of wisdom" (Proverbs 9:10).
[11] The Teacher gave a breathing formula that used these parts of the Lord's Prayer, to be said in the mind while breathing through the nose:

While breathing in:
May the Name of God be hallowed within me.
Holding the breath:
May the kingdom of God and His righteousness reign throughout me.
When exhaling:
May God's will be done.

Destiny, Obedience and Eternal Justice

Jesus said,

> Where two or three are gathered together in my name, there am I in the midst of them.[1]

Two people are needed to start any work in the world. You need to think about who these two are. Why do we want God? Because we need God in the same way as a pupil needs a teacher and a child needs a mother.

During times of suffering we need to call on the Lord. Call on the Lord in days of sorrow and He will manifest Himself to you, for only then does the Lord manifest Himself; otherwise He stays in the divine abode and does not come down to earth.[2] When the Lord gives you your medicine, you should accept it. If you do not want to take it, it means you do not want to be healed and, therefore, do not want to evolve.

It is said that whatever two or three ask in the Name of Christ, it will be given,[3] but you need to know that two elements cannot be combined if the necessary conditions for the chemical reaction are not present. Any chemist will confirm this. It is the same with us: the Lord will only answer a prayer if you have the necessary conditions for its realisation. For example, if you do not listen to the Lord and obey Him, He will not answer you.[4]

---

[1] Matthew 18:20. The Teacher actually read the whole chapter.

[2] "Thus saith the high and lofty One that inhabiteth eternity, whose name is Holy: 'I dwell in the high and holy place, with him also that is of a contrite and humble spirit, to revive the spirit of the humble, and to revive the heart of the contrite ones'" (Isaiah 57:15). "The Lord is nigh unto them that are of a broken heart, And saveth such as be of a contrite spirit" (Psalm 34:18). "He healeth the broken in heart, And bindeth up their wounds" (Psalm 147:3). Jesus said, "Blessed are they that mourn: for they shall be comforted" (Matthew 5:4).

[3] See Matthew 18:19-20

[4] "Your iniquities have separated between you and your God, and your sins have hid his

78

If you are sent unhappiness, thank God for it. Be grateful when times are good and also when you are unhappy. Never blame the Lord for your unhappiness, because you are responsible for it. In God everything is good; there is no evil in Him.[5] Suffering only comes when a person does not fulfil God's will. Suffering is the result of disobedience.

Why are 'two' needed? Because 'two' is the darkness and the light, the good and the bad, the truth and the lie. Do not expect to be happy in this life. Human beings are guests on the earth. The earth is a valley of tears for humankind. This earth is covered in the tears of millions of beings that have cried and cried and cried. If you build your happiness on earth you deceive yourself, for we have another home which is eternal.[6] When you hear the voices of relatives who have already passed away, you will understand the meaning of life. I do not, however, want you to complain. I want an end to all complaining. Everyone is creating his or her own destiny. God is the one who determines everything according to eternal justice.[7] If you feel ready for the path of the Lord, that is good. Whoever does not feel ready may stay in the world. You have been given husbands, wives and children. Why have they been given to you? Have you thought about it? Have you understood it? Make an effort to come to the right answer to this question.

The simplest thing for you now is to learn obedience. It is the only prayer with which you can successfully knock on heaven's door. Then whenever you knock, the door will be opened.[8] If you are not obedient, you can knock as much as you want and you can cry as much as you want but you will not be admitted. Power comes through obedience.[9] Obedience is a fruit, a result, a manifestation of love.

face from you, that he will not hear you" (Isaiah 59:2). "'As I cried, and they would not hear; so they shall cry, and I will not hear,' said the Lord of hosts" (Zechariah 7:13).

[5] "God is light, and in him is no darkness at all" (1 John 1:5).

[6] "We have not here an abiding city, but we seek after the city which is to come" (Hebrews 13:14). "For our citizenship is in heaven" (Philippians 3:20).

[7] "I the Lord search the heart, I try the reins, even to give every man according to his ways, according to the fruit of his doings" (Jeremiah 17:10).

[8] Jesus said, "Not every one that saith unto me, 'Lord, Lord,' shall enter into the kingdom of heaven; but he that doeth the will of my father which is in heaven" (Matthew 7:21). And the Teacher said, "We ought not to stand before God and ask a question if we have already made up our minds on the matter. Humility is a requirement of prayer" (22 January/4 February 1915).

[9] Jesus said, "The things which are impossible with men are possible with God" (Luke

18:27). The Angel Gabriel said, "No word from God shall be void of power" (Luke 1:37). And the Apostle Paul wrote, "The kingdom of God is not in word, but in power" (1 Corinthians 4:20).

Necessary Storms Are Coming

This is an important year, as I have told you before.[1] The storms that are rising are the things which need to happen to test your faith and love. Behind these storms stands One who watches the unfolding of all things,[2] One who never sleeps.[3] He is known throughout all ages and everything is sustained through His Name.

I am with you. Do not be afraid. Everything will be transformed for the good. We know the invaders who are coming – they have many names – but the Lord is the ruler of the world. Without Him nothing may happen.[4]

---

[1] Since the last recorded talk, the First Balkan War had ended (formally on 17/30 May 1913) and the Second Balkan War had started (16/29 June), when Bulgaria attacked Greek and Serbian forces. After events went rapidly against it, Bulgaria had to sue for peace, and an armistice began on the day of the present talk.

[2] "All things are naked and laid open before the eyes of God" (Hebrews 4:13).

[3] "Behold, he that keepeth Israel Shall neither slumber nor sleep" (Psalm 121:4). "The everlasting God, the Lord, the Creator of the ends of the earth, fainteth not, neither is weary" (Isaiah 40:28).

[4] God said, "All the earth is mine" (Exodus 19:5). "For I am a great king" (Malachi 1:14).

Always Be with the Lord

It is written in the Epistle of Jude,

> **Ye, beloved, building up yourselves on your most holy faith, praying in the Holy Spirit, keep yourselves in the love of God, looking for the mercy of our Lord Jesus Christ unto eternal life.** [1]

To build yourselves up in this way is the same process as purifying the heart, which means to cultivate it and to have One who helps you in the process. In Bulgaria we have a proverb: "A house cannot be built with one stone." When people think that they alone are able to purify their minds and to uplift their hearts, they are on false ground and their comprehension of life is delusional. If someone works together with the Lord, it is achievable. A disciple can work with his or her spiritual teacher only when keeping a permanent connection to that teacher. [2]

The material world and the spiritual world are the two poles in life. From the spiritual world there is descent into the material world, and from the material world there is ascent into the spiritual world. This descending and ascending is repeated eternally, because it is the unchangeable law for the progression and upliftment of humanity. This process enables human thought to develop and come to this progressive idea: everything that God has created is good. [3] This law expresses itself in self-sacrifice. It is love that pushes us towards this virtue. Without love, self-sacrifice is impossible. Without self-sacrifice there is no

---

[1] Jude 1:20-21. The original Bulgarian publication only quoted verse 20.

[2] It is still possible to have a living connection to the Teacher. Maria Mitovska, the Bulgarian translator, witnessed this powerfully on one occasion, the story of which is given in Appendix A (p. 381).

[3] "'My thoughts are not your thoughts, neither are your ways my ways,' saith the Lord. 'For as the heavens are higher than the earth, so are my ways higher than your ways, and my thoughts than your thoughts'" (Isaiah 55:8-9). And the Apostle Paul wrote, "We know that to them that love God all things work together for good, even to them that are called according to his purpose" (Romans 8:28).

progression in thought, there is no enlightenment in the mind.

Were we only to live in the spiritual world we would make no progress. We have to descend from the spiritual world and enter the physical-material world to uplift ourselves spiritually. We have our experiences, learn our lessons and take our examinations in the physical realm. It is at the physical level that we solve all the problems given to us as the purpose of any one human lifetime. It is in the spiritual world that we are assigned our missions, our work and our tasks in the material world. Descending and ascending is life and death, death and life. Each life ends in death, and from each death a new life begins.

The fallen angels, who left heaven a long time ago, understand how to manipulate the spiritual laws very well.[4] You can see this when a noble thought is born in you: the moment you have a noble thought, these angels immediately put the opposite thought in your mind as well. For example, you say to yourself, "From now on I will follow the Lord," and these angels immediately speak to you: "Wait until you are older. First establish a position in society, then it will be easier to follow the Lord." You accept their suggestion and fall into the trap of the young man who was put off going to church.

This young man decided to go to church one day. On his way there the devil met him and succeeded in convincing him that he was too young to go to church, as the church was a place for old people. Many years later, when the man had become old, he decided to go to church again. On his way there the devil met him once more. "You are old now," said the devil. "Where do you think you are going? Look at yourself! Stay at home and rest. The church is a place for young people."

The question is, why do the fallen angels try to divert people from the path of the Lord? The answer is clear: we know that were you to have a good servant, you would not want to lose him or her. I will give you another example. There are many drunks around and about, but no one tells them that they are not living well. When a drunkard decides to follow the Lord, however, there is a competition to convince him not to do it, that it is not the right path. I ask, where were these people earlier? They are the same people who influenced him to drink in the

---

[4] "Angels which kept not their own principality, but left their proper habitation, the Lord hath kept in everlasting bonds under darkness unto the judgement of the great day" (Jude 1:6).

first place. Yes, there is no moment in life when these angels do not try to possess you. Intrigues and quarrels are not true human affairs. The original human being was not so corrupted.[5]

Who brought the Romanian invaders to Bulgaria? It was the fallen angels. Who prompted the Bulgarians to fight the Serbians? It was the fallen angels. They want to persuade you to leave the path of the Lord. You wanted to fight, but now you see the consequences....[6] For many years I have been fighting to change this hypnotic condition, because I see that you are serving these angels and that they are beating you. This is why I am telling you to free yourselves from this slavery which you accept not because you want it but because you are bribed into it.

The following example shows how people are led into betraying the Lord. The devil comes and convinces you that all wealth and blessings are in his hands. You accept this and fall down, when instead you should have behaved like Christ, saying, "Away from me, Satan!"[7] You

[5] "God created man in his own image" (Genesis 1:27).

[6] During the First Balkan War, while the Bulgarian forces were fighting in eastern Thrace, Serbia and Greece partitioned Macedonia. The Balkan allies defeated the Ottoman Empire and almost completely drove it out of mainland Europe. However, the peace between the victors was short-lived. Although Bulgaria had made great territorial gains, it was denied that which it coveted. During the post-war dispute over Macedonian lands, Greece and Serbia signed a defensive military alliance on 19 May/1 June to protect what they held. Four weeks later, on 16/29 June, Bulgaria attacked its former allies, starting the Second Balkan War.

Bulgaria was also involved in a territorial dispute with Romania. Taking advantage of the situation created by the new conflict, Romania declared war on Bulgaria, and the Ottoman Empire followed suit. Romanian troops crossed the Danube and, with the Bulgarian forces occupied elsewhere, headed unopposed towards Sofia. The fighting ended after only a month, on 18/31 July, with Bulgaria, invaded by all its neighbours and its capital under threat, having no choice but to surrender.

On 28 July/10 August the Treaty of Bucharest was signed, formally ending the Second Balkan War between Bulgaria and Greece, Montenegro, Romania and Serbia. The Treaty of Constantinople, between Bulgaria and the Ottoman Empire, was concluded later, on 16/29 September. Not only had Bulgaria failed to capture Macedonia, its defeat cost it much of the territory gained in the First Balkan War, as well as Southern Dobrudzha, in the northeast of the country, to Romania, and left it in great financial debt. These, along with the destructiveness of the war, were "the consequences" for having "wanted to fight" that the Teacher was referring to, for war fever had preceded the conflict.

Several months into the First World War, the Teacher said, "Pride leads to a fall; it heralds a fall. This has happened to Bulgaria and it will happen to Germany. Each proud person and each proud nation and government will fall" (6/19 January 1915).

[7] "The devil led Jesus up, and shewed him all the kingdoms of the world in a moment of time. And the devil said unto him, 'To thee will I give all this authority, and the glory of them:

need to learn to recognise when you are being influenced by fallen angels, because hatred and lies are not your own but theirs.[8] People sometimes accept and imitate the way fallen angels behave, which causes them to slip and fall. The human soul always longs for divine love, but these angels have no way to bring happiness to the human soul. They only promise good things while neither doing good nor giving anything good. The human soul is a field, an arena in which both light spirits and bad spirits work.[9] We need to give room to the good spirits, because they will lead us to the right path. All of heaven and all good spirits are interested in saving humanity. When you are being possessed by bad spirits, a change comes over your face caused by the their hypnotic influence – a change you can see in the mirror.

Never ever become so powerfully attached to one thought that you are willing to do anything to realise it. A good or bad spirit will be living in the thought or feeling to which you are tied. If you succumb to the influence of a bad spirit, you will become ill and your body will suffer. This is why it is said, "Build yourselves on your most holy faith."

The crisis through which Bulgaria is now passing is our own crisis, because we were not careful, allowing ourselves to be hypnotised by bad spirits. We Bulgarians have travelled a long way under this self-deception. God allowed this crisis to happen to help Bulgaria return to its true self. When the Lord wants to save humanity from something terrible, He always sends some blessings in disguise, as when Jesus saved the men who were possessed by bad spirits by sending the swine into the sea.[10] The owners of the swine cried because they had lost some material goods. The Lord, however, says, "What good is it if a person gains the whole world but loses his or her soul?"[11] Some people lament that

for it hath been delivered unto me; and to whomsoever I will I give it. If thou therefore wilt worship before me, it shall all be thine'" (Luke 4:5-7). "Then saith Jesus unto him, 'Get thee hence, Satan: for it is written, 'Thou shalt worship the Lord thy God, and him only shalt thou serve.'' Then the devil leaveth him" (Matthew 4:10-11).

[8] Jesus said, "The lusts of the devil it is your will to do. He was a murderer from the beginning, and stood not in the truth, because there is no truth in him. When he speaketh a lie, he speaketh of his own: for he is a liar, and the father thereof" (John 8:44).

[9] "Ye are God's husbandry" (1 Corinthians 3:9). Jesus said, "Every plant which my heavenly Father planted not, shall be rooted up" (Matthew 15:13). "Now the serpent was more subtil than any beast of the field which the Lord God had made" (Genesis 3:1).

[10] See the miracle of the devils entering a herd of swine (Matthew 8:28-34)

[11] See Luke 9:25

Bulgaria has fallen. Yes, it has fallen, but I say the Lord did very well to send the swine of this nation into the sea to free its soul. The Lord may do anything to free a nation's soul.

The Lord is coming, and in what condition will He find your lives when He arrives? Well, you have given yourselves to Lucifer.... Perhaps you have several houses, perhaps you have taught your children to dance at balls and to style their hair beautifully, but what are the benefits of such things for your souls? What good is it for a person to gain everything but lose his or her soul? Hang on to your souls! Do not create illusions for yourselves, for you are in the eleventh hour. [12] Do not put it into your heads to live well on the earth at this time. That time will come, but only when conditions are better. Such conditions do not exist at present. It is now the last of times, times of difficulty and problems. [13] Find an example of a parent whose sons and daughters love him or her properly. Find some people who love their boss. You cannot. The Lord is coming to put things in order in a natural way. As you are now in the last hour, you should cut out and throw away everything which belongs to the world, [14] so that when your Master comes He

[12] To be at the "eleventh hour" is to have been called to work for God late in the day, with little time remaining before the wages are distributed (see the parable of the labourers in the vineyard: Matthew 20:1-16).

[13] God said, "Behold, I create new heavens and a new earth" (Isaiah 65:17). Jesus said, "The end is not yet. For nation shall rise against nation, and kingdom against kingdom. These things are the beginning of travail" (Matthew 24:6-8). And the Apostle Paul wrote, "In the last days grievous times shall come" (2 Timothy 3:1).

Years later, the Teacher said, "Christ said, 'I will be with you until the end of the age.' The 'end of the age' is the old order of things, which is being changed by the new order, the new heaven and new earth. A new order is coming in which love will reign in the world" (some time between 1929 and 1942). "Humanity needs to prepare itself for the great trials that are coming, for now it is the end of the age. When a woman gives birth her suffering is great, and humanity is a mother giving birth to a new consciousness. When the child is born everything will be easier" (some time between 1929 and 1942).

[14] "Love not the world, neither the things that are in the world. If any man love the world, the love of the Father is not in him. For all that is in the world, the lust of the flesh, and the lust of the eyes, and the vainglory of life, is not of the Father, but is of the world. And the world passeth away, and the lust thereof: but he that doeth the will of God abideth for ever. Little children, it is the last hour" (1 John 2:15-18).

Jesus said, "If thy right eye causeth thee to stumble, pluck it out, and cast it from thee: for it is profitable for thee that one of thy members should perish, and not thy whole body be cast into hell. And if thy right hand causeth thee to stumble, cut it off, and cast it from thee: for it is profitable for thee that one of thy members should perish, and not thy whole body go into hell" (Matthew 5:29-30).

does not find you without oil in your lamps.[15]

Some of you say, "You have no sympathy for us." To be sympathetic is to give you shoes when you are barefooted, to feed you when you are hungry, to visit you when you are housebound. To offer you sympathetic words would be useless. Words are not important; it is actions that are important. Love is the foundation. Love is the foundation of everything because it is a virtue that is blind to the mistakes of others. Love is not offended by anything.[16]

Read chapter thirteen of Paul's First Letter to the Corinthians and you will know the qualities of love.[17] You need this love now. Let us be with the Lord to compensate ourselves for the things we have lost at the material level. If the Lord is with us we will not have lost anything.[18] For this reason, learn not to be influenced by bad spirits. When the thought comes to you to criticise someone, ask yourself, "Why do I have this bad feeling?" If you want to heal yourselves, to be freed from your daily self-deceptions, do not connect yourselves to the cursed spirits who were ejected from heaven. Christ did not come to help them; he came to help human souls. For thirty years I have observed how proficient the fallen spirits are at greatly upsetting and disturbing our souls. You need to stand next to Christ, because I can see that a great danger is stalking you. If you want to stay in the world, I do not want to stop you, but I will continue my work. However, it would be much better for you to follow me. I tell you, the changing borders of Bulgaria are not important for you; it is your souls that you must not lose, and it

---

[15] Jesus said, "Be ye ready: for in an hour that ye think not the Son of man cometh. Then shall the kingdom of heaven be likened unto ten virgins, which took their lamps, and went forth to meet the bridegroom. And five of them were foolish, and five were wise. For the foolish, when they took their lamps, took no oil with them: but the wise took oil in their vessels with their lamps. Now the bridegroom tarried. And while the foolish virgins went away to buy more oil, the bridegroom came; and they that were ready went in with him to the marriage feast: and the door was shut. Afterward come also the other virgins, saying, 'Lord, Lord, open to us.' But he answered and said, 'Verily I say unto you, I know you not.' Watch therefore, for ye know not the day nor the hour" (Matthew 24:44; 25:1-5, 10-13).
[16] "Love covereth all transgressions" (Proverbs 10:12). "Love taketh not account of evil" (1 Corinthians 13:5). "Above all things be fervent in your love among yourselves; for love covereth a multitude of sins" (1 Peter 4:8).
[17] This is the famous passage on "faith, hope and love".
[18] "Thou wilt keep him in perfect peace, whose mind is stayed on thee: because he trusteth in thee" (Isaiah 26:3). "The peace of God passeth all understanding" (Philippians 4:7).

is now a dangerous time. This is what Lord Jesus Christ is telling you.

I will conclude this lecture with a story. A philosopher called Liao-Yang lived in China a long time ago. His wife wanted to leave him because of his unusual behaviour: he was often silent and grave, whereas she craved a life full of fun and pleasure. He allowed her to leave him, and she married a rich trader. When difficult times came to China, the country's leaders asked Liao-Yang what they should do. He gave them very wise advice for which he became famous and greatly treasured by the nation. His ex-wife then returned to him and asked him to forget the past and live with her as a couple again. Liao-Yang picked up a glass of nectar and emptied it onto the floor. He told her that if she could collect up the nectar and put it back into the glass without any impurities, he would take her back. But of course, she could not do it.

And when Christ comes, if he has to tell you to pick up the spilled nectar, you will not be able to do it.[19] Take care to protect your souls and Christ will be able to help you.

---

[19] "According to God's promise, we look for new heavens and a new earth, wherein dwelleth righteousness. Wherefore, beloved, seeing that ye look for these things, give diligence that ye may be found in peace, without spot and blameless in his sight" (2 Peter 3:13-14).

"And I John saw a new heaven and a new earth: for the first heaven and the first earth are passed away. And I saw the holy city, new Jerusalem, coming down out of heaven from God, made ready as a bride adorned for her husband. And I saw no temple therein: for the Lord God the Almighty, and the Lamb, are the temple thereof. And the glory of God did lighten the city, and the lamp thereof is the Lamb. And there shall in no wise enter into it anything unclean, or he that maketh an abomination and a lie: but only they which are written in the Lamb's book of life" (Revelation 21:1-2, 22-23, 27).

Developing Our Hearts with Spiritual Light

Jesus said,

> Walk while ye have the light, that ye may become sons of light. [1]

I will explain what Christ meant by the words, "Walk while you have the light." Spiritual light is as necessary to the soul as sunlight is to our bodies. Walk while you have spiritual light to become children of the kingdom of God. The human being grows like the seed of a plant grows, upwards. The word 'son' means one who inherits. Christ said, "Everything that my Father has is mine. [2] As my Father has eternal life, He has given me eternal life. [3] Walk in the spiritual light to know your path." [4]

We need to know to what we should aspire and what our occupations should be. For example, bees aspire to collect honey, ordinary people aspire to collect the benefits of earthly life, and spiritual people aspire to collect the blessings of heaven. Heaven is neither a refuge for poor people nor is it a hotel. Heaven is for purified, prepared souls, the children of spiritual light. Whoever purifies his or her soul is able to accept this spiritual light, which further purifies the soul. The human soul is like a plant in the soil, and this soil has to be cultivated for the soul to bear fruit. Walk while you have spiritual light to purify yourselves and produce the fruits of the soul, which are good deeds born of correct desires and thoughts. [5]

---

[1] John 12:35-36

[2] See John 16:15

[3] See John 5:26

[4] Jesus said, "He that walketh in the darkness knoweth not whither he goeth" (John 12:35). "I am the light of the world: he that followeth me shall not walk in the darkness, but shall have the light of life" (John 8:12). "I am the way, and the truth, and the life: no one cometh unto the Father, but by me" (John 14:6).

[5] "The fruit of the light is in all goodness and righteousness and truth" (Ephesians 5:9). "The fruit of the Spirit is love, joy, peace, longsuffering, kindness, goodness, faithfulness, meekness, temperance" (Galatians 5:22-23).

We can never sow a good thought without taking action: on the earth action is the connecting cord between a good thought and desire and their fruition. We ought to use each of our desires so that they bear fruit and benefit us – otherwise we will not be saved.[6] We say that God is kind and He will save us, but salvation involves changing conditions so that our hearts can develop within us. Once we are saved we ought to work for Christ, for to have been saved does not mean our work is finished. "Walk while you have spiritual light." If a person is ignorant of the profound meaning of the Gospels it is difficult for him or her to choose the right path in life, but when spiritual light penetrates one's soul, love appears. Love cannot appear within our souls unless it comes through spiritual light. When a person saves someone who is drowning, it creates a cord of gratitude and love between them. In the same way, when our souls are saved, a cord of the light of love for Christ is created within us. After having been saved by Christ, we ought to begin to work for him. Love always begins with the giving of something, just as a father passes on his knowledge to his beloved son. When God loves us, He likewise gives us the knowledge to save ourselves from bad conditions. God makes His divine presence known to us through spiritual light. When God enters us, when spiritual light enters us, we will already feel God without our needing to seek Him.[7]

Heaven is the heart, the pulse, of the whole world, of the whole universe, the heart through which life goes in and out. When we are in a good mood, which means when we are self-denying, virtuous and loving, we are in heaven. When we are in the opposite mood, we are in hell. Walk while we have spiritual light to be children of heaven.

There is mathematics in life. Addition is a mechanical process: we put some things together, or we put some people together, and so on. Subtraction is also a mechanical process: we remove someone from his or her home, or we take something away, or extract some of our thoughts from our minds. Quarrels involve adding and subtracting. For example, when neighbours quarrel, they subtract impure thoughts and desires

[6] "What doth it profit, my brethren, if a man say he hath faith, but have not works? can that faith save him? Faith, if it have not works, is dead in itself. By works a man is justified, and not only by faith" (James 2:14, 17, 24).

[7] "No man hath beheld God at any time. Hereby know we that we abide in him, and he in us, because he hath given us of his spirit" (1 John 4:12-13). "And this is the message which we have heard from Jesus Christ, that God is light" (1 John 1:5).

from themselves. When we arrive at the process of multiplying, however, the mind is required. To multiply means to sow the grain of wheat in the land: to calculate how, when and where to sow it to obtain plentiful fruit – three hundred grains from one sown grain! If we do not value a person, it means we do not know how to divide. The mind is a power, and we need to learn how to multiply and divide out this power so that we can use it to give us wealth, which we can, in turn, further multiply and divide out. The mind is a virtue from God, a virtue we need to know – not only do we need to know how to add and subtract but also how to multiply and divide. We should multiply and divide out the manifestation of our virtues, to increase our spiritual wealth and share out its benefits. We should want to become clever and powerful.

If we have a passion, it is like the current of a river. If this river flows from a high mountain, the current will be strong and cause problems. If we want to rid ourselves of the current, it means we do not want mountains either, although they offer us the most the beautiful springs, which are blessings. A passion can cause problems, but it also holds blessings if we know how to develop and cultivate it. For example, the River Iskar, whose source is in the Rila Mountains, used to carry muddy water, which made a bog, but since the river was developed it has been used to generate the electricity that lights the whole of Sofia. "Walk while you have spiritual light." In other words, use your power and your knowledge and develop them. What does this law teach us for our practical lives? We may apply it anywhere. We may always say, "I will walk while I have spiritual light," for it is good to acquire knowledge.

We need to conquer the devil with our minds and put him to work, and he will teach us because he has stolen the wealth that God gave humanity. The devil gives this wealth back to whoever masters him;[8] but if he masters us, we will serve him and will be in darkness.[9] When we have dusky thoughts, or when we hesitate, it means we are at the top of the mountain where God and spiritual light are on one side and darkness and the devil are on the other. At such moments we need to

[8] Jesus said, "When the strong man fully armed guardeth his own court, his goods are in peace: but when a stronger than he shall come upon him, and overcome him, he taketh from him his whole armour wherein he trusted, and divideth his spoils" (Luke 11:21-22).
[9] "Satan fashioneth himself into an angel of light" (2 Corinthians 11:14). Jesus said, "The lamp of the body is the eye. If thine eye be evil, thy whole body shall be full of darkness. If therefore the light that is in thee be darkness, how great is the darkness!" (Matthew 6:22-23).

keep our balance and reach for the spiritual light.

Freedom is a large space for the soul. We often feel burdened. When we feel burdened it is because our souls wish to break these restrictions so that they can develop. Our every suffering tells us that we need to escape restricting conditions and go out into spaciousness. We should not delude ourselves into loving the bodies of the people close to us; it is their souls that we should love. Seek the soul, not the body, the house. We often change our earthly homes – we were even in animal houses in the past.

Animals aspire to become human. Human beings need to aspire to become angels, to be children of spiritual light. We will not be children of God until we become children of spiritual light. We should not expect benefits on the earth, because purification, suffering and trials will be given to us here. We need to be powerful, strong, unhesitating and ready for Christ. Our thoughts must never be for material gain, but for having good, pure and light souls through which to give birth to good desires and thoughts. When we are suffering, our souls also suffer, because they aspire to pure and light thoughts and desires. Let us walk while we have spiritual light and be children of spiritual light.

Developing Ourselves with God

The Apostle Paul wrote,

> Be rejoicing in hope; patient in tribulation; continuing stedfastly in prayer.[1]

What does "hope" mean here? Hope comes from God. Hope is our mother: it feeds and supports us in the way a mother feeds her child. Hope gives us strength and life. It supports us so that we have faith and expect luck in the realisation of our good desires. Without hope a person is discouraged and loses the energetic impulse needed for work. It is said that a person without hope despairs. Such a person is without a mother, without the shelter of God. Hope gives us courage, so that sooner or later we achieve our aims. "Be joyful in hope." Our good desires bring us joy and contentment. When we are not joyful and content we complain. Were we to have hope, were we to believe that we will realise our good desires, how could we not be joyful? But we are almost always discontented, joyless and discouraged because we are not on the right path and are not making an effort to follow the divine laws.

We want love, but it is like the furniture we want before we have a home in which to put it. We first need to have houses made of good actions, well built with strong materials, and then we can furnish them.[2] We need intelligence and wisdom to organise the furniture well and to put a lamp inside our strong houses.[3] The truth must shine, because thieves do not enter where there is light.[4] Just as there are thieves here

---

[1] Romans 12:12

[2] God said, "Behold, I lay in Zion for a foundation a stone, a tried stone, a precious corner stone of sure foundation" (Isaiah 28:16). And Jesus said, "Every one which heareth these words of mine, and doeth them, shall be likened unto a wise man, which built his house upon the rock: and the rain descended, and the floods came, and the winds blew, and beat upon that house; and it fell not: for it was founded upon the rock" (Matthew 7:24-25).

[3] Jesus said, "The lamp of the body is the eye: if therefore thine eye be single, thy whole body shall be full of light" (Matthew 6:22).

[4] "In the dark thieves dig through houses: They shut themselves up in the day-time; They

on earth, there are also thieves in heaven. They steal our good deeds, our good thoughts, our love and other such things.[5] We are sent here to the earthly school, where we should learn from everything: from the sun, the stars, the grass, the stones and so on. Know that so long as the sun is shining in heaven and the stars also shine we should not lose hope, for we can correct anything when we have light. Anything can give us a lesson if we open our eyes and minds and think about it, for we then become open springs into which our Heavenly Father pours knowledge.

We need to gain knowledge from everything and to develop our minds so that we become capable of building ourselves strong homes. If we build with weak materials and bad minds, and if we do not support the beams, our homes will collapse. If we are unintelligent in the way we carry out our good actions, they will collapse. We may receive a lesson from anything when we have learnt how to read the divine book and have become able to understand the language of nature.[6] Our Heavenly Father is constantly working, creating, and we should create good thoughts, because they form our future conditions.[7] If we are suffering in the present, it is because of what we created in the past. We need to create good thoughts and actions and should not despair. We might make mistakes. Never mind, we will correct them. It is not so bad to make a mistake; it is far worse not to work. We need to work to attain good minds, and each one of us should make a plan for his or her life, for his or her work. We need to organise our knowledge well and have good materials, hope and joy when we build. We need hope, because we achieve things with hope; without hope we are discouraged and inactive.

"Be patient in sorrow." What is sorrow? We are sad and cry over many things in our lives. We are sad and sorrowful when we lose something. We are also sorrowful when we do not get something we want. We have sorrows, but if we look at these sorrows we will see that ninety per-

know not the light" (Job 24:16).

[5] Jesus said, "When any one heareth the word of the kingdom, and understandeth it not, then cometh the evil one, and snatcheth away that which hath been sown in his heart" (Matthew 13:19).

[6] The Teacher also said, "The fundamental things in the Bible are hidden in nature and in our souls, which are divine treasuries" (15/28 August 1912).

[7] Jesus said, "My Father worketh even until now, and I work" (John 5:17).

cent of them are without foundation. Only ten percent of our sorrows require our attention; as for the rest, we needlessly lose much energy.

We need to learn how to maintain and respect our bodies, because they are a great gift. We can only learn lessons on the earth with these bodies. We ought not to treat our bodies like workhorses. Instead, we should learn to understand and protect them. Our stomachs, lungs and minds need to be well maintained. The maintenance of our bodies does not mean to cater to the desires of the flesh as it is described in the Gospels. The 'flesh' is our low passions and desires,[8] but the body is a temple of the mind and soul.[9] It is through our bodies that we learn lessons, develop our minds, ennoble our souls and refresh our spirits.

If we review our sorrows with the intention of no longer wasting energy, we will free ourselves of at least fifty percent of them and retain the energy we would otherwise waste on them. Sorrow is not without use, however; it is necessary. Sorrow is like dew for our good thoughts, for it moistens our hearts by shading them from the sun so that good things can grow. But only sorrow of a noble kind is able to do this. For example, we may be sorrowful when we have not achieved our spiritual aims or have not succeeded in uplifting ourselves spiritually, when our good thoughts are stolen or when we fail to realise a good idea or to do something good, and so on. If we are sorrowful in these ways, we should not lose hope but instead be patient and work to achieve our aims. Let us always have a strong belief that we will achieve our aims. Sorrow is necessary because it teaches patience.[10] Remember that after sorrow the sun will shine and joyful days arrive.[11] It is important for us to learn patience.

"Be constant in prayer." People are always asking each other to help them materially, but no one is richer than our Heavenly Father.[12] What

---

[8] "Fleshly lusts war against the soul" (1 Peter 2:11).

[9] "Know ye not that your body is a temple of the Holy Spirit which is in you, which ye have from God? and ye are not your own; for ye were bought with a price: glorify God therefore in your body" (1 Corinthians 6:19-20).

[10] "Let us rejoice in our tribulations: knowing that tribulation worketh patience; and patience, probation; and probation, hope: and hope putteth not to shame; because the love of God hath been shed abroad in our hearts through the Holy Spirit which was given unto us" (Romans 5:3-5).

[11] "Weeping may tarry for the night, But joy cometh in the morning" (Psalm 30:5).

[12] God said, "The silver is mine, and the gold is mine" (Haggai 2:8). "For the world is

we should do is to constantly ask of Him, because He has everything in abundance and can give us anything.[13] Praying to God is the breath of the soul. We need to be constantly in prayer, just as we need to be constantly breathing, because just as breathing purifies the blood, so prayer purifies the mind and heart. We are connected to, and influenced by, whomever we pray to with our requests. When we constantly pray to God we are connected to Him and receive His good influence. When we constantly pray to God, sooner or later God will give us what we pray for – if we deserve it. If a person does not pray to God from the heart but only superficially, he or she is like someone who is suffocating. We should pray so that our hearts will be purified. The heart is the covering of the soul, it is the earthly crust of the soul.[14] Our good thoughts and desires are sown in our hearts and they grow like potted flowers. Our bodies are the pots and fertiliser for the good thoughts and desires that we need to cultivate.[15] If we do not purify our hearts, thorns will grow in them. If we dig and sow the grain of wheat, which represents our good thoughts, wheat will grow instead of thorns, our bad thoughts. The heart is like the soil. It cannot remain empty; something is always growing in it. The heart either feeds the grain of wheat and flowers or it feeds thorns, for there are always two sowers: the good Spirit and the evil spirit.[16] The good Spirit, like a good agriculturalist, wants well-prepared soil; the evil spirit only sows thorns everywhere. When we pray, we purify our hearts and lungs. Healthy lungs purify our thoughts and feed our minds. Healthy hearts purify our desires.

mine, and the fulness thereof" (Psalm 50:12).

[13] Jesus said to his disciples, "Whatsoever ye shall ask in my name, that will I do, that the Father may be glorified in the Son" (John 14:13). And the Apostle John wrote, "This is the boldness which we have toward him, that, if we ask anything according to his will, he heareth us: and if we know that he heareth us whatsoever we ask, we know that we have the petitions which we have asked of him" (1 John 5:14-15).

[14] The Teacher also said, "When we pray, we should feel warmth in the place where the soul resides. This warmth signals that the Spirit is at work. If there is no warmth, it means our minds are working weakly, which means we are not praying properly" (22 January/4 February 1915). "The soul is in the whole chest, but it also abides in the pit of the stomach, where pleasure is felt. The Spirit is in the head" (9/22 April 1914).

[15] "Ye are God's husbandry" (1 Corinthians 3:9).

[16] The Teacher also said, "A field cannot belong to two masters; it either belongs to good or to evil, and it is the same with a human being. The Lord teaches us everything that is good. Be faithful to God, who lives within you" (6/19 April 1914). And Jesus said, "No man can serve two masters" (Matthew 6:24).

With the words, "Be joyful in hope, be patient in sorrow, be constant in prayer," the spirit of the Apostle Paul would like to tell us to maintain the health of our bodies, to keep good hearts, to develop our minds, to ennoble our souls and to sanctify our spirits. Let us begin to listen to our new Teacher, Christ, who teaches us these things, and let us leave our old teacher, who always consumes whatever we gain.[17] For Christ wants all of us to have every blessing: healthy bodies, good hearts, pure thoughts and desires, and luminous minds.

---

[17] "Be sober, be watchful: your adversary the devil, as a roaring lion, walketh about, seeking whom he may devour" (1 Peter 5:8).

From Children of Lucifer to Children of God

The Apostle Paul wrote,

> So long as the heir is a child, he differeth nothing from a bondservant, though he is lord of all; but is under guardians and stewards until the term appointed of the father. So we also, when we were children, were held in bondage under the rudiments of the world: but when the fulness of the time came, God sent forth his Son, born of a woman, born under the law, that he might redeem them which were under the law, that we might receive the adoption of sons. And because ye are sons, God sent forth the Spirit of his Son into our hearts, crying, "Abba, Father." So that thou art no longer a bondservant, but a son; and if a son, then an heir through God. [1]

We are still slaves because we are young. We need to mature. As minors we are under the control of guardians. The house of the kingdom of God is building itself, and when it is built it will permit Christ, the Son, to enter it. [2] Here on earth we cannot live without homes. Everyone aspires to have his or her own house, for we can be ejected from rented accommodation. We also need to build our houses in the astral world. Both on earth and in heaven we each need to own a house. [3]

It is said in the Scriptures that in the beginning the Lord incarnated Himself in human sons, but they stopped wanting to learn from Him and became dissatisfied with His rules. That is why the Lord command-

---

[1] Galatians 4:1-7. The Teacher actually read the whole chapter and then said he would talk about the first two verses.

[2] "Know ye not that ye are the temple of God?" (1 Corinthians 3:16). "For other foundation can no man lay than that which is laid, which is Jesus Christ" (1 Corinthians 3:11).

[3] By the 'astral house' the Teacher was referring to the spiritual body. The Apostle Paul wrote, "If there is a natural body, there is also a spiritual body" (1 Corinthians 15:44).

ed the angels to make the earth formless and empty. People started to create their own laws, and, consequently, have suffered ever since.[4] The son of Hagar is a person of the flesh, whereas the son of Sarah is the child of the Spirit.[5]

When you were young your father took responsibility for you. If a father makes a mistake his child suffers and might even be put in danger, whereas if the child makes a mistake and suffers the father remains safe. If a father makes a mistake his child will be born with his sin, because a father and child are partners before the law. If the father errs, not only will he lose something but his partner will also have to pay for it, whether he is also guilty or not – this is the law.[6] A father's descendants carry his sins for four generations, but blessings are carried for a thousand generations.[7]

You are now children, partners, of your old father, Lucifer, who is the father on earth, the father of the flesh.[8] Lucifer, or Satan, who is the ruler of Saturn, is our father of the flesh. He is a great spirit of light who

[4] "God made man upright; but they have sought out many inventions" (Ecclesiastes 7:29). "The Lord saith, 'My people is foolish, they know me not; they are sottish children, and they have none understanding: they are wise to do evil, but to do good they have no knowledge.' And I Jeremiah beheld the earth, and, lo, it was waste and void" (Jeremiah 4:22-23).

[5] Abraham's wife, Sarah, could not conceive, so he had a child, Ishmael, by his wife's Egyptian slave Hagar, who became a wild, hostile man. Later Sarah gave birth to Isaac, the son God had promised Abraham. And God told Abraham that he would establish His covenant with Isaac, not Ishmael (see Genesis 16:1–17:22; 21:1-7).

"When Abram was ninety years old and nine, the Lord appeared to Abram, and said unto him, 'I am God Almighty; walk before me, and be thou perfect. And I will establish my covenant between me and thee and thy seed after thee throughout their generations for an everlasting covenant, to be a God unto thee and to thy seed after thee'" (Genesis 17:1, 7).

[6] "Lord God, thou recompensest the iniquity of the fathers into the bosom of their children after them" (Jeremiah 32:18).

[7] This principle is in the Ten Commandments (see Exodus 20:5-6). The Teacher said, "There is great meaning in carrying out a good deed in the right way. A good deed acts as capital that a human being deposits in the divine bank. If you do something good, God will remember it for twenty-five thousand years. Therefore, if you want God's blessings, do good" (18 October 1931).

[8] Jesus said, "I speak the things which I have seen with my Father: and ye also do the things which ye heard from your father. If God were your Father, ye would love me: for I came forth and am come from God. Why do ye not understand my speech? Even because ye cannot hear my word. Ye are of your father the devil, and the lusts of your Father it is your will to do. He that is of God heareth the words of God: for this cause ye hear them not, because ye are not of God" (John 8:38, 42-44, 47).

fell down because of his pride and was cast out and made the lord of darkness.[9] And we, while still the children of the flesh, of the material world, still the children of Lucifer, still minors and slaves, are as yet unready for the kingdom of God. As slaves we are paying with great suffering for the sins of our father, Lucifer, because we are in partnership with him and are not free of the old law.[10]

A river is mainly muddied from its source. If, however, most of the mud is coming from elsewhere in the water, it will soon be purified, for this means it is only the child who is making mistakes. But when the mud comes from the river's source, where the father, Lucifer, is making mistakes, the water will be very difficult to clean.[11] This is why God the Father sent His Son, who was born of a woman of flesh, to pay the debts of those who can deny old father Lucifer and who have agreed to adapt themselves to the Heavenly Spirit, for thus they will become free and enter the home of the Lord. We are still children under the law. When we are ready to be adopted and baptised of the heart, which is when the Son in the heart calls out, "Abba, Father!" we will be adopted by God and set free. Instead of being slaves, we will be the children and heirs of God through Christ.[12] When we did not know God and the

---

[9] "How art thou fallen from heaven, O day star, son of the morning! And thou saidst in thine heart, 'I will be like the Most High.' Yet thou shalt be brought down to hell, to the uttermost parts of the pit" (Isaiah 14:12-15). And Jesus said, "I beheld Satan fallen as lightning from heaven" (Luke 10:18). "For God spared not angels when they sinned, but cast them down to hell, and committed them to the pits of darkness, to be reserved unto judgement" (2 Peter 2:4).

[10] "As Jesus spake, many believed on him. Jesus therefore said to those Jews which had believed him, 'If ye abide in my word, then are ye truly my disciples; and ye shall know the truth, and the truth shall make you free.' They answered unto him, 'We be Abraham's seed, and have never yet been in bondage to any man: how sayest thou, 'Ye shall be made free?'' Jesus answered them, 'Every one that committeth sin is the bondservant of sin. And the bondservant abideth not in the house for ever: the son abideth for ever. If therefore the Son shall make you free, ye shall be free indeed'" (John 8:30-36).

"For the law was given by Moses; grace and truth came by Jesus Christ" (John 1:17). "There is therefore now no condemnation to them that are in Christ Jesus. For the law of the Spirit of life in Christ Jesus made me free from the law of sin and of death" (Romans 8:1-2).

[11] "Doth the fountain send forth from the same opening sweet water and bitter? Salt water cannot yield sweet" (James 3:11-12).

[12] "As many as are led by the Spirit of God, these are sons of God. For ye received not the spirit of bondage again unto fear; but ye received the spirit of adoption, whereby we cry, 'Abba, Father.' The Spirit himself beareth witness with our spirit, that we are children of

truth, we served those who are not gods. When we know God, or better still, when God knows us, we ought to serve only God and must not return to Lucifer.[13] It is not easy for Christ to be born in a human being, and he is not yet born in many people. The sons of Abraham, one by the slave Hagar, the other by his wife, Sarah, are both, of course, inside us. One is the son of the flesh, the child of the slave, the child of Lucifer, but the son of Sarah is the soul, the child of the Spirit. When Christ is born within us, the Spirit will descend and enter us.[14]

God" (Romans 8:14-16).

[13] "At that time, not knowing God, ye were in bondage to them which by nature are no gods: but now that ye have come to know God, or rather to be known of God, how turn ye back again to the weak and beggarly rudiments, whereunto ye desire to be in bondage over again? With freedom did Christ set us free: stand fast therefore, and be not entangled again in a yoke of bondage" (Galatians 4:8-9; 5:1). "For if, after they have escaped the defilements of the world through the knowledge of the Lord and Saviour Jesus Christ, they are again entangled therein and overcome, the last state is become worse with them than the first. For it were better for them not to have known the way of righteousness, than, after knowing it, to turn back from the holy commandment delivered unto them" (2 Peter 2:20-21).

[14] "It is written, that Abraham had two sons, one by the handmaid, and one by the free-woman. Howbeit the son by the handmaid is born after the flesh; but the son by the freewoman is born through promise. Which things contain an allegory: for these women are two covenants; one from mount Sinai, bearing children unto bondage, which is Hagar. Now this Hagar is mount Sinai in Arabia, and answereth to the Jerusalem that now is: for she is in bondage with her children. But the Jerusalem that is above is free, which is our mother. Now we, brethren, as Isaac was, are children of promise" (Galatians 4:22-26, 28). "Now to Abraham were the promises spoken, and to his seed. He saith not, 'And to seeds,' as of many; but as of one, 'And to thy seed,' which is Christ. And if ye are Christ's, then are ye Abraham's seed, heirs according to promise" (Galatians 3:16, 29). "Abraham believed God, and it was reckoned unto him for righteousness. Know therefore that they which be of faith, the same are sons of Abraham" (Galatians 3:6-7).

A Division in Love Causes Evil

Jesus said,

> Every kingdom divided against itself is brought to desolation; and every city or house divided against itself shall not stand.[1]

'Divide and Rule' is the motto of the contemporary world. If someone asks me what is the cause of humanity's suffering, I will say it is the motto 'Divide and Rule'. Consequently, for as long you have this motto, misery will follow you like your shadow. Christ said, "Any kingdom, organism, life or organised nation will not stand if it is divided."

It is said that people of the world quarrel over money. But why do religious people quarrel? Why do men and women quarrel? Why do brothers and sisters quarrel? Why do servants and masters quarrel? It is a false teaching that says people will be happier when they divide. Disorganised things can be divided; organised things cannot be divided and remain standing. Virtues cannot be divided, because if you divide them they will no longer be virtues and evil will be born. If you have a glass bottle full of water and the glass breaks into pieces, how will it store water anymore?

Christ said, "Each home divided against itself will not stand," which means spiritually wise life cannot progress for long once division has appeared. The home is the emblem of love. When a division appears in love it will not stand. When instability occurs, evil, hatred and controversy are born, and all these are nothing but gaps in the bonds of love. The first impression we have of a gap is an uncomfortable feeling. If we step on infirm, marshy ground where there is no solid foundation, we will sink. In the same way, dividing causes gaps in life, gaps which evil fills.

[1] Matthew 12:25

The Narrow Path of Development

Jesus said to Martha,

> Mary hath chosen the good part, which shall not be taken away from her. [1]

'Mary' means salt water. Christ said, "If the salt has lost its saltiness, with what will it be salted?" [2] Salt is useful in life. "Mary has chosen the good part." Do you know what this good part is? I will leave you to think about it. When Martha complained to Christ that her sister Mary was not helping her, he answered that although Martha was taking care of many things, only one thing was necessary: that which Mary had chosen. [3] What Christ meant was that people had been concerning themselves with material affairs for thousands of years and had not achieved anything. When you want to do something good, or if someone needs something from you, you should follow this rule of Christ: "Do not let your left hand know what your right hand is doing." [4]

The Lord sends souls here to develop themselves, and He determines each soul's place on the earth. Everything you have was given to you by the Lord, and you have no right to squander it, which is why Christ told his disciples not to waste the leftover bread from the feeding of the five thousand. [5] Why is a certain man poor? Because when he was rich he squandered his wealth, which means he did not know how to

---

[1] Luke 10:42

[2] See Matthew 5:13

[3] See Luke 10:38-42

[4] Jesus said, "Take heed that ye do not your righteousness before men, to be seen of them: else ye have no reward with your Father which is in heaven. When therefore thou doest alms, sound not a trumpet before thee, as the hypocrites do in the synagogues and in the streets, that they may have glory of men. Verily I say unto you, They have received their reward. But when thou doest alms, let not thy left hand know what thy right hand doeth: that thine alms may be in secret: and thy Father which seeth in secret shall recompense thee" (Matthew 6:1-4).

[5] See John 6:12

use the wealth God had given him. God later put him in the position of a poor person for him to become humble, to lose his pride. The Lord gives a certain woman a mind, but she does not know how to use it properly. Next time the Lord will send her here as an idiot so that she has to learn from others. You have come to the earth to cultivate the wealth that has been given to you and to use it well.

When you do not obey the divine laws, you burden yourself with useless work, and you look like a boat overladen with useless cargo sailing upon the sea. If there is a powerful storm, such a boat might capsize and sink to the bottom with its useless burden. To have sunk to the bottom is to find yourself naked, and that will be your condition when they call you to the next world.[6] You should now work to build yourself a body with which to live in the astral world.[7]

Mary chose that good part and accepted Christ in her heart. When Christ said, "The path is narrow," he meant for you to enter within yourself and become master of your mind, heart, soul and spirit. The wide path is the world.[8] In whatever position God has placed you in life, as a Christian you need to be courageous and resolute and to have a noble and grateful heart. I am telling you this because there are many trials you will have to face in this world. You would like Christ to come and put the world right. He will come, but from within you.[9] Your heart should be open and you should do good deeds, but they need to be done from an inner impulse and not out of a sense of compulsion.[10]

Before we can start to weave, we need to have a threaded foundation on a loom. The loom symbolises the cross. Spiritual clothing is woven on the cross. I see you are carrying crosses, but you should earn your

---

[6] Jesus said, "Behold, I come as a thief. Blessed is he that watcheth, and keepeth his garments, lest he walk naked, and they see his shame" (Revelation 16:15).

[7] Jesus said, "I counsel thee to buy of me white garments, that thou mayest clothe thyself, and that the shame of thy nakedness be not made manifest" (Revelation 3:18).

[8] Jesus said, "Enter ye in by the narrow gate: for wide is the gate, and broad is the way, that leadeth to destruction, and many be they that enter in thereby. For narrow is the gate, and straightened the way, that leadeth unto life, and few be they that find it" (Matthew 7:13-14).

[9] Jesus said, "If a man love me, he will keep my word: and my Father will love him, and we will come unto him, and make our abode with him" (John 14:23).

[10] "He that soweth sparingly shall reap also sparingly; and he that soweth bountifully shall reap also bountifully. Let each man do according as he hath purposed in his heart; not grudgingly, or of necessity: for God loveth a cheerful giver" (2 Corinthians 9:6-7).

crosses. The soldiers who have been awarded medals wear their crosses to show their heroism and self-denial. Suffering is weaving. When you pass through suffering it means you are being woven in the astral world. The upper part of the loom symbolises the head, the shuttle's movement from right to left symbolises the mind, and its movement from left to right symbolises the heart. This means that the mind and the heart have to be united to weave the cloth.[11] Whoever is fearful should stay at home, but courage to those who are willing to battle for the cross.[12]

When Christ comes I want him to find you ready to work. He is coming to read people's notebooks. What will he find written in them? He will see that you slept eight hours a night, ate three times a day and managed to do only one good deed during the entire year. Bad things are written about many of you.[13] You always ask for material things in your prayers, but you take less care of your souls, minds and hearts. Some people want to do the will of God, but how can they do it when they are permanently quarrelling? You are making a start here; they will give you greater work when you go to the astral world. You have been sent to the earth to save at least one other soul.[14]

[11] The Teacher also said, "Our thoughts and feelings should be in solidarity, which means the intellect, heart and soul should be united" (22 January/4 February 1915).

[12] Jesus said, "In the world ye have tribulation: but be of good cheer; I have overcome the world" (John 16:33). "He that overcometh shall be arrayed in white garments. I will give to him to sit down with me in my throne, as I also overcame, and sat down with my Father in his throne" (Revelation 3:5, 21).

[13] Jesus said, "The Son of man shall come in the glory of his Father with his angels; and then shall he render unto every man according to his deeds. Verily I say unto you, There be some of them that stand here, which shall in no wise taste of death, till they see the Son of man coming in his kingdom" (Matthew 16:27-28). And John of Patmos wrote, "I saw the dead standing before the throne; and books were opened: and another book was opened, which is the book of life: and the dead were judged out of the things which were written in the books, according to their works" (Revelation 20:12).

[14] This brings to mind a memory of the Bulgarian translator, Maria Mitovska. Maria often visited the home of Brother Boris Nikolov. On one of those occasions, Maria and Boris were in conversation in his garden when a man arrived. The newcomer greeted Boris and bent down and kissed his hand – a sign of great respect in Bulgaria at that time. After straightening up, he looked lovingly at Boris and said, "I thank you for turning me from a criminal into a human being." (Decades before, the communist authorities had imprisoned Boris for publishing the Teacher's lectures. It was in prison, as fellow inmates, that Boris's good influence was brought to bear on this man.)

The Right Desire in Life

Someone will say, "Is it possible to live without wishing for anything?" I do not say people should not desire things, but you need to learn to wish according to the great law of correct behaviour, which means you need to see whether your desire is good for you, for your relatives, for your nation and for all humankind. If you find it to be good in all these ways together, you are allowed to have your wish. There is a special commission in heaven that checks people's actions and accounts. Whoever would like to learn more about this has to study spiritual science. You may pray four times daily, but if in the past you did not think well and do good deeds, and if now you do not work, do not water your garden and do not help people and animals, no one will respect you when you go to the next world.

The style of my words is not important; the important thing is for you to apply the law, which is connected to the law of love and wisdom, because all the present laws will collapse. And that will be the end of the contemporary, rotten world and its debauched morality. A common brotherhood will be created around the whole world; the current human slavery will have disappeared, and the rich and the poor and the intelligent and the ignorant will all be aligned according to the law of wisdom and love. That will be the new culture. Arm yourselves with this thought, be heroes and do not fear anything.[1]

Until now you have been serving the devil. People believe more in the devil than they do in God.[2] You should say, "From now on I will

[1] The Teacher also said, "When people ask what it is to live correctly, the idea of brotherhood will come to them. Christ said that we should work in the way of brotherhood, which is love" (10/23 January 1915). "The meaning of the new culture is for everybody to have the right of freedom. All nations in the world are organs of the Divine Organism. Each organ has its function. The Slavic people have the mission to be the carriers of the new culture of brotherhood" (some time between 1927 and 1944). "The Slavic people now hold the power of the soul, which is love. They are people who love all humankind. They are very generous. One of the greatest features of the Slavic people is self-sacrifice. These are the reasons why they carry the culture of brotherhood" (1944).

[2] Jesus said, "Every one that committeth sin is the bondservant of sin. I came forth and am come from God. Why do ye not understand my speech? Even because ye cannot hear

106

believe in the Living Lord, who moves the world and has decided to transform it."[3] He has sent His servants to the earth to do this. If you do not transform the world, the stones will come alive and they will transform it,[4] and you will be last in the kingdom of God.[5] You will say that I am a little severe. I am sorry, but I am not being severe. I am only telling you that your relationships as brothers and sisters are not of the quality required by God. I am telling you the truth. Free yourselves of all the acrimony between you, because there is no reason for it.[6]

Let us turn to the great truth to which God is pointing us. God is calling us to great work. Start putting your minds and hearts to work. Let us create a great wave of love in the world that will place us on the path of consensus and the great laws of nature. Do this and you can

my word. Ye are of your father the devil, and the lusts of your father it is your will to do. He is a liar, and the father thereof. But because I say the truth, ye believe me not. He that is of God heareth the words of God: for this cause ye hear them not, because ye are not of God" (John 8:34, 42-45, 47).

[3] God said, "Behold, I create new heavens and a new earth" (Isaiah 65:17).

[4] "The word of God came unto John the son of Zacharias in the wilderness. And he came into all the region round about Jordan, preaching the baptism of repentance unto remission of sins. He said to the multitudes that went out to be baptized of him, 'Ye offspring of vipers, who warned you to flee from the wrath to come? Bring forth therefore fruits worthy of repentance, and begin not to say within yourselves, 'We have Abraham to our father,' for I say unto you, that God is able of these stones to raise up children unto Abraham.'" (Luke 3:2-3, 7-8).

[5] "And one said unto Jesus, 'Lord, are they few that be saved?' And Jesus said unto them, 'Strive to enter in by the narrow door: for many, I say unto you, shall seek to enter in, and shall not be able. When once the master of the house is risen up, and hath shut to the door, and ye begin to stand without, and to knock at the door, saying, 'Lord, open to us,' and he shall answer and say to you, 'I know you not whence ye are,' then shall ye begin to say, 'We did eat and drink in thy presence, and thou didst teach in our streets,' and he shall say, 'I tell you, I know not whence ye are; depart from me, all ye workers of iniquity.' There shall be the weeping and gnashing of teeth, when ye shall see Abraham, and Isaac, and Jacob, and all the prophets, in the kingdom of God, and yourselves cast forth without. And they shall come from the east and west, and from the north and south, and shall sit down in the kingdom of God. And behold, there are last which shall be first, and there are first which shall be last" (Luke 13:23-30).

[6] Among the "seven things which are an abomination unto the Lord" is "he that soweth discord among brethren" (Proverbs 6:16, 19). Jesus said, "Blessed are the peacemakers: for they shall be called sons of God" (Matthew 5:9). And the Apostle John wrote, "In this the children of God are manifest, and the children of the devil: whosoever doeth not righteousness is not of God, neither he that loveth not his brother" (1 John 3:10).

be sure that the future will be yours.[7]

---

[7] The Teacher also said, "Our planet is leaving the Thirteenth Sphere. We are passing into new regions where the new earth will be created" (10 December 1944). "The divine fire has two qualities: it will melt everything that is impure, but it will give life to good germinating seeds" (some time between 1929 and 1942).

Constancy in Life

It is written in Ecclesiastes,

Who knoweth what is good for a man in his life? [1]

Be constant in everything and do not become discouraged. Constancy is the touchstone of life on which the strengths of the human soul are tested.

I will tell you a story. Two frogs lived in a lake near the house of a rich landowner. One day they decided to see what the man was doing. The frogs entered his house and saw a large pot. Curious to know what it contained, they climbed up the pot to have a look. The frogs found it to be full of milk, but unfortunately they fell in. The frogs circled the milk's surface, trying to find a way to escape the pot, but it was impossible. One became tired and asked its friend to swim with it to the bottom so they could rest. The other frog replied that if they stayed down at the bottom they would die. But the tired frog went down anyway, and there it died. The other frog swam in a circle continuously until the milk was transformed into creamy butter. Then it stepped on the butter and jumped out of the pot. Similarly, you need constancy to make a firm foundation from which to ascend into the spiritual world. [2]

You are often misled when people talk to you about the truth. Leave everyone else to talk about whatever he or she wants to. People talk about what is true for them. You should look for the truth that is within your heart. What is this inner truth saying to you? Do not accept other people's truths. [3] Christ told you the truth, and it should be your guide

---

[1] Ecclesiastes 6:12. The Teacher actually read the whole chapter, and this verse was not quoted in the original Bulgarian publication.

[2] The Teacher also said, "It is necessary to learn to be exact in everything you do. You need to eat at regular times. You need to go to bed at a regular time and get up at a regular time. You need to learn to be exact in your lives. But what do you say? You say, 'I do things when the Spirit tells me to do them.' What is this 'spirit' you follow? It is the spirit of laziness" (8 April 1923).

[3] The Teacher also said, "The earth is a school and a place from which the spirit draws

in life. Be faithful and constant in everything you do. A person's character is determined by his or her constancy.

Some things are hidden in the spiritual life. There are things which you cannot be told; you have to sense them for yourself. You need to develop some qualities that will enable you to perceive them. You need to learn to work alone. If there are people to help you, that is good; if not, you have to work alone. This work is serious, not useless – you may do silly things when you are resting.

All people have their own fields in which to work. If someone does not work conscientiously, he or she will be held responsible for it before God. If someone says something bad about you, it does not matter.[4] Others can stain you externally, but you will clean yourself with water. Water cleans everything, and you need an abundance of it. The first life was born in water, which is why Christ said, "I am the living water,"[5] and this is the only water with which you can wash away your sins.[6] Guard against staining yourselves.[7] When you make a mistake with your mind, you trouble the spiritual world. When you make a mistake with your heart, you trouble the angels. To prevent you from obstructing them, the angels then start to work on you, which causes you to suffer.

Imagine a stone that could feel. Were a sculptor to begin to work on it, the stone would ask, "Why are you hurting me? What wrong have I done you?" The sculptor answers, "I am hurting you because you can be

strength and experience. Those who live well are well-educated people, even if they are ignorant according to our understanding. This is why we should learn how to live well" (9/22 April 1914).

[4] The Teacher also said, "When people offend us they are deluded in some way, so why are we angry if they are rude or do not understand us?" (9/22 April 1914).

[5] "Jesus said, 'Whosoever drinketh of the water that I shall give him shall never thirst; but the water that I shall give him shall become in him a well of water springing up unto eternal life. If any man thirst, let him come unto me, and drink. He that believeth on me, as the scripture hath said, out of his belly shall flow rivers of living water.' But this spake he of the Spirit, which they that believed on him were to receive" (John 4:13-14; 7:37-39).

[6] God said, "I will sprinkle clean water upon you, and ye shall be clean: from all your filthiness, and from all your idols, will I cleanse you. A new heart also will I give you, and a new spirit will I put within you" (Ezekiel 36:25-26).

[7] "Pure religion and undefiled before our God and Father is this, to visit the fatherless and widows in their affliction, and to keep himself unspotted from the world" (James 1:27). "God our Saviour is able to guard you from stumbling, and to set you before the presence of his glory without blemish in exceeding joy" (Jude 1:24).

made into a beautiful statue." When you are suffering and complaining, it means there is something in your souls that God must chip off. And God is chipping off large pieces at the moment, but you ought to be joyful because God's benevolence is working on you. A sinner is a stone out of which the divine chisel will form a graceful statue. The Lord is working on you to develop the new feelings and qualities that will enable you to live with the angels, who are much more advanced than human beings. They will put you in a larger world, and then they will teach you better arts and direct you towards a new object of study. Your present suffering is the divine hammer and chisel that would like to give you a more graceful form. Only patience is required from you. Patience is one of the qualities of God, and constancy is required to attain it.[8]

Someone says, "I am patient." That is what you say, but this patience of yours will be tested every day. You may be patient today and even more patient tomorrow but still lack divine patience. The Lord is patient when a person sends Him bad thoughts and desires, for He sends them down to the roots and transforms them into compost.

You constantly complain that you are suffering, but you have yet to experience real suffering. Your present suffering is like the suffering of a child crying for his or her dolls. When the child has grown up and faces bigger suffering in life, he or she will laugh at that early suffering. The darker your feelings, the more you ought to suffer. With time, as your feelings become more tender and your soul more sympathetic, you will see, looking back, that your previous suffering was sent to you as a blessing from God – yet how you cried for your dolls! God is great and kind, and He only sends people blessings, but you have to be able to make use of them. In the morning the sun sends its energy and revitalises everything in nature. Each sunbeam has its purpose and carries great power. It is up to you to receive the energy that is sent for you; the rest is for the other parts of nature.

When you get up in the morning feeling discontented, you look for the causes outside yourselves. You then blame each other – the husband

---

[8] "One day is with the Lord as a thousand years, and a thousand years as one day. The Lord is not slack concerning his promise, as some count slackness; but is longsuffering *toward you*, not wishing that any should perish, but that all should come to repentance. But the day of the Lord will come as a thief. Account that the longsuffering of our Lord is salvation" (2 Peter 3:8-10, 15).

blames his wife, the wife blames her husband – without suspecting the truth of the matter, which is that you closed the shutters of the window of your soul and barred any sunlight from entering it. You need to reopen the window so the light can re-enter your soul. If things like the weather can make you discontented, it means you are not in harmony with God, which means you are outside God's laws. If you do not want the weather to influence your souls, you need to make yourselves harmonious with God. In God everything is in harmony and balance. Balance is the fourth divine principle. Balance your minds, your hearts and your souls to be in accord with God and to draw energy from Him.

You aspire to become wealthy. That is not bad; you need wealth for your lives. But know that this wealth will be removed from you one day. For that reason, aspire to gain the type of wealth which you may always carry with you and which no one can take away from you.[9] You burden your minds with many thoughts and desires, and when you are unable to realise them, because you did not have the conditions to do so, you become discouraged. No matter what setbacks you have, you need to be constant in life and not to sink in spirit. The things which you cannot achieve now, you will achieve in the future. This is why you need to cultivate every good thought and desire. If you have any thoughts and desires which are not useful at this time, store them away in your granary so they do not cause you pain. To gain the benefit of any food, you need to send it to your stomach to be digested; if the food remains outside you, you will feel hungry. In the same way, every good thought and desire which you cultivate and apply in your life will provide you with the necessary juices for the development of your mind and heart.

Everything that you have is temporary, and anything that is taken away from you, causing you to suffer, is a stone that the Lord has placed on your path for you to step on and raise yourself. Obstacles, the difficulties you have, are the stones that form the steps on which you can uplift yourself. All the saints ascended this way. Without such suffering the saints would never have achieved divine wholeness. Constantly

---

[9] Jesus said, "I counsel thee to buy of me gold refined by fire, that thou mayest become rich" (Revelation 3:18).

"And the angel carried me away in the Spirit to a mountain great and high, and shewed me the holy city Jerusalem, coming down out of heaven from God, having the glory of God. And the city was pure gold, like unto pure glass" (Revelation 21:10-11, 18).

build yourselves upon a firm foundation to become fellow citizens of the invisible world and to attain the higher feelings necessary for you to have eternal life.[10]

---

[10] The Apostle Paul wrote, "We desire that each one of you may shew diligence unto the fulness of hope even to the end: that ye be not sluggish, but imitators of them who through faith and patience inherit the promises" (Hebrews 6:11-12). And the Apostle Peter wrote, "Brethren, give the more diligence to make your calling and election sure" (2 Peter 1:10).

Spiritual Light, the Nourishment of the Soul

Jesus said,

> **Walk while ye have the light, that ye may become sons of light.** [1]

Spiritual light is to the soul what sunlight is to the body. The nourishment, growth and development of the body are not possible without sunlight. Likewise, it is not possible for the soul to grow, develop and bear fruits without spiritual light. In the same way that light comes to the earth from the sun, spiritual light comes to the soul from God. Sunlight is not one and the same thing as the sun, nor is spiritual light the same thing as God. Just as sunlight reminds us of the sun, spiritual light directs us towards God. [2]

When it is cloudy and we cannot see the sun, we need to use our knowledge and experience to locate it; by thinking of the hour and the season we can guess the sun's position in the sky. Were we to look in the right direction, we would probably see a little more light there, recognising the sun, although unclearly. Similarly, when we have spiritual light sent to us by God, we should seek God with our efforts, experience and knowledge.

A mother and father give their newborn child the conditions for life and the growth of his or her body. When a human being is born, he or she is also given spiritual light, which is a condition needed for the development and growth of the soul. To achieve our aspiration to live in heaven, we need special conditions. These are the conditions that help the soul to be purified and to become spiritually rich, because heavenly life is only for souls who are spiritually rich, pure and "dressed in wedding garments". [3] A child of spiritual light is someone who has spiritual

[1] John 12:35-36
[2] "The invisible God" (Colossians 1:15). "Dwelling in light unapproachable; whom no man hath seen, nor can see" (1 Timothy 6:16).
[3] In the parable of the wedding feast, Jesus said, "The wedding was filled with guests.

light and uses it for his or her spiritual development.

The soul is like a plant; it ought to bear fruit. The soul makes roots into the material world through the heart. Desires and thoughts are the juices that feed the soul and give it the opportunity to bear the fruits of goodness. One's thoughts and desires can be good, but they only become valuable when they are manifested as actions. Only then does the soul bear fruit, using the conditions of life as its soil.[4] Just as sunlight transforms the juices in plants and fruits, it is through divine spiritual light that our thoughts and desires are transformed for the better and become good deeds, which are the fruits of the soul.[5]

Although we are the children of spiritual light, we each have a different attitude towards the source of this light, God. At different times God gives us different conditions for our development. Our souls understand their filial relationships with God in different ways at different times, according to the conditions in which God has placed us to work. God, as the best educator, teaches us how to understand and use these conditions to become good people.

People are given signs indicating whether they are free or not. These signs come in the form of suffering. When you suffer, it means your life needs to go into more appropriate conditions where the suffering will end. The angels are free, having the best conditions for the manifestation of their inner lives. The saints did not complain and they never suffered, because the lives of their souls were more fully manifested and placed in high conditions, in the divine atmosphere where they were free. Therefore, if we are suffering we should direct our inner lives towards higher conditions. When we uplift and strengthen our inner

But when the king came in to behold the guests, he saw there a man which had not on a wedding-garment: and he saith unto him, 'Friend, how camest thou in hither not having a wedding-garment?' And he was speechless. Then the king said to the servants, 'Bind him hand and foot, and cast him out into the outer darkness; there shall be the weeping and gnashing of teeth.' For many are called, but few chosen" (Matthew 22:10-14).

[4] The Teacher also said, "Why do branches grow up and roots grow down? This question is open, but it is necessary for growth to be both upwards and downwards. And we, like plants, have a double aspiration. Those who are only in the roots say that the world is only matter" (10/23 January 1915).

[5] "Ye were once darkness, but are now light in the Lord: walk as children of light (for the fruit of the light is in all goodness and righteousness and truth), proving what is well-pleasing unto the Lord; and have no fellowship with the unfruitful works of darkness" (Ephesians 5:8-11).

115

lives and make a connection with powerful, righteous and light spirits, we will be free and will no longer suffer. When we have achieved this state we will have become the children of spiritual light, because we made proper use of the conditions offered to us. A child of spiritual light uses both the light and dark sides of life. In other words, he or she is capable of using either condition for self-upliftment. Such a person is able to make good use of happiness or unhappiness, and of being helped or being hindered.

We often complain because of our passions, negative thoughts and desires. That is not right. They are the conditions which help the soul and the ripening of its fruits. Every such condition is given to us from our Heavenly Father for us to conquer it, to transform it from our master into our servant. That is how we become powerful in goodness and spiritually rich. There is no other way to be, because the kingdom of God is given to those who make a great effort for it. This effort is a fight. Our fight is not against flesh and blood, however, but against this century's rulers of darkness, against the cunning spirits. Our undertaking of this fight makes us the children of spiritual light, and we will receive help from heaven.[6]

If we would like to be the children of spiritual light, we have to use all the conditions, good and bad, in which we are placed at any moment. When we use these conditions for self-development we will be freed from bad conditions. This is how we can use our experiences and the knowledge we have gained to find God, the source of spiritual light. The child of spiritual light is joyful and his or her soul does not despair.[7] In these ways the child of spiritual light achieves the divine balance within himself or herself and transmits it out into the world.[8]

In people's relationships and behaviour there are two categories of law. The first category has a mechanical character with two sides: add-

[6] "Be strong in the Lord, and in the strength of his might. Put on the whole armour of God, that ye may be able to stand against the wiles of the devil. For our wrestling is not against flesh and blood, but against the principalities, against the powers, against the world-rulers of this darkness, against the spiritual hosts of wickedness in the heavenly places. Wherefore take up the whole armour of God, that ye may be able to withstand in the evil day, and, having done all, to stand" (Ephesians 6:10-13).

[7] "The kingdom of God is righteousness and peace and joy in the Holy Spirit" (Romans 14:17).

[8] Jesus said, "Ye are the light of the world" (Matthew 5:14).

ing and subtracting. The second category has a divine character, and its two sides are multiplying and dividing. Sin always accompanies the first category of law. For example, Adam and Eve were added to each other. Then the serpent was added to them and they subtracted their disobedience and pride from themselves, so God subtracted them from Paradise. When people come together they add their sins together, and when they begin gossiping they start to subtract their own and other people's weaknesses and sins.

A rich evangelist built a granary in which to store his grain, intending to save it all for himself rather than following the divine principle of sharing. He built it, but on the very night he completed it, God subtracted the man's soul from his body.[9] A diamond is very expensive but it only collects and refracts sunbeams without multiplying them. The grain of wheat is humble, cheap and plentiful on earth, yet it multiplies. A spiritual person is the same. The good and faithful servant multiplies the talents and gifts of his or her Master, fulfilling the divine law.[10] When a seed falls on good soil it multiplies thirty, sixty or one hundred times.[11] When God created human beings He commanded us to grow and multiply.[12] When you have good gifts and talents you are required to multiply them.

A wife needs to see her husband's good qualities and then try to multiply them. When they are multiplied he will divide his feelings with her, sharing them in recognition and acknowledgment of her contribution to his development. He will love her, appreciate her and help her. When a person sees bad qualities in his or her spouse, he or she must not subtract them in front of other people but should instead transform those bad qualities into good ones. And when they have become good, he or she should multiply them.

It is said that the kingdom of God is like leaven and a mustard seed,[13] which means that when the primary elements of the kingdom of God

---

[9] See the parable of the rich fool (Luke 12:13-21)

[10] See the parable of the talents (Matthew 25:14-30) and the parable of the pounds (Luke 19:11-27)

[11] See the parable of the sower (Mark 4:2-20, especially 8, 20)

[12] See Genesis 1:27-28

[13] See the parable of the mustard seed (Matthew 13:31-32) and the parable of the leaven (Matthew 13:33)

117

enter the human soul and spirit they multiply themselves. And when they are multiplied, God divides out His kingdom with the human soul and spirit. Bearing in mind that we should be the children of spiritual light, we need to multiply ourselves and use all the conditions in which we are placed for our own good and the good of those close to us. Just as the multiplying of plants and animals is only possible with sunlight, it is only possible for human beings to behave in accordance with divine law when they have spiritual light. The children of spiritual light ought not to be externally brilliant, fruitless, non-growing diamonds. They are meant to be grains of wheat that multiply.

Let us sow the seed of love and joy so that peace grows in our minds. Let us sow the seed of patience and kindness so that the fruit of compassion grows in our hearts. Let us sow the seed of faith and meekness to grow the fruit of restraint in our lives.[14] Only in these ways can the fullness of our lives be manifested, our hearts be ennobled, our intelligence come to shine, our love be developed and happiness be achieved. This is the ascending path of God for individuals, for societies and for humanity itself.

---

[14] "The fruit of the Spirit is love, joy, peace, longsuffering, kindness, goodness, faithfulness, meekness, temperance" (Galatians 5:22-23). In the 1914 Constantinople Bible it is "longpatience, kindness, compassion" and not "longsuffering, kindness, goodness".

The Beginning of the New Epoch

The Teacher began by reading the Gospel of Matthew, chapter 28; the Gospel of Mark, chapter 16, verses 12 to 20; the Gospel of Luke, chapter 24, verses 13 to 53; and the Gospel of John, chapter 21; which cover the time of Jesus's resurrection.

Not many people realise the importance of today's date, but for some it will be a day to remember, because today one epoch has ended and a new one is beginning.[1] Today is a great spiritual day. There is a gathering up above from where all our friends are sending you their greetings. If anyone does not believe this, the day will soon come in which he or she personally verifies the truth of my words.

Christ wants to restore three things in us: our stomachs, which make the vital juices that we need in life; our souls, which are the queens of our bodies; and the Spirit, which forms kind thoughts within us. In our lives we must not lie or allow others to lie to us, for only then will the Lord give us spiritual light.[2] Life is not found in material possessions but in communion with God. The contemporary

---

[1] Years later the Teacher would say, "We are at the boundary of two epochs. Human consciousness has passed, and is still passing, through a dark epoch, a night, which the Indian people call the Kali Yuga. The period of the dark night is long, but now we are at its end. We are crossing the boundary between two epochs, leaving the Kali Yuga and entering the new epoch. All people will pass through divine fire to purify themselves in preparation for the new epoch. Humanity will be uplifted to a higher level than the one we are at now. It is the only way that we may enter the new life. This is called the new birth. It will not be long before this fire arrives. It will change the world and bring a new morality. A great wave is coming at great speed from Cosmic Space. It will flood the whole world" (some time between 1929 and 1942).

"Our Solar System is leaving the Thirteenth Sphere, which has condensed matter. When the Earth has completely left this sphere the sixth race will come. The Solar System is entering a new field of the Spirit. This entering began in 1914. This zone contains virgin matter, which is why we can expect resurrection. Those who are ready will be able to accept the new wave" (some time between 1929 and 1942). "The Earth is still passing through a dark zone, but the future will be bright. We may call the new epoch the epoch of resurrection, because during this time divine love will vitalise and enliven human consciousness" (17 January 1940).

[2] "The Spirit is the truth" (1 John 5:7). Jesus said, "He that doeth the truth cometh to the light, that his works may be made manifest, that they have been wrought in God" (John 3:21).

situation contains the germ of the future life.

The divine things inside us are microscopic in size, but they multiply like the grain of wheat when sown. One divine thought sown in each of us would bring us the greatest happiness in the future. Christ will come, but in what condition will he find us? Spring and summer will come, but in what condition will they find the farmer's work? If he sowed his fields in time, he will make good use of the spring and will harvest his fields in the summer and fill his granary with the grain of wheat. If, however, he did not sow on time, the spring and summer will pass and he will have lost a moment of opportunity, leaving himself empty-handed. [3]

Today a new epoch is beginning in the spiritual world. In what way will your names be written in the new book of life? [4] Up to and including yesterday it was said, "Go and preach and tell people to repent," but from now on believers will be saved by faith, and the Lord will help them. [5] Nothing is harder than trying to save yourself without help. Were you to be in the sea after a shipwreck, could you alone save yourself? Christ is still saving us, one by one, with his ship. And after saving people, he teaches them righteousness and how to love one another. If we want to learn these things we need to uplift our spirits, regenerate our minds and resurrect our bodies. We cannot become citizens of heaven until we have done this. We punish our bodies with our desires and suffering. The physical body is a skeleton beneath which the true body is building itself. [6] This body will allow us to make ourselves vis-

---

[3] The Teacher also said, "In the spiritual life we must constantly be sowing if we want to harvest later on" (15/28 August 1912).

[4] "I beheld till thrones were placed, and one that was ancient of days did sit: his raiment was white as snow; his throne was fiery flames. A fiery stream issued and came forth from before him: the judgement was set, and the books were opened" (Daniel 7:9-10). "And another book was opened, which is the book of life. And if any was not found written in the book of life, he was cast into the lake of fire. There shall in no wise enter into new Jerusalem anything unclean, or he that maketh an abomination and a lie: but only they which are written in the Lamb's book of life" (Revelation 20:12, 15; 21:27). Jesus said, "He that overcometh shall be arrayed in white garments; and I will in no wise blot his name out of the book of life, and I will confess his name before my Father, and before his angels" (Revelation 3:5).

[5] Jesus said, "He that believeth on the Son hath eternal life; but he that obeyeth not the Son shall not see life, but the wrath of God abideth on him" (John 3:36).

[6] The Teacher also said, "The physical body is given to us as rough material that is used like a skeleton for the building of the spiritual body. When we pass into the spiritual world,

ible or invisible.[7] The Lord will manifest Himself to us if we have pure desires and thoughts.[8]

Christ is a teacher who will show us our mistakes in life, just as a schoolteacher points out the mistakes in a pupil's workbook and gives the work a mark. You should do the best you can so that when Christ comes he will find fewer mistakes in your workbooks and give you good marks. Just as full stops and commas provide meaning in a pupil's workbook, they are also important in your lives.

A great human being is one who loves. Who loves? The one who loves serves others. A person who is served but does not serve is one who does not love. A servant has the most thankless of occupations, but it is the most honourable occupation according to the Lord. The Lord will put into practice the new teaching of service.[9]

Do not fear the devil. Instead, cast him from you. When you think about evil, you cultivate it inside you. Women and men are not bad in themselves; it is the devil who makes them bad.[10] This is why each morning husbands and wives need to see that the other has improved a little since the day before. The stone is not put on the road so that we trip over it but so that we are careful not to.[11] We are responsible for all our suffering. The noble person is one who does not become angry. Do not judge each other.

Let us uplift ourselves and imagine the divine picture of today's celebration in heaven. The spirits will descend from heaven to make human

---

we will materialise and dematerialise with our spiritual bodies. If a soul fails to build a spiritual body during its time in the physical body, it will be left like an orphan when the physical body dies. This soul will be poor and unable to manifest itself, because it will have nowhere from which to draw energy" (9/22 April 1914).

[7] "When the doors were shut where the disciples were, for fear of the Jews, Jesus came and stood in the midst, and saith unto them, 'Peace be unto you'" (John 20:19). "When Jesus had sat down with them to meat, he took the bread, and blessed it, and brake, and gave to them. And their eyes were opened, and they knew him; and he vanished out of their sight" (Luke 24:30-31).

[8] Jesus said, "Blessed are the pure in heart: for they shall see God" (Matthew 5:8).

[9] Jesus said, "He that is greatest among you shall be your servant. And whosoever shall exalt himself shall be humbled; and whosoever shall humble himself shall be exalted" (Matthew 23:11-12). "If any man serve me, him will the Father honour" (John 12:26).

[10] The Teacher also said, "The human soul has none of the qualities of the fallen souls, the fallen angels. Our souls are purer than theirs" (22 January/4 February 1915).

[11] "God our Saviour is able to guard you from stumbling" (Jude 1:24).

beings satisfied with what they have, and Christ will come with them. Either they will come with a blessing, a renovation of the contemporary order, or, if it is seen that it cannot be renovated, they will come with a catastrophe that destroys everything from the foundations, after which the building will begin completely anew. We must not be afraid of this possibility.

Christ is always above us and among us. Let us leave this meeting with Christ in our souls. Let us open our hearts and souls so that Christ can enter them and bless us.

Behold the Man! The True Human Being[1]

It is written in John's Gospel,

Jesus came out, wearing the crown of thorns and the purple garment. And Pilate saith unto them, "Behold, the man!"[2]

Jesus, who was the embodiment of the original meaning of what it is to be a human being, came to the earth to be the brother of those who suffer.[3] When we go out before the world, can people likewise say of us, "Behold the man!" or "Behold the woman!"? To be a true human being, to earn the title 'the man' or 'the woman', a person has to have four things: wealth, strength, knowledge and virtue. You are wondering, "How does wealth fit in here?" By 'wealth' I mean the soil, the conditions, in which a person can develop strength. We need knowledge to understand our lives and to regulate them properly. Virtue is what we should aim for.

People often ask, "What should we do?" Sow a grain of wheat and it will show you what to do. You will ask, "How will it show us?" Put

---

[1] This was the opening lecture in *Power and Life, Volume One*, the first published book of the Teacher's lectures. It was surely not a coincidence that this new stage in the teaching began at the same time as the new epoch as described in the previous talk.

[2] John 19:5. It is evident in the text that the Teacher actually read the whole chapter.

[3] "God, sending his own Son in the likeness of sinful flesh and as an offering for sin, condemned sin in the flesh: that the ordinance of the law might be fulfilled in us, who walk not after the flesh, but after the spirit. The mind of the flesh is death; but the mind of the Spirit is life and peace: because the mind of the flesh is enmity against God; for it is not subject to the law of God, neither indeed can it be: and they that are in the flesh cannot please God. But ye are not in the flesh, but in the spirit, if so be that the Spirit of God dwelleth in you. If by the spirit ye mortify the deeds of the body, ye shall live. For as many as are led by the Spirit of God, these are sons of God. The Spirit himself beareth witness with our spirit, that we are children of God: and if children, then heirs; heirs of God, and joint-heirs with Christ; if so be that we suffer with him, that we may be also glorified with him. And we know that to them that love God all things work together for good, even to them that are called according to his purpose. For whom he foreknew, he also foreordained to be conformed to the image of his Son, that he might be the firstborn among many brethren" (Romans 8:3-4, 6-9, 13-14,16-17, 28-29).

moisture in the soil and the sunbeams will show the direction in which the wheat grows. It aims in one direction, towards the sun, the source of life. As individual grains of wheat, we should grow, which means we ought to aim towards God. Someone might ask, "When a grain of wheat is fully grown, does it reach the sun? Because I want to find God!" You do not need to know where God is; it is only necessary to aim for God.[4]

The grain of wheat understands what the sun is and receives what it desires from the sunlight. The same law applies to us, and we need to attain the same results as the grain of wheat.[5] We must be sown first. This means our lives will certainly have their difficulties, which represent the small but necessary obstacles which we, like the grain of wheat, must overcome. Some necessary pressure is applied to the grain, after which the process of growth begins. Knowledge comes with growth, and the fruit we bear is virtue. Consequently, we have to be sown: some soil must be placed on us to create the pressure, and then we need to grow and acquire knowledge. Once this knowledge is sufficiently grown it should be transformed into the ear of wheat. The Master will then have the grain harvested, and He will separate that which is useful from that which is not, the wheat from the chaff.[6]

We are born, which means we are germinated, we grow and we develop ourselves, we die and are buried in the grave. To die and be buried means to be trodden upon and threshed. The Lord will then pick what He needs from the threshing floor. This corresponds to the granary and the barn: the chaff is stored in the barn and the wheat is stored in the granary....

---

[4] Jesus said, "Seek, and ye shall find: for he that seeketh findeth" (Matthew 7:7-8).

[5] The Teacher also said, "The sun shines every day. The Lord is also before us every day. God lives above us as the sun lives above the earth. The sun sends us the light and warmth that we need so that we can grow. It eliminates the cold that rules the Universe and stops all progress. Through His spirits God enlightens us, warms us and grows us. When we are healthy, clever and fresh the Spirit and the Lord are within us. You do not need to follow a special programme to live like this but to fulfil the original divine plan. When you do, you will be rich. You suffer because you change the divine plan. You need to free yourselves of all deceitful ideas, of outer influences, and receive your advice from God, who is within you. May you listen to your inner voice, your souls" (6/19 April 1914).

[6] John the Baptist said of Jesus, "He shall baptize you with the Holy Spirit and with fire: whose fan is in his hand, and he will thoroughly cleanse his threshing-floor; and he will gather his wheat into the garner, but the chaff he will burn up with unquenchable fire" (Matthew 3:11-12).

I read the nineteenth chapter of John's Gospel so that you could see the four things which Christ carried on the cross, four things that we too should study. Once virtue is placed at the head, knowledge on the left side, power on the right side and wealth in the legs we have a crucified human being. And when this knowledge, power and wealth are nailed to the cross, their juices will ascend to the head, to virtue.

When the Lord wants to make someone good He nails him or her to the cross, nails his or her wealth, power and knowledge. What does nailing mean? It means a person has been put inside a locked safe where he or she is only available to the Lord. The Lord says, "When I am working you will be silent." People do not want to be quiet, however, so the Lord says, "Nail them so they become silent and I can work!" We should not cry when we are nailed to this cross, because it means the Lord is working for us. Unhappy are they who are not nailed to the cross. Those who want the Lord to work with them have to pass through this process of development. I am speaking allegorically.

Before this process of development begins, you must have faith, unshakeable faith in the general divine plan for all the creatures God has created. You should not doubt God, because He is perfect, almighty – as Jesus said, "Whatever is not possible for a human being is possible for God."[7] The divine paths are unknown. Do not allow the thought to come to you that these paths can be diverted or stopped – those are impossibilities. Once we have been invited to walk the divine path and are treading it, we need to have the simple faith of a child while avoiding the weaknesses shown in the following story.

A great English painter wanted to make a drawing expressing the plight of the poorest people. He walked around London for days and months to find exactly the right person to portray the state of abject poverty. Finally he found a boy in rags who fitted the image he had in mind. He said to himself, "This is the face I have been seeking for my painting." The artist gave the child his calling card and said, "Come to my home in four days' time. I would like to discuss something with you." Seeing how well dressed the man was, the boy said to himself, "How can I visit such a man dressed as I am?" So he went to his friends to try to find clothes that he could wear before kings. Having obtained

[7] See Luke 18:27

fine clothing, he dressed and went to see the man. "Who are you?" asked the painter when the boy arrived. "I am the boy you asked to visit you." "Go away!" the man replied. "If I wanted a child dressed like that, there are plenty to choose from. I need you the way you were on the day I found you."

And we too would like to dress well when heaven asks us to work, but our power is not in our clothing. Hats, clothes, shoes, ties and watches do not represent anything important. Our power is in our minds, our hearts, our noble impulses and our aspiration to do good things. When you have these things everything else will simply come of itself in its own time. When we go to heaven, should we take our earthly clothing with us? When calling us to heaven, the Lord undresses us here; He does not want our rags. The Lord says, "Bring that man here in his natural state."

When a person is buried and left in the grave, what does the Lord do? He begins to talk with the deceased, asking, "Did you understand life? Did you understand the meaning of the life I gave you?" During this conversation the Lord paints His great canvas. Then the following process is born: the people who buried the body begin to cry and enumerate all the deceased person's good qualities, because they see the divine painting depicting them.

We should endure all the suffering that comes to us and learn its lessons. Jesus, by his earthly suffering, wanted to show us how we should submit ourselves to this divine process.[8] He said, "Do I not have the power to ask my Father to send thousands of angels to save me? But if I do not fulfil that for which I came, how will humanity be uplifted?"[9]

---

[8] "Christ in the days of his flesh, having offered up prayers and supplications with strong crying and tears unto him that was able to save him from death, and having been heard for his godly fear, though he was a Son, yet learned obedience by the things which he suffered; and having been made perfect, he became unto all them that obey him the author of eternal salvation" (Hebrews 5:7-9).

[9] When one of the disciples fought to prevent Jesus's arrest, Jesus said to him, "Put up again thy sword into its place: for all they that take the sword shall perish with the sword. Or thinkest thou that I cannot beseech my Father, and he shall even now send me more than twelve legions of angels? How then should the scriptures be fulfilled, that thus it must be?" (Matthew 26:52-54).

Of the necessity of his upliftment, Jesus said, "As Moses lifted up the serpent in the wilderness, even so must the Son of man be lifted up: that whosoever believeth may in him have eternal life. And I, if I be lifted up from the earth, will draw all men unto myself" (John 3:14-15; 12:32).

And he also wanted to uplift himself.[10] You are on earth, and therefore storms and difficulties will come to you one day, and perhaps even the same destiny as Jesus. But you should not be unhappy when this hour comes, because where there is no suffering there is no enrichment, where there is sorrow there is joy, and where there is death there is resurrection. Those who do not want to participate in humanity's suffering will not gain anything.

What is suffering? It is the consequence of your previous mistakes that were caused by your own lack of competence. Suffering corrects these mistakes. The process of suffering is a method by which we can adapt ourselves and reach the higher, ascending vibrations that wait for us in heaven. We need to endure one hundred sorrows to receive one divine joy, which means we will value and keep this joy. The Lord prepares us with suffering, like a blacksmith tempering iron, so that we become strong enough to endure the joy to come. Every one of us is needed, very much needed by the Lord. It is possible for you to be a nought, a nothing, but you are an important one for God. Only the Lord, who sent you to earth, values your suffering. Consequently, you should not worry about what the world thinks of you. The One who sent you thinks about you and values you. What is important is that God approves of you. If the Lord is with you, you will be beautiful, and the world likes beauty.[11] If He is with you, you will be rich, strong and good, and goodness is always respected.

I will now speak about God, but not as the being that the philosophers describe: an abstract form dispersed throughout space, the exact whereabouts of which is unknown. I am talking of this Lord of whom I am preaching, who thinks about us and observes our behaviour, who corrects and punishes us, who dresses us in birth and undresses us in death. What

---

[10] God said, "Behold, my servant shall deal wisely, he shall be exalted and lifted up, and shall be very high. By his knowledge shall my righteous servant justify many: and he shall bear their iniquities. Therefore will I divide him a portion with the great, and he shall divide the spoil with the strong; because he poured out his soul unto death, and was numbered with the transgressors: yet he bare the sin of many, and made intercession for the transgressors" (Isaiah 52:13; 53:11-12). And Jesus said, "I have a baptism to be baptized with" (Luke 12:50).

[11] The Teacher also said, "The people of the sixth race will have correct features. They will be beautiful, their beauty having been formed by the high ideal they hold within themselves. They will be far more beautiful than the people of today" (1944).

is death? Sometimes the Lord makes an investigative operation on a person, and if He finds that she would lose much were she to stay alive, He will reduce her life, saying, "Take away the remaining capital that I gave this woman so that she does not accrue more debts. Let her capital be reinvested at another time, for the conditions do not favour her now. Bring her here to Me." During this process people think that the world has forgotten them – and it is right that the world goes on – but even when the world no longer remembers the departed, God never forgets us.

A young woman will never marry if she loves all bachelors. She needs to choose one and say, "This man is my world." It is the same in life: you should have only one Lord. There are many gods in the world who would like to take possession of you, but you need to find the God with whom you can live, develop and become rich. The Scriptures say, "God is not only in heaven; He lives in the hearts of humble people."[12] The first quality that you have to obtain so that God will come to live inside you is humility, but not the humility of a sheep. When they beat you and break your legs, do not say, "There is nothing I can do!" If your wealth is taken from you, and you say, "I have become humble," that is not humility. Humility is attained when a person who has riches, strength, power, knowledge and goodness becomes conscious enough to say, "Lord, all I have is at Your disposal." Instead, all people preach the Gospel and put the world to rights, but when the Lord touches their bulging wallets, they shut them, saying, "Hands off my money! I can give half, but not everything!" When people's strength is needed, they say, "You cannot use all my strength!" When people are in need, however, they beg for the Lord's guidance and help. This human way of understanding life has prevailed in all philosophies for thousands of years, and it still does. It is the cause of people's misfortunes and unhappiness. By his life, Jesus wanted to show us the right path.

Many people who become Christians think they should leave the world. You may renounce your home, wealth, spouse and children and yet still think about them. You can go and live alone in a monastery and still think, "What is going on with my wife and children, and how is our home?" Such thoughts show that you did not renounce these

---

[12] God said, "I dwell in the high and holy place, with him also that is of a contrite and humble spirit, to revive the spirit of the humble, and to revive the heart of the contrite ones" (Isaiah 57:15).

things and that you are not free. To renounce things is not to forget them but to let other people be free. Allow your spouse to behave as he or she knows how. Allow your children to behave as they know how. To renounce the world means to leave the world be, to leave it uninterrupted. Let it go its own way, for can any of us stop the river's flow? While we must allow the river to go on its way, there is one thing we can do, which is to make use of it. In the same manner, we cannot stop life, but we can make use of the things in it. Jesus clearly and positively said to us, "If you love me, keep my commandments,"[13] and we should love him.[14] Jesus did not say, "You had better love me or it will be most unfortunate for you!" No, the Lord never wants to pressure us into making sacrifices.[15]

People say, "As the Lord is almighty, why does He not set the world aright?" But how should He put it right? They answer, "By tying the tongue of anybody who lies and by removing the arms of those who steal." If He did that, we would have a world full only of amputees and dumb people! Instead, the Lord rules in the opposite manner, saying, "Whoever wants to be a master must be a servant."[16] Powerful people usually want all other rivers to be tributaries flowing into their rivers, but goodness works in the opposite way: the Lord overflows into small rivers and, instead of managing them, allows them to run themselves. You may make a small experiment of this in your own homes. You should think about management and put it in your minds to become

[13] See John 14:15

[14] The Teacher also said, "The meaning of love is to keep Christ's commandments, which is why you need to gradually study them. The Teacher will show you the correct sequence and the best way to learn them. Each morning you should read a chapter of one of the Gospels, find a commandment of Christ and try to apply it during the day. If you do this, Christ will enter you and make a home inside you. That is how you will come to understand the profound divine actions. Life is eternal, and there are many great things which Christ will reveal to you. He will reveal them gradually, however, because you are not yet ready for such great secrets" (11/24 January 1915).

[15] Even though he was sent to the earth to be a world saviour, Jesus made it clear his sacrifice was voluntary. He said, "No one taketh my life away from me, but I lay it down of myself. I have power to lay it down, and I have power to take it again. This commandment received I from my Father. The prince of the world cometh: and he hath nothing in me; but that the world may know that I love the Father, and as the Father gave me commandment, even so I do" (John 10:18; 14:30-31).

[16] Jesus said to his disciples, "Whosoever would become great among you, shall be your minister: and whosoever would be first among you, shall be servant of all" (Mark 10:43-44).

servants of the Lord. If you do this, you will descend to the place of the Lord.[17] You look for the Lord in heaven, but He is not there. The Lord is within you when you suffer.[18]

What people describe as growing, or advancing, is a process in which the Lord works – and He is the best worker. Some people complain, "Why does God not see my suffering?" God replies, "I have no time right now, as I am very busy with other, more important affairs of yours. When I have the time I will occupy Myself with your petty, external misunderstandings." This is not allegorical; it is reality. The suffering we experience here is also the Lord's suffering – He suffers and cries within you. You say, "I am crying. My soul is sad." But when we say, "Lord, forgive me for causing You so much suffering with my impure thoughts and actions," we will come to the true path, the path which will save us from the contemporary evil. We ought finally to allow our Lord to become stronger within us, for we tied Him up with ropes and nailed Him to the cross. Instead, we should place the Lord in the tomb and leave Him there in quietude. If we do this, He will resurrect Himself and make us free. And be sure of one thing: it is not devils but we human beings who obstruct the Lord's path. Having created the law of freedom, the Lord neither can nor wants to change it.[19] Until we arrive at the level of consciousness in which we voluntarily subordinate ourselves to the Lord, He will not save us.

The idea of being like the Lord needs to penetrate deeply into our consciousness. When it has, we will use our wealth, power and virtue to uplift. To uplift whom? To uplift our brothers, sisters and neighbours. We all ought to seek and value the souls of our brothers and sisters, but we should not fall in love with their bodies.[20] And I can tell you that

[17] No doubt this means humility as practised and taught by Jesus, who said, "Verily the Son of man came not to be ministered unto, but to minister, and to give his life a ransom for many" (Mark 10:45). Jesus also literally and symbolically lowered himself to wash his disciples' feet at the Last Supper (see John 13:1-17).

[18] "The Lord is nigh unto them that are of a broken heart, And saveth such as be of a contrite spirit" (Psalm 34:18).

[19] "For ever, O Lord, Thy word is settled in heaven" (Psalm 119:89). "The word of our God shall stand for ever" (Isaiah 40:8). "For I the Lord change not" (Malachi 3:6).

[20] The Teacher also said, "When Christ comes to someone, he or she will feel himself or herself to be Christ. This is the first delusion, and it is caused by the law of reflection. There are already such people in America, France and England. This delusion may result in spiritual love being converted into the love of the flesh. When this happens, many babies

since Jesus came to the earth he has not left it. He lives and works among people, and he needs to be resurrected within us. We need to have faith, but not the same faith and fear as the Jewish people had when they said, "We have no King but Caesar."[21] And when Caesar later destroyed Jerusalem and their temple, they denied him. Today people are still saying, "Caesar is my King," and the consequences will also be the same....[22]

We have to live in this world to prepare ourselves for heaven. We cannot yet live in heaven, as the heat and light there are too strong for us. When a gardener wants to graft a branch from a pine tree at high altitude to another at low altitude, the severed branch must be grafted and acclimatised at progressively lower altitudes until it is adapted for its new home. In the same way, the heavenly Father cannot take us directly from here and plant us in the Garden of Paradise. Even our educational system is structured this way. First we have to pass the first class, then the second class, and so on up through all the other classes in school. Then we go on to university, after which we finally enter the world. These are the methods of culture to which people who want to advance in life need to adapt themselves.

According to my understanding, a Christian should not be so foolish as to say, "I will accept whatever the Lord gives me." When you are ploughing your fields you need to sow wheat, because if you sow nothing, what will the Lord give you? He will give you weeds and thorns. Plant and cultivate your vineyards and they will give you fruit. The fruit you produce will correspond to the quality of the vines you have planted. A poor quality vine will produce sour grapes.[23] The Lord

are born.... That is the wrong path, and it leads to a reaction of persecution. A human being needs to realise that he or she is a manifestation of God. When a person understands this, God begins to act through him or her" (21 January/3 February 1915).

[21] See John 19:15

[22] The Teacher also said, "A town gave some of its population the task of finding out why the Lord had made the position of kings, for their king was terrible. They discovered that the Lord had only made human beings; He did not make the position of kings. People made kings, which is why they suffer at their hands. There is only one King, Christ" (6/19 January 1915). The Bible says that God did not want the Israelites to have a human king but instead wanted them to accept God Himself as their king. The people, however, ignored God's warning that they would rue the day they chose their own king (see 1 Samuel 8:1-22).

[23] Jesus said, "I am the true vine, and my Father is the husbandman. I am the vine, ye are the branches: He that abideth in me, and I in him, the same beareth much fruit: for apart

gave your children good minds, but what did you yourselves plant in your children's minds? Did you sow the seeds which would produce good fruit? We want to be good, powerful and rich. Not only can we have virtue, power and wealth, it is necessary for us to have them. The development of virtue, power and wealth require the divine balance, the divine seed and the divine law. To develop virtue we need the divine balance. To build wealth we need the divine seed. To become powerful we need to know and understand the divine law and to have the conditions for its development.

You will ask me, "How can we find the Lord?" It is very easy. One man told another, "This orchard is full of beautiful apples." The other man, wanting to tease, closed his eyes and replied, "But I do not see any." His friend then slapped him in the face, which made him open his eyes and see. Sometimes the Lord also slaps us so that we open our eyes and see. Those of you whose eyes are closed should want them to be opened. Contemporary people argue over whether God exists or not, over His whereabouts, but when unhappiness comes everyone looks up and calls out, "Lord!" This is the purpose of misfortune and unhappiness. They are the Lord's slap with which He tells us, "I created you to see, not for you to keep your eyes closed." If we want to uplift ourselves, we have to develop the inquisitive, receptive state of children.[24]

I will now tell you something else. What is the method by which you should work? From now on we need to be constantly connected to all the people on earth through our minds and hearts, because salvation comes from our collective prayers: "Unity Is Strength."[25] When people's minds and hearts are connected, the kingdom of God will come on earth. Do not look for the weaknesses of a friend whom you love – anyone might have weaknesses.[26] Weaknesses are the external

---

from me ye can do nothing" (John 15:1, 5).

[24] Jesus said, "Verily I say unto you, Except ye turn, and become as little children, ye shall in no wise enter into the kingdom of heaven. Whosoever therefore shall humble himself as this little child, the same is the greatest in the kingdom of heaven" (Matthew 18:3-4). "Verily I say unto you, Whosoever shall not receive the kingdom of God as a little child, he shall in no wise enter therein" (Mark 10:15).

[25] 'Unity Is Strength' is an ancient Bulgarian saying and had been the country's motto since 1887. It was later removed during the communist time and then restored with democracy.

[26] "Love covereth all transgressions" (Proverbs 10:12). "Love taketh not account of evil" (1

clothing in which the human being is dressed, for the human soul is pure and can neither be contaminated nor destroyed. No one is in a position to pervert your divine souls. They can be spotted externally but not internally, because God dwells inside them. Although we can be subordinated by the world, it is impossible to destroy anything protected by God. When Pilate told Jesus, "I have the power to crucify you," Jesus replied, "I am only subordinate to the One who has given you that power. My soul remains free." [27] We should submit ourselves to the present suffering in the world, even though we cannot understand why it is happening. Only once we have passed away and been resurrected will we understand. Until now everybody has been tortured by his or her fears in life, but they do not make for a real life. A true life is lived when a person is filled with noble feelings. A happy person is someone who is joyful in having done a good, unselfish deed.

If somebody has offended you, you neither want to acknowledge him nor to shake his hand the next time you meet. Nevertheless, you should take off your hat and shake his hand, but do so without giving him your respect. We usually take off our hats to a person in a higher social position than ourselves. There is sometimes a message in this gesture: "Can you give me a higher position in life?" There is a devilfish in the sea that likewise greets all the creatures it meets…. A person grasps another's hand in greeting. Why? Because the hand's 'devilfingers' are doing a lot of talking. The little finger asks, "Can you give me money?" The ring finger says, "I want the knowledge and glory of a great painter." The middle finger says, "I want rights and privileges." The index finger says, "I need respect." The thumb says, "I want strength and skill." But people will never find everything they need from each other. Finally Jesus comes and says, "The things for which you search – wealth, strength, knowledge and goodness – I can give them to you. [28] Without exception, whoever leaves his mother and father for me receives the future life one hundred times over." [29]

Corinthians 13:5). "Love covereth a multitude of sins" (1 Peter 4:8).

[27] See John 19:10-11

[28] After his resurrection, Jesus said, "All authority hath been given unto me in heaven and on earth" (Matthew 28:18).

[29] Jesus said, "Verily I say unto you, There is no man that hath left house, or brethren, or sisters, or mother, or father, or children, or lands, for my sake, and for the gospel's sake, but he shall receive a hundredfold now in this time, houses, and brethren, and sisters, and

Behold the man who can shake hands with us, who can give us wealth, strength, knowledge and goodness – all these things. But the people said, "Crucify him!" Pilate answered them, "But you will lose him!"[30] And Jesus is also standing before us today, and I say to you, "Behold the man for whom you search, the man who is able to place peace in your hearts. He is the only man who is able to give you good minds, good health and good social positions, who is able to uplift you, to show you the path and to clear your minds." You, however, are doubtful, saying, "Show him to us so that we can see him!" I will answer you with an example. In the evening a man comes to you holding a small candle. I say to you, "Behold the man who is bringing you light!" You see the light but you do not see the man who is carrying the candle. When will you see him? When the sun rises. Seek for yourselves the light that the man carries, for it will help you to find the path on which you should walk. This is how you need to understand the matter.[31]

I will give you another, clearer allegory. I take you into a darkened room and say, "This room is stupendously decorated with enormous riches." You answer, "Maybe. Who knows? I do not see anything."[32] I light a small candle and the nearer objects become discernible. I light another candle and they become a little clearer. With the addition of more and more candles the room gradually becomes lighter and lighter. Then an electric light is switched on and everything can be seen. Finally, when the daylight enters the room, all becomes perfectly clear. The world is like this room, and each of you should carry a candle and

mothers, and children, and lands, with persecutions; and in the world to come eternal life" (Mark 10:29-30).

[30] "Pilate saith unto the Jews, 'Behold, your king!' They therefore cried out, 'Away with him, away with him, crucify him.' Pilate saith unto them, 'Shall I crucify your king?'" (John 19:14-15).

[31] Jesus said, "I am the light of the world: he that followeth me shall not walk in the darkness, but shall have the light of life" (John 8:12). "I am the way, and the truth, and the life: no one cometh unto the Father, but by me" (John 14:6). And John of Patmos wrote of his vision, "The glory of God did lighten the holy city, and the lamp thereof is the Lamb. And his servants shall do him service; and they shall see his face; and his name shall be on their foreheads. And there shall be night no more" (Revelation 21:23; 22:3-5).

[32] "The mystery of God is Christ, in whom are all the treasures of wisdom and knowledge hidden" (Colossians 2:2-3). "The Lord is rich unto all that call upon him. O the depth of the riches both of the wisdom and the knowledge of God! For of him, and through him, and unto him, are all things" (Romans 10:12; 11:33, 36).

become a bearer of light. Were we all to enter the room with lighted candles and put them together, we would see a lot. Your minds are the candles. I do not like people who carry unlit candles. I like those who carry lighted candles. Every one of you needs to be a lighted candle. A faithful, loving and good person is a lighted candle. It is a great mistake to extinguish a candle's flame.[33]

You ask, "What should we do?" You ought to pray for one another. Send good thoughts to your friends and pray for them to be blessed. And when the Lord blesses them He will bless you as well. When people gather to pray, join them. Prayer has great power. People need to become prayerful. We prepare our minds and hearts through prayer. Do not pray only for your individual selves, for that is egotism. I do not want to occupy myself with people's minds; I want to occupy myself with their hearts, because all evil is in the heart. God Himself said, "My son, give me your heart."[34] You now need to begin a process of purification like spring cleaning, opening the windows and washing the floor. Everyone is suffering under a burden. There is a general disharmony everywhere. Men and women cannot come to agreement. They argue over who should control the household's money. They argue over who should rule the house – who should be the cock and who should be the hen. However, those are not the important things in life. I tell you, something else is important.

Jesus has come and he is working. When the light comes to you, it will do so gradually and silently. Jesus will not come as thunder, as some people expect.[35] There may be thunder, but it will not be Jesus.

---

[33] Jesus said, "I am come a light into the world, that whosoever believeth on me may not abide in the darkness" (John 12:46). "The lamp of the body is the eye: if therefore thine eye be single, thy whole body shall be full of light" (Matthew 6:22). "Ye are the light of the world. Let your light shine before men, that they may see your good works, and glorify your Father which is in heaven" (Matthew 5:14, 16).

[34] See Proverbs 23:26

[35] "And the seventh angel sounded; and there followed great voices in heaven, and they said, 'The kingdom of the world is become the kingdom of our Lord, and of his Christ: and he shall reign for ever and ever.' And there was opened the temple of God that is in heaven; and there was seen in his temple the ark of his covenant; and there followed lightnings, and voices, and thunders, and an earthquake, and great hail" (Revelation 11:15, 19). "And I heard as it were the voice of a great multitude, and as the voice of many waters, and as the voice of mighty thunders, saying, 'Hallelujah: for the Lord our God, the Almighty, reigneth. Let us rejoice and be exceeding glad, and let us give the glory unto him: for the marriage of the Lamb is come, and his wife hath made herself ready'" (Revelation 19:6-7).

The prophet Elijah entered the desert and dedicated himself to fasting and prayer. And when the storm and fire came, Elijah covered his eyes. God was not in the storm or the fire but in the gentle voice that spoke.[36] The Lord is neither in your suffering nor in your power or knowledge. Where is He then? He is love. If you love, He is within you. If you do not love, He is absent.[37] And you must love – it is the law.[38] We do not love others but instead wait for others to love us. This means we are sitting by the fireplace waiting for others to bring us wood so we can be warmed. But we should have this fuel for ourselves, and we ought to offer it to others as well.

We followers of Jesus, who has given us strength, should at last allow him to enter us. I now give you this man. Will you accept him or will you crucify him? Will you permit him to enter you, or will you say, "We do not want him!"?[39] This is the problem which you need to solve. If you say, "Let him in, he is our lord," you have solved the problem and a blessing will come to you. And then the words of the Scriptures will be fulfilled: "My Father and I will come and make our home within you,"[40] and the light will be within you and you will all be reconciled.[41]

---

[36] See 1 Kings 19:1-13

[37] "Beloved, let us love one another: for love is of God; and every one that loveth is begotten of God, and knoweth God. He that loveth not knoweth not God; for God is love. No man hath beheld God at any time: if we love one another, God abideth in us, and his love is perfected in us" (1 John 4:7-8, 12).

[38] Jesus said, "'Thou shalt love the Lord thy God with all thy heart, and with all thy soul, and with all thy mind.' This is the great and first commandment. And a second like unto it is this, 'Thou shalt love thy neighbour as thyself.' On these two commandments hangeth the whole law, and the prophets" (Matthew 22:37-40). "A new commandment I give unto you, that ye love one another; even as I have loved you, that ye also love one another. By this shall all men know that ye are my disciples, if ye have love one to another" (John 13:34-35).

[39] The Teacher also said, "We seek Christ and we find him, but when he appears inside us we crucify him. Christ then resurrects himself and leaves us. But when will he return to us? Perhaps he will return in ten years, or one hundred years, or one thousand years, and so on" (11/24 January 1915).

[40] Jesus said, "If a man love me, he will keep my word: and my Father will love him, and we will come unto him, and make our abode with him" (John 14:23).

[41] "And this is the message which we have heard from Jesus Christ, that God is light" (1 John 1:5).

Sofia, Sunday 23 March/5 April 1914

The Grain of Wheat, the Emblem of the Human Soul

Jesus said,

> Verily, verily, I say unto you, Except a grain of wheat fall into
> the earth and die, it abideth by itself alone; but if it die, it
> beareth much fruit.[1]

The grain of wheat is the emblem of the human soul. It represents
the great history of nature's development. If you were able to unfold a
grain of wheat's leaf and read its history, you would completely understand the history of the human soul.[2] Just as a grain of wheat falls to
the ground and dies, then sprouts, grows and produces seeds, so the
human soul develops.

Perhaps a grain of wheat seems nothing special to you, something
of almost no value and weighing only one sixteen-thousandth of a
kilogram. How can you calculate one grain's price when a whole kilogram of grain costs so very little? But a single grain of wheat has power,
potential and the spirit of self-denial. It uses its power to nourish itself
and others, but when you sit down at the table to eat, you do not think
about what the grain of wheat gives you. You do not know what joy it
brings you and what kind of thoughts it carries. You do not know its
origin. People value it no more than hens do. The grain of wheat is a
great enigma in the world.

What is hidden in a grain of wheat? It is an emblem of life. The first
letter in the Bulgarian word for 'grain', жито (zheeto), has a shape like
the growing grain of wheat: in the lower part are the legs, the roots,
and above them, the branches: Ж. When we sow the grain of wheat, it
grows and shows us the direction in which we should aim. The grain
of wheat tells us that we should aim towards the One out of whom we
came, God. To aim towards God we need to be rising branches which

[1] John 12:24

[2] Here the Teacher said "лист" (leest), which means 'leaf' or 'a sheet of paper', poetically
equating the plant's anatomy with the pages of its 'history book'.

137

blossom and bear food for the world; or, as the grain of wheat would say to us, "Help your neighbours and make sacrifices for them, just as I, the grain of wheat, am doing." This is why Christ said, "I am a living bread that has descended from heaven."[3] What is bread made from? It is made from the grain of wheat.[4]

People today say their lives are unfortunate and unhappy. Everybody is discontented, even kings and princes. All people, from the highest position to the lowest, want something to be given to them. And when they receive what they have wanted they become discontented again and want something else. Ask them why they are discontented. It is because they are looking for something more in life.

Let us return to the history of the grain of wheat. When the grain of wheat is sown in the earth, what would you say if you were in its place? You would say, "My life is ending! I am decaying away!" The grain of wheat, however, has more faith than us. When a grain of wheat is buried in the soil it begins to decay but immediately understands the language of the sun. When the first sunrays appear, the grain of wheat says to itself, "I will not die. I will resurrect and bear fruit for others," and energy is born inside it and it begins to sprout, aiming towards the sun.

It later fertilises and ripens. People do not leave the grain of wheat alone, though; they take sickles and cut it. Its suffering does not end there either. The wheat is harvested: it is bundled-up into sheaves, gathered up with pitchforks, thrown onto a wagon and transported to the threshing floor. And still its ordeal is not over. The sheaves are untied and the stalks spread out over the threshing floor. Horses tread upon the stalks and drag threshing boards over them. What would you think if you were in the wheat's place? Well, human life also passes through the same process. You will ask, "Why must I pass through it?" And I will answer that you need to learn from the grain of wheat's example.

After the threshing boards and the horses' hooves have passed over the grain of wheat, it is taken to the granary. And still its suffering continues. The grain is sifted, bagged and transported to the mill, where it

---

[3] Jesus said, "I am come down from heaven, not to do mine own will, but the will of him that sent me. I am the bread of life. I am the living bread which came down out of heaven: if any man eat of this bread, he shall live for ever: yea and the bread which I will give is my flesh, for the life of the world" (John 6:38, 48, 51).

[4] Jesus said, "The seed is the word of God" (Luke 8:11).

is ground between two millstones until it is totally crushed up. If you were in its place, you would lament, "What kind of life and world has the Lord created!" The grain of wheat, however, has great patience. It says, "See more of my history." The grain is taken from the mill as flour and ends up in people's homes, but still it is not left in peace. The flour is sieved to extract any impurities. The pure flour is then mixed with water and yeast and is kneaded into dough. If you were in the grain of wheat's place, you would say, "Surely my suffering is over!" No, it is not.

When the dough has risen it is put in the oven, and once it is baked we behold beautiful loaves of bread. If you were in the bread's place, you would say, "Finally, my suffering is at an end!" But after a short time the beautiful loaves are broken up and eaten. The grain of wheat enters the stomach, and juices are formed there which enter the mind. What happens then? Great thoughts are formed in our brains and new desires in our hearts. The grain of wheat carries the garments which clothe our feelings – it flows through the pens of writers and poets and the bows of violinists.

So, you see what the grain of wheat gives us. And if the grain of wheat were not to pass through its process of development, we would never see the beautiful things in nature. Why not? Because the grain of wheat gives us the power to see and perceive them. This is why Christ said, "I am a living bread." To be truly alive, a human being has to be in communion with his or her environment, which means to be helpful to others and to receive help from them. Just as a grain of wheat passes through the process of sacrifice, so should we. It is not so difficult to make a sacrifice.[5]

Let us now turn to the history of Christ's life, to the history of the Jews. How do you explain the following contradiction? A nation waits a

[5] The Teacher also said, "We love someone very much because he or she gives something to us. We love Christ because he feeds us and because he sacrificed himself for us, like the grain of wheat that we eat. This is why he said, 'Whoever eats my flesh and drinks my blood has eternal life.' People are unhappy because they seek love, but to have love is to be ready for self-sacrifice. If you want to be loved, you need to be prepared for self-sacrifice. To love means to make sacrifices, which means to 'sow'. We have to sow love to harvest love. Our lives are only valuable when they are valuable to our neighbours. Life is a force that God has given us. As God gives us life, He can also take it away. Life requires people to be healthy, to have deep peace and to self-sacrifice for the Lord. Christ has shown us the path of life. First comes self-sacrifice, which means to be ready to sacrifice your mind, your heart and your belongings for your neighbour" (6/19 April 1914).

thousand years for its Saviour, its King who will come to set it free,[6] but when he appears the high priests and princes oppose him.[7] You might say that if Christ came now, you would behave better than they did. I doubt it, though, and I will give you an example why. Look at how men behave with their wives and how women behave with their husbands, then you will know how you would treat Christ.... When the truth appears in the world it does not wear the best clothes but dresses in the most modest way. That is why Christ appeared in such a simple form among the Jews, and it is the reason why people could not understand the truth. Such are the laws of this world.[8]

But there is another law in the world, which is manifested by sunlight. When the sun begins to shine on all sprouting seeds and the creatures of the earth, its light produces joy and gladness in some people but hatred and malice in others. The light which produces a good mood in some, makes others violent. The light and warmth make a wolf think about where it can find a sheep to eat. When receiving the light and warmth, a criminal begins to think about how to steal money from you. When receiving the light and warmth, a good person thinks about where to find someone who is poor and in need of help.

Give the grain of wheat to a chicken and it will grow beautiful feathers; give it to a pig and it will grow beautiful bristles; give it to a wolf and it will grow beautiful teeth and nails; give it to a fish and it will grow beautiful scales. Each creature adapts the food, warmth and light according to its development and understanding. You will be able to

---

[6] There are references to a coming Messiah in the Old Testament: "And beginning from Moses and from all the prophets, Jesus interpreted to them in all the scriptures the things concerning himself" (Luke 24:27).

[7] "The chief priests and the Pharisees gathered a council, and said, 'What do we? for this man doeth many signs. If we let him thus alone, all men will believe on him: and the Romans will come and take away both our place and our nation.' But a certain one of them, Caiaphas, being high priest that year, said unto them, 'Ye know nothing at all, nor do ye take account that it is expedient for you that one man should die for the people, and that the whole nation perish not.' So from that day forth they took counsel that they might put him to death" (John 11:47-50, 53). "And the chief priests and our rulers delivered him up to be condemned to death, and crucified him" (Luke 24:20).

[8] "Who hath believed our report? and to whom hath the arm of the Lord been revealed? For he grew up before him as a tender plant, and as a root out of a dry ground: he hath no form or comeliness; and when we see him, there is no beauty that we should desire him" (Isaiah 53:1-2). Jesus said, "The foxes have holes, and the birds of the heaven have nests; but the Son of man hath not where to lay his head" (Matthew 8:20).

comprehend this law only when you have experienced the two opposing worlds. The reason why evil exists in people is inexplicable – why they prefer hatred instead of love, and lies instead of the truth. It cannot be explained. Many questions beginning with 'why' will be left unexplained. The Bulgarian word 'why' is a questioning word, but it tends to imply, "I want …!" Why do people have such desire? Because there is a law stating that we must strive to advance ourselves.

Christ said that if the grain of wheat that falls to the ground does not die, it will remain alone in this world. What is loneliness in life? It is the greatest suffering a person can experience. The meaning of life is to multiply oneself. All the suffering in the world is due to people wanting to live for their individual selves. Every evil is born from the desire to live only for oneself and to become the centre of the world. To live like that is impossible according to divine laws. Our thoughts and desires fail because we build them on sand.[9] We can only be happy in the world when we live for the Lord. We need to live for Him.

The example of how we ought to live can be found in nature. When the sun rises in the morning it rises for all, because it loves all.[10] The sun attends to all creatures, from the lowest to the highest, which is why they turn their eyes to the sunrise. The energy from the sun resurrects and uplifts. Does the sun say that we should enter it?[11] No, it only tells us to make use of its blessings.[12] We should radiate light in the same way as the sun, enlightening the people around us.[13] You have some false ideas in your minds that come from your individualistic lives. Imagine that you enter a house where there are twenty or thirty people but there is only one window. You tell them, "You have no right to the view outside! I want it for myself alone!" And while you stand

---

[9] Jesus said, "Every one that heareth these words of mine, and doeth them not, shall be likened unto a foolish man, which built his house upon the sand" (Matthew 7:26).

[10] Jesus said, "Your Father which is in heaven maketh his sun to rise on the evil and the good, and sendeth rain on the just and the unjust" (Matthew 5:45).

[11] "God is the blessed and only Potentate, the King of kings, and Lord of lords; who only hath immortality, dwelling in light unapproachable; whom no man hath seen, nor can see" (1 Timothy 6:15-16). "For man shall not see the Lord and live" (Exodus 33:20).

[12] "Every good gift and every perfect boon is from above, coming down from the Father of lights" (James 1:17).

[13] Jesus said, "Ye are the light of the world. Let your light shine before men, that they may see your good works, and glorify your Father which is in heaven" (Matthew 5:14, 16).

at the window looking out at the sun, everybody else is deprived of its light. Instead, you ought to show them the way out of the house so that they too can see the light.

Do not think the Lord has prepared only small things for you; He has prepared greater things for you. Ask a frog what its conceptions of life are. It will say, "For the benefit of my life, I want more flies to fly near me so that I can catch them." That is the frog's philosophy of life. When we ascend the staircase of progress, we should not think that we human beings are at the summit of our development. There is still much further to climb on this staircase, from where we are now to the path to which we aspire. The distance between human beings and the angels is enormous, almost the same distance as that which exists between tadpoles and human beings. From the angels' point of view, we are still tadpoles.[14] Some people say, "Is it not true that human beings are made in the image and likeness of God?"[15] Yes, we were, but we have yet to regain that image and likeness – you can see how we conduct our lives.... For us to be able to say, "We are made according to the image and likeness of God," we have to have the features of God. But what are His features? They are virtue, love, wisdom and truth. Virtue excludes evil. Love excludes hatred. Wisdom excludes mindlessness. Truth excludes lies. If these things are excluded from you, you have the likeness of God; if they are not excluded from you, you are still a tadpole.

We need to be purified so that we can understand the words of Christ. Our eyes and minds need to be purified. The mind is a perfect weapon when we know how to use it,[16] but it is a very dangerous weapon when we cannot handle it properly. You are within your rights to plough a field for seeding, for then you are following natural law, but when you plough a field which is already sown, you are being foolish. Some people say, "We must think and criticise," because they believe there cannot be progress without criticism. But how should you criticise? Criticism that acts like surgery cutting out unhealthy tissue from the human body, that I understand; it is useful. But to cut out healthy tissue, that I do not

[14] Jesus said, "Among them that are born of women there hath not arisen a greater than John the Baptist: yet he that is but little in the kingdom of heaven is greater than he" (Matthew 11:11).

[15] See Genesis 1:26-27

[16] "The sword of the Spirit is the word of God" (Ephesians 6:17).

understand. It is not difficult for a person to be that type of surgeon. Anyone can remove someone's leg with a saw, but few people know how to perform skilful surgical operations. For you to learn this, the laws of virtue and love have to take possession of you. When I speak of love, do not think I am preaching a teaching of peacefulness and calmness – a person who wants to have love has to experience the greatest suffering in the world. The person who has not suffered cannot experience the divine principle of love. To love God we have to be ready to make sacrifices, just as God makes sacrifices for us.[17] In your attempts to know God, you say, "Lord, give me what I want. Give me! Give me! Give me!" And this demand sounds all over the world.

It is not material wealth that we need but the fundamental things which make for a good life.[18] We abandoned the development of our hearts, and now we need to return to a fundamental principle: the development and ennoblement of our hearts. Evil does not nest in the mind but in the heart.[19] Every one of us ought to ask his or her heart what it wants. We are guilty of corrupting our hearts. We have made our hearts lie and think evil thoughts or other wrong things many times. The Lord said in the Scriptures, "My son, give me your heart."[20] God knows and sees people's mistakes,[21] and He wants nothing more from us than for us to open our hearts and allow Him to enter. You will ask, "How do we do that?" You do it in the same way that you open a window so light can enter your home. It is said, "The doctor does not visit sunlit rooms." Sickness does not reign there. To put it another way, "The doctor never leaves a room that is never sunlit." Similarly, the devil does not enter a human heart that the Lord has already entered.[22]

A camel travels through the desert, carrying its heavy burden with

---

[17] "Herein was the love of God manifested in us, that God hath sent his only begotten Son into the world, that we might live through him. Herein is love, not that we loved God, but that he loved us, and sent his Son to be the propitiation for our sins" (1 John 4:9-10).

[18] Jesus said, "A man's life consisteth not in the abundance of the things which he possesseth" (Luke 12:15)

[19] Jesus said, "Out of the heart come forth evil thoughts" (Matthew 15:19).

[20] See Proverbs 23:26

[21] "The eyes of the Lord are in every place, Keeping watch upon the evil and the good" (Proverbs 15:3).

[22] "We know that whosoever is begotten of God sinneth not; but he that was begotten of God keepeth him, and the evil one toucheth him not" (1 John 5:18).

great difficulty. Its owner finds a fox skin on the road and adds it to the camel's load, but the animal's spinal cord breaks and its carcass and the entire load is left there in the desert. A camel's back can only carry a certain amount of weight. And we often treat ourselves like that camel. We are travelling on our lives' journeys, and if we put more on our backs than we can carry, we will impede our development. I am not recommending poverty, though. I recommend three types of wealth: physical, mental and spiritual wealth. Heaven wants people who are rich in these ways because they can be generous.[23] When Christ said, "Collect treasures,"[24] he meant such kind of treasures. Deposit this capital of yours in heaven so that God will use the interest to feed the poor people on earth. It is not the angels who will attain our salvation for us; we ourselves have to attain it, and we have all the conditions that we need to do so. The law is not that we be equally educated; everyone needs to know only what is necessary for him or her. Someone says, "I have a small brain." I reply, "If you cannot look after a small pony, how will you look after a large horse? If you have a small heart yet you cannot manage it properly, how will you rule a much larger heart with its greater desires?"

What should we do? We ought not to think about the future, but instead we should use all the blessings given by this day for the sake of goodness, for what we do today will bring us all future blessings. God, who has provided the conditions for today, will also provide the conditions for the days to come – such is the law. There is no sense in thinking about what will happen to us; we need to be calm about the future.[25] There are some laws that regulate the relationships between

[23] The Teacher also said, "The existence of everything in our lives comes from Christ, which is why we love him. He left us this wealth not so that we love him, but for us to make use of it without keeping it only for ourselves. This is the wealth for which Christ sacrificed himself. If we do not use this wealth, Christ will take it back from us. He gave us this wealth for us to use it to develop spiritually so that he can prepare us for the angelic life" (13/26 April 1914).

[24] Jesus said, "Lay not up for yourselves treasures upon the earth, where moth and rust doth consume, and where thieves break through and steal: but lay up for yourselves treasures in heaven, where neither moth nor rust doth consume, and where thieves do not break through nor steal: for where thy treasure is, there will thy heart be also" (Matthew 6:19-21).

[25] "Ye know not what shall be on the morrow" (James 4:14). Jesus said, "Your Father knoweth what things ye have need of, before ye ask him. Seek ye first his kingdom, and

people. If somebody does something mischievous, it is not an arbitrary occurrence; it happened according to the law itself. Misfortune and unhappiness will bring you blessings, however. Each difficulty will reveal a new horizon to you. You may verify this at any time, which is why you should not worry about what misfortunes and unhappiness might happen to you.

We do not even begin to think wisely about the laws that regulate life. Instead, we think about who is guilty of social wrongs, but we will not find the guilty people. The guilt belongs to the individual lives of people as a whole. When a person wants to become king over others, he or she is guilty, and anyone who wants to dethrone this regent is also guilty. It does not matter who is the king, one person or another, or a third or a fourth, for they all walk on one and the same path. I am not saying a person should not desire to become a king or a queen. The question is, whom should you rule over? Become the ruler of your mind, your heart and your will. How are your citizens? They are your thoughts, your feelings and your desires. Have you brought them under your authority? Have you set up order in yourself?[26] First become an example for the world. What kind of preacher would I be if I turned to people and said, "Be generous!" when I am a miser, "Do not steal!" when I am a thief, and "Do not lie!" when I am a liar? Each teacher ought to be a model, an example for others. Jesus, when he descended to teach people on earth, gave them a model. If we had assimilated his teaching, the world would have immediately changed. A dynamic power is hidden within us, but we are unable to use it because we do not yet know how to work properly.

A thorn bush grew in the road, blocking the way. Passers by would hit it with sticks, but no matter how much they hit it, the thorn bush grew larger and larger until it upended the wagons trying to get past it. Nobody knew what to do, until a man arrived with a pick and declared, "I will demonstrate my skill." He then took the pick and began digging into the ground a little distance from the bush, gradually undermining its roots. At first the thorn bush laughed and said to itself, "So many

his righteousness; and the things ye need shall be added unto you. Be not therefore anxious for the morrow: for the morrow will be anxious for itself. Sufficient unto the day is the evil thereof" (Matthew 6:8, 33-34).

[26] "He that ruleth his spirit is better than he that taketh a city" (Proverbs 16:32).

people have failed to harm me, so why should he frighten me?" But the man dug deeper and deeper, until the thorn bush said to itself, "He has found my weak spot!" Unless you put a pick to work in yourself, the inner thorn bush will laugh and say, "I will continue to grow!" You need to understand this allegory. What is the pick? Think about it and find it.

We always need to be wise judges in life. Let me explain with an example. During the American Civil War two criminals were brought before a judge. One of them was blind and the other had no legs. Their crime was stealing apples. The gardener had caught them with the apples and took them to the judge. In his defence, the blind man said, "I am blind. How could I have stolen apples from the tree? I only picked some up from the ground." The man who had no legs said, "I have no legs. I cannot walk anywhere to steal anything." The judge thought it over before saying, "Put the man without legs on the back of the blind man." He then made his ruling: "The one who has eyes but no legs found the apples and picked them from the tree while the blind man carried him." And he was right, because that was how they took them.

The same crooked partnership exists inside human beings. Everyone has two inner beings, one blind and the other without legs. When the Lord takes them to the crime scene, one says, "I did not pick the apples. How could I have found them?" and the other says, "I could not have walked here without legs." But the Lord answers, "Put one on top of the other," and judges them thus. Who is the one without eyes? It is the human instinct. Who is the one without legs? It is the human mind. They say to each other, "Let us steal something together," and the mind climbs onto the back of the instinct and they go off to steal apples. And when the gardener captures them, they ask him, "Why are you beating us?" but they are both guilty.

We need to evolve, for there are greater blessings awaiting us, but we need to become clever enough and good enough to mature and be trustworthy of such an inheritance. Three of the things I mentioned earlier – virtue, righteousness and wisdom – are great riches, and you will be healthy and happy when you have them. But you will say, "How can we apply this teaching in the world?" We are not required to rearrange the world; it is already well arranged. There is no abnormality in the world; everything proceeds according to a determined order. We know why natural and political events occur. We do not need to turn this current around, but one thing is necessary in the world: the individual personality needs to be put right, no matter whether you are a man or a woman. Once parents put themselves right, their children will also right themselves. And when the children have put themselves right, their neighbours will right themselves too. It is in this way, person by person, that the whole world will be set right. The quality of the dough depends on the quality of the yeast. This is the principle that Christ set, and he acts for its realisation.[27]

The world will start to transform itself for the good in the same way as a pupa starts to transform itself.[28] This transformation must occur in our hearts, minds and wills. When we have completed our own transformations we will feel a certain inner power, and then we will come into contact with the higher, advanced beings whom we call saints. When we make this connection our minds will be enlightened, just as pupils are enlightened by their teachers. The saints are the teachers of humanity, and they should guide us all. They teach the world how it ought to live. But you will say, "Where are these teachers? Where do I find them? We only see their images in the church...." Everything has its shadow, and by following the shadow we can find the object that

[27] Jesus said, "The kingdom of heaven is like unto leaven, which a woman took, and hid in three measures of meal, till it was all leavened" (Matthew 13:33). And the Teacher said, "It is impossible for everyone to become spiritual; only those who are ready may do so. The world will be saved by only one person who has turned to God, because he or she will have a leavening effect. It is not the quantity of people that is important but the quality" (6/19 January 1915).

[28] The Teacher also said, "We ask, 'Why does the Lord keep us in this suffering?' He does so so that we learn what He can do for us. What does a caterpillar say? 'My world is the leaf, my food. Only give me leaves. I do not care about flowers!' Our lives are like the life of this caterpillar. People say, 'Material things. Material things. Talk to us about material things. We do not care whether there is life after death, whether another world exists or not. We do not care!' After the eating and eating of leaves, the caterpillar enters a condition in which to form a cocoon. And when it has been transformed into a butterfly, it says, 'Flowers. I only need flowers!' When we are like caterpillars we are attached to the physical world, but when we have been transformed like butterflies we will have an idea of the spiritual world. When we have no idea about the spiritual world, it is a foreign place for us. Imagine that a top-class violinist visits your town. He may play very beautifully, but if you are deaf or if you have not developed your appreciation of music, you will be unable to benefit from his performance.

"When we accept Christ's teaching we will love a very high culture and the earth will become a garden managed by the most intelligent people. This is why we are required to form cocoons and transform ourselves" (10/23 January 1915).

casts it. Your desires in the world are shadows, and so are your aspirations. If you want to understand the essence of life, you have to follow this spiritual law: first direct your attention to your heart, then link it to your mind and think about God. What idea do we need to have about God? We may imagine Him as the most good and perfect person, in whom there is no malice or hatred and who loves us as a father loves his children. That is how God relates to us.[29]

What do you think? Is God listening to us right now or not? He listens to our minds and works inside them. Our daily moods are due to Him. Just as the sun improves our mood as it rises, so the happy moments of life are due to this Inner Sun that shines inside us. In the spiritual life there is rising and setting. In your mature years this sun is powerful, for you are between noon and mid-afternoon. In old age you are setting, as at sunset, so that you can rise again tomorrow. The Lord will rise in the hearts and minds of many people, but He will also not rise in many others. Those in whom the Lord rises will feel joy and gladness. Those in whom the Lord does not rise will say, "My life is unfortunate and unhappy and sorrowful and full of suffering." These people will have to wait. Why? Because they are not yet in a condition for the Lord to rise within them. If the Lord rose in them prematurely, it would be disasterous for them. For the moment it is better for them to rest. I do not say they will die; I only quote the law as it is. Someone says, "I love you." But in what way do you love? You love as the cat loves the mouse and the wolf loves the sheep. That is love, but it is a love which causes suffering in the world. The world needs the following kind of love: for us to love others and to help them to be as happy as we are. That is why Jesus said, "Those who believe in me will do as I do, and whoever loves me will be loved by my Father, and my Father will come and make a home inside him or her."[30]

The devil is to blame for all suffering,[31] but you should not be angry with him. I approve of the devil for one thing only: he is very hard-

---

[29] Jesus said, "Your heavenly Father is perfect" (Matthew 5:48).

[30] See John 8:31; 14:21, 23

[31] "God himself tempteth no man" (James 1:13). "He that doeth sin is of the devil; for the devil sinneth from the beginning" (1 John 3:8). Jesus said, "The devil was a murderer from the beginning, and stood not in the truth, because there is no truth in him. When he speaketh a lie, he speaketh of his own: for he is a liar, and the father thereof" (John 8:44).

working and never discouraged. If you throw him out of one doorway, he re-enters through another. If he fails in one way, he seeks another, then a third and a fourth. This is a perfect and encouraging feature of his. The Lord says to us, "Take an example from the devil. He teaches people, and he will educate everybody." After the devil has lied and lied and lied to you, you will finally say, "I have learnt about your lies. You cannot fool me anymore." And the next time the devil comes to you, you will say, "My eyes are now open to your tricks!"

When you start to suffer, say, "I have not yet completed the cycle of the grain of wheat." When your thoughts and hearts have transformed and become excellent, you will attain the image and likeness of God. Then God will resurrect you, just as the sun brings the sown grain of wheat back to life.

The Spirit Manifests Itself to Every Soul

The Apostle Paul wrote,

> **To each man is given the manifestation of the Spirit to profit withal.** [1]

There are many questions which currently occupy the human mind that also occupied humanity in the past. We will have such questions in the future as well. Today I will give you a brief definition of the meaning of 'the Spirit'. Many minds have a vague understanding of the Spirit. Even knowledgeable people have only a vague idea about it. You will ask, "How is it possible for a well-educated person to have a vague understanding of the Spirit?" And I will answer, "Most naturally." If you were deprived of your sight and a picture was put in front of you, you would have only vague ideas about it. Similarly, a well-educated person can have a vague understanding of the Spirit. When considering this question, keep in mind whether we have the necessary feelings and abilities to connect with the true reality of things. For we may directly or indirectly understand the order of the world, but our understanding will be different in each case. [2]

We may understand the Spirit in the way it manifests its essence. Our direct experience of the sun is through sunlight, but the true nature of the sun is much more profound. The light is a spirit that descends from the sun and directly contacts our lives. Were the Sun itself to come to the Earth it would melt everything. For the same reason, God does not want to come down to us but instead sends His Spirit, which is light. [3] God says, "I will not come down Myself, but will deliver My blessings

---

[1] 1 Corinthians 12:7. It is evident in the text that the Teacher actually read the whole chapter.

[2] "The natural man receiveth not the things of the Spirit of God: for they are foolishness unto him; and he cannot know them, because they are spiritually judged" (1 Corinthians 2:14).

[3] "Invisible God" (Colossians 1:15). "Thou covereth thyself with light as with a garment" (Psalm 104:2). "Dwelling in light unapproachable; whom no man hath seen, nor can see" (1 Timothy 6:16). "God is light" (1 John 1:5).

to people through My Spirit."[4] This Spirit, this creative power, is what builds everything that we have within us. This wise power, which is manifested by God, is the source of all the natural laws. No matter what names scientists give these laws, there is always a single, spiritually wise essence that is operating, a Spirit who creates laws.

The Spirit directly communes with our souls. We have an idea about its origin through the changes occurring in the realms of our souls. We could have no understanding of the Spirit without the soul. The divine world is presented to us from within, by the way in which the soul thinks. If there is anything divine within us, it is our luminous, thinking souls. This is why when we speak of a human being, we should mean his or her soul. A person who is separated from his or her spiritually wise soul becomes indistinct from a four-legged animal: living to eat and sleep and having all of an animal's needs and weaknesses. The Spirit manifests itself in the human soul, which is why human beings are distinct from other creatures. Human beings walk upright. Why do animals not walk upright? Because they live in contradiction to the Lord. Their walking on four legs shows that their wills are discordant with the manifestation of God. Perhaps many thousands of years will pass before animals are uplifted to the human stage of development; in other words, before they can walk upright. We have uplifted ourselves to some extent, and we aspire to rise further because we want to be near to God and in accord with Him. We desire to walk the divine path. If we make mistakes, they are not due to a wickedness of will but to other causes lying in our pasts.

Some people are idealistic, but what are their ideas of the ideal life? I understand the ideal life as having harmony and accord in all one's relationships. Some people want to live in heaven. But where is heaven? I understand the word 'heaven' to mean a state of order in which people respect their rights and their duties.[5] A man wants to advance himself,

---

[4] "The Spirit searcheth all things, yea, the deep things of God. For who among men knoweth the things of a man, save the spirit of the man, which is in him? even so the things of God none knoweth, save the Spirit of God. But we received, not the spirit of the world, but the spirit which is of God; that we might know the things that are freely given to us by God" (1 Corinthians 2:10-12). "Every good gift and every perfect boon is from above, coming down from the Father of lights" (James 1:17).

[5] The Teacher also said, "We are bound with thousands of obligations in life: first to our parents; then to our brothers and sisters; then, after we have married, to our spouses and

but you hinder him and slow down his progress by forcing him to respect your rights, when instead you should have consciously realised that you have an obligation to him. The chapter of the Gospel that I read at the beginning shows how relationships should be.

Here is an analogy to help you understand how misconceptions are formed. I give a woman a fresh walnut and tell her to study it. Examining it by taste, she bites into its green covering and then throws it away. Next I give a walnut to a more intelligent woman. She peels off the green covering, bites into the hard shell that was beneath it and breaks a tooth, then throws the walnut away. I give a walnut to a third woman, who is wiser than the other two. She removes the green outer cover, breaks the hard inner shell with a rock and eats the walnut. I call the three women together and ask them, "What is a walnut?" The first one answers, "It is an astringent fruit, spicy and poisonous." The second one says, "The fruit is hard and will break your teeth." The third woman describes it as "delicious". This analogy can be adapted to help us understand our own mistakes.

Everything in the world is covered in layers, and if we have insufficient knowledge we will not discover the essence of things. Food is necessary for the body, but the mind and the soul also need their foods. When I say that it is not good to overeat, I mean that the body, the mind and the soul need to be equally nourished: a human being is formed of a threefold circle.[6] The three women who examined the walnut were not clever enough. The one who ate the actual walnut thinks herself to be the most intelligent of people when in fact she is not. I now give a walnut to a fourth woman, who, instead of eating it, plants it, and after ten or fifteen years this single walnut produces thousands of walnuts.[7]

children; then to society; and so on. It is an art to know how to meet each of these obligations. Freedom has rights and duties. A society that only has rights, or which only has duties, cannot survive; it is necessary for these two processes to go together" (13/26 April 1914).

[6] The Teacher also said, "The human being is a tripartite being, simultaneously living in the physical, astral and spiritual worlds" (5/18 January 1915). "Contemporary science has studied the human body in detail, but this is the external side of a human being. A human being is like a walnut with three shells, three coverings. The innermost part of the nut is the soul, which is the real human being. Thinking, feeling and action are the real the human being, the soul" (15/28 January 1915).

[7] The Teacher also said, "From a religious point of view there needs to be layers. Some people are nuts, some people are the shells covering the nuts, and other people are the shells' outer coverings. Both theory and experience are necessary. One person believes in

There are, therefore, four categories of people in the world. One says, "The world is perverted, immoral and undeserving of life." The next says, "Egotism reigns in the world. It could not be worse." The third one describes the world as "nice and pleasant", and this is near the truth. But what is the fourth type of person? He or she is someone who has entered the divine school and begun to study, learning to plant beautiful things.[8] The earth is best understood as a divine school in which human beings have been placed to study, to learn how to remove the outer covering and the inner shell and then plant the nut instead of eating it. When a person has learnt the properties of all things, he or she will understand the real meaning of earthly life.

When a master sends his servants out to work in the vineyard, he gives them bread and the tools they need to complete their task. Likewise, God has given human beings brains as the tools for their work. Why have we been given brains? Is it to taste a walnut's bitter outer covering? No. We have been given brains to learn how to plant walnuts. Someone says, "Would I be better off if I planted walnuts? Surely not." Here we should understand the word 'walnut' to mean the good thoughts, the good desires and the good actions which we can plant within others. You will prosper by such work.[9]

When you encounter difficulties in the realisation of a desire, do not despair and give up. God clothes a thought in three or four layers. One of them might not be favourable for you but another will be. If you remove the unfavourable layer and plant your thought in good soil, it will definitely produce good fruit. That is how I see the world. Evil seems really to exist, and it does exist, but only at the outer layer of things. People can also seem bad, and indeed they can be bad, but they are not bad in their essences, because nothing bad can come out

himself or herself, another believes in society, but only the highly spiritual person goes deeply into the cause of things, and only he or she profoundly believes in God. God is a necessity for humanity. Contemporary people have no idea about God. They do not understand His philosophical side. When people reach the truth they will achieve balance" (6/19 January 1915).

[8] Jesus said, "Every plant which my heavenly Father planted not, shall be rooted up" (Matthew 15:13).

[9] The Teacher also said, "Each thought, feeling and deed that we understand is a great blessing for us. Whoever values understanding becomes a great human being" (16 July 1939).

of God.[10] Bad things originate from certain relationships and attitudes that we have in the world. For example, two families live together in a four-room house. One family has more children than the other, and they argue over which family should have more rooms. Each family speaks ill of the members of the other one, considering them unreasonable people. Actually, they are all unreasonable, because reasonable people never argue.

The Bulgarian word for 'quarrel' originated from the root of the Sanskrit word for 'darkness'. People who live in spiritual light never argue. There is a certain manifestation in the brain which darkens our thoughts and is followed by bad desires. When we have light thoughts we are ready to live in peace and accord, but when a little darkness appears we are ready to change our relationships with others. Therefore, evil originates from the darkness of the human mind.

The Lord knows that darkness exists on earth and causes harm – darkness always causes harm. Were we to live in permanent darkness, all of our feelings, our eyes and our ears, and so on, would atrophy. The Lord sends the Spirit to work on us, on our thoughts, feelings and bodies, so that we come to think in the correct way about things and form a true understanding of them. First of all we should each form a correct self-understanding. In other words, we should understand what our correct personal relationships with God should be. According to my understanding, the earth is a school only for the individual human soul. If anything at all is real in the world, it is the human soul.

If you want divine love to be manifested, the Spirit has to be within you and you have to give it the internal space to manifest itself. The Spirit is a very delicate being; do not think that it will come and knock hard on your door. No, it will knock very gently on the door of your heart, and if you open the door it will change your life dramatically – it will show you how to live. If the Spirit knocks on the door of your will, it has come to tell you what you consciously should do. If you do not open the door, you will soon learn what you have lost.... When you meet an idiotic person, you need to realise that sometime in the past when the Spirit knocked, he did not open the door. You call someone else a fool. Why? Because when the Spirit knocked on the door of her

---

[10] Jesus said, "Your heavenly Father is perfect" (Matthew 5:48).

mind in the past, she turned it away. A cruel person is also someone who did not accept the Spirit when it knocked on the door of his or her heart. So, we should always be ready to give the Spirit the space to penetrate us and manifest itself within us.[11]

Some people say, "I want to see the Spirit." But the only thing you see is the Spirit! It talks, but, as your ears are insensitive, you do not hear it – just like when you try to speak to a deaf person. You want to hear. Good. So adjust your ears so that they hear what the Spirit is saying. "I want to see the Spirit." That is good, but if your vision is blurred, how will you see it? I repeat, the only thing that we see in the world is Spirit. The flower I am now holding is Spirit, and if you were able to see properly, you would see the whole human figure in it. Why do you not see it thus? Because your sight is limited. You see only the dense parts of the flower and not its finer form.

Let me explain. Something appears spherical to you, like a walnut on a tree, but if you plant the nut, will the stem grow spherically too? No. Actually, it will immediately manifest its essence. If you want to know things, you need to plant them in their true soil. If you could plant this flower I have here in that way, you would immediately see that it is a spiritually wise being. What is the flower saying to you? Why does it have this colour? It has been given this colour to show that life without love is meaningless. For thousands of years this flower has told people what they ought to do: that they should love, that their minds should be neither very sharp nor very dull.

In some instances the mind should be sharp, but it is not necessary when you are among intelligent people. When you are among your enemies your hearts should be strong, but they should be soft when you are among friends. You need to know how to love. When you smell a rose, two things are manifested: one, its gentle, kind fragrance; two, its thorns. Everyone has his or her thorns, but they are not the true person. Thorns are needed for those conditions of life in which you have to fight to defend yourselves, when you must not be soft. It is not good to make friendly appointments with devils. You need to have thorns to keep them away from you.

[11] Jesus said, "Behold, I stand at the door and knock: if any man hear my voice and open the door, I will come in to him, and will sup with him, and he with me" (Revelation 3:20).

You have friends and you say that you know them, but until you learn about both their dark and light sides you do not know them well. You always want to be good, but you ought to be gentle in certain situations and hard in others. When a friend of yours is angry, you need to know how to protect yourself. To know how to protect yourself, you need to know how to fight. If you fight an enemy, you are doing your duty, but if you fight with peaceful or defenceless people, you are doing something foolish. Fighting has to exist, but only against the parts of nature which need to be subordinated. When rock has to be exploded in a mountain to make a tunnel, I understand it as a good act. But to use such methods among people in an organised society, that I do not understand. A person who does such a thing does not understand his or her relationship with the Spirit and does not understand its guidance. [12]

In the chapter I read, the Apostle Paul described how the relationship between the individual and the Spirit should be. You may ask, "But are there not thousands of relationships in the world?" Yes, there are, but we should select only the ones which are favourable to us. For example, we need to know the nature of our relationship with water. When we put water in our stomachs the results are positive, but it would be completely different were we to put water in our lungs.... When we put air in our lungs the results are favourable to us, but they would not be so were we to put it in our stomachs. And so on.

Different things have different relationships with particular organs. You will say, "But I know all this. Eyes need light, ears need sound, and so on." Good, but do you understand the inner meaning of that light? When the sun rises in the morning, what do you do? You say to yourself, "The sun is rising." But when someone says, "The teacher is coming," what do the pupils do? They take out their books and sit at their desks. At sunrise we ought to take out our books and say, "The Teacher Spirit is coming." Then we should sit at our desks and ask, "What should I do today?" The sun will speak to us, saying, "I will listen when you talk to me. I will teach you, and you can make a report back on what you have learnt." This is the meaning of sunrise. When we are able to learn the programme that the Spirit has prepared for each of us each

---

[12] The Teacher also said, "Our ideal should be to love God, who has given us life. God participates in our thoughts and deeds and advises us not to make mistakes so that we do not create suffering for ourselves" (15/28 January 1915).

day, our lives will unfold favourably. You will say, "But today's sun looks just as it did yesterday. It has risen in exactly the same way." No. Never in my life have I seen two similar days or two similar sunrises. Each day is different from all others, each day has its own programme, and one day's light is different from that of the previous day. Therein lies the greatness of the Divine Spirit, who brings innumerable riches and invisible worlds to us and reveals to us from within what God is – God is something great.

Say that you have a physically unattractive friend who eats and drinks too much. Those things are unimportant. One day you start to love him, and all of his inner and outer weaknesses disappear for you and you begin to see something else in him. This means you have removed the outer covering of the walnut and you see his mind. If you plant this walnut, half of the tree's fruit will be for you and half will be for him. But if you eat the walnut, how will you benefit from it? You will not, and neither will your friend. Therefore, when the Spirit comes, it will say that you should sow better thoughts and desires.

Sometimes when you meet a friend, you do not know what to talk about. People can also talk a lot without saying anything important. You should first plant a walnut, and afterwards you may talk as much as you want. Do not speak before you have planted a walnut. First thing each morning, you ought to ask yourself a question: "What fruit should I plant today?" If you plant a walnut, it will produce its riches and abundance after a certain amount of time. You will only understand this parable after you have returned to the other world from which you came. There you will learn of the beneficial results of the good thoughts and desires you planted here and the good things you did for your neighbours, your friends, your spouse and your children. As this is unclear to you, I will give you another example. Raise your children well and do not expect them to do anything for you in return. If you have planted a good walnut inside them, not only will they look after you in your old age, they will love you as well. If a mother is not loved by her children, it means she did not bring them up well. A parent's priority ought to be to receive the guidance of the Spirit, for it will show you how to raise your children so that they love you.[13]

---

[13] "Train up a child in the way he should go, And even when he is old he will not depart from it" (Proverbs 22:6).

I will conclude my lecture with a comparison. There are three categories of relationships that we need to attend to and protect – for
God, society and the individual all exist in the world. Some people
put themselves first, saying, "I come first, then comes society and then
comes the Lord." That is a misconception. Others say, "Society comes
first. I live for my nation, for society. I come next and then comes the
Lord." That is also bad prioritising. The third type of person says, "God,
the Lord, and the Spirit inside me come first. Second comes my spiritually wise soul, which should serve God. Society comes third and I
come last." That is the correct order of things; anything else is wrong.
All mistakes originate in people wanting to know whether society or
the individual is at the head. A three-headed body will always be stuck
in disagreements about which way to go. Sometimes you struggle to
come to a decision, which means you are being three-headed. Cut off
two of them and put the Lord as the only head, for everything ought to
be in its proper place.[14]

Now ask yourself, "Who is my head?" If you answer, "The Lord is
my head," I will be pleased. Put the Lord at the head. Do you know what
state you would be in were you to do so? You would have no double-
mindedness, no fear, no trepidation and no uncertainty. Instead, you
would be strong-willed, courageous, resolute, decisive, clever and good
people. You would be rich in all things – whatever you were to take
in your hands would turn into gold. Some people fear money. Only
foolish people have such a fear. Why? Because they are spiritually weak
people. It is up to us what use we make of things.[15] How many times
has the Lord sent you the Spirit only for you to reject it?

What rules are you required to observe? When you return home
from work, take off your backpack, leaving all your relationships,
everything that you have given and received in life, there in the hallway.
Enter your rooms free of outer affairs, and say, "Thank You, Lord, for
everything You have given to me." Eat a good meal and thank the Lord
again. Get up the next morning, take your backpack or briefcase and

[14] "In Christ dwelleth all the fulness of the Godhead bodily, and in him ye are made full,
who is the head of all principality and power. Seek the things that are above, where Christ
is, seated on the right hand of God"(Colossians 2:9-10; 3:1).

[15] Jesus said, "I say unto you, Make to yourselves friends *above* by means of the mammon
of unrighteousness; that, when it shall fail, they may receive you into the eternal tabernac-
les" (Luke 16:9).

go out again to work. But what do people do? They return home in the evening with heavy packs on their backs, and, instead of taking them off, wear them in bed. Then they spend the whole night tossing and turning. And all the while the Spirit says, "Take off your pack. This is not the place for it."

If you sit down to eat feeling heavy-hearted, it is because you still have your pack on your back. Take it off before eating – this is the message of the Spirit. If some people's sinfulness is bothering you, leave that problem outside in the hallway. Do you think the Lord is unaware that people sin? Is it your job to set the world to rights? There is already One who will set it right. When you return to your home in the evening, you ought to thank God for having sent you among sinful people so that they could give you some good lessons. When you meet a sinner, say, "You carry your pack very well." Sinners are people who are carrying backpacks. One day their packs will be removed. Someone is rude or sour. Why? Because he did not remove the baggage from his heart. Someone else cannot think. Let her remove the baggage from her mind, and then she will think properly.

There are two extremes, two opposite poles in life that you should keep in mind. These poles are good and evil. Do not try to reconcile the good and evil inside you; it is not possible.[16] They were both given to you so that you could come to know the profound affairs in the life of the Spirit. Your ailments will be lifted from you when your heart opens and the Spirit comes to you and your soul unites with it.

---

[16] "Ye adulteresses, know ye not that the friendship of the world is enmity with God? Whosoever therefore would be a friend of the world maketh himself an enemy of God. Or think ye that the scripture speaketh in vain? Doth the spirit which he made to dwell in us long unto envying? But he giveth more grace. Wherefore the scripture saith, 'God resisteth the proud, but giveth grace to the humble.' Be subject therefore unto God; but resist the devil, and he will flee from you. Humble yourselves in the sight of the Lord, and he shall exalt you" (James 4:4-7, 10).

Divine Gifts: The Parable of the Talents

In the parable of the talents, Jesus said,

> Unto one *servant their Lord* gave five talents, to another two, to another one; to each according to his several ability. [1]

I will talk to you about this verse in Matthew's Gospel. You have no doubt read the chapter many times and have stopped to consider the parable of the talents more profoundly. Maybe you drew certain conclusions about it, some closer and others further from the truth. I will address this verse in its usual meaning.

When Jesus said a sentence or a parable he had in mind the fundamental divine thought, the divine law. Now, we may put this question forward: why did God give one person five talents, another person two talents, and another person one talent? Was this purely chance or was it a considered decision? In nature nothing that God creates is by chance; chance does not exist. We sometimes describe as 'chance' something which we cannot explain. We meet someone unexpectedly, and later we say to ourselves that it was just chance. One of the laws of life says that every meeting is predetermined, that each meeting has some previous causes. If you are unaware of this law you will think that you meet people without there being a reason, but that is not true.

What should we understand by the five talents, the two talents and the one talent? There are three kinds of people: five-talent people, two-talent people and one-talent people. Who are the single-talent people? They are those who live only for themselves. They say, "I have come to the world to eat three times a day, to drink and to lie down and rest sufficiently to stay healthy. I am also here to be well-dressed." Such people are egotists – fruitless, seedless people with one talent. Who are the two-talent people? They are those men and women, single talents, who have married, becoming two talents, and then gained two

---

[1] Matthew 25:15. The parable of the talents is told in Matthew 25:14-30.

more talents, their children, to become a four-talent partnership. They say, "Lord, we have used the two talents that You gave us. We raised two children and gained two more talents." The second type of two-talent person is someone who lives for his or her home, for society and for the nation. Five-talent people are those who have something more. The five talents correspond to our five senses. Five-talent people are those who have correctly developed their senses of sight, hearing, smell, taste and touch. They think and conclude correctly on everything that God has created; they understand nature, understand things in general and understand cause and effect. They are the spiritual teachers of the world and they live for all humankind.

Let us now make a calculation with these talents: $1 + 2 + 5 = 8$. Does it come to eight by chance? No, eight is the number of work. The Scriptures say that the Lord made the world in six days and rested on the seventh day.[2] Every rest is followed by a new workday.[3] We are now in the eighth day, and the Lord is telling us, "Look, I made the world. Now your workday is beginning. You work, and one day I will come to inspect what you have done." We are living in the eighth day and we make mistakes because we do not know how to work properly. The Lord, however, says, "Work, go forwards. Of course you will make mistakes." On the path of our development we should not ask the impossible. We should constantly expect change and wear and tear. You are frightened of death, but what is death? It is the discarding of our worn-out clothing. It is a law that the body gradually changes.

The Scriptures say, "The Lord made the human being in His image and likeness."[4] Yes, that is the divine plan. The Lord left us here to work, to build our brains and hearts, which means to build our characters and to educate ourselves. When we are fulfilling this divine plan, it is unimportant if there is a little disorder and dirt around us. When

---

[2] See Genesis 1:1–2:3

[3] The Teacher also said, "You need to follow the law of rhythm. After six years of work, the seventh year should be spent in rest. Villagers work a field for six years and then leave it to rest during the seventh year. When you do this, the blessings, the fruitfulness, will be unceasing. This law applies to all professions. The invisible world directs all human work through many laws. In matters of trade you should work according to divine law. If you cannot apply divine law in your trade, at least act according to human law" (21 January/3 February 1915).

[4] See Genesis 1:26-27

a house is being constructed, there are many stones, tiles and sand strewn around the place, as well as much else. After the house is built, everything is cleaned up and the new occupants enter it. We are now in the eighth day and we are building ourselves.

There are three categories of workers: those with a single talent, those with two talents and those with five talents. The person with five talents gained five more, ten in all. Add the four talents from the couple and there are fourteen. Include the single talent that is buried in the earth and the total is fifteen. If we then subtract the original eight given talents, we are left with seven. What does the number 'seven' mean? I said earlier that seven means rest. Now we have the law, the thoughts which Christ hid in his words. Only someone who knows the Scriptures can understand these thoughts. Their meaning is that a person who wants to rest first has to work, and those who have not yet worked should not rest, for the Lord worked for six days and rested on the seventh. We often say, "When will I be able to rest?" But you have not yet started to work – what kind of rest are you looking for? You have just picked up your hoe and put it on your shoulder. And you want a rest! You should only want to rest after you have dug and planted the whole vineyard. When you have done it you will be given the rest you need. We need to understand the fundamental divine law which states that rest follows work.

Only those who have worked are joyful and glad. Christ said, "Those who have worked will enter the joy of the Lord. All the blessings that I have, they will also have."[5] But what did Christ say to the man who had not worked but instead hid his talent in the earth? He said, "Take the single talent from him and give it to someone who has made five. Take him to the outer darkness, where he will learn the necessity of work."[6] What

[5] "His Lord said unto him *that gained other five talents,* 'Well done, good and faithful servant: thou hast been faithful over a few things, I will set thee over many things: enter thou into the joy of thy Lord.' *And he said unto him that gained other two talents,* 'Well done, good and faithful servant; thou hast been faithful over a few things, I will set thee over many things: enter thou into the joy of thy Lord'" (Matthew 25:21, 23).

[6] "His lord said unto him *that hid his talent in the earth,* 'Thou wicked and slothful servant. Take ye away the talent from him, and give it unto him that hath the ten talents. For unto every one that hath shall be given, and he shall have abundance: but from him that hath not, even that which he hath shall be taken away. And cast ye out the unprofitable servant into the outer darkness: there shall be the weeping and gnashing of teeth'" (Matthew 25:26, 28-30).

is this outer darkness? It is down in the earth where the worms work. If you do not learn to work, God will turn you into a worm and put you in the earth, the outer darkness, until you have learnt. All those who spend their time philosophising on the divine law will experience whether these words are true or not.... This morning I am speaking about a fundamental law: we have to work. And it is only true work when we work for God; it is mere labour when we work for ourselves alone.

To work means to attain knowledge. The five-talent person has fully developed the five senses through which the Lord gives us human beings every ability and necessary knowledge. The Lord has also given the person with two talents the abilities corresponding to his or her knowledge. I will make a comparison. The single-talent person is like a mineral that cannot multiply itself; it is always alone. Certain minerals can refract sunlight, but they cannot become spiritually wise beings. Were your hearts to harden like a mineral, you would become one-talent people. There is a danger in this, because the Scriptures say, "I will take away your stony heart."[7] The single talent needs to be transformed so that it begins to give birth and develop itself. The other talents symbolise the grain of wheat and the plant kingdom, which are a little higher placed than the mineral realm, because they have the ability to multiply and gain something. What can beautiful minerals provide for our lives? We would all die were we to rely on them for the necessities of life. Thanks be to the grain of wheat, which carries two talents. Thanks be to those people who love to work. And may there be even greater thanks to the five talents, those abilities we possess for the higher, spiritual life.

This higher, spiritual life shows us how we should cultivate the blessings God gives us so that we can save ourselves from many of the calamities in this world. We need to ask ourselves, "What is the meaning of the words 'each according to his ability'?" The meaning is that each person ought to know his or her strengths. People often say, "I want to have more talents, greater abilities." Good, but if we do not use the talents which we already possess, or if we do not know how to develop them, why should we be given more talents? Every one of us has received sufficient gifts that, were we to develop them, they could

[7] See Ezekiel 11:19; 36:26

be made into a foundation for the development of five talents.

Not many people have five talents. I can positively say that all of you listening to me here have two talents. Were you to transform these two talents into four, things would be different. What does the number 'four' mean? It means you should discover the process by which to purify your lives. You need water, but your water is muddy and you need to learn how to filter it. If you drink muddy water it will be harmful to you. The number four symbolises the divine process through which our desires and thoughts in this world are filtered. Everyone who has two talents should work until he or she has made a filter. Do you know the cost of this filter? Your filters are your discerning minds, and discernment is necessary in life.

When a person is known to be discerning, you should realise that he or she has a filter that retains whatever is valuable while allowing the rubbish to drop through it. Of course, it depends what you are filtering. If you are filtering cheese, the cheese remains in the filter, but if you are filtering water, the pure water passes through the filter while the mud remains in it. Therefore, your filters need two essential qualities, two essential talents: when you use the first talent the valuable things should remain in the filter; when you use the second talent the valuable things should pass through the filter. The first talent is the ability to recognise the fruit that God has given to us for our personal benefit. The second talent is the ability to recognise the fruit that should be sown in the field, which is to say, should be worked with in life.

You each have different assignments in the world. Sometimes you succeed and sometimes you fail. Do not be discouraged by failure, though, because the person with few talents who wishes to gain more has to work hard – this is the law. To have only one talent and not to have used it is a dangerous condition to be in. Knowing how to work is a primary requirement of ours.

I told you that you have two talents. You will ask, "What are these two talents?" They are your mind and your heart. But you will say, "In what ways can I use my mind?" Well, if you pass somebody whose car has broken down and you know how to repair it, fix it and the owner will be grateful to you. Sometime in the future your turn will come when he or she helps you back. In such a scenario you both benefit. The second talent is your heart. If someone that you know is ill, your heart will urge you to visit and help him or her. The heart is the root of our lives, and the mind is the branches and leaves. You know that there is a correlation in nature between roots and branches. Each branch has a corresponding small root down in the earth. When a root dries up underground the corresponding branch also dries up above the ground. There is law to be followed: you need to know that if a desire dries up within you, a corresponding thought will dry up as well. If two desires dry up, two thoughts will also dry up. If three desires dry up, three thoughts will dry up. And one day, when your feelings have completely atrophied, all the branches will be dry and you will have been transformed into a one-talent person.

Let us take the five human physical senses: sight, hearing, smell, taste and touch. What role do these senses play in our lives? They are the five doors through which a human being enters this world. We examine nature through them. They are five realms from which we can draw wealth. Each of our senses corresponds to a great divine virtue, and we need to observe whether what we sense is in harmony with our hearts and whether it is connected to the truth. If we look clearly at this world, we will see it is the clothing of the truth. The visible world is an expression of the truth. There are great blessings in every leaf, stone, spring and rock; great knowledge is hidden inside them all.

What truths nature can reveal to us! Were we to pick up a pebble, we would roll it around and then throw it away, saying, "It is worthless." That would show that we had not understood the meaning of the stone. Or we pick a flower, pluck it and throw it away, saying, "It is worthless." That shows we do not understand the meaning of the flower. Now, consider the sense of hearing. We hear the word 'love'. It is a flower. Did we understand the meaning of this word? No. We ask ourselves, "What is this?" and decide, "It is nothing," and throw it away. We hear the word 'truth' and say, "An empty word." In that case, what is the most important thing to us? Some people would say, "A person needs to eat well and afterwards drink a glass of wine." That is true when one's taste needs satisfying. Eating, however, does not cover everything. It is true, a human being needs to be nourished, but, according to the law of five talents, we need to be nourished by five kinds of food. Each of our senses needs to receive its corresponding food. If we do not feed all of them thus, the deprived senses will atrophy.

165

You see, Christianity is a science; it is not an entertainment. And do you know what kind of science Christianity is? It is a great school with its classes, departments, academies and universities. Everybody who comes to listen in this school needs to understand what he or she is hearing. In the school in which I teach, I do not want people with one talent that they have buried; I want people with two talents. Why? Because I do not want to waste my time on fruitless work. Would you like to keep and raise lice or fleas? They are creatures with one talent. All parasitical people are one-talent people. They are sponges, lazy people who live on the backs of others. A great punishment awaits them.... When a spirit comes to guide you, the first thing you should do is examine it. If it has two talents, you should accept it and feed it. If it has one buried talent, do not accept it. Send it away. It is a louse. It is a flea. It is a wolf that cannot be ennobled. Some people say, "This man can be ennobled," but I say that he can only keep lice. How did the master act towards the servant who had one talent? He threw the servant out so that he went away and learnt to work. We ought never to encourage a person who wants to keep his or her single talent buried. Instead, we ought to warn him or her, "Friend, you can expect the greatest danger ahead in your life." We should not lie to or comfort such a person. Instead, we ought to tell him or her the truth.

Of course, I do not wish to scare you with this lecture. That is not my purpose. When school pupils are beginning to work in the science laboratory, the teacher should explain the properties of the substances they will use. The pupils need to know that if they are not careful the experiments they will undertake might be very costly. Many people have lost their sight or other senses due to carelessness.

Christ's rule also applies in society. I am often asked, "Why does Bulgaria suffer?" It suffers because you do things like putting a man with one talent at the head of the government and expect him to put the country right. According to Christ's words, this politician should be removed from office and thrown out. The head of the government should be someone with five talents – even two are not enough. People with two talents should be policemen or soldiers. Army officers should have four talents; generals and ministers should have five. Kings, who take the highest position in the state, ought to have ten talents. Corrupt heads of government are foolish people, but those who gave them their positions are even more foolish. It is like when a master chooses an incapable servant, expecting him or her to be a good worker. If later on the master wonders why the servant's work is unfinished, we ought to wonder more about the master than the servant. We in Bulgaria need people of two, four, five and ten talents. Were we to have them, I assure you, no misfortunes and unhappiness would befall us. This is why you should pray for such people to be created, and they will come in the future. Let us put these two, four, five and ten talents to work.

Finally, I ask, why do we need the minds that the Lord has given us? The mind is primarily a filter. After transforming milk into yoghurt or cheese, the liquid is removed by filtration. Let us apply this law of filtration in life. If you frequently lament, "I have no friends in the world," I will ask, "Why do you have no friends?" If you answer, "I do not even have one friend," I could safely say that you are a one-talent person. If you say, "No one loves me," I will conclude that you are a one-talent person who has buried all your divine gifts in the ground. Egotistical people, who only live for themselves, deserve to be friendless and to be cast out into the outer darkness. This is what Christ meant by the parable of the talents.

You will ask, "All right, but what is the leaven with which I should work?" You already have this leaven, but you need to know how to make yoghurt and cheese from milk. If you add leaven to milk that is too cold, can you make yoghurt from it? No. If the milk is very hot, can you make yoghurt from it? Again, no. Just as you need to follow a fundamental law while making yoghurt, you have to have good feelings and good desires to be able to transform another person for the better. A person needs to be transformed with good yeast so that he or she does not go sour. People should be transformed with the truth. Two-talent people can transform others with the truth. Having done so, they will receive two more talents and become four-talent people. Those with four talents are people who have already been saved, which means they have already passed through the law of Jesus. In other words, they have passed through the process of self-improvement and have purified themselves of bad desires. These are the two talents which you need to apply in your lives.

You might have heard other sermons on this parable which said that the talents represent money or abilities that have been developed.

A talent, however, is always an ability that originated externally of ourselves and which can be given to us and also taken away. Talents can never be human possessions, as they belong only to God, and He gives them and takes them back according to the way we behave. When you are born on the earth, you are given two talents and told, "Work with them. If you gain two more talents, I will increase them so that you have five talents and enter My joy." Even if God has only given you one talent, there is a place for it in the world. If a one-talent person says that she would like to gain one talent more, she will be saved. And if she makes efforts and suffers, it shows that she truly wants to gain another talent, because when she suffers it is the originally sinful one-talent being within her that suffers. She needs to pass gradually from her 'one', from her 'I', from her egotism, to divine love and self-sacrifice. A person who has only one talent should self-sacrifice to gain a second one, which means to cultivate his or her heart and mind.

Once you have developed all of your senses to perfection, you have five talents. Do you know what it means to develop all of your senses? Many people look without seeing, listen without hearing, and eat without understanding the blessing of taste. For example, when you taste bread, do you sometimes say, "Lord, I thank You for this bread You have given me. Thank You for the life which enters me through it"? If you do not give thanks, it means you have not only misunderstood the purpose of taste, but also that you do not understand what the mouth was made for. The mouth is necessary primarily so that the life of love, which is the foundation of everything, can enter it.[8]

Keep this thought within you: if the Lord has given you one talent, pray for Him to be with you and to give you a second talent, for therein is salvation. Christ came to save the world, to save mainly those with only one talent. But do you know how much sorrow those lazy people cost him? He paid a great price for them.[9] If a man has one talent, leave that talent to the Lord. I tell you, send him away. Why? Because you

[8] The Teacher also said, "Thank the Lord when you eat, for He has given you the opportunity to feed yourself and thus collect new strength with which to continue your life on the earth. Also be thankful when you read a book, because through it you are being given the opportunity to collect new knowledge" (9/22 April 1914).

[9] Jesus said, "The Son of man came to give his life a ransom for many" (Mark 10:45). "The Son of man must suffer many things, and be rejected of the elders and chief priests and scribes, and be killed" (Luke 9:22).

cannot help him to correct himself. Only the Lord is in a position to help him, to save him. When I tell you to throw him out, it is because it would be a good thing for you to do. Being thrown out would enable him to find the Lord, for he will never work while he clings to you. Finding himself alone, however, he will turn to the Lord and be saved. Do not feed him, but let him hunger for two, three or five days. Let him suffer a little. How many times a day does a baby cry? The baby cries so that his mother knows it is feeding time.

There is no life in one-talent people; they are as useful as a corpse. One-talent people are as willing to help others as stingy people are willing to sacrifice their money. I tell all of you here, each of whom has two talents, that if any of you transforms himself or herself into a one-talent person, he or she will have committed a great crime. You are people who may obtain four talents, and when the Lord finds that you are working, and you say to Him, "Lord, using the two talents that you gave me, I have gained two more," He will reply, "Good servant, enter My joy!"

Love, Patience and Benevolence

The Apostle Paul wrote,

> **If I speak with the tongues of men and of angels, but have not love, I am become sounding brass, or a clanging cymbal.** [1]

'Love' has become a very prosaic word in people's mouths, so prosaic that it has lost all meaning, and when a word has lost all meaning it is 'saltless'. Anything that is saltless has lost all its strength, which results in its degradation. [2]

In the organic world, when some food enters the stomach and the correct reaction does not take place, a state of bodily discomfort occurs which doctors call indigestion. This law is valid not only in the physical world but also in mental life. When a thought is presented to you that cannot be processed correctly in your brain and your mind is unable to accept it, a mental form of indigestion takes place. The same thing also happens in the human heart. When a desire enters the human heart that the heart cannot process properly, it results in an emotional form of indigestion.

Human nature understands things in a threefold manner. For example, you have a beautiful red apple. You are first attracted to the apple with your eyes, then by its smell and finally by its taste. Your tongue says, "This apple is delicious." In the same way, love has a threefold

---

[1] 1 Corinthians 13:1

[2] The Teacher also said, "Human life is made of two substances: acid and alkali. Like an acid combining with an alkali to form salt, spirit and matter combine in a human being to form life.

"What can renovate us? Love can. Love is the acid added to the alkali, which is the soul. Love is expressed in the organism by the beating of the heart and the circulation of the blood. Love expresses itself in great deeds. Spiritually wise love creates. It is a force that can change the heart, the mind and the will. And we should change ourselves. Wherever change occurs, there is life. Where there is emotion, there is movement. Motion is the carrier of our emotions. When the heart is constipated, spiritually wise love is the medicine which can heal it" (15/28 January 1915). "A person needs to be ever young of heart and mature of mind" (20 May/2 June 1912).

manifestation in people's lives, but as they do not understand its structure, a miscomprehension of love is born inside them. Some people say love is a feeling, others that it is a power, others that is an illusion, and so on. A person's mind determines his or her state, and therefore it determines his or her understanding of love.

Everything should to be tested on its own territory. Of course, when we come to talk about the broad meaning of love, not every one of you will be ready to understand what I could tell you about it. To make my thoughts comprehensible to you, I need to dress them in a simple form. A newborn baby is fed milk before progressing to soft food. Once the child's teeth have grown, he or she is ready for solids, but while the teeth were emerging the child suffered pain. We pass through a similar state in human life when we are being prepared for the solid food of love: we pass through the process of suffering. Therefore, when we say, "Suffering is necessary," we mean that we need to pass through pain while our teeth grow so that we can nourish ourselves with this solid food. I can explain what these teeth are later, but for the moment I only tell you that when your suffering begins in the world it is a sign that your teeth are beginning to grow. When you have passed through this process you have been formed, you have thirty-two teeth and you are the age of Christ, thirty-two years old.[3]

I will make a short analysis of how the Apostle Paul understood love. To understand love, we need to compare it to its opposite idea. When making a description we usually describe the external side of things, but we can also analyse inner qualities.

Today all people want to be eloquent speakers, because everybody knows that an eloquent speaker can influence a crowd. But Paul said,

---

[3] The Teacher also said, "There are three things which can deceive us and three things which always tell us the truth. Decayed food can be made acceptable to our taste if it has been prepared with delicious sauces and spices. When the food enters the stomach, however, the stomach will tell the truth – it might even vomit back the food. Our intellects may also lie to us. If we have bad thoughts, they will be rejected when they enter our higher minds, our spirits. The third thing which can lie to us is our emotions. When we accept someone with our feelings, our souls will say what value he or she really holds for us. We would therefore be wise to trust our stomachs, our higher minds and our souls. We should rely on these three things: the soul, the spirit and the higher mind. There are people feeding on milk and others who are feeding on solids. We should take the food which is useful to us, milk or solids. No matter what we want to do, we ought to begin by finding out what God thinks about it" (15/28 January 1915).

"Even if I have all the eloquence possible in human language, even if I have all the eloquence of the angels, but do not understand love, I will gain nothing useful." That type of eloquence can do no more than describe the outside of an apple. At this time, everyone is asking, "What will happen to me? And what will happen to Bulgaria?"[4] Were you able to prophesy, everybody would come to ask you about the future, and you would be respected if your prophecies proved true. But Paul said, "If I can prophesy and know all secrets and all knowledge, and have enough faith to move mountains, but have no love, I am nothing."[5] The events of today do not constitute life. You can move mountains and towns, you can organise kingdoms, but these things are only the external side of life. Paul also said, "Even if I give away all my belongings to feed the poor, and even if I give my body to be burned, but I have no love, I will gain nothing useful."[6]

Even if we have every gift that Paul spoke about but do not have love, we do not have the most important thing. It is not that those other things have no value, but that they are only the externality of a human being; they are not from the soul. Next Paul began to describe the positive qualities of love.[7] The first quality of love is patience. Do you know the meaning of patience? It is the fundamental pole of life. If you have patience you can achieve anything. If you have no patience you cannot achieve anything in life. A patient person is a ship with an

---

[4] This lecture was given three weeks into the month of uncertainty that followed the assassination of Archduke Franz Ferdinand, heir of the Austro-Hungarian Empire, in Sarajevo on 15/28 June 1914. Although the assassin and his fellow conspirators were Bosnians, and thus Austro-Hungarian citizens, suspicion of culpability swiftly fell on Serbia. Europe awaited Austria-Hungary's response. Bulgaria was still recovering from its defeat of the previous year, so the possibility of a third Balkan conflict in three years – let alone a general European war – would have been extremely worrying. The likelihood of war appeared to have receded, though, three weeks having passed since the assassination without any apparent action. However, several days after this talk, on 10/23 July, Austria-Hungary handed Serbia an ultimatum whose severity was designed to ensure its rejection, making it clear that it was intent on war.

[5] See 1 Corinthians 13:2

[6] See 1 Corinthians 13:3

[7] "Love suffereth long, and is kind; love envieth not; love vaunteth not itself, is not puffed up, doth not behave itself unseemly, seeketh not its own, is not provoked, taketh not account of evil; rejoiceth not in unrighteousness, but rejoiceth with the truth; beareth all things, believeth all things, hopeth all things, edureth all things. Love never faileth" (1 Corinthians 13:4-8).

anchor. An impatient person is a rudderless ship. Patience is the distinguishing quality of love. It is said, "God is love,"[8] for God has great patience. God's great patience is a sign of His great love for us. If God did not love us so, He would not have been able to tolerate us for so long; He would have been unable to tolerate our ignorance and baseness, and He would have long since purified the world of us.[9] Therefore, whatever kind of blessings we want to attain in life, patience is an absolute necessity. Many people say, "Patience is for oxen." No, patience is a great quality. There is no nobler feature in the human character.[10] People are not born with patience; it has to be acquired. Love can come as a gift, but patience is something we have to attain. Suffering is a process through which patience can be acquired. It is a method of obtaining patience.

Patience requires three basic qualities: wisdom, truth and virtue. Why does a mother tolerate some of the faults of her child while trying to bring him up properly? Because she sees that although he has weaknesses he will become a good man one day, useful to his home and homeland. She therefore acts wisely. There is a divine soul in a child that attracts the mother's love so that she is ready to meet and indulge the child's needs with great patience. The proper fulfilment of any kind of work in this world absolutely requires love – it is a great quality in the hearts of those who have it.

I am talking about love in its broad sense, not its essence. Some people consider love simply to be a sensation, a pleasant mood of heart. That is not love, because a person can have a pleasant mood of heart after drinking some wine. A massage can also give pleasant feelings, but it is not the same pleasure as love gives. When someone loves you, he or she might cause you pain. Love simultaneously causes suffering and joy – this is a quality of love. Love is a double-edged sword: it caresses everyone but also punishes everyone. How does it punish us? When it leaves us, we become sad and say, "I am unhappy." Why? "Because of love's absence." "I am happy." Why? "Because I have love inside me."

[8] See 1 John 4:8, 16

[9] "One day is with the Lord as a thousand years, and a thousand years as one day. The Lord is longsuffering toward you, not wishing that any should perish, but that all should come to repentance. Account that the longsuffering of our Lord is salvation" (2 Peter 3:8-9, 15).

[10] The Teacher also said, "A primary quality of a saint is patience" (5/18 January 1915).

173

But love also says something else: patience is the way by which love comes to the human heart. Patience creates the conditions for love's manifestation. It is the first fundamental quality of love's arrival, its vanguard. When you acquire patience in its broad sense, you will see it is a great power in the hands of someone who is brave and resolute. A great future lies before such a person.

I will now consider the word 'benevolence'. Benevolence is the positive, active side of love, whereas patience is the passive, preserving side by which a burden can be endured.[11] Benevolence is the love which is ready to build, to do someone a favour, no matter whom. If you meet a beggar who wants a favour from you, do it. If a friend of yours with noble qualities would like a favour from you, do it; it does not matter if he or she does not have the same convictions as you. We want people to love us and to be polite to us, but we often break this rule towards others. Not only are we impatient, but often we also do not show people the benevolence they are due.

Some people say they love somebody yet they speak badly of him to others. One day the echo of those words will be heard, because we reap what we sow.[12] If you plant apples, you will gather apples. If you sow thorns, you will reap thorns. I am not talking about how my relationship with you should be, but instead I look at how my relationship with God should be, how my attitude towards love should be, towards what I am required to do for my brothers and sisters. How I understand my actions is a secondary issue. What is important for me is whether I am ready and able to obey the fundamental law of fulfilling what love demands of me. Am I able to be patient when love wants me to be? Can I be benevolent in the way love wants? This law is necessary for everybody, for the whole world, for those who really have hearts. I will leave those who do not understand this alone.

Some people say, "I have no chance to succeed in this world. I am an unhappy person." And I reply, "You are unhappy because love does not visit you." "But why does it not come to me?" "Because you are impatient." "But I try to be patient...." "Good. You are making a start." "But still, I have no chance in life." "That is because you are not benev-

[11] A literal translation of the first part of 1 Corinthians 13:4 in the 1914 Constantinople Bible is, "Love is longpatient and benevolent."

[12] "Whatsoever a man soweth, that shall he also reap" (Galatians 6:7).

174

olent." You will say, "Those things are good and easy to do, and I will do them." But you do not.

I say to you as a doctor, "You are all ill," because I have yet to meet a healthy person in the full sense of the word. Only the saints and the angels who live in heaven are completely healthy. All people are ill, but to different extents, of course. A doctor will advise that you need the good conditions for health: hygiene, light, fresh air, good food and so on. And love also offers advice for your health, saying: "You ought to be patient and benevolent, for they are my two hands with which I constantly work, the hands of love." And do you know how much these hands cost? They are beyond value. When you have these hands you are in a position to do any kind of work. I emphasise, you absolutely require patience and benevolence for these spiritual hands to grow. If you reject these two qualities, your external organs will not be able to react, and your inner organs will not be able to develop, in a way that allows you to express virtues. Why do you need to be virtuous? Because virtues will bring you all the materials necessary for the building of your home, all the juices necessary for your growth. Virtue is not an abstract idea; it is a real thing that is always in a position to create.

Therefore, those of you who are able to understand need to realise what patience is in the full sense of the word. It is not simply the enduring of offenses, for that is not enough. The secret of patience is this: when someone offends you, you should find the good aspect of the offence and make use of it. An offence is a very hard walnut that someone has given you. You need to break the shell, remove the nut and eat it. If you can feed yourself in this way you will be completely healthy. When people speak badly of you, when they blame you for something, they are providing you with food. If you know how to use this food correctly, you will be most satisfied. When people throw stones at you, you should break them up, because there are treasures inside the stones which you can use to enrich yourself. When you arrive home, begin to think about patience and pray to the Lord to help you understand it.

Love does not envy. If you want to know whether love has visited you, you need to ask yourself whether you are envious of anyone. If you have envy, you do not have love. Love should always be present in our actions. We need love in this lifetime, in the next lifetime, in the one after and all our future lives. The higher we ascend, the deeper the meaning we will discover in love. We should start on this path now, for there is no other way to heaven. You will say, "This is a difficult path. Do we have to follow it?" You can enter any place without taking this path except the kingdom of God. Love does not envy, love does not reply to injustice with injustice, or to evil with evil, but instead it endures everything. Of course, I am not saying envy and pride will never visit our hearts. Sometimes they will visit us as guests. We will not be judged for that, though. The key is not to make friends with them. But we sometimes go hand in hand with envy and say to others, "She is a bad person. You should avoid her," and thus make that woman's life unhappy. Envy is not an abstract idea. There are even people on earth who are the very embodiment of envy.

Only when we learn these two qualities, patience and benevolence, will we learn the history of our lives and why we have descended to earth. Again, I give you the example of the grain of wheat. Of all the fruit in the world, there is none more exemplary than the grain of wheat. If you would like to learn the process of patience, observe the patience of the grain of wheat. Without patience you will meet with disappointment.

You may follow other people, but if you do you will sometimes be deceived. Only by following God will you never be deceived. There is only one path: as Jesus Christ said, "I am the path."[13] A man says, "I do not believe," and takes another path. However, one day he will be convinced that Christ's is the right path. Life will tell him as much, because life is a great teacher. You will say, "Convince me first and then I will follow this path." I do not want to convince you. I am simply saying that this bread I give you will nourish you.[14] You ask, "But tell me what it is made of." I do not have enough time to explain. Will you take the bread and eat it? "I do not want it." So I put it in my bag and continue on my way. You will also ask, "What is love? Of what does it consist?" If you ask too many questions, I will not have time to answer them, and I will put love in my bag and continue on my way. Life is a positive thing. Taste and eat of this bread and you will see. Love is the food of life; you cannot live without it or achieve anything useful in the world.

[13] See John 14:6

[14] Jesus said, "I am the bread of life: he that cometh to me shall not hunger" (John 6:35).

Some people have such an obscure idea of love with regard to study-ing, business or war. We need love in everything we do, for it is a great power. The strength with which I lift this glass is love. The same force can be placed in a weapon so that it kills many people. This same power can also be manifested in an earthquake. It is a power which could even destroy the whole earth or create a new world. It is a question of how it is used. Love is a power that, through a certain regulation, can be put to use. But people are selfish. When love comes to them, they want to imprison it inside themselves. However, if love is imprisoned inside a person, it will destroy his or her walls and escape. Love cannot stay in the type of homes in which people want to imprison it. Death is born that way. Death is a process that destroys every egotistical thought and desire. Through death God destroys all the fences in which bad spirits are incarnated.[15]

Our hearts and minds need to have all the conditions with which to accept love. Love is quiet and calm, but when it acts it is also an incred-ible power. When we are in harmony with love, the world is blissful. If we are not in harmony with love, there is no more dangerous power in nature. That is why people say, "The person who is capable of great love is capable of great hatred." Love's positive power is equally matched by its negative power. This is why we ought to be very careful with it. When we have love, we should not act negatively – or it will act as a destructive force, causing illness, suffering and all social destruction.

Many people say, "As the Lord is love, He ought not to punish peo-ple." The Lord is very kind but He is also demanding. When He sees you discontented, the Lord says, "Put one kilogram's burden on that per-son's back." You ask, "Why has this weight been put on me?" Instead of answering you, the Lord orders for another kilogram to be added. "But I cannot carry it!" The Lord adds another kilogram. And when you are so weighed down that you cannot move, you begin to say, "Lord, forgive me." And He responds, "Remove one kilogram." You repeat the prayer. "Remove another kilogram." The number of kilos lifted from your back corresponds to the extent of your prayers. And having taken off all the weight, the Lord asks, "Did you learn your lesson?" "Yes, I have learnt it well." "If you do not want Me to put more burdens on

---

[15] "The wages of sin is death; but the free gift of God is eternal life in Christ Jesus our Lord" (Romans 6:23).

you, you have to be benevolent and patient with the world around you, just as others should be with you. Your little brothers and sisters may well make mistakes, and you need to be as patient as I am. The day you break this law I will burden you again." "But I could not bear it!" "You would have to."

I have told you before how you can liberate yourselves from the burden of discontentment: you have to speak to the Lord from the heart and say, "Lord, I am grateful in my heart and soul for everything You have given me." For God has given thousands of blessings to each person, but people do not know how to use them. In life it is not the quantity of one's possessions that counts but in having what is useful at any given moment. If we are grateful for everything that God has given to us, He will give us even greater blessings. [16]

We ought to apply what is written in this chapter of Paul. Let us begin working to be useful to our brothers and sisters around us. We are here to study as in a school. This school is like a garden in which we should learn to plant and cultivate only beautiful and useful things. [17] There is a connection between the school and the heart and the mind. We should not only think, though; we also need to cultivate and apply the fundamental laws which are necessary for the development of life.

You say, "Why did God not give me greater abilities, more power and more money?" I can see many reasons why not. For how many times has God sent you and your ancestors to the field to work, but instead of cultivating your minds and hearts, you spent your time tasting the forbidden fruit and trying new things which cost you all your capital? How many times have you come together in this field and, instead of working, run away, only to return to God later and ask for a free gift? You are like schoolchildren whose parents wish to educate you, but you run away from the school to which they have sent you. Many of you run away from this divine school. The person who would like to learn the divine law, to obtain a higher degree, to be uplifted

---

[16] The Teacher also said, "Gratitude is a medicine which frees human beings from all difficulties and sufferings. It is a medicine that transforms evil into good, the negative into positive. Gratitude is a requirement in the awakening of consciousness. Through gratitude a human being attracts God's attention. When we attract God's attention to ourselves, He transforms evil into good" (20 September 1936).

[17] "Ye are God's husbandry" (1 Corinthians 3:9). Jesus said, "Every plant which my heavenly Father planted not, shall be rooted up" (Matthew 15:13).

to the sphere of the saints, from where life can be seen clearly and in which the Lord will look benevolently upon him or her, has to finish the divine school on earth and pass the examination of maturity.[18] It is a blessing to graduate from this school. You will say, "This teaching is difficult!" Yes, that is true. It is difficult for lazy people, but this teaching holds riches for those who are diligent, hardworking and humble.

I will return to the word 'love', which people have made 'saltless' and perverted.[19] They have trampled on its goodness and beauty and destroyed its harmonious sound to the extent that only its coarse sound remains, a sound that scratches our ears. And we say to ourselves, "Love is the illusions in life. It is the empty dreams of the young, those innocents who chase the ungraspable shadow of life." Yes, love is a shadow, but behind this shadow is a reality from which the juice of life flows, from which the soul constantly quenches its thirst like a weary traveller at a cold, clear mountain spring. What invaluable wealth and what knowledge are hidden in this one word! And if people had known how to say it correctly, in its original pronunciation from the Divine Mouth, everything around them would have smiled and tenderly listened to this heavenly call. They would have possessed the magic wand of the ancient sages, before the force of which everything tilted to the good. Many people will say, "Imagine how happy a person would be to own such a wand." Yes, it is the greatest happiness a human being can attain on earth, and if someone has an invincible aspiration to attain this blessing, he or she can acquire it.

For the moment I will only tell you this: if you begin to learn patience in life, to endure everything with humility and joy, you will find the truth. Your impatience and bad thoughts create a heavy atmosphere in your homes. We attain benefits through difficulties and hard work, which is why we should be content with what God gives us through His goodwill and great wisdom.

I never advise you to act solely upon the advice of others. You can make use of people's advice, but each person needs to listen decisively to the advice which God places in his or her conscience. Consider

---

[18] Jesus said, "Ye shall be perfect, as your heavenly Father is perfect" (Matthew 5:48).

[19] Jesus said, "Ye are the salt of the earth: but if the salt have lost his savour, wherewith shall it be salted? it is thenceforth good for nothing, but to be cast out and trodden under foot of men" (Matthew 5:13).

what others say, and if it agrees with what the Lord tells you in your conscience, listen to them. If, however, it does not, never follow their words. If you would like to avoid making mistakes, you must listen to the Lord. Whoever does not listen to the Lord is not an intelligent person but a slave to external attractions, to other people and to all things.

You search for the Lord, but where do you look? The Lord is within you, in your mind and heart. The Lord is manifested in these two gifts. Listen well to your mind and heart, because the Lord speaks to you through them. If someone tells you that the mind and heart are spoiled, that person is wrong. If our minds and hearts were spoiled, what else could we use to come to know the Lord? There are spoiled things within us, but not everything is spoiled. I ask you, if you do not believe and trust in your mind and heart, in what will you believe and trust? In whom should we believe and trust? In the Lord who lives within us. And when we believe and trust in the Lord within ourselves, we will also believe and trust in the Lord in our brothers and sisters. People who do not believe and trust in the Lord who lives inside them cannot believe and trust in the Lord who lives inside others either. Those who are not benevolent to their neighbours are displeasing to God. This is why the Lord tells us to love our neighbours.[20]

But your neighbour is hurt, crucified, nailed to the cross. Your Lord is not in heaven because you nailed him here. And your salvation can only be attained by the same nailing, the suffering through which you will develop patience and benevolence. Then your liberation will come. You will say, "That is a difficult task." Have no fear. It is not difficult. To be nailed to the cross is a most pleasant work. The Lord has endured such nailing for thousands of years. You will say, "But will we not suffer?" No, you will not suffer. We do not want those who are afraid of suffering to be in our spiritual school. You should thank God for your suffering, for He sent it to you. You have earned the suffering that is being given to you now and you are worthy of enduring it. Had Christ not worn the crown of thorns and been nailed to the cross, how would he have manifested his love?[21] Would you love him today if he had cho-

---

[20] Jesus said, "The second great commandment is this, 'Thou shalt love thy neighbour as thyself'" (Matthew 22:39).

[21] In his Farewell Discourse, Jesus said to his disciples, "The prince of the world cometh: and he hath nothing in me; but that the world may know that I love the Father, and as the

sen to live as a king?[22] You love him because he was nailed to the cross for our salvation.[23] This is why you should be heroes from now on. Do not be afraid of suffering. Say to the world that you are a strong person who is ready to carry not just one but ten crosses.

A person complains that the cross he carries is very heavy, so the Lord says, "Remove the cross from that man." The Lord then places the man in a large hall and tells him, "There are many crosses in this hall: big ones and small ones, gold ones and silver ones, iron ones and stone ones. Choose one for yourself." The man walks around until he finds a small cross. He says, "This little cross is the one I want." The Lord replies, "But that is the cross you were carrying! That is the same cross as I gave you before...." And thus do we often exaggerate our suffering, but this is not good, because suffering is the path of our ascension to God. This is why when someone is suffering, we ought to say, "This man is a sinner who is on the path of salvation." I would congratulate him and say, "Brother, you are nearer to heaven. I would like to be in your place."

When someone says, "I have never experienced suffering," I reply, "You are still green." The green colour is pleasant. Suffering does not come until ripening begins. I have given you this last thought for you to meditate on it on behalf of the Lord. When suffering comes to you, you should be happy and enjoy it, thanking the Lord for loving you and sending you the suffering. Suffering is a sign of divine love. Let all of us carry this cross, for the Lord has given suffering to the Bulgarian people as one soul so that they acquire the two great qualities of patience and benevolence. Do not complain about the situations of

---

Father gave me commandment, even so I do" (John 14:30-31). "Even as the Father hath loved me, I also have loved you. Greater love hath no man than this, that a man lay down his life for his friends. Ye are my friends, if ye do the things which I command you" (John 15:9, 13-14).

[22] "Again, the devil taketh Jesus unto an exceeding high mountain, and sheweth him all the kingdoms of the world, and the glory of them; and he said unto him, 'All these things will I give thee, if thou wilt fall down and worship me.' Then saith Jesus unto him, 'Get thee hence, Satan: for it is written, 'Thou shalt worship the Lord thy God, and him only shalt thou serve''" (Matthew 4:8-10). "My kingdom is not of this world" (John 18:36).

[23] "The Lord hath laid on him the iniquity of us all. He was oppressed, yet he humbled himself and opened not his mouth; as a lamb that is led to the slaughter; yea, he opened not his mouth. By his knowledge shall my righteous servant justify many: and he shall bear their iniquities" (Isaiah 53:6-7, 11). "Behold, the Lamb of God, which taketh away the sin of the world!" (John 1:29).

your neighbouring countries. The time will come for them to study the lesson which you received first. [24]

Do not complain, "We are being crucified!" for God will answer, "Never mind, you are nearer to Me because of it." Being crucified means the time has come for you to enter the kingdom of God. Let us be joyful that we have something more in this world. Let all of us be followers of Christ and worthy on this earth of the title 'Christians'. Leave aside what others say. Let us have patience and benevolence. Let us fulfil our duty to God as we understand it in our pure thoughts and desires. Let us never stumble on this great path. Let us fight bravely and resolutely, encouraging everyone who battles alongside us. This is the power by which we will overcome the present hardships.

[24] The Teacher also said, "The Bulgarians are saying, 'We have been beaten and they took away our butter.' Have no fear, your butter is neither with the Greek nor Serbian people. They only took the buttermilk; your butter went up to heaven. What will happen to Bulgaria? Bulgaria has been sown and it needs to germinate and grow, which means it needs to suffer" (5/18 January 1915).

Nobility of Character: The Example of Joseph

It is written in Genesis,

> *Joseph's* brethren saw that their father loved him more than all his brethren; and they hated him, and could not speak peaceably unto him. And Joseph dreamed a dream, and he told it to his brethren: and they hated him yet the more.[2]

We often ask this question: "Why do misfortunes happen to me?" It is thought that people suffer to pay for their past or present sins, and they seek the causes of their karma. We see that Joseph experienced misfortune because of the two dreams he told his brothers.[3] Of course, they interpreted the dreams to mean that Joseph had secret ambitions, and so, to prevent him from becoming their leader, they desired to be rid of him. And these were not strangers but his brothers! At the first opportunity, they seized him and sold him to some Ishmaelites. The Ishmaelites sold him on to an Egyptian man, and then Joseph's examination began: God tested his character.[4] Human life is nothing but tests

---

[1] Five days earlier, on 15/28 July 1914, Austria-Hungary had declared war on Serbia, Bulgaria's neighbour, commencing what would become known as the First World War. Austria-Hungary had Germany's unconditional backing, which meant this Balkan conflict risked turning into a general European war should Russia intervene on behalf of Serbia. Not unexpectedly, Russia began mobilising, to which Germany responded, on 19 July/1 August, the day before this lecture, by declaring war on Russia.

[2] Genesis 37:4-5. The Teacher actually read Genesis 37:5-11 and 39:1-23. The story of Joseph is told in Genesis 37:1–50:26.

[3] "*Joseph* said unto *his brethren*, 'Hear, I pray you, this dream which I have dreamed: for, behold, we were binding sheaves in the field, and, lo, my sheaf arose, and also stood upright; and, behold, your sheaves came round about, and made obeisance to my sheaf.' And his brethren said to him, 'Shalt thou indeed reign over us?' And he dreamed yet another dream, and told it to his brethren, and said, 'Behold, I have dreamed yet a dream; and, behold, the sun and the moon and eleven stars made obeisance to me.' And his brethren envied him" (Genesis 37:6-9, 11).

[4] "Joseph was sold for a servant: His feet they hurt with fetters; He was laid in chains of iron: Until the time that his word came to pass; The word of the Lord tried him" (Psalm 105:17-19).

of character. Character is the most precious thing in the human soul, and it must pass through fire, its trials, its tempering. Character is a human being's true home. Only when a person has passed through fire and withstood all of his or her trials can it be said that he or she has a valuable, stable and eternal character.

We see that Joseph passed through one misfortune after another. After the misfortunes that followed his initial two dreams, Joseph went to on to have more problems, as described in chapter thirty-nine of Genesis. As Joseph was a handsome young man, his master's wife fell in love with him. When she propositioned him, he told her, "No, my master has placed everything in my hands except you. You belong to him. I cannot commit such a sin before God." We can see that the Lord reigned in the soul of this young man. Before doing anything, he made the following measurement: "Is this right? Would it please the Lord or not?" He knew the problems which would follow his refusing such a woman, but he preferred to suffer them than to commit a sin. After being tested in this way he was imprisoned, but the Lord helped him during his imprisonment. If you read the whole story, you will see that God did not abandon Joseph but had him freed from prison by ena-bling him to interpret the two dreams of the king of Egypt.

While we are being tested we do not know the purpose God has in giving us the test.[5] You would like to go to heaven, but if someone asked you what you understood by 'heaven' or 'Paradise', you would not know exactly how to answer. You have a certain idea about heaven, but it is not a clear one, just as the meaning of the two dreams were not clear to Joseph's mind. And really, what meaning could the sheaves, the sun and the moon have had for him? The dreams were showing Joseph certain future events: his being sold by his brothers, his being tempted by the woman, his being imprisoned and, finally, his liberation and upliftment.

Now, what do the kingdom of Egypt and the temptress repre-sent? Egypt symbolises the kingdom in which we live, and the king's wife who tempts us symbolises the world. You are slaves who have been sold and driven away by your brothers. You are in Egypt and

---

[5] After their father's death, Joseph said this about his ordeal to his brothers: "Ye meant evil against me; but God meant it for good, to bring to pass, as it is this day, to save much people alive" (Genesis 50:20).

your master's wife desires you and is offering you a certain pleasure, which means the world is tempting you with certain benefits. Sexual pleasure is not bad in itself, but some things are forbidden.[6] When Adam was in Paradise, the Lord told him to eat anything except the one forbidden fruit. Adam's disobedience resulted in all his subsequent suffering.[7] There are forbidden things in this world, and if you try to eat the forbidden fruit it will result in your suffering. How many people would like to steal other people's money, perhaps needing money to build houses, or wanting it for their pleasures or for travelling abroad? Joseph did not look at things that way, however. The favours and benevolence of his master's wife were offered to him, but he thought thus: "I would prefer to have the benevolence of God than another man's wife." The world is a woman who does not belong to us. Tomorrow, having had her pleasure, she might discard you, for she is only attracted to your outer beauty.

There is a contemporary delusion: when people respect us, we think it is because we are simply worthy of it in ourselves. Everybody respects a famous singer until her larynx is damaged, after which she is ignored. All that respect had only been given to her vocal cords. It is the same with a great violinist, who is respected by everybody until his arm cannot move the bow. If the violinist's arm is paralysed, no one will remain interested in him. As long as a woman is beautiful, men will try to win her affection, but once her beauty has faded their attention will move on to someone else. Joseph was aware of this type of self-delusion, and therefore he sought only inner things, things which are stable and eternal, things which always give a person peace. With this attitude he attained the benevolence of God.[8]

This is why we need to be careful of those small causes that might result in misfortunes. If Joseph had not told his brothers of his dreams, the same misfortune might not have befallen him. But is it possible that

---

[6] "Thou shalt not commit adultery" (Exodus 20:14) and "Thou shalt not covet thy neighbour's wife" (Exodus 20:17) are parts of the Ten Commandments.

[7] See Genesis 2:15-17; 3:17-24

[8] "Love not the world, neither the things that are in the world. If any man love the world, the love of the Father is not in him. For all that is in the world, the lust of the flesh, and the lust of the eyes, and the vainglory of life, is not of the Father, but is of the world. And the world passeth away, and the lust thereof: but he that doeth the will of God abideth for ever" (1 John 2:15-17).

185

he could have arrived at the same misfortune another way? There are trials which cannot be avoided. I will not speak about these inner laws now, but I will say that there are things which are absolutely predetermined by God. If we run away from the smaller predetermined things, they will come to us in a greater way. We need to learn from the behaviour of Joseph to be able to neutralise suffering.

We must not delude ourselves that if all is well with us today, our lives might not be changed tomorrow, bringing unexpected misfortunes.[9] Destiny, or providence, has predetermined what kind of trials each human life must pass through. These tests are necessary. Why are they necessary? I will explain with an example. To cross a deep river you need a small boat, but you need a ship to cross an ocean. And to pass from one world to another, you need the ship called Faith. Trials and misfortunes are necessary because they are the fuel for your journey; they are your ticket. Anybody who does not want to follow the path of this necessary law is a foolish person. Whoever complains, saying, "Why did the Lord give me this suffering?" is a foolish person. Whoever says, "I want to learn the meaning of my suffering and my trials," and is also grateful for them, is an intelligent person. Notice how Joseph did not complain when misfortunes came to him but instead met them with joy in his soul. When later he took a high position in the house of his master, he also thanked God for it and did not grow proud. And when his master gave him greater blessings, Joseph was not tempted by the 'blessings' offered by his master's wife. He said to himself, "There is a law that I have to obey: I must not sin." In such circumstances sexual pleasure would have been sinful.

What is sin? Whatever does not give birth to anything, whatever does not bear fruit, is a sin.[10] A prostitute or a promiscuous woman sins because she is not giving birth. Conception atones for sin. Each action which does not bring life with it is a criminal waste of divine energy. When someone encourages you to sin, he or she wants you to waste your divine energy. You drink too much wine and have a headache the

---

[9] "Ye know not what shall be on the morrow" (James 4:14). "In the day of prosperity be joyful, and in the day of adversity consider: God hath even made the one side by side with the other, to the end that man should not find out any thing that shall be after him" (Ecclesiastes 7:14).

[10] "Have no fellowship with the unfruitful works of darkness" (Ephesians 5:11).

next day. What have you attained? Have you become nobler? No. Why do we desire things and perform actions which do not improve our characters? We ought to limit ourselves to those pleasures which are within the framework of what is permitted, natural and spiritually lawful. For example, children gain pleasure from playing with their toys, but their toys are also educational for them. There are some pleasures in adult life that are useful, but there are also pleasures which always cause the destruction of human feelings, human vital forces and human salvation. The unnatural life, or the so-called illicit affairs that some men and women have, act destructively on their hearts and minds.[11]

If you love and desire someone, ask yourself whether to act on your desire would please God, whether it would be beneficial for the one you love or corrupting to his or her soul and mind. Joseph was young and unspoiled. When a corrupt woman wanted to defile him, he did not succumb to her temptation because he did not want to ruin his name. Had he succumbed, nothing would have been left of his reputation. Notice that the first woman, Eve, was put to the test and was unable to withstand it. Afterwards her husband was tested and also failed. The serpent told Eve, "If you eat from this tree, what knowledge and what power you will receive! You will become like God." She succumbed, saying, "I am ready for glory. I can do it!"[12] And it really was infidelity.[13] Now it was Joseph's turn to be tested by the same serpent that had seduced Eve in the garden. This time the serpent presented itself as a woman who said to Joseph, "Come with me...." But he told her, "No, I cannot." Much suffering followed this choice, but so did his upliftment.

'Man' and 'woman' represent two principles, two great and spiritually wise forces: masculinity and femininity. One of these forces is active and the other is passive, one acts and the other accepts. These are two processes in nature that interchange. God does not always give; sometimes He takes away. A person might receive something while losing something else. Masculinity and femininity are two principles at

[11] The Teacher also said, "You should avoid sexual intimacy with promiscuous people, because they are energy vampires. They drain others of their energy and strength, which leads to illness and spiritual degeneration" (some time between 1929 and 1944).

[12] See Genesis 3:1-6

[13] The Teacher also said, "It was not long before Eve became dissatisfied with Adam. He was old, so she looked for a younger companion, and found him in the serpent, the black adept" (24 December 1916).

work. One principle is creative and is called 'man' or 'God'. The second principle is passive and is called 'woman' or 'the Lord'. Both of these principles are one and the same. Consequently, whether in an active or passive moment, we need to be faithful to both principles. We will attain real benefits in life only if we keep these sublime, divine principles. If you are faithful to God, all the dreams and desires of your mind and heart can be attained. You may only obtain these things in one way, through God. Only God can fulfil your thoughts and desires. The mother nourishes and raises her child, and the teacher educates the pupil. Just as the child cannot nourish and raise himself or herself without the mother, neither can the pupil learn without the teacher. Joseph listened to the voice of his inner teacher, God, who was teaching him to obey the great law of the movement and action of life.

Our purpose in life should be focussed on the development of our characters. How? Character is formed by thoughts and feelings, by positive powers. We should not comprehend life in the limited framework of the ordinary contemporary understanding; we need to understand life in the framework in which God made it. A person can be strong of mind only when his strength is connected with all the divine laws and he is in harmony with all the beings that surround him, from the lowest to the highest. Then his mighty character can do anything, because all those beings will be helping him. When we are at odds with these divine laws, contradiction appears in our minds and we meet with misfortunes in life.

Why do we sometimes not succeed in our endeavours? Because we want to do something good without realising that it is not actually good. We believe our plans to be clever and destined to succeed, but they do not. If you break God's law you will be bothered unceasingly. A person needs to fear punishment before making mistakes, not afterwards – tears do not save people.[14] Salvation is attained by organising the heart, the mind and the body. This is our task on earth, and we have the great character of Joseph as our example. When we read these chapters of Genesis, we ought to study Joseph's character well. Do not think that he was foolish; he was highly intelligent spiritually, which is why, as you may see, his father loved him so much. Joseph also had

[14] "Be not wise in thine own eyes; Fear the Lord, and depart from evil" (Proverbs 3:7). "The fear of the Lord is the beginning of wisdom" (Proverbs 9:10).

a noble heart. His father realised this, but his brothers thought their father loved Joseph for his external qualities. That is why they sold him. But no matter what the conditions in which he was placed, Joseph's character uplifted him. Due to his valuable qualities, Joseph's master gave him a powerful position. Another test sent him to prison, but he also uplifted himself there. The Lord finally removed him from prison after two years, which is the given time for a test. What are your prisons? They are your present human bodies. One day you must escape from these dirty, unhygienic prisons....

Let us return to Joseph's character. We see that he had common sense and a mind that worked well and comprehended the fundamental laws of life. He had a noble heart, and he did not want to be unfaithful to the promise that he had made to God: "I have given my honest word to my master and also to my Lord, to serve Him faithfully. I cannot be unfaithful to the Lord." Joseph was not the kind of young man who followed his bad inclinations and desires. In every situation Joseph was prompted by noble motives and kept his heart and mind in balance. For the Lord to be able to live within us, it is necessary for our minds and hearts to be in accord and balanced. When discord arises between them, the Lord cannot live within us. Human conflict is caused by the discord between people's minds and hearts, with all people wanting to take more than they are due while themselves giving nothing. Far too many people intend to steal from their neighbours, which is why there is always confrontation between them – it is a law that governs all beings, from the small to the large.

Many people would like to live good lives. Some people are still living with their fathers, telling of the dreams they dreamed. A second category of people are those who are sold by their brothers in Egypt and tempted by the wife of their master. A third category consists of those who are imprisoned. The best position is to come out of prison and stand before Pharaoh, but first you must pass through the other three categories, the three stages. They are the three schools, the three courses. The first course is being with the father. The second course is to have one's wisdom tested by the woman – a test Joseph passed very well, leaving his garment and running away with his integrity unstained. What does it mean to leave one's clothing? It is to leave the covering of your soul, which is the flesh. The world speaks to you like this woman:

189

"I am very beautiful. Come with me or you will go to prison!" She tests whether you will give in to temptation or follow the divine law.

You need to free yourselves of your weakness for seductive benefits so that you become able to conquer temptations and to follow the divine law. Believe in God. Have faith in Him and you will have a great future like Joseph. There cannot be two opinions on this. I am showing you how a young man, who followed the path that God showed him, rose from being a common shepherd to the highest position in Egypt. He achieved this without committing crimes, neither by lying nor killing, but through self-denial, suffering and obeying the divine law. This demonstrates that the wisdom and knowledge you have in your mind and the goodness you have in your heart are the only things which can help you to progress honestly in life. Never be deceived by external things that can attract your eyes. The kind of houses you may build for yourselves and the kind of windows they will have depends on your minds and hearts. Anyone can use his or her mind and heart to change his or her social position, to climb from poverty to wealth. To make such a change honestly is possible only if a person obeys the divine laws.

If we look at what happened when Joseph's brothers came to him in Egypt, we can see the second noble aspect of his character. He did not avenge himself on them but instead cried with them and poured out all his love to them. Likewise, if someone does something wrong to us, we should not take vengeance upon him or her. Evil thoughts, vengefulness and gossiping do not make character. The act of forgiving builds character. It is the only path upon which you can rise to the level of nobility. We have an example of this in Christ. When the soldiers mocked him while he was on the cross, he said, "Forgive them, Lord."[15] The time will come when you will be asked, "Have you forgiven those who caused you sorrow, those who sold you?"

A father said to his son, "You will achieve nothing in your life." The son went abroad to study. After he returned, he rose in society until he held a powerful position in the government. Once he had attained this post, the first thing he did was to send some policemen to collect his father and bring him before him. When he arrived, the son asked his father, "What do you think now? Have I not made something of

[15] In the Bible the soldiers mocked Jesus after he had said these words (see Luke 23:33-37).

myself?" The father replied, "Was it wise to bring me here like this, to frighten me? You are an unwise man who does not know what he is doing. You should have sent a carriage to bring me here."

Everyone uses the method of fear: "Let the Lord give me power and I will know how to rule. I will hang people!" People have been using this method for thousands of years. Everybody is fighting and there are tears in every home. And how much better has it made the world? Not one bit. Only love can plant noble elements in the human soul. Punishment is useful only when it is imposed by love with the purpose of uprooting evil. A surgeon who cuts out healthy parts of the body is not intelligent but foolish.

In life, you need to obey the fundamental law that requires you to keep a balance between your mind and heart. Many people doubt whether God exists. Some of you say, "I believe there is a God." Were you to be put in Joseph's situation, however, you would say, "If there really were a God, He would not have put me in prison like this. To have taken me from my father and mother, for my brothers to have sold me … Could a good God have done this? I do not believe so."

You ought to accept all the suffering dealt out to you by the Divine Hand. You should learn how to enjoy suffering. Sufferings are the stones with which you will build the steps of your house. Suffering will form your character. Suffering is the connecting cord between a human being and God. Only by suffering is it possible to pass from one world into another, better world. There is nothing better with which to uplift yourselves in this world than suffering. You loathe suffering, but it is actually the greatest blessing. After a soul has suffered for a long time, the suffering will bear fruit and the soul will begin to rejoice. If a tree's roots did not draw up the juices, how would we get its sweet fruits? If a mother does not suffer, if she does not carry her baby in her womb, how would she be able to have a child to enjoy? If a father does not sacrifice his individualistic life for his family, how will he be happy? If a teacher does not make an effort, how will the pupils respect him or her? Who, having lazed around in life, has been taken to heaven and put in a high position there? You cannot escape suffering. There is suffering from one end of the world to the other. Suffering is the chiselling and modelling of the Sculptor making a statue. When we learn the deep meaning of suffering, we will understand that it is a process that forms our characters. And when we are making the final hits with the hammer and chisel and completing our characters, all suffering will cease and the great statues of our lives will be ready.

We are preparing ourselves to go to heaven. And what will we take there? We will take our characters. They are our true wealth. You would love to be a good-looking person, to have a well-shaped figure and be noble of manner; but when you enter the world, what would people say if you have all of those things but not a noble character? When people look at your face, do they see a virtuous person? When somebody is not handsome or beautiful but is strong of mind and good of heart, people say, "That person has a good, strong character," and this is the best compliment the world can give us. The world will need us if we have such minds and hearts. There were many Egyptians in elite positions during the time of Pharaoh, so why did he not put any of them in the highest position in the land but instead chose a foreigner? Was it for his good looks? No, it was because of his mind and his goodness. If we are like him, the world will give us the same place that he attained. If we are foolish, the world will discard us. Contemporary people rely on the opposite concept: they say one should not be virtuous, because virtuousness is foolishness. They do not know what they are talking about, because external things can be taken from anybody, but character remains with a person eternally. Character is therefore the most valuable of things.

Today you are passing through the same trials as the Egyptians of Joseph's time, and you are worried like they were, not knowing what will happen tomorrow. Fate, the future, is not in our hands. You cannot predict the turn of future events, but your destiny would be in your own hands if you had the faith to rely on God as Joseph did. Then you would certainly change your destiny. No matter where you were and in what circumstances you were placed, you would rise like oil in water. The first thing is neither to be scared nor worried. You need to be brave and resolute, unafraid. Fear should give way to spiritual kindness and wisdom. You should hesitate only when you have an unresolved problem, not knowing whether it is correct to do something or not. Once you have solved the problem and consider your solution to be the right one, you should announce it and stand by it. Joseph did this when he said to his master's wife, "I cannot do this with you." Bad consequences followed his refusal, but God was with him throughout.

Patience is a necessity in the construction of character, for it is the foundation of things. And we mostly see patience in Joseph's character. He did not spend his time in prison worrying. Instead, he worked and studied and was prepared to endure anything. Patience is an aspect of character with which a human being is not born; it has to be obtained through effort. All the suffering in the world has only one purpose, to build patience within us. No matter what difficulties and disappointments come our way, we need to learn to be patient, to develop self-control, to view the future with faith and never be discouraged. A young woman says, "It is my dream to marry my ideal man." After marrying him, she says, "My life is over!" No, her life is just beginning. Some people say, "I have lost my money!" So what? You are at the beginning of your life. You have not lost anything. "I have lost my health!" You are at the beginning of your life. You will be healthy again. No matter in what position of life we find ourselves, we need to be patient and to rely on God right to the end. In everything you do, this faith needs to be deep in you.

Some people would like to live in polite society, to be surrounded with good people. Although Joseph lived as a foreigner among Egyptians, owing to his good heart and mind he managed to make friends with them. But some of you say, "People are sinful." So make friends of those sinners, for there are noble souls among them. Today's Christians say, "That man does not believe in God. He is still green." If he were not green, how could he ripen? Things that grow in the earth are green at first; they do not ripen immediately. The green state is the one in which juices are drawn from the ground. When sufficient juices have been accumulated, ripening begins. "She offended me, calling me green!" It is very good that you are green. You have not really been insulted. If you work and are noble, one day you will ripen. A person who is never green cannot ripen and will instead become dry. There is no process of development in something that is all dried up. If you are green, I am pleased for you. It is a noble condition. You will become golden yellow when you ripen. Everybody loves money – 'ripening'. There are people who are not yet ripe. Do you know what having money means? It means you are ripe. Life is the gradual development from the green state to the ripe one.

This process of ripening will continue to be necessary until all people have completed their development and obtained all the knowledge and goodness of their hearts. When people have obtained all these juices, the Lord will send them divine blessings and the fruits within them will ripen. Then the Lord will appear. While you are green the Lord observes you from afar, but when you have ripened He will come and pick your ripe fruits. The Lord needs these fruits. When you begin to understand life, to discern the essential from the unessential, the constant from the transitory, when your characters are well-developed and have become strong, when the fruits on the trees in your gardens begin to ripen, you will be taken out of prison and presented to the Master of this world to interpret the two dreams of life, to give the truth not as prisoners but as people who are free. When you have succeeded in this, the truth will be the crown of your heads, the sheaves in the field will bow to you and the sun and the moon and the eleven stars in heaven will greet you. Then, because you have come to understand the deep meaning of earthly life, the Lord will appear and establish the kingdom of God on earth.

The Law of Service

Jesus said,

> If any man serve me, let him follow me; and where I am,
> there shall also my servant be: if any man serve me, him
> will the father honour. [1]

Many people will ask, "What is the hidden meaning in the words,
'Whoever serves me will be honoured by my Father'?" There are different aspirations in the world. Contemporary people aspire to knowledge, wealth, land, houses, glory, greatness and power – they aspire to
many things. Jesus, however, insisted on only one thing: service, for a
person to know how to serve.

'Servant' is a word with a monotonous connotation, expressing the
lowest position in society. There are, however, different kinds of servants in life: servants in the restaurant, servants in the kitchen, servants
in the theatre, servants in the university, servants in the government,
and so on. Every person is a servant in a certain sense, but not everyone acknowledges it. There are therefore two kinds of servants in the
world: one who knows his or her duties and how to perform them,
and another who does not know how to serve. The latter are usually
called rulers, masters who sit and wait for others to serve them. They
teach others how to work, how to serve them. Everybody would like to
be in the category of masters, but Christian teaching takes the opposite
position. It holds the principle that whoever wants to be a master has
to be a servant. It is said that the Son of God did not come to be served
but to serve. [2]

We are obliged, according to the law of necessity, to be servants. A
man declares, "I am a master!" No, it is a self-deception for this man to
believe he is completely free and not in service to anyone else. He is, at
the very least, in the service of his stomach. The stomach puts a person

[1] John 12:26
[2] See Matthew 20:25-28

in the position of performing work that is not always pleasant: to prepare food well and chew it properly. If we do not serve our stomachs correctly, they will punish us....

Service is a quality. How many misfortunes happen in the world because people do not know how to serve? The world will change when mothers have learnt to raise their children well, when teachers have learnt to teach their students properly, when governments have learnt how to serve the people and meet their needs, creating the laws necessary for their correct development. Contemporary civilisation is being put to great tests, with millions of people being called to serve in armies in various ways.[3] But what awaits these 'servants'? Their heads, legs and muscles will be ripped to pieces and mixed together with those of their comrades.[4] And this is what people call civilisation, culture....The people of today say, "We do not need the Lord; science will uplift us." But what is this science teaching us? It is teaching us to be hard-hearted, to make guns and grenades. Yes, science has brought us to this dangerous test. Heaven is now testing how we serve the Lord.

The world requires its servants to serve it, and the Lord requires us to serve Him.[5] Christ said, "Whoever serves me will be honoured by my Father." We are forever arranging our affairs, and yet they forever remain unarranged. For example, we become ill and call the doctor to heal us, but death still takes us away; we build houses and hire security guards to protect them, but still our wealth is stolen. Christ is now saying, "You have served your own principle for so many years, and now you can see the consequences of it.... But if you serve me, you will see

[3] Since the last lecture, a week earlier, the military situation in Europe had moved with great rapidity. On 21 July/3 August Germany declared war on France, Russia's ally, and the next day invaded Belgium as a key part of its plan to attack Paris. Britain, a signatory to a treaty guaranteeing Belgium's neutrality, declared war on Germany that same day, 22 July/4 August, an hour before midnight, British time. The great imperial powers of Austria-Hungary, Britain, France, Germany and Russia were now involved in a war that would be of unprecedented scale, casualty and cost.

[4] The Teacher also said, "Human beings have created weapons that destroy houses. A person builds a house, a body, and someone throws a grenade that explodes and throws him out of it. It is important that anyone who is thrown out of his house like this comes back to consciousness in the other world as soon as possible" (5/18 January 1915).

[5] Jesus said, "No man can serve two masters: for either he will hate the one, and love the other; or else he will hold to one, and despise the other. Ye cannot serve God and mammon" (Matthew 6:24).

the true meaning of your lives."[6] We need to serve as Christ did. He did not come to be served but to serve. People ought to be servants to those who are weaker and less able than them, but we should not put bad people in positions where they 'serve' others.

Do you know why contemporary society is rotten? It is because too many mothers who ought to be educating their children themselves instead leave the job to paid servants so that they can go out to restaurants, to the theatre, to balls and other pleasures. This does not just happen in Bulgaria but everywhere. If a female servant does not love a child in her care like a mother, because she did not give birth to the child, she cannot educate that child properly. She will say, "If my mistress only cares to spend her time sitting in restaurants, why should I care for her children?" If mothers were servants, in the fullest sense of the word, to their children in their upbringing and education, the world would change. It would also change if fathers educated theirs sons properly. When parents neglect their duty and leave the upbringing and education of their children to others so that they can go out and find pleasure in the world, the results are bad indeed.

I will explain to you the true meaning of service and the qualities that a servant needs. First, a servant needs to have a noble heart, to be sensitive, obliging, humble, flexible and adaptable to all conditions, to work well and not be lazy. Life requires a great deal from us and we need to serve it well. For example, when a tailor makes a mistake, the clothing is returned and the tailor has to pay for its alteration. Nature is the same: it gives us material, life, and tells us, "Cut and sew this cloth." And if we cannot make good clothing with the material of life, nature fines us for it.[7] If we want to learn how to serve, we should turn to Christ for him

[6] Jesus said, "If ye love me, ye will keep my commandments. And I will pray the Father, and he shall give you another Comforter, that he may be with you for ever, even the Spirit of truth. The Spirit of truth shall guide you into all the truth" (John 14:15-17; 16:13).

[7] The Teacher also said, "You can do many things when you are connected to the forces working in nature. There are different levels of intelligence in nature, and you will develop according to the level with which you are connected. You definitely need to connect to the spiritually wise laws in nature. However, you say, 'We do not see any such laws....' That is because you have not trained your sight with constant exercises. A man had a collection of insects and butterflies. When he started out he could not distinguish between the smallest butterflies at fifty metres away. Through constant concentration and effort he was able to develop and enlarge the centres of his brain related to vision. As a result he became able to distinguish between the smallest butterflies at a good distance" (10/23 January 1915).

to teach us. A person who is a servant ought to be highly intelligent; a foolish person cannot serve properly. Teachers and priests are servants. The first task of a teacher who understands the nature of her vocation is to learn about her pupils' souls, to be able to know how to direct them to knowledge. A priest needs to understand the souls of his parishioners, to be able to give them the appropriate food for their hearts.

There is a quality that we all need, which is patience. Patient people are often referred to as 'oxen', but to be patient is not to be an ox; being patient is a spiritually wise act. To be able to endure the external hardships in life, we need an inner balance of the soul, heart and mind. I give you the example of a mathematician who lived several centuries ago. He worked for twenty years on certain calculations, and his study was littered with all the papers on which he had written his research. The man always locked the door to his study when he left it. One day, however, he forgot to lock it. His servant entered the study and found the floor covered in paper. Thinking it to be discarded rubbish, she collected the paper, burnt it and cleaned the room thoroughly. When the mathematician returned and asked his servant where the papers were, she replied, "I put them in the fire. Look how tidy your study is now!" He did nothing except tell her, "Never do this again!"

We serve like that mathematician's servant: we collect all the papers and decide that some are valuable and that others are not.... The mathematician did not behave in the way we would have in his position, however. Instead, he showed great patience with his errant servant. You are now in the same situation as the mathematician: your house is open and your servant is collecting your papers and putting them in the fire. And when you find your house has been cleaned according to your servant's understanding, what will you say? I know there will be tears as you lament, saying, "Lord, am I the most sinful person? Why has such a fate befallen me?" And we think we are people who understand the divine law.... Instead, we should be like the mathematician, saying, "Please, do not do this again." For our part, we need to keep our affairs in order and not leave the doors to our studies unlocked and at the disposal of the servants.

Christ said, "Whoever serves me will be honoured by my Father." You all think only of this world, of temporary things, to look after your own affairs and those of your family; but in doing so you leave many important things unarranged, like your relationship with your Master, who will one day call you to give an account of yourself. That day is coming. Do you know where you will be in several years' time? Do you know what will happen in Europe during these coming years? Do you know what situation you will end up in? You do not. The present world will be thoroughly cleansed and given an injection to uplift it for a new life. The people who will help civilisation will have to apply Christ's principles and learn how to serve. Those who do not know how to serve in the way that Christ wants will not have the chance to develop themselves spiritually.

We all spend our time thinking about how to make our bodies healthier: what kind of food to give them, what kind of homes they should live in. We are all working for external things, but no one is focussing on the internal side of human life. Not only should our homes be arranged beautifully, but our minds need to be well ordered as well. If our bodies need hygienic homes to live in, so do our hearts. I do not consider someone who has a hygienic home but an unhygienic heart to be an intelligent person. We usually put most of our attention on serving external things, whereas we ought to first give priority to our hearts, then to our minds and then to our bodies. If we build our lives in this way, we will receive God's blessing.

Christ said, "If anyone serves me, let that person offer me his or her heart."[8] Christ mainly came to the earth to cultivate the human heart. What is this cultivation? It is the weeding out of all the defects of our lives. You have been Christians for a long time. All of you follow Christ, but were he to call you to an examination, how many of you would be able to endure the test of patience and humility? Were he to give you such a problem to solve, not only theoretically but also practically, or to give you another problem concerning any of the other human virtues – righteousness, love, truth and wisdom – do you think you could not fail the test? You know when other people love you or not, but you have not learnt to recognise whether you love others or not. As the Lord requires us to love others, we need to arrive at self-denial.[9] We

[8] Jesus said, "He that hath my commandments, and keepeth them, he it is that loveth me: and he that loveth me shall be loved of my Father, and I will love him, and will manifest myself unto him" (John 14:21).

[9] Jesus said, "This is my commandment, that ye love one another, even as I have loved

often say, "These people have worn me out. They have taken so much from me." But do we human beings not take from the Lord all the riches we find here on the earth? The Lord has now descended to the earth, and He is speaking to all His servants who have stolen and lied: "Enough thieving and lying! Come and give an account of yourselves." This account is the present European war.

The Lord is saying, "Give Me a report on how you have used everything that I have given you." And this is our answer: everybody wants to be the ruler. Each race on the ascendant wants to rule over the other races. Every nation would like to rule over other nations. These are the reasons why conflicts arise. If all people were guided by Christ's principle of serving humanity, if everyone had his or her own sphere of work and contributed the right amount to humanity, disputes would no longer exist.[10] All nations are now arming themselves to become rulers, but what is happening at the international level is also taking place in our everyday lives – enter any house and see what is happening there. Two young people marry and everybody is joyful, saying, "This couple will live in peace and harmony." After two or three months, however, the wife would like to take charge, but her husband declares, "I am the master of this house!" Actually, both are deceiving themselves, as neither one is the master; they are both servants. It is said that the man is the head of the house, but to be a head does not mean to be a master. To be the head of the house means to be an intelligent servant who, by example, teaches the other spouse how to serve, so the couple can say together, "We are servants of the Lord, our Master."

We are sometimes discontented and dissatisfied with ourselves. Why do we sometimes not have enough willpower and are weak of mind? It happens when we come into contradiction with the Lord, with the great law. Every time a person comes into contradiction with a divine law, inner suffering appears and his mind is divided. Then he does not

you" (John 15:12). "By this shall all men know that ye are my disciples, if ye have love one to another" (John 13:35).

[10] The Teacher also said, "Let us be faithful to the Lord, to Christ. Christ is the life, the love and the living thoughts that teach the nations to love one another. He is a collection of the higher spirits who teach the nations how to live, who gives them laws and supervises them. Christ is the One who can save us from the chains with which we voluntarily bind ourselves. If we do not see him now, he will appear one day and demand his ten percent...." (6/19 April 1914).

know what to do and bad thoughts and desires come to him. These thoughts and desires do not have the power of God, and the man's mind changes colour. Bad desires and thoughts are like a snake coiled around you that constantly sucks out the juices that feed your mind and heart, until you are dried out and feel paralysed.

Look how many people drive themselves mad in their desire to become rich. No matter how much money they gain, they are never satisfied. They pile up their wealth, but for what? There is no inner meaning in this. People are learning new methods of becoming rich, influencing other people's thoughts and actions through magnetism and suggestion. In the past thieves lurked in the forest with guns, but now they are in the cities carrying new tools with which to steal from their neighbours. There were three hypnotists in America who hypnotised the owner of a bank into writing them a cheque for a large sum of money. The method of robbing people has changed. Everybody wants the gift of hypnotic trickery, but do you know what misfortune it brings? There is the legend of King Midas, whose desire that anything he touched be turned into gold was granted. Everything seemed perfect until he touched his food and his wife.... He then prayed to the Lord to save him from this great curse. We may each obtain such power, but it will destroy our lives. Our true wealth is within us and not outside ourselves. This is not to say that wealth is found in a person's physical strength. Human strength is not found in muscles but in the tender, delicate feelings that develop all other strengths and powers.

God made the world so that nature is subordinate to the seemingly weakest power there is: love. Love is so gentle and delicate, but actually it rules the world. When love enters someone, it takes that person apart and transforms him or her.[11] Christ said, "Whoever serves love, serves me," which also means, "My servant will have everything that I have."[12] That this is true may be verified by reading the parable of the mustard

---

[11] "God is love; and he that abideth in love abideth in God, and God abideth in him. This is the love of God, that we keep his commandments: and his commandments are not grievous. For whatsoever is begotten of God overcometh the world" (1 John 4:16; 5:3-4).
[12] Jesus said to his disciples, "All things whatsoever the Father hath are mine" (John 16:15). "Whatsoever ye shall ask in my name, that will I do, that the Father may be glorified in the Son. If ye abide in me, and my words abide in you, ask whatsoever ye will, and it shall be done unto you" (John 14:13; 15:7).

201

seed.[13] Were we to deposit the small yeast of love in our hearts and the hearts of our neighbours and those who run governments, it would transform the whole world.[14]

The disregarding of Christ's teaching created the present cataclysm. The Lord has put the milk, 'humanity', in the churn, and this war is the churning process. Some of the milk will be turned into butter, which will rise to the surface, and the rest will become buttermilk. In other words, some people will become butter and others will become buttermilk. The Lord has a good purpose in mind for both the butter and the buttermilk: the butter will be eaten and the buttermilk will be drunk. This churning has been predetermined, and you will either become butter or buttermilk.

Christ turned to the Judeans and asked who among them wanted to be his disciples. Some of us say, "I am a believer. I believe in Christ." Those who only 'believe' in Christ are only listeners, but his question concerns those who actually want to apply his law.[15] If you have stopped to think on the words, "I serve Christ," and have been learning to serve Christ the whole year, you have been learning the great secret of these words – a secret that cannot be revealed here. It is very easy to learn this secret, but first you have to have light. Only Christ can give you this light and the conditions in which it can be developed. I can give you the seeds, but only Christ can give you the conditions for the seeds to grow. The love we feel does not depend on our strength and desires; it depends on the contact that we have with Christ. Some people ask, "Where is Christ?" They expect him to come down from heaven. Christ is already in the world and the world can hear him. He comes in two ways, for he has two faces. One face is kind, saying, "Peace be

---

[13] Jesus said, "The kingdom of heaven is like unto a grain of mustard seed, which a man took, and sowed in his field: which indeed is less than all seeds; but when it is grown, it is greater than the herbs, and becometh a tree, so that the birds of the heaven come and lodge in the branches thereof" (Matthew 13:31-32).

[14] "Another parable spake Jesus unto them: 'The kingdom of heaven is like unto leaven, which a woman took, and hid in three measures of meal, till it was all leavened'" (Matthew 13:33).

[15] "As Jesus spake, many believed on him. Jesus therefore said to those Jews which had believed him, 'If ye abide in my word, then are ye truly my disciples; and ye shall know the truth, and the truth shall make you free'" (John 8:30-32).

with you." [16] The other face scowls and comes with fire and guns. This scowling face is now calling out, "Gather up those who do not obey my teaching. Let them taste the bitterness of disobedience. They did not want to serve me. Let them taste all the bitterness of their actions. Everyone reaps what he or she has sown." [17]

Christ says, "If anyone serves me, let him or her follow me." You reply, "It is easy to follow Christ. We can follow him and call him Teacher." But he might respond, "You say that not because you want my teaching but because I fed you with bread and fish." [18] He will ask you, "Have you helped a sick person? Did you heal him or her?" You should not be looking to serve the Lord himself but to serve him by serving his 'little brothers'. [19] People want God to ensure the health of their families, to give them money and high positions in society. This is how

---

[16] After his resurrection, Jesus said this to his disciples three times (see John 20:19, 21, 26). "For unto us a child is born, unto us a son is given; and the government shall be upon his shoulder: and his name shall be called Wonderful, Counsellor, Mighty God, Everlasting Father, Prince of Peace" (Isaiah 9:6).

[17] Six months into the First World War, the Teacher said, "If we do not understand Christ's teaching, it will act destructively. If we had accepted his teaching two thousand years ago, we should have had the opposite results to those we have today. The present world is a lesson for humanity; it is the result of our having not known the laws which govern human life.

"When the Son of Man comes, people will ask him, 'Why did the Lord give us this evil?' Christ is coming and he will explain why: 'Two thousand years ago I came to prevent this, your present misery. I told you not to oppose evil.' You, however, make room for evil. If you had applied this law that Christ gave you, the present war would not have been permitted. Christ is saying that we are now experiencing the consequences of our not having accepted him two thousand years ago. We are paying for what happened then" (10/23 January 1915).

"Things which are more awful are coming. The causes of these events are not of the present but have been building for thousands of years, and now they are erupting. Human beings have not corrected themselves, which is why things have not changed and these terrible events have come. If all people were to pray now, these events would pass in a less severe form" (21 January/3 February 1915).

[18] When the multitude found Jesus on the day after the feeding of the five thousand, he said to them, "Ye seek me, not because ye saw signs, but because ye ate of the loaves, and were filled" (John 6:26).

[19] Jesus said, "When the Son of man shall come in his glory, then shall he sit on the throne of his glory: and before him shall be gathered all the nations: and he shall separate them one from another. And the King shall say unto the righteous on his right hand, 'Inasmuch as ye helped one of my brethren in need, even the least, ye did it unto me.' Then shall he say unto them on his left hand, 'Inasmuch as ye helped not one of the least in need, ye did it not unto me.' And these shall go away into eternal punishment: but the righteous into eternal life" (Matthew 25:31-32, 40, 45-46).

God has been 'served' for two thousand years. And God is now asking Europe a question: "What have you done for Me during all these past years?" And were Christ to appear, what would you say to him? Think about what you would be able tell him of what you have done for him....

I advise you to use the short time you have left to learn how to serve the Lord, so that when Christ comes he will not find you unprepared.[20] Do not think there is more time. There is no more time for this whole generation. All people – children, adults, priests and those in the government – need to learn how to serve the Lord. Christ wants all of you to serve him. Those who want to be his disciples should serve him in the broad sense of the word, which means to serve and uplift the spirits of those who suffer, those who are upset and those who are sad. There are despairing people who are asking themselves, "What will become of me?" You need to show them the path.

I will conclude this talk with a story that exemplifies your current predicament. A heavy sleeper was staying in a hotel in New York that caught fire during the night. When another guest tried to wake him up, telling him the hotel was on fire, the man pushed him away. Later, when the entire building was ablaze, the heavy sleeper could be seen on the roof calling out for help, but there was no one to help him anymore. I tell you, the hotel in which you are temporarily staying is burning. I advise you to save yourselves now, because otherwise there will come a time when you climb to the roof and call out for help, but there will be no one to help you. When you are told that the hotel is on fire, dress yourselves and leave. Everything that is burning will be ruined. All the things which have impeded human progress are going to be destroyed. The Lord will then build something good on the ruins. Do not think that life is ending. A new epoch, greater than any previous one, is coming. We may anticipate this bright future with joy.[21] We should not be

[20] Jesus said, "Be ye ready: for in an hour that ye think not the Son of man cometh. Who then is the faithful and wise servant, whom his lord hath set over his household, to give them their food in due season? Blessed is that servant, whom his lord when he cometh shall find so doing. Verily I say unto you, that he will set him over all that he hath" (Matthew 24:44-47).

[21] The Teacher also said, "Be sure that something very beautiful is coming into the world, something that humankind has never seen before" (some time between 1929 and 1942). "And he that sitteth on the throne said, 'Behold, I make all things new'" (Revelation 21:5).

afraid of the storms that are coming to disinfect and purify the world. We should thank God that they are coming. It is no good trying to prevent them, as they cannot be prevented. They will come, and pass, and good will come of it all.

As for us, we only need to ready ourselves for the coming of Christ.[22] For some he has already come,[23] and for others he is still coming.[24] When Christ comes and says, "If anyone serves me, let him or her follow me," we ought to follow him. Will you follow him or not? In following him you will find the ideal for yourselves as individuals, the ideal for your homes, the ideal for society, the ideal for your nation and the ideal for all humankind. This is the meaning of human life here on earth.

---

[22] The Teacher also said, "People all over the world, of all nations and races, are now forming the nucleus of a new race, with a new understanding" (1944). "In the future there will be many more people of the sixth race on the earth than there are at present. They will be the leaders on the earth. The spiritually wise people throughout the world will form the sixth race. You are heading, slowly but surely, towards becoming people of the sixth race" (1944).

[23] Jesus said, "There be some of them that stand here, which shall in no wise taste of death, till they see the Son of man coming in his kingdom" (Matthew 16:28). "And being asked by the Pharisees, when the kingdom of God cometh, Jesus answered them and said, 'The kingdom of God cometh not with observation: neither shall they say, 'Lo, here!' or, 'There!' for lo, the kingdom of God is within you'" (Luke 17:20-21).

[24] "Behold, he cometh with the clouds; and every eye shall see him" (Revelation 1:7).

The Importance of Small Things

Jesus said,

> See that ye despise not one of these little ones; for I say unto
> you, that in heaven their angels do always behold the face of
> my Father which is in heaven.[2]

In general, men and women aspire to great things, to great activities.
An inner weakness causes everybody to despise small things. If you are
given a penny, you say, "It is worthless. A large sum of money would
be acceptable, but a penny ... I am not a beggar!" If you are given a
walnut, you say, "How offensive! To have given me five or ten kilos
of walnuts would have been acceptable, but one walnut ... Are you
mocking me?" When we aspire to great things we are trying to become
acquainted with those in high positions: kings, prime ministers, direc-
tors, scientists and philosophers. Of those in lower positions, we say,
"They are ignorant, simple people." From one end of our lives to the
other we despise small things and seek only great ones. Christ, however, warned his disciples not to despise small things. But why? "Do not
despise them because you will offend the angels who serve them in
heaven. If you despise the little ones, you also despise those angels for
whom the little ones are like their children."

If you want to split a log, you begin by making small, sharp wedges. Using an axe, you make a crack in the log. You then drive the small
wedges into the crack to make space for larger wedges to be driven
in and split the log in two. If those initial wedges had been large and
blunt, how could they have been driven into the wood? Small things
can prise open the way for larger ones. In the world, the whole process

---

[1] Austria-Hungary had followed Germany in declaring war on Russia. In the days since
the last lecture, given a week before this one, Britain and France had declared war on Austria-Hungary. The great imperial powers were now fully set against each other: the Allies
of Britain, France and Russia against the Central Powers of Austria-Hungary and Germany.
[2] Matthew 18:10

of development begins with the small things that you despise – the whole progress of the universe is due to them. The farmer and plough produce great fruitfulness, but we should not forget the role of the countless small worms that also ploughed the field.

As we were brought up to despise small things, when we begin the Christian life we still carry the instincts of the wolf under our sheep-skins.[3] We still show our nails sometimes, as we have not entirely forgotten our old habits. Great thieves do not acquire their habit immediately. At first they would have stolen only a very small amount of money from their fathers, but with time they go on to take larger and larger amounts – and this really is a law. When we despise small causes we are blind to their great consequences. I can say that all our present unhappiness and misfortunes, both general and private, are due to the despising of small things in the past. This is why Christ told his disciples, "Do not despise these little ones." Now, who are these little ones? Someone might say, "They are our children." It is true, they are our children, but when we begin to apply Christ's law fully we will see there are also many other things that we should not despise.

"Do not despise these little ones." I will explain the hidden meaning of these words. A Hindu man gave his son a walnut and told him to examine it. The son broke the shell and ate the kernel. His father asked him, "What does a walnut contain?" "Nothing special," replied his son, "Just a few pleasant-tasting bits of kernel." The man asked his son, "Did you not find anything else in the walnut?" "No, nothing." "Son, a great power was hidden in that walnut. If you had not eaten it but instead had planted it in the earth, a great tree would have grown from it. You would have seen the greatness of this small thing which is the germ of the great thing." And when the Lord sends you a small thought, an apple seed, you say, "It is nothing," and throw it away. But the Lord says, "Ask yourself what kind of power it contains. Plant it, and you will see what grows from it." The truth is, it is because we have constantly despised small things that we have come to a state of saying that the world is bad. And we consider ourselves to be so intelligent....

Christ said, "Do not despise these small things and do not aspire

---

[3] Jesus said, "Beware of false prophets, which come to you in sheep's clothing, but inwardly are ravening wolves" (Matthew 7:15).

to great things. Instead, learn about the great power hidden in small things and use it. Small things will help you attain great things." Are your houses not built of microscopic grains? Our daily lives are built on the grain of wheat, fruit and other small things. Nourishment concerns not only the body but also the mind, for our joy and gladness in life come from our small thoughts and desires.[4]

Why ought we not to despise the little ones? Why should we not break the second divine commandment, which is to love our neighbours?[5] It is because each living being that has a useful relationship with another being should not be despised. This being could be a pigeon, a hen, a sheep, an ox, a horse or a donkey. There is a book for each animal in which the extent to which you used it on any particular day is written down. If an animal served you in some way for its entire life, how much do you owe it? One day you will be called to repay your debt to it. You will then say, "I do not remember this debt," but the Lord has it in writing.... We all are indebted to the small ones who have served us. Our present development, thoughts and desires are due to the small ones of whom Christ spoke. As we are indebted to them, we ought to love them and recognise that they have worked for us in the past. And now we should work for them.

I am often asked why the angels are interested in human beings. People want to know what we could have in common. The answer is that, once upon a time, when the angels were in the equivalent position to us human beings now on earth, we were in the same position in comparison with them as the animals are now in compared with us. We served the angels at that stage of their development. They therefore owe us a great deal, and the Lord requires them to pay us back now. The great angels do not despise us, their smaller siblings, because we

---

[4] The Teacher also said, "We should always begin with the smaller things and proceed towards the greater ones. Every one of our actions in the world is collective, because every one of us is connected with many spirits. Each of our thoughts comes with an obligation to the spirit who gave it to us, for it directs us in its realisation and we are in its hands. This is why we should not desire great things. It is permitted for us to receive the fulfilment of a great desire, but the spirit who gives it to us will demand that we pay for it. And if we are unable to pay, suffering, poverty, illness, and so on, will come to us.

"The most important thing now is to discern which of our desires and thoughts will be useful to realise, for these are the desires and thoughts that the Lord has already selected for us" (13/26 April 1914).

[5] See Matthew 22:35-40

worked for them in the past. You might have an ignorant servant, but you do not know what relationship your servant had to you in the past and why the Lord has put him or her in your home. Your connection with your servant did not originate in the present; he or she has been in your home on many occasions. You do not know this, but the Lord does. Perhaps your servant saved your life many times in previous incarnations. You should therefore be loving and benevolent to your servant. If you are, you will understand this great divine law, to love small things.

Love is not for great people, angels and saints; it is for the small things, for the little ones, for poor people, for fallen brother-beings. A mother develops this love for her child, according to the divine law which requires her to love her son or daughter. The mother loves her child because of an inner fire, for the Lord, incognito, has entered the child. You want to see the Lord, but when He comes to you in your child, you say, "Why did the Lord give me this child?" You call the Lord every day while also sending Him away from you. And you consider yourselves intelligent people.... This behaviour is not only confined to you; it is displayed by the whole world. The Lord tests your minds each day to see how much you love Him and to see to what extent you tell the truth.

A man sells a blind horse, telling the purchaser, "In the name of the Lord, I assure you this horse is not blind." The purchaser replies, "If you said that in the name of God, I believe you," and buys the horse. What will the Lord say to such a liar? He will say, "I do not know you, because you did not use My name for My glory but instead used it to deceive people, to commit crimes and to hide them." These small things create unhappiness. You have a blind horse that you want to sell in God's name, but you need to be careful, for you will not only be held responsible for what you do but also for its consequences.

Do you know what the blind horse is? It is your bodies. People speak against the body and punish it. They blame the body for everything, but the body is not guilty. Do not despise the body and do not mix the flesh with your desires, with your lusts. You need to be freed of your desires and lusts but not of the flesh, for to be freed of the flesh would mean to be removed from all of the thoughts and actions it may perform. Do not torture your bodies, these temples created by the Lord. You need to be very kind to your bodies, because you can only work properly when your bodies are healthy.[6]

When Christ said "their angels in heaven", he meant the intelligent beings who keep account of our actions. What we call the 'conscience' is the voices of the angels who live within us and make note of our every act, good or bad. They tell us, "You did well," or, "You did badly." If you offend somebody, his or her angel will tell you, "You behaved incorrectly." You apologise and make your excuses – "I am sorry, I was irritable and in a bad mood" – but these excuses have nothing to do with the divine law which says you should not despise the little ones.[7]

These small things sometimes cause great benefits or great damage. Many times in our lives small causes either contribute to our development or impede us. The causes which make us good or bad are never bad in themselves; the problem comes when things are used in a bad way. By analogy, if you put air in human lungs it will purify the blood and feel pleasant, but if you put air in the stomach it will cause pain. In each case the air has a different effect. Therefore, in saying that we should not despise little things, Christ meant that we should not despise any part of the wholeness of human life with which we are closely connected. For example, were I to ask you to tell me how your human hearts, minds and bodies are formed, could you explain it? In the beginning, when human beings first appeared on the earth, we were not large but microscopic. Under certain conditions we developed and became human beings who are a million times larger than we were at first. Originally human power was deposited in the germ from which we evolved. Thus, contemporary human thought has a great, divine foundation, and if it falls on good soil we will be reborn by it.[8] What we call 'rebirth'

---

[6] The Teacher also said, "It is said that the flesh is the devil, but if we can yoke the devil, he will be a very good worker for us. As contemporary people are unable to yoke the devil, he makes us work for him instead. He is teaching us, and we will become more intelligent in the future" (10/23 January 1915).

[7] The Teacher also said, "Angels help us, and they are all guided by a Spiritually Wise Power. Intelligent beings direct evolution. Christ came to tell us that these guiding powers are spiritually wise. He said, 'If you lose the salt that God has given you, what will happen to you?'" (15/28 January 1915).

[8] When explaining the parable of the sower, Jesus said, "The seed is the word of God. And that in the good ground, these are such as in an honest and good heart, having heard the word, hold it fast, and bring forth fruit with patience" (Luke 8:11, 15). And the Apostle Peter wrote, "Ye have been begotten again, not of corruptible seed, but of incorruptible,

exists as a law of the Spirit.[9] This is a divine inner process which uplifts and renews the human heart, the human mind, the human soul and the human spirit. It is a process of ascent, from below to above. It is through this divine aspiration that we build our upliftment and salvation. This is why all beings, from the greatest to the smallest, aspire to renew and uplift themselves. Youthful vitality is needed for the blossoming of the human soul.[10]

The reason we should be benevolent to small ones comes from the principle of not embittering the Lord. When someone becomes bitter because of our bad actions, it is not the person we embitter but the Lord who is within him or her. It is also true that when we do something good we help the Lord. When we help someone, his or her angel in heaven will offer us a favour in return. So, if we want to have friends in heaven, we have to serve the little ones. Then their 'parents', the angels in heaven, will receive us in their home and feed us and make us feel at home there. Favour for favour, love for love – this is the way of the world.

Now, do you know why Christ presented the thought about the little ones to his disciples? He did so because contempt is a state that you need to remove from your souls. For example, you meet a stranger and become contemptuous of him, thinking that he is lower than you. It is one thing if you only notice his ignorance and then help him, but if you despise him it is poisonous. Contempt gave birth to our hierarchical system, castes in which some are ennobled and others kept down, in which some are rich and some are poor. Were you to understand the relationship between things, you would see that you do not need to be ashamed if you are poor, for it is an assignment given to you to bear. Therefore you are small that you may grow, you are poor that you may become rich. These are two opposite poles between which development lies. The movement is always from great things towards smaller

through the word of God, which liveth and abideth" (1 Peter 1:23).

[9] Jesus said, "Except a man be born anew, he cannot see the kingdom of God. Except a man be born of water and the Spirit, he cannot enter into the kingdom of God. That which is born of flesh is flesh; and that which is born of the Spirit is spirit" (John 3:3, 5-6).

[10] "According to his mercy God saved us, through the washing of regeneration and renewing of the Holy Spirit, which he poured out upon us richly, through Jesus Christ our Saviour" (Titus 3:5-6). "They that are planted in the house of the Lord Shall flourish in the courts of our God. They shall still bring forth fruit in old age; They shall be full of sap and green" (Psalm 92:13-14).

things, which means to say that the Lord is always interested in small things. He does not engage Himself with great things.[11]

The Lord created the world, but managing the whole world does not give Him the same pleasure as engaging with children.[12] God works in this way: when He sees people making mistakes, He teaches them. Thus, by example, God shows us that we ought not to despise small things but instead should endure them and teach them. To do so is our rest and pleasure. A teacher feels pleasure when occupied with pupils and praises those who study well. The saints and priests occupy themselves with sinners to turn them to the Lord. And the task for all of us is to turn our attention to weak people and small things. When a man declares, "I am never able to rest," I understand him to be occupied with great things, with great thoughts. How can he rest when carrying a sack of gold too heavy for his strength: ten, twenty or fifty kilos of gold? He could rest were he to empty his pack of everything but one gold coin.[13] And now the Lord is coming to say to everybody, "Down with the baggage you carry! Free the world of it. Down with the weapons that destroy your minds and hearts! All of you should become as

[11] The Teacher also said, "Everyone should follow the teachings of Christ, no matter what position he or she holds in life. This is a commandment of Christ, and when we obey it the Lord will help us and uplift us, turning us from small people into great ones" (11/24 January 1915).

[12] "*Jesus* called to him a little child, and set him in the midst of them, and said unto the disciples, 'Verily I say unto you, Except ye turn, and become as little children, ye shall in no wise enter into the kingdom of heaven. Whosoever therefore shall humble himself as this little child, the same is the greatest in the kingdom of heaven'" (Matthew 18:2-4). "In that same hour he rejoiced in the Holy Spirit, and said, 'I thank thee, O Father, Lord of heaven and earth, that thou didst hide these things from the wise and understanding, and didst reveal them unto babes: yea, Father; for so it was well-pleasing in thy sight'" (Luke 10:21).

[13] "When *Jesus and his disciples* were come to Capernaum, they that received the half-shekel came to Peter, and said, 'Doth not your master pay the half-shekel?' He saith, 'Yea.' And when he came into the house, Jesus spake first to him, saying, 'What thinkest thou, Simon? the kings of the earth, from whom do they receive toll or tribute? from their sons, or from strangers?' And when he said, 'From strangers,' Jesus said unto him, 'Therefore the sons are free. But, lest we cause them to stumble, go thou to the sea, and cast a hook, and take up the fish that first cometh up; and when thou hast opened his mouth, thou shalt find a shekel: that take, and give unto them for me and thee'" (Matthew 17:24-27).

The Teacher said, "In the future people will cast out the nets of their personal occupations and catch the fish with the gold coin in its mouth so they can pay the tax collector – just as Peter cast out the net into the world to pay tax for Christ" (21 January/3 February 1915).

children and not despise the small things I have created."

The Lord wants to turn us human beings back towards the pure original state that people call 'wild', but which is not in fact wild in its essence. I want people to become wild, pure, in that way. Our Bulgarian word for 'wild' means 'pure' in Sanskrit. Let us become pure and come close to God, instead of becoming rude and evil. I would like the whole world to become wild, pure and noble as soon as possible. I would like people not to despise the small things that God loves. I would like people to place love, righteousness, wisdom, truth and power on the high place where they belong. Salvation is found in these things.

Immortality: Attuning Ourselves to the Lord

It is written in John's Gospel, of the day of Jesus's resurrection,

When it was evening, and when the doors were shut where the disciples were, for fear of the Jews, Jesus came and stood in the midst, and saith unto them, "Peace be unto you."[2]

Immortality is an ideal to which the soul constantly aspires. The human soul lives on earth to find the path to immortality. Immortality is regulated by a great divine law which people need to investigate and apply in each area of human life. With this in mind, we should constantly study to discover the conditions in which immortality can exist. A human being can become immortal and also lose immortality. Death and immortality are two states. In scientific language, immortality is a balance of the forces acting in nature. Death is the loss of this balance. Immortality has harmony within it, whereas death has division, discord and disharmony. People who desire immortality need to know what it contains.[3]

When you enter a concert hall to listen to an orchestra, you will see the violinists tuning their instruments before they play. Do you know how long it takes a violinist to become good enough to join an orchestra? It takes at least twelve years of learning to attain mastery of the instrument. We may say the violin has been the most perfect instrument since the great master Stradivari made it two centuries ago. It has not undergone any changes since then because it was already made almost to perfection.

I can compare the violin to the human soul, which also has four strings and a bow. The soul's strings are the four human temperaments,

---

[1] Unusually for a *Power and Life* lecture, this talk was not given on a Sunday. The day before this lecture, on 10/23 September, Japan declared war on Germany.

[2] John 20:19

[3] The Teacher also said, "Death is just decayed matter. After thousands of years we will return to the earth as more perfected beings. We cannot perfect ourselves in one lifetime" (15/28 January 1915).

and the human will can be considered as the bow. The violin's four strings are mi, la, re and sol, and the violinist knows how to attach them to the instrument and tune them. I said there were four human temperaments, which are choleric, phlegmatic, sanguine and melancholic. They correspond to the human soul, the human mind, the human heart and human life. There are these four main strings, and you need to know how to tighten and loosen them to get the right tones. For example, the heart and the mind need to be tuned to one and the same tone.

The four strings of a violin are made to produce four different tones, and there are four tones difference between each string. Therefore, when the whole violin is tuned there are four times four tones, sixteen in all – the steps upon which the strings are tuned. When the violinist has tuned the violin, he takes the bow and begins to play. When played, the violin and bow form the shape of a cross. The violin is the instrument that produces the most pleasant music, the tones of which are the closest to those of the human voice.

When you play your violin, your cross, you cry out and say, "Lord! Why did you give me this heavy cross?" I tell you, the Lord has given you a wonderful instrument, but you do not know how to tune it, which is why you carry it as a heavy burden on your back. Take it off your back and start tuning it in readiness for playing. When the Apostle Paul said, "I will glory in the cross,"[4] what do you think he meant? I see people carrying their crosses everywhere – in the churches and everywhere else – but I have not seen anybody 'playing' his or her cross. People in the concert hall applaud the violinists they see playing their crosses, but the audience does not realise that they themselves are also carrying crosses and need to become 'violinists' in life. The most important thing when playing the cross is keeping the rhythm. When the conductor's baton is raised, all the musicians need to pay attention to its direction. The movement of violin bows is pleasurable because the movements follow certain rules. When we arrive at the profound inner meaning of life, when we tune the strings (the mind, the heart, the soul and life itself) and start working the bow (the human will) as directed by the Spirit of the Great Conductor, we will create the most pleasant music in our lives.

---

[4] The Apostle Paul wrote, "Far be it from me to glory, save in the cross of our Lord Jesus Christ, through which the world hath been crucified unto me, and I unto the world" (Galatians 6:14).

Notice that the cross is a great blessing by which the Lord visits us on earth. The cross produces the greatest symphony of all, with music and singing, and it is called 'salvation' itself. When Christ suffered on the cross, the angels above in heaven were not crying but singing, and all the prisoners in hell rejoiced that their Saviour was coming.[5] At Christ's birth the angels sang in heaven to proclaim his coming,[6] to proclaim the creation of this divine instrument, the strings and the bow of our faith.[7] Contemporary Christians say, "How piteous we are! The earth is a valley of tears, and life is a meaningless burden." For foolish people, who neither know how to play their violins nor desire to, who do not know how to tune their strings, who do not follow the Great Conductor, life really is meaningless. But life has great meaning for those who can tune and play their violins.

Christ often comes to you and asks, "Do you know how to play your violin?" When I ask someone, "Do you know how to suffer?" what I mean is, "Do you know how to play your violin?" If you do not want to suffer, it means you do not want to play. Those who do not know how to play their violins are gloomy people; there is no hope in them. It is said, "A person who sings and plays an instrument does not think evil thoughts." A person who is suffering is somebody who is singing and

[5] "Unto each one of us was the grace given according to the measure of the gift of Christ. Wherefore he saith, 'When he ascended on high, he led captivity captive, And gave gifts unto men.' (Now this, 'He ascended,' what is it but that he also descended into the lower parts of the earth? He that descended is the same also that ascended far above all the heavens, that he might fill all things.)" (Ephesians 4:7-10). "Christ suffered for sins once, the righteous for the unrighteous, that he might bring us to God; being put to death in the flesh, but quickened in the spirit; in which he also went and preached unto the spirits in prison, which aforetime were disobedient, when the longsuffering of God waited in the days of Noah, while the ark was a preparing, wherein few, that is, eight souls, were saved through water" (1 Peter 3:18-20).

[6] "The angel said unto the shepherds, 'I bring you good tidings of great joy which shall be to all the people: for there is born to you this day in the city of David a Saviour, which is Christ the Lord.' And suddenly there was with the angel a multitude of the heavenly host praising God, and saying, 'Glory to God in the highest, And on earth peace among men in whom he is well pleased'" (Luke 2:10-11, 13-14).

[7] Jesus said, "I love the Father, and as the Father gave me commandment, even so I do" (John 14:31).

"Christ was a Son, yet learned obedience by the things which he suffered; and having been made perfect, he became unto all them that obey him the author of eternal salvation" (Hebrews 5:8-9). "As many as received him, to them gave he the right to become children of God, even to them that believe on his name" (John 1:12)

playing his or her violin in life, saving himself or herself. Will a violinist who plays well ever go hungry? Anyone who does not know how to play will end up begging. A person who knows how will sit down and play his or her violin and receive money from appreciative people. Whoever knows how to suffer, how to play the violin, will never go hungry.[8]

Now, when we have learnt this great law of 'singing and playing' or 'suffering' (these words have one and the same meaning to me), through suffering we will come to another great law, immortality. Everything in immortality is harmonious; there is no disharmony in it. Christ, who is coming to the earth, is coming to teach people how to sing and to play their violins.[9] He will teach you how to tune the strings of your souls. The string of the soul is mi, the highest string. The string of the mind is la. The string of the heart is re. The string of life is sol. This is the first lesson that Christ will give you.

Many times people ask themselves, "Why has the Lord given me this useless heart?" Is it your heart that is useless, or is it you? "Why has the Lord given me this foolish mind?" Is it your mind that is foolish, or is it you? "Why has the Lord given me this meaningless life?" Is your life meaningless, or is it you who does not know the meaning of your life? Sufferings are the laws by which the Lord acts for our development.[10]

We should sing and play our violins, which means to feel and think. To think means to play one's violin, and to feel means to sing. Were two neighbours now to tune and play their violins, things would be most pleasant between them. Over a year ago I visited a family in which everyone could play a musical instrument. Most people today do not know how to play a musical instrument; instead, when they have nothing to do, they start quarrelling. Life is meaningless for such people. Christ is saying, "Tune your violins, move your bows, learn how to

---

[8] Jesus said to his disciples, "I have meat to eat that ye know not. My meat is to do the will of him that sent me, and to accomplish his work" (John 4:32, 34).

[9] Jesus said, "Whosoever doth not bear his own cross, and come after me, cannot be my disciple" (Luke 14:27).

[10] The Teacher also said, "When you do not understand a feeling, it causes a depression in your heart. When you do not understand a thought, it causes a depression in your mind. When you come to understand a feeling or thought, you feel great joy and inner peace and calm. The feelings and thoughts that are understood in the divine world are the fruits that nourish the human spirit. Without these fruits the spirit is weakened, just as an undernourished human body weakens" (16 July 1939).

play. When you gather together in the evening, start playing music and singing with a good rhythm: one song, another song, and so on. Eat together and then again play music and sing. Afterwards go to bed, sleep and the next day go out to work in life again."[11]

Now you will say, "What is the connection between those last words and Christ's resurrection?" Christians discuss the question of the resurrection, and conclude by saying, "I will learn everything when I go to heaven." To think like that is human illogic. The relevant question is, what should we do in this world? We are very clever in this world but we are not clever about the next world. If you want to study at a university, can you just go there? No. First you need to go to kindergarten, then to primary school, then to secondary school, where you prepare yourself to receive higher learning, and then, finally, you may enter university. Why has the Lord sent us to the earth? What is the earth? It is a kindergarten and primary school from which we need to graduate. If we do not graduate here, how will we enter secondary school in the other world? When we go to the next world, do you think they will simply accept us in their school? Absolutely not.

The word 'resurrection' contains a great idea: it holds divine secrets. To have resurrected oneself is to have mastered all the elements and forces and all of one's thoughts, desires and actions. How can you resurrect yourselves without having mastered all of those things? How can you be ready for resurrection if a frog or a snake can frighten you? If you cannot endure the slightest sadness to serve God while on earth, how can you resurrect yourselves? If it takes twelve years of constant work, of between one to twelve hours each day, to learn how to play the violin, how much do we Christians need to work to learn Christ's resurrection? One weakness of the contemporary church is that it thinks everything can be received as a gift. The Lord could give us gifts of violins, strings and bows and find us music teachers and pay for our lessons, but we would still need to practise for ten hours daily to learn how to play – that part depends on us. Anyone who cannot practise like this is lazy, incapable and unworthy of the kingdom of Christ.

I am interpreting Christ's words to his disciples, "Peace be with you," in their broad sense. To have this peace, people need to be like an

---

[11] The Teacher composed many spiritual songs and melodies. Listening to music and communal singing are an important part of the Brotherhood life.

orchestra ready to play under the authority of the conductor's baton. When Christ says, "Peace be with you," everybody needs to be ready with his or her violin and bow, listening to the divine beat that constantly moves from one end of the world to the other. All people sing and play their violins before the Lord, who is observing them.

Whoever has not learnt to sing has a downward-curving mouth. Crying is singing with a downward-curving mouth. When we smile, the ends of our mouths rise, but they curve downwards when we cry. A person who cries is young. He or she has not yet learnt how to sing. To cry is to sing badly, which is a preparation for singing well. It is not bad to cry, because with time the crying will be transformed into beautiful singing. We need to be tolerant while somebody is learning to sing.

The new energy that Christ brought into the world with his resurrection shows humanity the path of the divine art of salvation.[12] This is why we need to study the Gospels profoundly. You say, "I do not understand this and that. This bit is useful and that bit it not. This bit is right and that bit is wrong." I ask you, what is right? Some people do not want to suffer, do not want to sing. Others do not want to work. What do they want then? Crying is an exercise, a transition to singing. The spade also has its beat. When you lift a spade and dig, you ought to think this to yourself, "The Master is watching me. I need to know how to work with this spade in a rhythmical way." If you are chopping wood, do it by all the rules of that art. We say, "This is meaningless. That is meaningless," but in that case, what does have meaning in life? The seemingly smallest works, to which we give the least significance, hold the greatest content.

Resurrection is a process that the Spirit of God performs in our lives, a great process through which God restores the original state of harmony. At present your ears are coarse and you do not have any musical ability, and you comprehend only the roughest tones. One day your ears will open, and you will begin to hear more and from greater distances than you are able to now. You will then notice that certain tones move through the whole universe – tones which objects such as springs, trees and leaves emit – and you will hear great music spreading from one end of the world to the other. Then you will understand

---

[12] Jesus said, "If I go away, I will send the Spirit of Truth unto you" (John 16:7). "I, if I be lifted up from the earth, will draw all men unto myself" (John 12:32).

the inner meaning of life. Christ, by his resurrection, wanted to bring you to this concert hall. He will pay for your tickets, but will you have good enough ears to understand the divine music when you enter the hall and hear the concert? This is the deep inner meaning of Christ's resurrection. This is life as the angels, from the lowest to the highest, experience it. This divine manifestation is everywhere in the world, but, as we cannot find this inner connection, we consider there to be no link between all events.

When you hear the words, "Peace be with you," you need to be ready for whatever the Conductor will direct you to play, be it to sing or to cry. If the Lord raises the baton and says, "Peace be with you," but you do not know how to play or to sing, He will stop you and teach you again and again, as many times as is necessary. You need to understand that artistry is attained with great patience and hard work lovingly done. There is no heaven for lazy people.[13] This is why the Lord says, "If you do not become as receptive as children, you will not enter the kingdom of heaven."[14]

Children have the desire to learn things, but adults say, "We do not need this. We do not need that," until their backs are the shape of question marks, their heads being attracted down towards the ground until they are buried in it. The Lord says, "These violins were not well made, so put them down and remake them." They will be remade and they will re-enter the world to begin studying again, for the Lord has decided that all people have to learn how to sing and to play their violins. The Lord does not want children in heaven who have neither wanted to learn how to sing nor to play their violins. The Apostle Paul said that when he was in the third heaven he heard something unutterable in human language.[15] He heard singing and music playing. In Revelation, John also said that he heard singing and music playing from heaven.[16]

I would like to leave you with this. Do you know which is the fundamental tone of your soul? Do you know how to tune your violin? You

---

[13] The Apostle Paul wrote, "We desire that each one of you may shew diligence unto the fulness of hope even to the end: that ye be not sluggish, but imitators of them who through faith and patience inherit the promises" (Hebrews 6:11-12).

[14] See Matthew 18:3; Mark 10:15

[15] See 2 Corinthians 12:2-4

[16] See Revelation 14:1-3

need to learn. When you get up each morning, tune your nervous system. If you are a little angry or upset, it shows your violin is not tuned. Stop and tune it. In doing so your sorrow will gradually disappear. How can you tune your nervous system? By praying. Prayer is tuning. Some people ask, "Why should I pray?" To tune your violin. When you have tuned your violin in this way, say to God, "My violin is tuned," and the Lord will tell you, "Begin today's work." Then peace will be with you and you will work well.

The first thing we should do in the morning is to pray – to tune our minds, our hearts, our souls and our lives – and go before God ready to work. Let us be grateful for our experiences and say, "Today I had a very good singing and violin lesson. When my Father returns He will be pleased with me." Christ has come to see how we sing and play our violins on earth. He is nailed to the cross, and today five hundred million people are singing and playing the cross. Christ gave us a teaching with which to make the perfect civilisation. Christianity is divine music and divine singing. Learn to sing and to play the cross. Tune your violins correctly, move your bows and listen to the commands of the Great Conductor. When you do this, the whole world will follow this divine law and be prepared for another life that is coming.[17]

---

[17] "The mind of the spirit is life and peace. And ye are in the spirit, if so be that the Spirit of God dwelleth in you" (Romans 8:6, 9).

"In the visions of God brought he me into the land of Israel, and set me down upon a very high mountain, whereon was as it were the frame of a city on the south. And he brought me to the gate, even the gate that looketh toward the east: and behold, the glory of the God of Israel came from the way of the east: and his voice was like the sound of many waters: and the earth shined with his glory. And he brought me unto the door of the house; and behold, waters issued out from under the threshold of the house eastward, for the forefront of the house was toward the east. Then said he unto me, 'These waters issue forth toward the eastern region. And by the river upon the bank thereof, on this side and on that side, shall grow every tree for meat, whose leaf shall not wither, neither shall the fruit thereof fail: it shall bring forth new fruit every month, because the waters thereof issue out of the sanctuary: and the fruit thereof shall be for meat, and the leaf thereof for healing'" (Ezekiel 40:2; 43:1-2; 47:1, 8, 12). "And I heard as it were the voice of a great multitude, and as the voice of many waters, saying, 'Hallelujah: for the Lord our God, the Almighty, reigneth'" (Revelation 19:6).

Knowing God Is Eternal Life

Jesus said,

This is life eternal, that they should know thee the only true God, and him whom thou didst send, even Jesus Christ. [1]

Life is the most natural and most powerful aspiration of the human soul, it is the wealth which the soul desires. This aspiration has existed for thousands and millions of years, and it is not only restricted to human beings: birds, fish and even plants also have it. The only difference is in the methods which the various beings use to obtain life. The human aspiration towards life is what concerns us, it being very important for our development. For example, you enrol at a music school not only to listen to music but also to study it. You are given a violin, strings and a bow and you are taught how to string and tune the instrument. You are given a teacher to teach you the main rules of music, and you start to exercise your mind, hands and fingers. In this way, over the course of time, you learn the artistry of the excellent violinist. By the same law of education, the Lord wants to teach us the methods, the way, to attain life.

Humankind had eternal life in the past, but we lost it. This loss was due to a simple reason, and now we aspire to correct the mistake that caused death. It was only when people began to feel the continual destruction of their souls, their minds, their hearts and their organisms, and of everything which builds, that they realised what they had lost.

It is written in Genesis that God put the first two human beings in Paradise and told them to cultivate it and use everything within it, only forbidding them to touch one tree, the tree of the knowledge of good and evil. They, however, wanted to make a small experiment in disobedience, with the woman trying it first. It is written that the serpent coiled around the tree of the knowledge of good and evil and began

[1] John 17:3. It is evident in the text that the Teacher actually read the whole chapter.

to speak to Eve, asking her a question: "How can it be that you, as the masters of Paradise, who use all the trees in Paradise, do not use the tree which hides a great secret?" Eve asked, "What secret?" The serpent answered, "If you eat from this tree you will have the knowledge of God, you will know why you live, you will know good and evil and you will be as powerful on earth as God." At that moment vanity was born in Eve. She said to herself, "To be like God is my great desire," and plucked the forbidden fruit and tasted it. Then she went to her husband to convince him to taste it as well, which he did. It is written in the Scriptures that as a result of these acts they both became naked, which means they saw themselves as naked.[2]

When does a person become naked? A rich, dying man left his son money, farmland and forests. After his father died the son began to live a life of leisure and pleasure. He squandered away all his money and property and became naked. He gradually became naked through excessive eating, drinking and laziness. This brings us to the thought that Adam and Eve ate of the forbidden fruit for a long time and gradually pawned away Paradise. Finally the Lord said to them, "What are you pawning? Is it your own property? Get out of here! From now on you will earn your bread with labour, so that you learn the great law of valuing the life I have given you."[3]

A person can easily become poor. An American man who inherited a vast fortune from his father had a weakness for flowers. He started to collect different flowers from all over the world. He even sent special expeditions off to gather rare flowers. After several decades he had spent all of his money, and when he died the community had to finance his burial.

But you will ask, "How does somebody lose his or her life?" I will tell you. Imagine that you once had a healthy, good son who studied and graduated abroad. The idea grew in his mind to become a great, glorified man by attaining the Cross of Saint George. He said, "I will go to war and get my glory." He was hit by a bullet and received his glory, but he also died.[4] Adam and Eve wanted the same cross, so the Lord sent them off to the battlefield. They left Paradise to conquer the world, but in doing so they lost eternal life.

[2] See Genesis 2:15-17, 25–3:12

[3] See Genesis 3:17-24

[4] The Cross of Saint George was a Russian military medal.

Now, let us return to the thought of Christ. We know how to spend money and we know how to lose our lives, but we do not know how to gain life. Christ came to teach us how to regain the lost life, which is why he told us, "I am the life."[5] What is the difference between life and other forces? Life is a force that builds, uplifts, connects, integrates and gives joy and gladness to the human soul. There are three important words in the third verse of the Chapter that I read to you: "life", "know" and "God". Life is what we aspire to. Knowing is the method by which we achieve our aim. God is the medium, or the conditions, from which we may draw life.[6]

There are two ways I can teach you about eternal life. I could talk about it, presenting it from its philosophical side and explaining its biological origin and its physiological and psychological manifestation, but that would be of no use to you. It would be like explaining how bread is made to a hungry man instead of offering him bread to eat. The man would interrupt, saying, "I am hungry. Give me something to eat. I do not care how bread is made. All I want is to feed myself. After I have eaten I will be able to listen to those things." We should now say to the philosopher, "We do not want to know from what elements life is made, from where it originates. We want to feed ourselves, to eat of eternal life. We can discuss those things with you afterwards. Right now we want to be saved from death." I think that is the best approach.

How can you attain eternal life? You have yet to become truly alive, although you think you are really living. Actually, you do have life, but it is not wholly in your possession; it is pawned. One day the one to whom you are indebted will come along, hand you your bills, put you in prison and take your life. What does burial mean? It means to be put down in a prison cell to pay for one's debts. Everyone who seeks the Cross of Saint George instead of paying his or her debts will be buried in the ground, first to pay off the debts and then to learn how to gain life. People cry when someone close to them dies, but crying cannot save the deceased. The one who has something to collect from us will not have mercy, no matter how much we cry. The debt collector will say, "Pay your debts!"

It is now necessary to learn the fundamental law of life and free

[5] See John 14:6
[6] "Only God hath immortality" (1 Timothy 6:16).

ourselves from death. I will show you how with a story. During the Turkish occupation of Bulgaria a Turkish man forcibly took control of a whole region and its population. He ruled them with violence and fear, and no one dared fight him. The people prayed to God to save them from this evil situation. One day a young shepherd was passing through the region. He had good, neat clothing and carried a shepherd's crook. When he entered the forest he was confronted by the Turkish tyrant, who said, "Stop! Who are you? And who gave you permission to pass this way?" "I am a shepherd passing through with my flock." "Throw away your crook!" commanded the tyrant. The shepherd replied, "But I have brought you this crook as a gift – it is full of gold.[7] My grandmother told me that my grandfather brought the crook from Paradise. It has never lied to me and it directs me on my way." "What foolish words," said the Turkish man, drawing his sword. "I will tell you from which 'paradise' it came when I stick your head on it!" But the brave shepherd chopped the Turkish man's sword in half with the first stroke of his crook. With the second stroke he chopped off his right arm. With the third he chopped off his left leg, and the tyrant fell to the ground. "I told you my crook comes from Paradise and it always tells the truth. For the time being the three lessons it has taught you are sufficient. God always makes you pay properly, though. My crook tells me that the next time I pass here I will give you three more lessons and chop off your head." "I believe your crook," said the Turkish man. "I will apply what it has taught me. Can I oppose this crook of truth from Paradise? From now on the population in this region is to be free. It is the will of Allah."

I have told this poetic story to explain a truth in the form of a folk tale. The population in the story represents us human beings, and the Turkish man represents death. And is there any place in the world where this Turkish man does not enter? There is no home he has not visited – what are the crosses and graves telling us? Everybody believes the Turkish man to be invincible. If anyone says it is possible to be freed from him, people always reply, "You are crazy. It is impossible." But we only need one young shepherd to disprove the false theory of the Turkish man's invincibility with three strokes of his crook of truth from Paradise. However,

[7] In the past, to hide and protect their wealth when travelling, Bulgarians would hollow out an object and fill it with their gold.

willpower and courage are required for such a great fight.[8]

Someone will say, "I do not see any deep meaning in that simple tale." You are correct from your point of view, because you have not made the effort to interpret it. But what would you say if you realised that the following truths were hidden in the story? The young shepherd represents the spiritually wise, morally untainted human being. His grandmother represents divine love, which constantly tells our souls that freedom is a human right. His grandfather represents divine wisdom, which brings the crook, which symbolises the divine laws, and entrusts it to the hands of this spiritually wise being so that he can protect his soul from slavery. The sword represents the natural forces that oppose human progress. The right arm is the tainted human will. The left leg is the tainted human heart. We may avoid destructive actions by directing these forces in a particular way. It is from this point of view that the words, "Whoever conquers to the end will be saved," need to be understood.[9] Conquering is necessary for attaining life, and Christ's words, "When a stronger man enters a strong man's home, he can take his possessions only after he has tied the strong man up," have the same meaning.[10] We need to learn the laws governing the process of obtaining life.

A weaver follows the entire process of weaving. The artist who wants to paint a valuable painting needs to understand the laws of that art, to know how colours combine and to be a master with the brush. The sculptor who wants to make a great statue needs to be a master with the hammer and chisel. Whoever builds a house needs to know how to do so. The doctor who wants to be useful and respected needs to know the elements used to heal the sick. The teacher needs to know the human soul and human mind very well, and should behave in accordance with that knowledge. A Christian who wants to obtain eternal life needs to know the foundation of this life and apply the laws by which it is

[8] Behind the story is the idea of Jesus as the good shepherd who conquered death. Jesus said, "I am the good shepherd: the good shepherd layeth down his life for the sheep. Therefore doth the Father love me, because I lay down my life, that I may take it again. No one taketh it away from me, but I lay it down of myself. I have power to lay it down, and I have power to take it again. This commandment received I from my Father" (John 10:11, 17-18).

[9] Jesus said to his twelve disciples, "He that endureth to the end, the same shall be saved" (Matthew 10:22).

[10] See Matthew 12:29

obtained. Life can be compared to the material that needs to be woven, made into clothing and worn. Life is the first piece of clothing in which the human spirit should be wrapped. When we waste this material we become outwardly naked. This nakedness is called moral degradation.[11]

Christ put it clearly, saying, "It is life eternal to know God." 'To know God' is the secret of obtaining eternal life. But you will ask me, "Do we not know God?" If you knew God in the way that Christ spoke of it, you would not die. But you will respond, "Who does not die?" Death is the fact that disproves a person's claim to know God. You will point out that Christ also died. No, he did not die in that he resurrected and showed himself to his beloved ones.[12] When you die, will you resurrect and appear to your beloved ones? This is an important question for you.

You may have a philosopher's idea of God, a pantheist's, a material-ist's or a churchgoer's, but none of them will bring you eternal life, the eternal genesis, the eternal blessing to which we aspire, our purpose. Instead of receiving eternal life, you will be like an ill woman who exposes her body to the moonlight in the expectation of being warmed for the good of her health; or the hungry man who only observes bread from a distance; or a thirsty woman who believes she is drinking pure water when it is actually far off upstream. I tell you, those things are not knowledge; they are ideas of the external shadow of things. When you obtain true 'knowing of God', eternal life will be realised in your soul. Then you will face death like the young shepherd, and afterwards there will be no gravestone newly inscribed: "Here lies a young, green man who was taken by death."[13]

I will return to our topic and give further analogies. Each living being wants an environment and the conditions in which it can live. Plants need soil, moisture and light. Fish need water. Birds, mammals and human beings need air. The external human senses also have their environments. The environment of the human eye is light, for the ear it

[11] Jesus said, "He that overcometh shall be arrayed in white garments. I counsel thee to buy of me white garments, that thou mayest clothe thyself, and that the shame of thy nakedness be not made manifest" (Revelation 3:5, 18).

[12] The Apostle Peter said, "God raised Jesus up, having loosed the pangs of death: because it was not possible that he should be holden of it" (Acts 2:24).

[13] The Teacher also said, "The people of the sixth race will not die. When the time comes for them to leave the earth, they will simply dematerialise and become invisible. They will not need graves. Graveyards will remain for others, who are not of the sixth race" (1944).

is sound, for the nose it is smell – flowers constantly emit etheric vibrations that nourish the sense of smell. Food, which is all the organic substances, the juices, which flow and deliver life, is the environment of the taste.

If we climb higher, we will further observe how this great law functions. The environment in which our hearts can live is our desires. The environment in which the human mind can live and develop is human thought. Without thoughts the human mind atrophies, as does the human heart without desires. The environment for the human will is the force of action, the activities and energy of work. Without work the human will atrophies. By the same law, the environment for the human soul is God. This is why it is written in the Scriptures, "In Him we live, move and exist." [14] Through God the soul can reacquire its original life, in which it is dressed in immortality. God, therefore, is an inner environment, an inner condition, an inner power from which we have to constantly draw. Our eyes are connected with the light. Our lungs are connected with the air. Our stomachs are connected to our mouths so that we can feed ourselves. In the same way, the heart and mind are two tools through which the soul can receive life. The heart and mind are preparatory environments for the Divine Environment, the Universal Divine Consciousness in which our souls are immersed. It is a fact that when a being loses its connection to its environment it is exposed to death. It does not matter whether the being is a plant, a fish, a bird, a mammal or a human being – this law applies itself equally. Christ, who understood this law profoundly, insisted that it is necessary to know God, or, to put it in scientific language, that it is necessary for us to be connected with our environment.

We say, "We will know God when we go to the next world." But the other world is God! People who think that, when they have died, they will freely be able to go to God in the other world, are like a criminal son who, when he was being led to jail, said, "I am going to see my father." How will he be able to see his father when he is in prison? If you behave like a criminal son, you will not go to your Heavenly Father in the next world. Instead, you will be sent to a correctional centre. To be able to go to your Heavenly Father in the other world, you first

[14] See Acts 17:28

have to have conquered death, to have escaped the prison and become free. That is why Christ said, "I am the door. Whoever enters and exits through me will find pasture."[15]

Tell me, have you entered and exited through this door? If so, how did you do it? Were I to ask you to tell me about the house of a friend of yours, you would say, "The garden gate faces west. The front door faces south." You would then go on to describe the house's size and colour, and so on. Churchgoers say, "Christ is the door." If Christ is the door, tell us of what it is made? Is it made of wood or iron, of gold or silver, of precious stones or something else? What are its hinges, and to what kind of base is it fixed? You will say, "It is symbolic." Good, then interpret this symbolic door, telling us what Christ is and explaining in what sense he is a door. "Christ saved us." How did he save us? "He died for us." Can a dead person save you? "But he rose again." How did he rise again? "By the divine life." That is correct, and it means that Christ was connected with and knew God, and through this knowing of God he conquered death, resurrected and comes to our souls.

First Christ was imprisoned here with us for thirty-three years, during which time he taught us how to escape this prison, how to conquer death and evil. Since then Christ has been outside the prison, in the other world with the Father of Light; but he is now coming here to visit our minds and hearts, and the world will see him in the crook of truth's blows to the sword, the arm and the leg. He will destroy all false teachings. What are the false teachings? They are those elements, thoughts, desires and actions that destroy human happiness and the human mind and the human heart and the human soul and the human spirit, which everywhere bring death, anarchy and slavery and which paralyse our lives. What is the teaching of life? It is to learn about those elements that bring happiness, blessings, goodness and enlightenment and which uplift the human spirit and the human heart, bringing the love of all things to the heart. The Living Christ is in all these things.[16] This is why he said, "To receive the fundamental elements that bring you eternal life, you need to know God." You ought to fight in the world, but with whom? With death. But you have to understand this art correctly, otherwise mistakes will follow you unceasingly.

[15] See John 10:9

[16] Peter said to Jesus, "Thou art the Christ, the Son of the living God" (Matthew 16:16).

A Bulgarian woman sent her son to study in Germany and gave him sufficient money to live on, although it did not seem enough to him. One day he wrote to his mother asking for a much larger monthly allowance. She wrote back that she could not afford to give him more money, and therefore he needed to find some work to supplement his allowance. Her son replied, "If you do not send more money, I will kill myself!" To his threat she responded thus: "Commit suicide and I will spit on your grave! I do not want a cowardly son who does not want to work, who is frightened of facing the struggle of life and instead prefers to live as a feeble old man." That is not the exact wording of the story, but the sense is correct. Anyway, the son came to his senses. The mother's telegram is now framed, and her son points to it and says, "It saved me." Similarly, in the world we need to struggle against the elements of death. And how will we conquer death? There is only one way, which is to know God, the Genesis of Life.

To acquire life we have to have knowledge. To acquire knowledge we have to have fresh minds that are receptive and flexible. Once you are in a condition to be constantly receiving good, sublime thoughts in your mind – in the same way as you are in a condition to be constantly breathing – you will be on the path to the eternal life you seek. If you make the following small experiment each day, you will train your will: when bad thoughts and desires come to you, send them away. Only accept good thoughts and desires. Do this for a year and you will produce miracles for yourselves; there will be no obstacle which you cannot subordinate to the efforts of your wills. Now, whoever would like to attain immortality has to have a strong will in the true meaning of the word. You say, "I cannot do it." Whoever 'cannot do it' will be sent to prison – for so it is written in the divine book.[17] When you say, "I cannot attain immortality," God says, "Imprison that man. I will teach him that he can." There is no other means of escaping the prison. This is our fate.

If we want to unite with God, to live with Him and attain eternal

[17] "I saw a great white throne, and him that sat upon it. And I saw the dead standing before the throne; and books were opened: and another book was opened, which is the book of life: and the dead were judged out of the things which were written in the books, according to their works. And if any was not found written in the book of life, he was cast into the lake of fire" (Revelation 20:11-12, 15).

life, we absolutely have to serve Him.[18] If we are not prepared to serve God, we will still be servants, but to whom? To the devil, the prince of this world who will yoke us three times daily. The devil will take his whip to you and command, "On with you! You do not want to work for the Lord, so now you have to take a whipping from me."[19] Eventually you will say, "There is nothing else for it, I have to do my real work." Of course you will come to this conclusion, for otherwise you will continue to feel the whip. These are the only two paths.[20] Someone says, "I do not want to serve the Lord." If you do not want to serve the Lord, you will have another lord. "But I want to be free!" You are deceiving yourself; there is no freedom in this world. Only the person who is united with God is free. Whoever has a fully conscious life is free. If you beat up someone today, tomorrow someone else will beat you up, and so on and so on, and that is not freedom.

Christ said, "You need to come to understand the fundamental principle of knowing God." I want you to apply what I tell you. You go to church, stand up, cross your hands, close your eyes, raise your consciousness and pray to God. Then you leave and forget it all. People say, "That man goes to church and believes in God but then lives differently in the world outside." This means that man has not found the path of salvation. It is said, "Christ came and saved us." Christ saves people who are intelligent and good; he never saves people who are bad and foolish. Christ saves intelligent, good people who obey and apply his teaching. Initially Christ teaches us how to work for ourselves. He says, "I am the way, the truth and the life."[21] 'The way' is a method. 'The

---

[18] Jesus said, "I and the Father are one" (John 10:30). "And I know that his commandment is life eternal: the things therefore which I speak, even as the Father hath said unto me, so I speak" (John 12:50). "If a man love me, he will keep my word: and my Father will love him, and we will come unto him, and make our abode with him" (John 14:23). "If a man keep my word, he shall never see death" (John 8:51).

[19] Jesus said, "No man can serve two masters: for either he will hate the one, and love the other; or else he will hold to one, and despise the other" (Matthew 6:24). "My kingdom is not of this world" (John 18:36). "The prince of the world hath nothing in me" (John 14:30).

[20] Jesus said, "Enter ye in by the narrow gate: for wide is the gate, and broad is the way, that leadeth to destruction, and many be they that enter in thereby. For narrow is the gate, and straightened the way, that leadeth unto life, and few be they that find it" (Matthew 7:13-14).

[21] See John 14:6

truth' is your mind, with which you should come to know how to discern which things are good and which things are bad. 'The life' is the artistry with which you know how to make fabric and turn it into the clothing you wear.

Make a small experiment with yourselves. If you are ill, irritable or in a bad mood and there is also a problem with your children, let the children be, do not worry about them but think a little about yourself, for there are deep reasons for your condition. If you say to me, "I am thirsty," I will tell you, "So drink." "I am hungry." "So eat." "But how will I drink? There is no glass." "Kneel beside this mountain spring. It can quench your thirst." "I do not want to kneel!" "Kneel or remain thirsty." "But my new trousers will be ruined." "If you want to keep your trousers clean, you will stay thirsty. It is better to receive the benefit of the water and dirty your trousers." "I am hungry," you say. "So come with me to a room where I have bread for you." We arrive in the room and I ask you to sit on the floor and eat. But you tell me, "I am not used to eating like this. I need a knife, a fork and a plate." "Forget about those things," I say. "Take this bread, break it with your hands and eat." You reply, "But people will see me! It is shameful!" "If you are ashamed, you will remain hungry. If you are ashamed to go to school with a primer, you will remain ignorant."

When a person is called to follow Christ, she should not answer, "But what will people say?" Instead, she should come close to Christ and apply his teaching. Then she will become strong. The devil only threatens people if they are weak. I do not want you to be weak. I want you to feed yourselves. How? By feeding your minds and your hearts. You will not attain eternal life by knowing how to feed only your bodies. To obtain eternal life you also need to know how to feed your mind, your heart, your soul and your spirit. This is a method of nourishment according to the profound teaching of Christ.[22] I would title this morning's lecture, "Learning How to Nourish Ourselves." So far you have only learnt how to chew, an art you have mastered well.

---

[22] Jesus said, "My meat is to do the will of him that sent me, and to accomplish his work" (John 4:34). "Behold, I stand at the door and knock: if any man hear my voice and open the door, I will come in to him, and will sup with him, and he with me" (Revelation 3:20). "Work not for the meat which perisheth, but for the meat which abideth unto eternal life, which the Son of man shall give unto you" (John 6:27).

Now continue from there. Nourish your hearts, nourish your minds and nourish your spirits. When you can feed yourselves in these ways, I will tell you that you are most intelligent and have embodied Christ's teaching, and that you will attain eternal life because you know how to connect yourselves with God.

I have experimented with this and understood it, and I place it before you to do the same. The only thing impeding you is your hesitancy and philosophising. Philosophising is useless in matters of practical living. If you ask a woman to teach you how to spin and weave wool, you would not be able to do it properly right away. However, were you to keep at it, you would gradually learn how, despite any obstacles that might arise. Let your first experiment be like this: try to keep your mind free for a minute or two and do not think of the ordinary things of daily life. You say, "I have stopped thinking. I am thinking of nothing," and yet your grandmother, children and possessions are going through your mind – and you think you are free. Your minds are chaotic. Finally say, "I want to be free. Today I will think of the Lord, the Great Love in life. Everyone else go out into the garden and leave me alone, because I have very important work to do." Try it for only two minutes at first. If your children come to you quarrelling and crying, leave them to it. Forget everything else for two minutes and dedicate this small amount of time only to the Lord of Love. This is the smallest art, and you will say, "That is simple." Actually, it is not so easy. The next time try it for five minutes, then for ten.

First of all Christ wants you to free your hearts of the things that pollute your sanctuaries. I can see your hatred and hypocrisy. How do those things benefit you? Not at all. Remove them and put yourself in order. Then call your priest: "Come, servant of the Living God, put on your vestment and take the censer and offer up your incense to God." Call the bishop of your life. But who is this bishop? Your bishop is your spirit. Call your choir. Who are your choristers? They are your good feelings and desires. Say, "Come, let us sing and serve the Lord in this temple." Then Christ will come to you, and when he sees that your temple is free of those who sell pigeons and other such things,[23] he

[23] "Jesus entered into the temple of God, and cast out all them that sold and bought in the temple, and overthrew the tables of the money-changers, and the seats of them that sold the doves; and he saith unto them, 'It is written, 'My house shall be called a house of

will say, "Peace be with you. The day of your resurrection has come. Today you will be with me in Paradise." Do you know the profound meaning of the words spoken by the criminal who was crucified on the right hand side of Jesus? "Lord, remember me in your Kingdom." He was a man who had driven away all the vermin from himself with a whip, which is why Jesus assured him, "Today you will be with me in Paradise."[24] So drive away all the vermin from yourselves. What did the other criminal, the one crucified on the left hand side of Christ, say? "If you truly are the Son of God, descend from the cross and free us."[25] How could Jesus free this man when he had not driven away all the vermin from himself, when he was still a slave to his egotism?

I think you understand me. The meaning of my words is clear. I want to speak to you perhaps as you have never been spoken to before. The first priority is for you to learn to love the Lord. This love will unite you with Him. You have thousands of opportunities to connect with the Lord and make your lives happy ones. And when you have united with the Lord and entered eternal life, everything will be transformed in you and all things will take their correct places. So make it your task first to give two minutes, and then five minutes, to driving away alien thoughts from yourselves. And when you have made this time to be alone, enter a state of deep contemplation and think over the following great problems. "Why am I here on earth?" "Why am I not in a good mood?" "Why are my thoughts and my heart not noble?" "Why do I not have the willpower to solve a certain problem?" And Christ will answer you, "I am the way, the truth and the life," which means, "When you have driven everything bad away and accepted me in yourself, when you have come to know God, my Father, who lives in me and who has given me eternal life, He will also give the same life to you." We have to accept Christ within ourselves if we want to connect ourselves with God. Christianity will be meaningful only when we have learnt how to conquer this life and have attained another life which is really valuable for us; because it is a life that brings knowledge, power, nobility of feeling and happiness; it is a life that gives us the power of the Spirit with which to conquer everything. Let the fear of poverty in

prayer,' but ye make it a den of robbers'" (Matthew 21:12-13).

[24] See Luke 23:33, 39-43

[25] See Luke 23:39

the world end. All these things are Christ's teaching.

You are afraid of death. Instead, face it, saying, "I will fight you!" Perhaps you will be threatened with imprisonment. If so, tell yourself, "Through the power of the One True God, who lives inside me, I will fight against the one who brings death." The whole world might turn against you, wanting to frighten you, but do not be frightened. A frightened person cannot become a citizen of the kingdom of God. You are now battling in the world, and when you go to heaven you will be awarded the true Cross of Saint George, which is a living cross. Afterwards, when you return to the earth for your next incarnation, Christ will say to you, "Come, good servant who has fought on the field of battle." Human beings have suffered for thousands of years, but they have yet to suffer for humanity itself, for righteousness. Until now people have suffered only for themselves, for possessions. At last people should suffer for Christ. You will find life in this suffering, which is why the Apostle Paul said, "If we suffer like Christ we will be like him in the resurrection."[26] For as God resurrected Christ, so He will resurrect us when we live for Him. Let us allow the Spirit of Christ to incarnate in us, and let us come to know the true God and attain eternal life. Then we will go out and work for our younger brothers and sisters, that they may also learn the art of attaining the wealth of this divine life.

---

[26] "They that are of Christ Jesus have crucified the flesh with the passions and the lusts thereof" (Galatians 5:24). "If we have become united with Christ by the likeness of his death, we shall be also by the likeness of his resurrection" (Romans 6:5).

The Value of Human Life

It is written in Matthew's Gospel,

> Jesus went into the synagogue: and behold, a man having
> a withered hand. And the Pharisees asked him, saying, "Is it
> lawful to heal on the sabbath day?" that they might accuse
> him. And he said unto them, "What man shall there be of
> you, that shall have one sheep, and if this fall into a pit on the
> sabbath day, will he not lay hold on it, and lift it out? How
> much then is a man of more value than a sheep! Wherefore
> it is lawful to do good on the sabbath day." Then saith he to
> the man, "Stretch forth thy hand." And he stretched it forth;
> and it was restored whole, as the other.[1]

We ought to thank the Pharisees for provoking Christ into speaking
this great truth: "How much more valuable is a human being than a
sheep!" for otherwise he would not have said it. According to the Pharisees, and the law of Moses, the Sabbath was a day of rest, of inactivity.[2]
A Bulgarian man does not work on Sunday. Instead, he puts on his best
clothes and goes to the tavern, where he orders half a litre of wine. He
says, "Today is Sunday. For six days we must work, and on the seventh
we should drink and have a good time." The Jews saw Saturday, the
Sabbath, purely as a day of rest. Therefore, when Christ healed a man's
hand on the Sabbath, the Pharisees criticised him for breaking the law.
In response, Christ showed them up by making a comparison: "If one
of your sheep fell into a pit on the Sabbath, you would pull it out,
would you not? Of course, you would do it not out of love for your
sheep but because your material interests were threatened."

If you ought to do something good for a person in need, you will
arrive at a great problem caused by limited human understanding, as
did the Pharisees who said, "You must not heal people on the Sabbath!"

[1] Matthew 12:9-13. The original Bulgarian publication only quoted verse 12.

[2] One of the Ten Commandments is to keep the Sabbath as a holy day of rest (see Exodus
20:8-11).

Christ had the answer: "Surely a human being is of far more value than a sheep!" In other words, surely a spiritually wise being is far higher than a spiritually unwise being. If you spend much time each day cooking to satisfy the insistent bleating of your stomachs, why, when it comes to uplifting the thoughts and heart of a spiritually wise human being, do you say, "This cannot be done on the Sabbath! There is another time for it. Let us wait until then." Christ, however, said, "Just as you would take care of one of your sheep, so I, according to the same law, should take care of a spiritually wise being. Just as you would go and free your sheep from the pit, I have come to the earth to liberate spiritually wise beings, to rescue them from the 'pit'."

The man in the synagogue had a paralysed hand. Do you know what a paralysed hand signifies? It means the man's will was paralysed. Christ said, "I want to restore his will so that he can act freely and apply his thoughts and feelings, because this man was sent to the earth to work. No matter whether it be a Monday, a Tuesday, a Wednesday or a Saturday, I will fulfil my mission." Whatever work does not break the divine law may be performed by anyone at any time, because rest is intended for the body alone and not for the spirit. Only lazy people rest on the earth, and they rest every day. Hardworking people say, "We will rest only when Christ has returned to the earth." That is how a Christian needs to understand work.

There is a fundamental principle that we need to keep in mind: there are certain laws we need to understand, but it is not enough only to understand them; they have to be applied in our lives. Without application, each teaching, each religion, no matter what it might be, is fruitless. It is not enough for a plant to grow, develop, blossom and bear fruit; the fruit needs to ripen. The purpose of the plant is only achieved when the fruit has ripened. By the same law, a person can be born, grow, develop and bear fruit, but if the fruit does not ripen, his or her life is fruitless. Christ freed the man's hand, which means he restored the man's willpower.

If you read further into this chapter, you will find that a man who was possessed by a demon, another who was blind and another who was dumb were brought to Jesus, who healed them.[3] There is a con-

---

[3] See Matthew 12:22. The Bulgarian and English Bibles describe only one man with all three afflictions.

nection between this miraculous healing and Jesus saying that a human being is higher than a sheep. You might say such miracles only happened in the time of Christ, but they also happen in our time as well.[4] Who are the possessed, blind and dumb ones? They exist inside you! Right now you all look like angels: how beautiful and pious you are. Were a demon to enter any of you, however, there would be weeping and gnashing of teeth.…[5] You, spiritually wise people, should stretch out your hands and heal those who are possessed by demons, saying, "Peace be with you." Just as the demon left the man at Christ's words, so you can also say the same words and heal a sick person. Animals can also be possessed. If your horse begins to kick out when there are children around, what do you do? You bridle the horse. The bridle is a law. Each spiritually unwise being should be bridled.

People need to be healed of their blindness. You protest, "But I am not blind!" I believe that you are not blind, but many people are. An illiterate woman was asked to read something. Ashamed of her illiteracy, she answered, "I cannot read it because I am blind." Can you open this woman's eyes? Open them! Teachers are people who open the eyes of the blind – they perform miracles. If you send your children to teachers, they should return them with open eyes in ten to fifteen years' time. Some people are deaf, and you should clear their ears so that they can hear and comprehend. This is easy to do, because human beings have spiritual wisdom, which is why Christ said, "Surely a human being is much higher than a sheep!" Of what does a sheep's life consist? It consists of grazing, growing wool on its back, producing milk and bleating. Some people today are like sheep: they constantly

[4] There are many stories of the Teacher miraculously healing people. The Bulgarian translator, Maria Mitovska, was a friend of an older disciple called Nadezhda, who gave her one such account first-hand.

One day, when Nadezhda was with friends on Vitosha Mountain, a snake bit her. They brought her back to her home in Izgrev (the Brotherhood community near Sofia) and laid her down on her bed, where she lost consciousness. Fearing that she was near to death, her brother went to find the Teacher for help. As he ran down the street towards the Teacher's rooms (which were beside the Brotherhood lecture hall), he saw the Teacher running towards him, heading for their home, having perceived what was happening. Once he was with Nadezhda, the Teacher put his hands on top of her head and she immediately opened her eyes, healed. Afterwards she slept for a long time, before waking up in normal health.

[5] Jesus said, "The sons of the kingdom shall be cast forth into the outer darkness: there shall be the weeping and gnashing of teeth" (Matthew 8:12).

bleat, complaining about other people three hundred and sixty-five days a year. Christ said, "Surely a human being is much higher than a sheep!" because a human being can think.

A paralysed hand should be freed. A person possessed by a demon should be released. Blindness and deafness should be healed. This was what Christ wanted to express with his words. He told the Pharisees, "You do not understand the fundamental divine law. I know why you want people to have paralysed hands. Your self-interest dictates that you have crippled people around you. You say of the blind, 'It is better that they are blind so they do not see our crimes.' Of deaf people, you say, 'It is in our interests that they be ignorant.'" If some people do not want others to be enlightened, it is because of certain practical considerations. Christ, however, held the opposite view. He said crippled hands should be freed, possessed people should be released, and blind, deaf and dumb people should be healed. Christ wants intelligent people who are able to understand and fulfil the will of God. The Bulgarian word for 'man' has a deep meaning. It comes from the Sanskrit word *manas*, which means 'a being that thinks'. This is why people say, "Be a man!" To be a man means to be a thinking being, who reasons and who has the will do that which is good. This is what it means to be a human being.

You need to be certain of the following law: a person cannot have will unless he or she is doing good things.[6] Some people say, "I have willpower," but they do not know what it means. If I start to roll a wheel at the top of Vitosha Mountain,[7] it will roll downwards, but it cannot roll back up towards the top. The river runs down the mountainside, but it cannot flow upwards. In the same way, many people are rolling and walking downwards. Only the person who can climb up the mountain has willpower. Such a person can conquer and remove certain obstacles in life.

Christ told the Jewish people, "You should not be sheep. You should not be beings who only roll downwards like rivers and river stones. Instead, you ought to be people who are ascending towards God,

[6] The Teacher also said, "To kill someone is not a manifestation of will. To destroy a town is not a manifestation of will. To burn a house down is not a manifestation of will. Children do such things. The creation of a town and other such positive things are the manifestation of spiritually wise will. The will is manifested in the creation of something sublime" (10/23 January 1915).

[7] Vitosha Mountain lies to the south of Sofia, the capital of Bulgaria.

which means to be fulfilling God's will." This is what Christ wanted to tell them, and they understood him. Today people are constantly descending, rolling down Vitosha Mountain and asking themselves why they are unhappy. Whoever rolls downwards is unhappy. Happy is the person who begins to ascend. A person will be unhappy until he or she begins to think and reason. When someone begins to think and reason properly, he or she becomes happy and previously impossible things begin to become possible.

"Surely a human being is of far more value than a sheep!" Christ hid a thought in these words that is of great significance to us. When, in the first chapter of Genesis, God said He made the human being in His own image and likeness,[8] He meant that He wanted us to think and act in the way He thinks and creates, to have willpower like Him. Here 'likeness' means having the ability to distinguish between good and evil and the ability to create harmony. 'To think and act' is a divine principle that the Lord has deposited in each of us. Anyone who does not think and act as prompted by God does not have the image and likeness of God but is merely a sheep. This not to say that a sheep is bad, but a sheep's function is to graze and produce milk and wool; a human being's function is completely different. Human beings were created to rule all other beings, to regulate the atmosphere, to regulate all other elements, to organise the earth.[9] We human beings need to become good masters, which will be possible only when everyone understands what God has deposited within him or her.

People say, "I believe Christ came to save the world." That is good, but they have been preaching it for two thousand years.... And how will Christ save the world? "He gave his blood to redeem people." All right, but when a farmer pays for a pair of oxen in the market, what does he do with them? He puts a yoke around their necks and ties them to the plough, takes his stick and walks them to the field. You believe in Christ and that he paid for your sins,[10] but if you have not voluntar-

---

[8] See Genesis 1:26-27

[9] See Genesis 1:26-28

[10] "Ye are not your own; for ye were bought with a price" (1 Corinthians 6:19-20). "For thou the Lamb wast slain, and didst purchase unto God with thy blood men of every tribe, and tongue, and people, and nation, and madest them to be unto our God a kingdom and priests; and they shall reign upon the earth" (Revelation 5:9-10).

ily yoked yourself to work for him, do you actually serve Christ? You believe Christ came. Very good, but do you listen to him? No, you do not. I advise you to go and listen to Christ when he speaks in his school, to learn to understand his teaching and apply it in your lives.[11]

I do not want people to throw away what they have now – not at all. What you have now is the fact that you are still in primary school. You have been studying only primers for thirty to forty years, and they are totally worn out. It is now time for you to pick up readers. I understand it when a person works with a primer for one, two or three years, but I do not understand someone using a primer for one hundred years. Christ says, "From now on, use readers." And those who have finished with their readers should go on to books on grammar, arithmetic, physics, chemistry, and the law of God, and use them to advance in life.[12] You have bleated enough.

People ask, "Do you believe Christ came to the earth?" It is not enough simply to believe; more is required of you. Listen to what Christ said and learn the teaching that he brought. Only then will you learn the deep meaning of this life. And when you have the ability to think, act and create, you will have a hidden advantage in life: you will have wealth. This wealth is your mind and your will, which together form a mine that you should exploit. I ask you, have you worked on your minds and your wills, or have you only been bleating over your primers until now?

Christ is coming, and if he inspects your home, he will thoroughly check whether you have been working or not. I am not talking about the ordinary homes you have built but those homes in which you came to earth and in which you live. Christ will see whether these prison cells, these rooms, contain spiritually wise thought and action or only sheep excrement. Sheep excrement is a good fertiliser, but it is a sin for a human being, whose Father has sent him or her to school and who has been given all the necessary conditions to become a spiritually wise being, to remain outside the house bleating.[13] And when the angels

---

[11] Jesus said, "Take my yoke upon you, and learn of me; for I am meek and lowly in heart: and ye shall find rest unto your souls" (Matthew 11:29).

[12] 'The law of God' was a subject taught in Bulgarian schools until the communists came to power in 1944, after which it was removed from the curriculum.

[13] Jesus said, "I am the door of the sheep. I am the door: by me if any man enter in, he

descend to observe us and return to heaven to make their report on humankind, what will they say? They will say, "They are still bleating down below." This bleating needs to be transformed into speech. Christ now wants to make these sheep spiritually wise, because the conditions are suitable for it.

Christ says that the sheep's wool should be spun and made into cloth. Anybody can shear wool from a sheep, but it then needs to be used. If a sheep is not sheared on time, its wool will fall off like the leaves on a tree. The wool needs to be sheared and turned into cloth, which means our thoughts and desires need to be transformed into actions – for then the naked people could be clothed.[14] When did human beings become naked in Paradise? It was when they became foolish, became sheep who bleated. It was when the man's hand was crippled and his wife succumbed and they left the wholly wise life for the external gloss of things. The man followed his wife's example and both gave themselves over to loose living. They thus became foolish, losing their sight and their ability to think properly. Christ came to the earth especially for those people who have been made in the image and likeness of God, to untie their hands so they can keep the divine law.[15]

All of you are required to think correctly, to be spiritually wise, to feel correctly and to act correctly, so that your lives will be beautiful and good, both in form and content. Let me put it as it was said two thousand years ago: "Be perfect, as your Heavenly Father is perfect."[16] This is the motto of the new life, and we should aspire to it. It is a divine law, and you need to make a little more effort to follow it.[17]

---

shall be saved" (John 10:7, 9).

[14] Jesus said, "I counsel thee to buy of me white garments, that thou mayest clothe thyself, and that the shame of thy nakedness be not made manifest" (Revelation 3:18).

[15] Jesus said, "I counsel thee to buy of me eyesalve to anoint thine eyes, that thou mayest see" (Revelation 3:18). "If ye abide in my word, then are ye truly my disciples; and ye shall know the truth, and the truth shall make you free. Every one that committeth sin is the bondservant of sin" (John 8:31-32, 34).

[16] See Matthew 5:48

[17] The Teacher also said, "There are three laws in our society which connect us. The first law is, 'Love God with all your heart, with all your mind, with all your will and with all your soul.' The second is, 'Love your neighbour as yourself.' The third is, 'Be perfect as our Father is perfect.' Everything is based on these three laws. Follow them in all your affairs or you will not succeed in life. You need to free yourselves of all fear and doubt. They will leave you when you achieve boundless love" (16/29 August 1912). "To 'Be perfect as our

There is one thing I approve of in worldly people. See how much effort a lady makes before going out to a party, to a ball or to the theatre. She prepares herself in front of a mirror for a whole hour until everything is just right. For that I praise her. And how many times have you Christians stood in front of your mirrors in order to correct your characters? You say, "I can correct myself without a mirror." No, you cannot. You need a mirror. Follow the example of the worldly lady. I approve of the mirror, but the mirror of the heart and mind. When you see yourself in that mirror, everything ought to be correct. Only then can you present yourself to the Lord. Do not think that the Lord will accept you in heaven as you are; He will not. Worldly people understand the need for preparation much better than you, which is why Christ said, "The sons of this world are cleverer than the sons of spiritual light."[18] You should not criticise worldly people. Instead, you ought to learn a very good lesson from them. I recommend worldly people as an excellent example of comprehending the necessity of preparation in life and the effort it requires. If we had taken their example and applied it to the spiritual world, we would be much higher than we are now.

You say, "Worldly people do foolish things that are of no use to us." But what do you need then? Heaven? Heaven does not want foolish people. If you cannot build yourself a house of stone, how can you build your character, when it requires a far greater effort? You have not earned the money to build yourselves ordinary houses, yet you want to build yourselves fine characters.... When the Lord tells you not to pay attention to worldly affairs,[19] He means this: "Now that you have spent lifetimes becoming an expert in material affairs, I want you to stop aspiring to build more houses than you need, and instead learn to build the house of your heart. And once you have built the house of your heart, build the house of your mind." This is why Christ said, "Surely a human being, who thinks and who is able to develop his or her character, is much higher than a sheep, which spends its time grazing and bleating!" The

heavenly Father is perfect' means to be perfect as God is perfect in compassion, goodness and tolerance" (10/23 August 1914).

[18] Jesus said, "The sons of this world are for their own generation wiser than the sons of the light" (Luke 16:8).

[19] Jesus said, "Lay not up for yourselves treasures upon the earth: but lay up for yourselves treasures in heaven: for where thy treasure is, there will thy heart be also. Ye cannot serve God and mammon" (Matthew 6:19-21, 24).

spiritually wise element of a human being should master the spiritually unwise element. The animal nature needs to be transformed by the human nature. It is normal for a sheep to be an animal, but it is abnormal for a human being. Christ wants intelligent people to help him, people who know well how to build according to all the rules of divine science. Doing what benefits the kingdom of God takes first priority in the minds of such people. We now need people who can neither be tempted nor deceived by the outer appearance of things.

Let us move on to the stage of spiritually wise living that has the purpose of improving all nations and all humankind. To achieve this, we have to keep in mind the human soul, the home, society, the nation and humanity itself. Christ referred to all these categories; they form one whole. The home is greater than the individual, society is greater than the home, the nation is much greater than the societies within it, and humanity is greater than the nation. This is why we aspire from that which is smaller to that which is greater, from the manifestation of the animal nature to the manifestation of spiritual wisdom. Christ presented the thought, "Surely a human being is much higher than a sheep!" because a human being is capable of working on, and completing, the construction of his or her life.

When you arrive home, the first thing you should do is to cast out the one who possesses you. The second thing is to open your blinded eyes. Third, heal your deafness. Fourth, free your crippled hand, which means to put your mind into action. This is a serious problem, but you have the rules by which to come to the solution. Of course, one, two or three days could pass without success, but you will solve the problem if you persist at it. While you are working on the problem, the results will show you how to continue.

Were a maths teacher always to answer the problems that should be solved by the student, the student would never learn to calculate independently. The maths teacher gives the student some tasks and says, "Bring me the solution to these problems." The whole world around us forms the problems that the Lord has given us to solve – our tasks in life. In the chapter I read from, Christ gave us many problems to solve. I have been focussing on one of them, but the other ones are more difficult, because they accord to the complicated rule of three. At the moment I am giving you a problem requiring only four simple processes: addition, subtraction, multiplication and division. When you begin to work with the complicated rule of three it becomes a little more difficult, but you can still solve such problems very well using those four simple processes.

Some of you say, "I do not know how to add." You will learn. Some people do not know to whom they should be added, which means they do not know to whom they should be married. Some people no longer love their spouses and want to be rid of them, wanting to subtract them from their lives. That, however, is not the right time for subtraction. A man and wife multiply by having children, whom they then need to educate. What a great law is hidden in these four processes! You need to learn how to add, subtract, multiply and divide. It is a profound science, which has been put in front of humanity for thousands of years. So far, we have only learnt the mathematical side of calculation. When we begin to add the saints, the angels and God to ourselves, we will learn the truest form of addition. Someone says, "I know how to add." And I ask him, "But how do you add, with a plus or a minus?" He replies, "I have minus two thousand Leva."[20] And I ask, "For how long will you have to work to repay that debt?" Another person declares, "I have plus two thousand Leva." And I say to her, "You have some capital, which means you can use your wealth to help others." This is a fundamental law of Christ.

When a sheep sees a wolf, it stamps its feet to convey something to the predator: "Go away! Can you not see that I am grazing?" But the wolf pounces on the sheep and eats it anyway. That exemplifies the intelligence of a sheep. And when you see the devil, do not stamp your feet; that will not frighten him. The devil is only afraid of those people who have good minds and willpower, whose hands are unbound. Christ came to untie human hands and to give us the strength to fight the wolf, the devil.[21] Wolves have the right to walk in the world, to use their teeth, but we have the right to use our minds and wills against them. They have the right to eat, but we have the right to remove their-

---

[20] The Lev is the principal unit of Bulgarian currency.

[21] "Resist the devil, and he will flee from you" (James 4:7). Jesus said, "The prince of the world hath nothing in me" (John 14:30). "There is no truth in him. For he is a liar, and the father of lies" (John 8:44). "I am the truth" (John 14:6). "The Spirit of truth shall guide you into all the truth" (John 16:13).

teeth. They have the right to use their nails, but we have the right to clip them. Uproot the teeth of this devil and remove his nails. Once you have turned the devil into a sheep that gives you milk and wool, you will no longer have anything to fear. You can also turn the devil into an ox, yoke him and make him plough for you.

Christ spoke of another problem: when a bad spirit goes out of a person it becomes very restless and would be seven times worse if it returned.[22] All foolish people who are freed will become seven times worse, which is why Christ said, "I came to save spiritually wise people."[23] He came to save human beings, not animals. The salvation offered by the profound Christian teaching needs to be applied in our lives. Our minds and hearts should be an example to others and our homes should be ideal gardens. This is the real purpose of our lives, and it is the reason why you ought to begin working on yourselves.

Here in Bulgaria, when someone visits a friend's house, the owner shows the guest over all the property. The guest enjoys the tour and praises his friend's accomplishment. One day the Lord of Heaven will come to visit you, and what will be the quality of the tours you give Him? The buildings on your properties are in ruins, as are your churches and schools.... But if any of you gives a tour which shows everything on your property to be in good order, after visiting you, the Lord will say, "Behold the human being who has worked with spiritual wisdom!"

This is what Christ meant when he said, "Surely a human being is much higher than a sheep!"

---

[22] See Matthew 12:43-45

[23] Jesus said, "Every one which heareth these words of mine, and doeth them, shall be likened unto a wise man, which built his house upon the rock: and the rain descended, and the floods came, and the winds blew, and beat upon that house; and it fell not: for it was founded upon the rock. And every one that heareth these words of mine, and doeth them not, shall be likened unto a foolish man, which built his house upon the sand: and the rain descended, and the floods came, and the winds blew, and smote upon that house; and it fell: and great was the fall thereof" (Matthew 7:24-27).

The Pharisee and the Publican:
The Basis of All Human Types

Jesus said,

> Two men went up into the temple to pray; the one a
> Pharisee, and the other a publican. The Pharisee stood and
> prayed thus with himself, "God, I thank thee, that I am not
> as the rest of men, extortioners, unjust, adulterers, or even
> as this publican. I fast twice in the week; I give tithes of all
> that I get." But the publican, standing afar off, would not lift
> up so much as his eyes unto heaven, but smote his breast,
> saying, "God, be merciful to me a sinner." I say unto you,
> This man went down to his house justified rather than the
> other: for every one that exalteth himself shall be humbled;
> but he that humbleth himself shall be exalted.[1]

I will take these two people, the Pharisee and the publican, as the
subject of my lecture today. They represent a very old culture in an
important way. Let me compare their distinctive features, to shed light
on their customs and spiritual characters.

Christ was describing two distinct types of people. A talented artist
who knows the science of humankind could paint these two types with
all their distinctive features. Such an excellent painting should be hung
in every home as an example to its occupants. What were the charac-
teristics of a Pharisee and a publican? It is not enough to say, "He was
a Pharisee," or, "He was a publican." We need to know the external
features of their faces and hands, their physiques and the structure of
their heads. After that, we need to come to the particulars in the storage
of their souls. Only thus can we obtain a clear picture of what has been
deposited in this biblical text and make use of it.

Christ was a great artist presenting two of the distinctive traits of these

---

[1] Luke 18:10-14. The original Bulgarian publication only quoted verse 10.

247

two different characters. I will use them to describe the Pharisee and the publican in more detail. You will say, "How can you describe a person when so few words were said about him?" It is a science. There are scientists in comparative anatomy who, when given only the smallest part of an ancient creature, are able to describe the structure of the whole animal. Similarly, were you to give a leaf to an expert in botany, he or she could describe the whole tree. By the same law, I will try to describe the Pharisee and the publican, to show what kinds of people they were.

You will ask me, "What do we have in common with these two men who lived two thousand years ago?" Well, there are two kinds of people in the world: publicans and Pharisees. Many other types have originated from them, but they remain the fundamental ones. You may belong to one kind or another, no matter what your social position, be you a priest or not, an aristocrat or not, a scientist or not, a philosopher or not, be you a man or a woman. These two character-types are interwoven and can be seen in the lives of everybody. They will forever remain in human history as the two distinctive types of people. Christ's artistry was demonstrated by his ability to describe them clearly in very few words.

The outer appearance of a Pharisee was respectable and pleasant. He was tall, upright in posture and elegant in his movements. From a physiognomic point of view, his physical features say much about what kind of person he was. His hands and fingers show that he was intelligent, resolute, confident in his worldview and strong-willed, doing everything he could to realise his ideas. His digestive system worked well and he ate and drank temperately, having no weakness for gluttony. His taste was refined. His chin shows that he was mentally flexible and quick to comprehend things. His smile shows that he considered others to be beneath him. His forehead shows that he was an individualist and that he was observant and had a practical mind. His ears show that he was well organised. His beard shows that he was determined and tenacious. The shape of his head shows that he was a man with great self-control; that he was self-respecting, proud, demanding and vain; that he had religious feeling, but that it had been developed narrowly; and that he was merciful, but only to himself and those close to him. His face shows that his aesthetic taste was refined but unpoetic, with love neither for nature nor for the sublime and ideal; and that he had faith, but only in his own mind. He was religious, but he respected and adored only himself in his devotion. Were you to have entered his temple, you would have found his own portrait as the centrepiece, not the image of Christ; you would have found icons of his ancestors in the places of those of the Virgin Mary, John the Baptist and the other saints; you would have found him burning incense and worshipping his ancestors, saying, "Glorious and great is my family tree." The Pharisee was an intelligent man who gathered knowledge in life, who knew the Jewish Kabbalah and the principles of the civilisation of his time. Were he alive today, he would be a well-known writer, or a philosopher, or an artist, or a statesman, or a spiritual leader.

Why did Christ select this type of person? What was wrong with the Pharisee's prayer? His was a philosophy that had outlived its time. He was a person who had fallen in love with his own portrait and saw only himself wherever he went. It is strange when someone falls in love with his or her own image. When the Pharisee prayed to the Lord, see how he spoke: "Thank You, God, that I am not as other people but am something more." That was the wrong philosophy, because God is the creator of all human beings. The Pharisee said, "I am not like other people." But what was he then? He was not an angel but was made of the same mess as every other human being, with the same blood flowing in his veins. He wanted to deceive both himself and the Lord, and that is the first lie in human life. The Lord said to him, "You are not telling the truth." The Pharisee's statement worked negatively. He did not compare himself with higher beings, with angels, but with lower types, with criminals, saying that he was not like them. Were I to compare myself to very low creatures, saying, "Thank You, Lord, that I am not like oxen, donkeys, dogs, lizards and snakes," what kind of comparison would that be? This weakness exists in everybody.

The Pharisee said, "Thank You, Lord, that I am not like a thief." The Lord replied, "If I had put you in the place of a person who became a thief, what would you have become?" Once upon a time, an angel in heaven observed a man committing many sins. The angel turned to the Lord and said, "How do you tolerate that low creature? If I were in Your place, I would free the earth of that man." The Lord then incarnated the angel on earth in the same position as the man, and the angel went on to commit twice his sins. So, people should not judge someone else's actions from their own positions, for they would behave in the same way were they to have been put in his or her place.

Many people come to me and start speaking thus: "I am not a bad person. I was brought up well, because my family has respectable ancestry." I reply, "I do not doubt you. I believe what you have just told me, deep in my soul. I agree, we all have respectable ancestors. Our ancestors, however, were not really as noble as you and I believe. Many of them were great scoundrels, criminals, evildoers and hooligans, and the Lord's account of them is written throughout us. Although something's outer appearance might look good, the interior does not necessarily correspond to the exterior. That our ancestors were not as pure as we suppose is shown in the bad traits we have inherited from them, traits we display at least twice a day. If your grandparents were as pure and as good as angels, where did your bad traits and bad behaviours come from? Were you to add a little of a bitter or poisonous substance to a pure liquid, it would be noticeable; it would be known that something bad had been mixed into something good."

We can describe people who have a philosophy like the Pharisee as being conservative, people with a high opinion of themselves. It is no bad thing for you to have a high opinion of yourself as long as it is accurate and is not mixed with any bitterness. The greatest conservative and regulator in nature is nitrogen, which extinguishes fire and suffocates all life. Nitrogen is the oldest and most balanced element in nature, but everything in nature would be dead if only nitrogen existed. However, the organic world should be very grateful for the existence of nitrogen.

The Pharisee did not ask God to smooth some of the rough sides of his character; he only thanked God that he was not like other people: blasphemers, extortionists, murderers and adulterers. As a scribe and a philosopher, he ought to have instead focussed on the causes of blasphemy, extortion, murder and adultery. According to Christ's teaching, when we meet someone who is in a lower moral condition than ourselves, we should not judge him or her in our souls. Instead, we should learn a lesson by discovering what causes brought him or her to such a state. If we find that there is something similarly wrong inside us, we need to uproot it. The One who laid down the great laws of life says, "Do not judge others and you will not be judged."[2] There is a deep

---

[2] See Luke 6:37

meaning in these words, and whoever understands it has arrived at the great law of human welfare.

Contemporary zoologists study animals and have given the world valuable knowledge about them, but no one has investigated the deep causes of their creation. Why do some animals have horns while others do not? Why do some animals crawl while others walk on four legs? Why do some animals eat meat while others eat grass? Why are animals deprived of human intelligence? There are deep, fundamental reasons for these things; it is not as arbitrary as people might think. When people understand these deep causes, they will arrive at the spiritually wise philosophy on which the order of the future society will be built, the dawn of the new civilisation. The entirety of contemporary civilisation is based on the views of the Pharisee – it is a 'Pharisee civilisation'. This is a civilisation in which people make distinctions based on form, on external appearance and etiquette. This civilisation was born in the distant past in Egypt, India, Babylon, China, Persia, Judea, Greece and Rome. And today it is in Europe, clothed in the beautiful cloak of Christianity. I am not saying the foundations of this civilisation were bad, but I am saying that outer form ought to always have a corresponding content. Without content a form is nothing but a simple shell in which only parasites can live.[3] It is said of someone, "What amazing eyes that man has." So what? "They are beautiful." What is beautiful about them? "They are shiny and pleasant to look at." Look at your eyes in the mirror and you will see the state of your soul. The eyes are the only things which never deceive and are never hypocritical.

When the Pharisee prayed, Christ, who was watching, spoke to him: "Your soul is muddy. Your ancestors did not live such pure lives as you imagine. You think you are not like other people, but you were like them in the past and you are not far above their level now." It does not matter how you interpret these words of Christ, be it by the Hindu philosophy of reincarnation, the transmigration of the wise Egyptians, the emanation and perfecting of the spirit of the Kabbalists and the occultists, or by the contemporary philosophy of heredity. These teach-

---

[3] Jesus said, "Woe unto you, scribes and Pharisees, hypocrites! for ye are like unto whited sepulchres, which outwardly appear beautiful, but inwardly are full of dead men's bones, and of all uncleanness. Even so ye also outwardly appear righteous unto men, but inwardly ye are full of hypocrisy and iniquity" (Matthew 23:27-28).

ings and theories only exist to help us understand certain things and the events of human life more clearly, but the fundamental principle which lies at the base of all things always remains one and the same, no matter how we explain and interpret its manifestations.

The great law of cause and effect, of action and retribution, never lies; it always tells the absolute truth. If you are good, it is written in the book of life that you have been good. If you are bad, it is written that you have been bad. If you speak the truth, it is written in the book of life that you have spoken the truth. If you lie, it is written that you have lied. If you help your neighbours, or sacrifice yourself for your nation, or work for the good of humanity, or serve God out of love, it is written down in the book of life. If you rape your neighbours, or betray your nation, or impede the development of humanity, or are unfaithful to God, it is written down in the same book. It mercilessly records people's actions on their foreheads, noses, mouths, faces, heads, hands, fingers and all the other parts of the human body. Each bone testifies for or against us. We read this recorded history of human life every day.

The lives of our ancestors were recorded in earlier pages. It is written that some of them were terrible criminals, thieves and bandits. If we further turn the pages of the book and follow the line from which Abraham, Isaac, Jacob, David, Solomon and many others came, we will find a full record of their actions printed there. It records that Abraham was a righteous man who was highly intelligent, big-hearted, very faithful to God and sublime of spirit, and that he knew of the deep wisdom of the divine rules for the great future of humanity. It can be read that Jacob was originally a two-faced, cunning and selfish man, who, with lies and treachery, succeeded in taking his brother's birthright. When he was around thirty-three years old he went through a transformation, after having served his uncle Laban for fourteen years in exchange for marrying his two daughters. A change for the better took place in him then. It is written that David was a brave man who was resolute and had an excellent natural and poetic mind, but he had a weakness for beautiful women. He took Uriah's wife by deception, and that was the day David's trials began. Nathan, the brave prophet, was not afraid to unmask David to his face and show him the bad consequences that this law would write about him in the book for future generations to read. Of Solomon, it is written that he had an excellent philosophical mind and a good but stained heart, that he was a man of immeasurably strong feelings and passions, with great vanity and a weak will – he was a first-class epicurean in eating, drinking and having pleasure with women.

Christ knew these things. He knew about the lives of his ancestors.[4] When, therefore, people addressed him as "Good Teacher", he answered, "Why do you call me good? Only God is good."[5] What he meant was this: "The family in which I was born was not as noble as you think, for God has another measure of which you are unaware. God requires total purity in all things. Many of my ancestors did not live in a way that pleased the true God, whose will I am fulfilling." That is why Christ said to the Pharisee, "You are deceiving yourself, other people and God. Many of your ancestors committed crimes, which is why you do not have any right to say, 'I am not like those people.' Since there is no humility in your soul, your prayer cannot be accepted and you cannot be pardoned. You Pharisees have perverted the divine law by clothing it in hypocrisy. Stop presenting yourselves falsely, because God is not a human being who can be deceived by your external appearance. God looks at the condition of your hearts and values you by them."[6]

I will now describe the other type of person, the publican. He was of medium height, a little overweight and slightly short-legged, with fat hands and a round face. His digestive system was very strong. He liked to overeat and to drink excessively. If he needed something, he would take it from others by force or theft. His nose and respiratory system show that he was an emotional man, impulsive like a child, who could easily express his joy, especially when drinking, but when he sobered up he would start crying because his wife was ill. His ears show that although he was capable of theft, he was also giving. He would say, "My father and mother stole things. Let me give to others and do good so that, hopefully, God will forgive my family's sins." His eyes show that he had a natural softness and good-heartedness. His head shows many

[4] Jesus said, "There is nothing covered up, that shall not be revealed: and hid, that shall not be known" (Luke 12:2).

[5] See Mark 10:17-18

[6] "The Lord seeth not as man seeth; for man looketh on the outward appearance, but the Lord looketh on the heart" (1 Samuel 16:7). "I the Lord search the heart, I try the reins, even to give every man according to his ways, according to the fruit of his doings" (Jeremiah 17:10).

253

things about him: his familial and social feelings were very strong, as were his devotion, benevolence and compassion; he had a correct understanding of life, an excellent, sophistry-free mind and a well-developed conscience that would point out his mistakes, mistakes he was not afraid to confess before God, before other people or to himself; he had no false perception of his own nobility; he was devout, keeping an image of the good God and not a god of his own imagination; he always had faith that this good Lord would lead him to the light, and he trusted the Lord more than he trusted himself. His philosophy was correct because he did not compare himself to those who were lower than him, but instead said, "Lord, when I see You, the angels and the saints, I wonder what it makes me. I need to uplift myself and become like You. I am a sinner. My ancestors did not become true human beings, and neither have I. I eat, I drink and I live like a pig. Forgive me for being unable to make use of the blessings You have given me."

And what did Christ say about the publican? He said, "This man, who realises his errors, has a high ideal and will one day surpass the Pharisee." How could this be? It is so because rich people rely only on their rental incomes and do not work. All they do is talk about politics and their social issues. Other people get up early in the morning and work ten hours a day. They meet misfortune after misfortune in life but persist on anyway. Over lifetimes, people who work hard gain knowledge and become eminent.

You need to be able to recognise whether a person is primarily a publican or a Pharisee. The purpose of my lecture is to teach you how to be able to make this distinction as a practical tool in your lives. My apologies, but I can see both of these types among you. As Christ described these two opposite poles, I tell you to take the good in each one of them and create a simultaneously noble Pharisee-and-publican character. Create the third type of Christian person, the new human being.

When there is misfortune in your life, you say, "Why has this happened to me, Lord? There are other people who are greater sinners than I am." But your words show that you are in the position of a Pharisee, a person who argues with the Lord, do they not? The Lord answers, "You are very righteous, but do you know the terrible things that your ancestors did, things in which you were their partner? Here is the receipt that you signed many years ago, and now you have to pay it." "But I do not remember signing this!" "That makes no difference," replies the Lord. "Your debt has been noted in My book, which never lies." When misfortune happens to you, be thankful for it and say, "This is only a small misfortune." Then you will be in the position of the publican, and Christ will say to you, "You will enter my Father's home."

You sometimes judge the Pharisees, saying, "They were insincere people." But do you know that you who judge the Pharisees are actually the contemporary form of Pharisee? Learn a lesson from the Pharisee's character so as not to develop his bad features. If you already have them, uproot them and stop treading the negative path of life. There is no benefit in keeping the bad qualities of your ancestors. You also should not rest on their laurels. Do you know the story of the geese? A man was herding a flock of geese to town to be sold in the market. The geese said among themselves, "What an awful thing this man is doing to us. Does he not know that our ancestors saved Rome?" The man asked them, "But what have you yourselves done in life?" "Nothing." "In that case you deserve to be boiled in a pot." Your ancestors might have been noble people, but what are you? If you do not have a noble character, form one. Your ancestors might have left you certain capital, but you can squander it away.

There are also religious Pharisees. "I am from the Orthodox Church." "I am from the Evangelical Church." "I am from the Catholic Church." "I am a freethinker." I am pleased that you are Orthodox, you are Evangelical, you are Catholic and you are a freethinker, but do you have the noble traits of Jesus?" "We do not." In that case none of you is really Orthodox, Evangelical, Catholic or a freethinker; you are nothing. Attain the traits of Jesus. "But I am a freethinker!" Really? Do you have the traits of an honest freethinker? By a 'freethinker' I mean a person who is a friend of the truth. If you are not a friend of the truth, you are a first-class liar.

People often say to one another, "You are a fine person." Contemporary people come together in groups of three or four and begin to praise each other for their nobility and excellence. "We read your story and were enraptured by it." After the author leaves, they say, "What an idiot!" When the next person leaves, the remainder speak of her in the same way. Do not be deceived by what people say about you; they might say many unpleasant things. Nobody tells the truth. However, the bad things your enemies say about you are nearer the truth than what is said by those who flatter you. You may be good, but you are not as good as you think you are. Sometimes you feel very self-important, thinking there is no one else like you and that you will rule the world. Christ, however, says, "Listen, many years ago your ancestors were rulers, and I remember that it is written in my book that they committed many crimes. You might take the same path, so do not be too self-confident." For this reason, no matter what situation you are in, you should only have the Lord God as your ideal.

You will have many bitter experiences in this world. If one hundred people praise you, perhaps only three are telling the accurate truth; the others will also tell you the truth, but in either an overly rude or an overly flattering way. The truth is not in those two extremes but in the middle path, on which you take and combine the good features of the Pharisee and the publican. The Pharisee's good features were his excellent mind, his perception and his sense of order. The publican's good features were his compassion, his deep devotion and his conscience, a conscience with which he recognised his mistakes and formed the aspiration to rectify his life.

Pharisees and publicans also exist in families. A husband is a Pharisee, handsome and of noble birth, while his wife is from a humble background with uneducated ancestors. The man belittles his wife for this, in order to have the upper hand in their relationship. The reverse also happens: a wife is a Pharisee and her husband is a publican whom she belittles. Both publicans and Pharisees now need to correct their lives. When Christ said that the publican was more justified than the Pharisee, he did not mean that the publican was a wholly correct person. What he meant was that the publican had a better understanding of life and the divine order than the Pharisee. Christ wanted to say that one day the publican would have a higher position than the Pharisee. If you do not want to become humble, the Lord will make you humble, because the Lord humbles the proud and uplifts the humble.[7] 'Pride' is synonymous with 'Pharisee'. 'Humility' is synonymous with 'publican'.

You do not know what will happen to you in the future. You might end up in a situation from which neither your noble qualities nor

---

[7] "God resisteth the proud, but giveth grace to the humble. Humble yourselves therefore under the mighty hand of God, that he may exalt you in due time" (1 Peter 5:5-6).

your ancestors can save you. Some years ago, in London, I think, one of the richest and most eminent of Englishmen went down to his cellar to look at his treasures. He entered the cellar, closed the door and enjoyed beholding his riches. When he had had enough and tried to open the cellar door, he discovered that he had locked himself in and that the key was in the other side of the door. He remained in the cellar, surrounded by his gold and great wealth, for three days, neither able to get himself out nor to call out to anyone for help. Finally he died, having left a message: "If somebody could have given me a piece of bread, I would have given him half my riches." That is why Christ said, "My bread can save you, but those things for which you struggle cannot."[8] Do you know how many people die like that, closed in themselves? Despairing people sometimes commit suicide. What type of person commits suicide? Publicans do not; a Pharisee might. Poets, artists and statesmen who feel their work is unappreciated might commit suicide. It is always Pharisees, noble thinkers, who commit suicide.

Today people preach that if anybody wants to succeed in life, he or she needs willpower. The human will can be applied in three ways: first there is self-will; second is the will to benefit oneself primarily and then one's nation; third is the will to act in the interests of one's society, one's nation, all humankind and God. If you have the third type of will, you will fulfil all of your obligations in this world and there is no force that could divert you from your duty. This is true willpower. The will to work for the glory of God, for humanity, for your nation, for your home and for the uplifting of your character is real willpower

Some people say, "You should have a noble mind." A mind which understands the nature of its relationship with God, which works to apply sublime thoughts in life, is a noble mind. You all have the

---

[8] Jesus said, "Work not for the meat which perisheth, but for the meat which abideth unto eternal life, which the Son of man shall give unto you. I am the bread of life: he that cometh to me shall not hunger. I am the living bread which came down out of heaven: if any man eat of this bread, he shall live for ever" (John 6:27, 35, 51). And the Teacher said, "We should not burden our hearts with many of the cares of life. We only need our daily bread, which comes from God. Many other things are from the cunning one. Purify your hearts and minds and strength will come to you – this much, I know. You should not only be content and of a good disposition when you are rich, but also in days of poverty. When we are with God, we are given what we need and empowered" (21 January/3 February 1915).

potential to develop such qualities. "But my nose is not as I want it to be!" It will develop over time. Look at baby birds in the nest, whose wings are undeveloped. All they can do is open their mouths, chirp for food and wait for their mother to bring them worms. The more they pray for food, the more they are fed. Their wings grow until finally they can fly away. You can progress by the same law: simply open your mouths and pray. Those of you who do not open your mouths are Pharisees, and Christ will tell you, "The world is not for you. The kingdom of God is not for you. The future is not for you." This is what Christ wanted to say.

There are people who do not want to open their mouths and instead remain silent. I understand a person being silent, but when ought you to be silent? When you are angry, when you want to offend somebody, when you are envious, be silent.[9] When you are joyful, when someone needs comforting, open your mouth and speak.

Parents are not educating their children correctly because they teach too much like Pharisees. The traits of the Pharisee are on display in the home in front of the children. They are also on display in the church. They are on display everywhere. And we are astonished that the kingdom of God has not yet arrived....

Moreover, the Pharisee criticises the rest of the world – priests, teachers, rulers and so on – while considering himself or herself a saint. Never forget that you are the same as those whom you judge and blame.[10] Stop it, because your Divine Mother is here with you, and when you say, "Chirp! Chirp!" you will be fed. This may seem funny to you, but it is a great truth. It is a small thing, but we need to learn from the birds' example. In comparison with the heavenly life we are paupers, but the Lord is constantly giving us food. Greet your Mother, because She is bringing you food. How many places She had to travel to find a worm for you! How are we to thank God, who thinks about us every day and delivers food to us? Each morning we should say, "Chirp! Chirp!" praying to God. Do you know what this means? It has a deep

[9] "Let every man be swift to hear, slow to speak, slow to wrath: for the wrath of man worketh not the righteousness of God" (James 1:19-20). "A fool uttereth all his anger: But a wise man keepeth it back and stilleth it" (Proverbs 29:11).

[10] "Wherein thou judgest another, thou condemnest thyself; for thou that judgest dost practise the same things. And we know that the judgement of God is according to truth against them that practise such things" (Romans 2:1-2).

meaning. What does a chirp contain? If you knew it, you would know the words with which heaven speaks.

You are now in the temple, and Christ is asking you, "How do you pray, like the Pharisee or the publican? Will you go out into the world and begin working as a Pharisee or as a publican?" Christ wanted to tell us not to be like Pharisees. Nothing in the world concerns me as much as Pharisees and their criticisms. We ought to purify ourselves before we try to purify others.[11] First we have to educate ourselves, then we can educate others. "But we have to preach and educate people." If I were to preach prematurely, I would delude people. "Go out and say such and such." What should I say? Should I lie to people? When you go out into the world, you should tell the great truth with both your words and the way in which you live. What Christ wanted to say was that, when we begin studying, we need to work simultaneously with our words and our lives.

I very much approve of those teachers who teach their subjects, such as physics or chemistry, by working with practical experiments right from the start. In learning carpentry, the student is taught both in theory and practice. It is the same in tailoring. Christ says, "Enter the workshop and take your rulers, scissors and cloth."[12] Some people need to begin with the needle and later go on to scissors. What are the scissors? The scissors are your tongues. When you cut the cloth and sew correctly there are no more beautiful scissors than your tongues. However, when your scissors cut this way and that without thinking, they are not being used correctly. "May we not speak?" We may speak, but in the right way, for if we do not speak correctly we will cut thoughtlessly and ruin the cloth.[13]

---

[11] Jesus said, "Why beholdest thou the mote that is in thy brother's eye, but considerest not the beam that is in thine own eye? Or how wilt thou say to thy brother, 'Let me cast out the mote out of thine eye,' and lo, the beam is in thine own eye? Thou hypocrite, cast out first the beam out of thine own eye; and then shalt thou see clearly to cast out the mote out of thy brother's eye" (Matthew 7:3-5).

[12] This tutoring in tailoring is a metaphor for building the spiritual body with Christ's guidance. Jesus said, "He that overcometh shall be arrayed in white garments. I counsel thee to buy of me white garments, that thou mayest clothe thyself, and that the shame of thy nakedness be not made manifest" (Revelation 3:5, 18).

[13] "If any man thinketh himself to be religious, while he bridleth not his tongue but deceiveth his heart, this man's religion is vain. If any stumbleth not in word, the same is a perfect man, able to bridle the whole body also" (James 1:26; 3:2). Jesus said, "I say unto you, that every idle word that men shall speak, they shall give account thereof in the day

I do not say all these things to discourage you. I do not want to tell you that you are born Pharisees, but that you have a tendency to be like Pharisees. Everybody has this tendency, and it is good to have it to some extent; but whenever you start saying, "Thank You, Lord, that I am not like other people," the Pharisee is alive in you and it is hard to free yourself of him. He lives in your heads, in your ears and behind your eyes. Where will you find this Pharisee? You will find him in all of your features and behaviour.

Christ, therefore, is now asking us, "What is the most correct way to pray to God?" And the answer is for prayer, in its general sense, to be made for the benefit of society. Some people think true prayer can only be made in a church. Do your prayers in church relate to your family lives? And do those prayers help you? You should find the 'church' that you need, but where is it? The teacher begins by teaching the pupils something and then leaves them to use it to solve a problem for themselves and discover a certain law. It is written in the Scriptures, "You are the temple of God."[14] If we are the temples of God, in what manner should we enter our secret room and go before Him?[15] If we enter them like Pharisees, Christ will tell us, "Your prayer has failed."[16] If we enter them like publicans, confessing our mistakes and promising to correct them, our prayers will succeed, and Christ will respond, "You are pardoned. You have a future."[17]

A teacher might find mistakes in a pupil's notebook, but the pupil should not complain, "How petty my teacher is, highlighting three mistakes!" If the teacher crosses out four or five incorrect words, the pupil says, "My teacher has spoiled my notebook!" True, but if you would like to become perfect, you ought to thank your teacher, because if those few mistakes are left unaddressed, they might increase themselves. Correct them. Do not leave them as they are, for a mistake is

of judgement. For by thy words thou shalt be justified, and by thy words thou shalt be condemned" (Matthew 12:36-37).

[14] See 1 Corinthians 6:19

[15] Jesus said, "When thou prayest, enter into thine inner chamber, and having shut thy door, pray to thy Father which is in secret, and thy Father which seeth in secret shall recompense thee" (Matthew 6:6).

[16] "If we say that we have no sin, we deceive ourselves, and the truth is not in us" (1 John 1:8).

[17] "If we confess our sins, God is faithful and righteous to forgive us our sins, and to cleanse us from all unrighteousness" (1 John 1:9).

like a louse. If a louse is left alone for one week, it will multiply into thousands of lice. One mistake is sufficient to send someone to the pillory.[18] By the same law, one virtue can uplift you to heaven and place you among the angels. Given the necessary conditions, one erroneous action will cause you to descend but a virtuous one will uplift you. Consequently, pay attention to your virtues and vices alike. If you have lived a wicked life but have retained one virtue, it will be the rope cast into the stormy sea of life by which you can haul yourself to shore. A last remaining vice is bad enough to kill you, just as a last remaining virtue is powerful enough to save you. Either of these two things may change your life. This is the law, and it is the reason why Christ said, "Do not be negligent."[19]

The Pharisee had more noble traits than the publican. In many respects he was higher than the publican, but he had a last remaining vice, pride, which pulled him down to hell. The publican was a great sinner, but he had one remaining virtue, humility. He said, "I will work for my salvation!" He hoped to correct himself in the future, which is why God blessed him. I ask you this morning, in which of these two conditions are you? Do you have a last remaining vice or a last remaining virtue? If you have a last remaining vice, I am sorry for you. Take care, for you are in a dangerous place in life. If you have a last remaining virtue, you are in a safe place and I congratulate you, for you are on solid rock. Hold on to this last remaining virtue and Christ will walk beside you.

---

[18] The Teacher also said, "Some people go away from Christ because he shines light on them, which reveals their dark spots; but we should not be afraid of Christ, for he is our friend" (15/28 August 1912).

[19] Jesus said, "Be ye ready: for in an hour that ye think not the Son of man cometh" (Matthew 24:44). "Take heed to yourselves, lest haply your hearts be overcharged with surfeiting, and drunkenness, and cares of this life, and that day come on you suddenly as a snare" (Luke 21:34). "Behold, I come as a thief. Blessed is he that watcheth, and keepeth his garments, lest he walk naked, and they see his shame" (Revelation 16:15). "Take ye heed, watch and pray. I say unto all, Watch" (Mark 13:33, 37). And the Apostle Peter wrote, "Be sober, be watchful: your adversary the devil, as a roaring lion, walketh about, seeking whom he may devour" (1 Peter 5:8).

Temporary Life and Eternal life

Jesus said,

This is life eternal, that they should know thee the only true God, and him whom thou didst send, even Jesus Christ. [1]

With these words on eternal life Christ revealed a great law of life to his disciples. Two essential elements are determined and distinguished by this law. They function in both temporary life and eternal life, in both conscious life and supersensitive life. People who do not understand the profound meaning of the original language can interpret these words in different ways, changing the order of the words 'life' and 'eternal'. There are, however, certain laws regulating human thought which do not permit such changes. Until people learn to think properly, they will continue to make mistakes and pay for them with suffering. The things that are written in the great book of life are for spiritually wise people; they are not for lower beings who do not understand these laws. No matter whether someone reads "eternal life" or "life eternal", he or she will ask, "What is meant by the word 'eternal'?" This word has an inner and an outer meaning. For Bulgarians 'eternal life' means a boundless, endless life. We often mix the idea of eternal life with human existence, but a human being can exist without really living.

The main thought in this verse is "eternal life". God and Jesus Christ are the two sources from which eternal life comes; or to put it another way, they are the two points of support, the two pillars, on which eternal life rests. In the terms of syllogistic logic, God is the main premise, Jesus Christ is the minor premise, and eternal life is the conclusion. Let me make this thought clearer to you. 'God' means the source of the Spirit and the conditions, forces and laws in nature on which the great order of things are built and sustained. 'Jesus Christ' means the spiritually wise genesis that is emitted by the one God, which directs

[1] John 17:3

and protects all living beings. 'Eternal life' means the spiritually wise movement of the soul.

When you say "eternal life" you think you understand its meaning and essence. But what is knowledge? We can only truly know the things which we can test or do. We do not know the things that we cannot test or do. Such things we can only imagine or guess at. Having seen a person making cloth, you would all say, "I now know how cloth is made." Were you asked to actually make some yourselves, however, you would have to concede, "I cannot."

Each living being needs an environment and the suitable conditions for its life. For example, the environment of fish is water. What do we need to understand by the word 'environment'? It is the surrounding medium, the foundation and the soil, which are words with many touching points. In Bulgarian and other languages there is no word with which to show the essential difference between these three things. The primary element of eternal life is the medium in which the soul is immersed, just as fish are immersed in water. When we begin building a house, we first lay a foundation, then build the walls and make a roof. When cultivating a plant we sow a seed in the soil. A fish needs water. A house needs a foundation. A plant's roots need soil. What is the environment of eternal life? It is God. We human beings live in the air; we are surrounded by it. Although air is our environment, there are certain other things that we need as well: water, food and light. Air, food, water and light are the necessary elements for organic human life.

The word 'eternal' refers to the spiritual world and the materials from which immortality can be built. The word 'life' refers to organic life in matter, which grows and develops but cannot be unending, eternal, for its form can be changed, a change we call 'death'. Human death does not mean the end of consciousness, but the loss of the conditions in which human life exists.[2] The deceased's consciousness remains beyond the death of the body, just as the bones remain physically.[3] Consciousness is a human being's spiritual spine. God is the

---

[2] The Teacher also said, "The soul has one physical body at a time. When it has finished its mission with a body, the soul leaves it and prepares the matter for the next body in which it will live. When it is time for its next incarnation on earth, the soul enters its new body. The process repeats itself again and again, and this is what eternal life means" (15/28 January 1915).

[3] "If there is a natural body, there is also a spiritual body" (1 Corinthians 15:44). "The

supreme power, or the necessary environment, in which human beings are spiritually immersed.

The human soul needs to be immersed in God. If you do not immerse your soul in God, it means you are outside your true environment, living as an unplanted seed. There have been grains of wheat stored in Egyptian pyramids for five to six thousand years waiting for the conditions in which they could be sown and grown. Some such grains have recently been planted, producing excellent results. And the human soul is like a grain of wheat in the divine granary waiting for the conditions in which it can start its life anew. For us Christians, this means that we need to find the conditions which enable us to immerse ourselves in God. Every spiritually conscious person should make efforts in this direction and attain this state. Otherwise you will live, you will exist, but your existence will be no more than vegetating, for you will be existing in storage without the conditions to germinate and grow, limited by the Divine Essence that created you as grains of wheat and fruit seeds.

You cannot escape your existences. You cannot commit existence-suicide, for your genesis is beyond time and space. The human soul existed deep within the Divine Consciousness for billions of years in a state that was not individualised. During this time, before it knew separate, individual life, the soul lived in a dreamlike state, contemplating the divine bliss. Now, through its awakening, the soul comes to earth to learn the inner meaning of individual life, to obtain its own immortal life and become a citizen of heaven with certain rights and duties. God imposes this inner aspiration on the soul. Some people want both to be incarnated and to live like God. It is impossible to live like God, however, because had you wanted to live like God, it would have been unnecessary to go outside Him. What need could there be in this Divine Consciousness to separate Itself and look for another kind of existence? The human soul has always existed in God, but its eternal aspiration is to seek God in all His manifestations and imitate Him.[4]

The scientific aspect of achieving eternal life is the mastering of these three fundamental things: the environment, the conditions and the elements of existence. In the church they are expressed as the Trin-

---

body apart from the spirit is dead" (James 2:26).

[4] "Be ye imitators of God, as beloved children" (Ephesians 5:1).

ity of God. What is the Trinity? It is three different Beings who share one thought and one will: the Father, Son and Holy Spirit. In the terms of syllogistic logic, they are the major premise, the minor premise and the conclusion respectively. The environment of all beings, and of our souls, is God. The element that brings life in itself is Christ. The conditions that help to manifest life are in the Holy Spirit.

When you change environments, you simultaneously need to change your form in accordance with the laws of the new environment. For example, you may take a dip in water, but if you actually wanted to live in water, you would have to change your human form into that of a fish. That, however, would be a degradation of life. A fish that wanted to change its environment from water to air would need to change its form accordingly, transforming its gills into lungs. A human being who wants to pass into the spiritual world is like a fish in the water wanting to experience life in the air. Therefore, if you want to experience the conditions in which the angels live, you have to transform yourselves accordingly. I recommend this teaching I am giving because it involves making yourselves 'lungs' for the other world. Without such lungs you cannot enter it. You need to prepare yourselves so that your lives can continue upwards without interruption when you leave the earth.

What did Christ mean when he said, "This is life eternal, to know You, the one true God"? He meant that God is the supreme power that is in constant motion within us, which bears life in Itself and creates the conditions by which we can know It. A being cannot know the environment in which it is immersed. For example, a fish cannot know the water in which it lives. Some people want to know God. If you are only immersed in God, you cannot know Him because you are inside Him. That would be to live in Him without knowing Him. If you want to know God, you have to go outside Him.

The cells in the human body are spiritually wise beings with certain intelligence. For one of the cells in your body to say, "I want to know what a human being is," would be the same as you saying, "I want to know what God is." If you want to try to know God, He cannot remain your environment; you have to go outside Him. "But can I do that?" Yes, you can. You only need to change your form. "But I cannot do that!" Then you have to wait until you can. For a cell to know what a human being is, it has to travel through billions of different conditions, through all the tissues of the human body: the stomach, the heart, the lungs, the brain and so on. Only when it has done so can it stop and say, "I have formed my opinion about the human being. I now understand what a human being is." And the philosophers in this world, having travelled everywhere, stop and say, "Now I understand what God is. Come, I will tell you. He is almighty." No, you have not understood anything. Only when you have exited this environment, when you have passed through the door known as 'death', will you know what God is. That is why people die. When the desire is born in a soul to know God, its human life has to end. The soul says to itself, "I must die so that I may know God." And this is the most accurate definition of knowing God.

The first letter in the Bulgarian word for 'knowing', познаване (poznavané), has the shape of an upside-down glass: П. While blossom grows it has the shape of an upward-facing glass, but once it has formed its seeds the blossom begins to turn downwards until it hangs like an upside-down glass, or the Bulgarian letter P: П. I say that, when we are receptive to knowledge our glasses are turned up to face God, so He can pour something into them. When we have received some knowledge, we want to taste it, to experience it, to learn about it. To return to the organic description, this means that the tree has blossomed, pollination has taken place and the fruit is growing and needs to ripen. You cannot learn something until you are pollinated and your fruit is growing. Otherwise you are just an empty, upward-facing soul. When your soul turns and faces down, it means the Lord has put something inside you. It is possible for fruit to drop prematurely, in which case the process of pollination and ripening needs to be repeated – there is no success in life without hard work. It is said that the letter O, or nought, is nothing, but in mathematics a nought has the power to increase or decrease a number ten times, which means that 'nothing' is actually 'something'. According to my understanding, time and space exist in nothingness as two elements necessary for our organic development. Light and warmth act in space, which means that when we put nought (O) after P (П) the flower has the conditions with which to develop, for it is knowing: познаване (poznavané).

Fruit trees have two environments: the soil for the roots, and the air for the branches and blossoms. The tree of life also has a double life, a material life in the roots and a spiritual life in the branches. The world of the spirits, of the angels, which some people call the astral world, is the connection between the physical-material human world and the divine world.[5] God is the one who speaks in the divine world. He is the source of knowledge, power and life. The human being in the physical world represents the soil preparing the juices of life. The angels connect the physical and divine worlds and apply the laws so that the two function harmoniously together. It is through the angels that we can know God, and we cannot have life within us unless we know Him. Imagine that you go outside on a cold winter's night and bask in the moonlight. Seeing that you are shivering, somebody asks you, "Why are you standing out here?" "I am sunbathing." "But there is no sun!" "Are you blind? That sun up there will slowly warm me." When you have no true idea of God, it shows that there is a gap between you and Him, a certain obstacle cutting off the connection between your life and the divine life.

I see this is unclear to you. Do you know why? It is because of the gap between the two worlds. I have to convey things from the other world to you here in this world. Human beings can perceive sound waves and light waves within certain ranges. Our speech is logical when we remain within the narrow circle of those things which we comprehend, those things which we can experience and test. When we pass instantly from sound to light we cannot remain logical, for there are vibrations between sound waves and light waves which we miss, due to our having no idea about them. There is an unimaginably large range of vibration between sound waves and light waves that is imperceptible to us. The things we do not understand form a desert for us in which nothing grows and nothing can be found.[6]

When Christ spoke about eternal life he was very careful. He filled all the gaps and connected all the worlds into a unified whole. He con-

---

[5] The Teacher also said, "Many people maintain that Christ's teaching is for the other world, but it is not; it is for this world. There is a relationship between the invisible world and the visible world like that between the roots and branches of a plant. When we walk the paths of Christ, we are connected to saints and light beings, which causes them to rejoice. These saints and light beings feed us spiritually. A tree nourishes itself from its roots and branches, from below and above" (11/24 January 1915).

[6] Nine years later the Teacher would say, "For a long time I have made an effort to translate the angelic language into the language of the earth, but I have not succeeded because their emphases and rhymes do not fit each other" (16 September 1923).

nected the spiritual world to the world of the angels. He connected the divine world to the world of the Trinity. He connected the physical world to the world of human souls. This is why Christ said, "I am the path from the truth to the life.[7] I join these two worlds, leading you to both the world of the angels and the world of God, the world of truth. Whoever follows me and walks on the path that I show him or her will find the necessary blessing for his or her soul, which is divine peace." This is why Christ also said, "My peace I give to you. My peace I leave with you."[8] Peace is the child of heaven, nurtured in the home of God. We may therefore come to the following conclusion: "the path" is the movement of the Spirit in the spiritually wise application of the laws of nature; "the life" is the harmonious organisation of the elements, and the development of the forces, in the Divine Soul; "the truth" is the manifestation of the one God, who creates the conditions in which the human spirit and the human soul can aspire to something better and brighter in this vast world.

Let us consider eternal life as a spring flowing from the divine mountaintop.[9] The water is the element that brings life, and the river's current is the descending path to a lower world. Christ said, "I came out from the Truth, from God, and descended to the material world to help human beings by giving them this living water."[10] It is also why elsewhere he said, "I am the living water."[11] These three things of

---

[7] Jesus said, "I am the way, and the truth, and the life: no one cometh unto the Father, but by me" (John 14:6).

[8] See John 14:27

[9] "In the visions of God brought he me into the land of Israel, and set me down upon a very high mountain, whereon was as it were the frame of a city on the south. And he brought me unto the door of the house; and behold, waters issued out from under the threshold of the house eastward, for the forefront of the house was toward the east" (Ezekiel 40:2; 47:1). "And he that sitteth on the throne said, 'I will give unto to him that is athirst of the fountain of the water of life freely'" (Revelation 21:5-6).

[10] Jesus said, "Whosoever drinketh of the water that I shall give him shall never thirst; but the water that I shall give him shall become in him a well of water springing up unto eternal life. The hour cometh, and now is, when the true worshippers shall worship the Father in spirit and truth: for such doth the Father seek to be his worshippers. God is a Spirit: and they that worship him must worship in spirit and truth" (John 4:14, 23-24).

[11] "Jesus stood and cried, saying, 'If any man thirst, let him come unto me, and drink. He that believeth on me, as the scripture hath said, out of his belly shall flow rivers of living water.' But this spake he of the Spirit, which they that believed on him were to receive: for the Spirit was not yet given; because Jesus was not yet glorified" (John 7:37-39).

which I am speaking – God, Jesus Christ and eternal life, or "the way, the truth and the life" – are all connected. If the water did not come from the mountaintop spring and did not flow down the riverbed of which Christ spoke, it would not bring the expected blessings. According to the Christian point of view, we should be near this spring. The Living Christ is the spring, and all we need to know is how to drink from it. I am not saying you do not know how to drink this water, but that you are drinking from it at between five hundred to one thousand kilometres downstream of the spring. You say that you know Christ, but you are unaware of how many other, impure elements have entered the water before it reaches you, deceiving your taste. You need to walk upstream. The path is long and your feet will blister, but when you arrive at the spring you will say, "This, truly, is water." Those who cannot make the journey will have to drink impure water, which is better than having no water at all. I am telling you to go, despite the blisters, and drink from the spring. When you return you will have a clear, fresh mind, a good heart and a broad perspective. You have to do much hard work on yourselves so that you can apply Christ's teaching and achieve those favourable results that will someday uplift you to citizenship of heaven and life among the saints and angels.

When we talk about eternal life, immortality, everybody will say that such a life is impossible here on earth. Actually, you could acquire eternal life right now, today, were you to have the bravery of the Bulgarian shepherd who knew how to fight with his crook.[12] To know how to fight with the crook of truth means to have attained the state of being in which you know how to react appropriately to any obstacles that come to face you in life. You often say, "It is the Lord's will," and do nothing. Observing this, the Lord responds by saying, "That coward's sheep will be taken from him and he will be enslaved." I am teaching you the necessity of work. Somebody might repossess your property and your heart and sell them, but no one can repossess and sell your mind. So many hearts, so many souls, are pawned or sold, yet the people who have pawned or sold them still believe they own them. We see many people who do not know how to think and act correctly. They can hate but they cannot love. All these people, with their rotten minds and

---

[12] For the story of the shepherd with the crook of truth, see p. 225 of the present volume.

hearts, create bad karma, and the whole population will have to suffer in the future because of the human laws and rules they create.

Christ said that to attain eternal life a person first has to learn to think and act correctly.[13] You are now saying to yourselves, "I understand. When I get home I will begin to apply the law correctly." But what will you apply? You will apply the old law. A small, unpleasant incident will derail you and you will forget about eternal life. Perhaps your dinner will be overdone and you will speak angrily to your spouse, who cooked it, losing your mind and heart over the food. If your meal is brought to you overcooked, do not let it disturb you.[14] While preparing yourself for eternal life you need to have the patience and self-control of the philosopher who had been working on certain mathematical problems for twenty years. He did not get angry when he returned home to find that his servant had put all his notes, made over twenty years, into the fire.[15]

It is also important that you protect your work. You often collect all the pieces of paper on which the Lord has made notes for you, saying, "What is all this rubbish?" and throw them into the fire. When the Lord arrives and asks you, "Where are your papers?" you answer, "I have cleaned the room." "This must not happen again!" says the Lord. That is not the way to clean your divine rooms. These pieces of paper are the different centres in a human being in which the Lord has written many things that are very precious for you. Everything should be put in order. There is a great mess in the buildings that the Lord is making out of you. Although the bricks, sand and stones are scattered all over the place at the moment, they will all become part of the structure of your new homes. You need to prepare this material yourselves, which is why Christ said, "When you know within yourselves the one true

[13] Jesus said, "I know that the Father's commandment is life eternal" (John 12:50).

[14] In linking "the old law" and an overcooked meal, the Teacher was possibly referring symbolically to the divorce law controversy of Jesus's time: an interpretation of Mosaic law – that, "When a man taketh a wife, and marrieth her, then it shall be, if she find no favour in his eyes, because he hath found some unseemly thing in her, that he shall write her a bill of divorcement, and give it in her hand, and send her out of his house" (Deuteronomy 24:1) – had allowed easy divorce for men, even for as trivial reason as a wife spoiling a meal. It was in this sense that the Pharisees asked Jesus, "Is it lawful for a man to put away his wife for every cause?" (Matthew 19:3).

[15] For the story of the servant and the mathematician's papers, see p. 198 of the present volume.

God, who builds, who is your environment, conditions and elements, you will gain eternal life."

I want to leave you with three things to think about: your environment, conditions and elements. If you are unable to do it, think on whatever you can. If you are able to, think on the following questions. Is your soul immersed in the environment called 'God'? Do you have the right conditions and elements? Is your air pure? Are your windows open? Are your eyes and tongue in their proper places?

The tongue is not as limited as it appears. This tongue that creates and destroys in the world is small and barely seen, but it can achieve so much: it breaks bones and causes people to fight one another.[16] If your tongue is loose, you need to tighten its screws and bolts, for when the Lord comes He will see whether or not your tongue is functioning as He designed it to.[17] Some screws and bolts must be damaged, as the tongue is jabbering away non-stop. Tighten the loose screws and bolts. And so many of them are missing! You need to find all the lost screws and bolts and all the lost parts of your tongue, mind and heart and put everything in its proper place. Christ is now coming to help you with this process. You, however, have already discarded something small that you erroneously believed to be unimportant....

Today's scientists consider the appendix to be useless and think it should be removed if it becomes painful. How can they say it is unimportant? It has taken God millions of years to make the appendix, and the time will come when it begins to function. If the appendix is removed, the illness will reappear somewhere else in the body. An appendix might well protest at your diet, saying, "You should not eat meat! Animals should not be killed!"[18] Beans, lentils and the like will not cause you pain in the appendix. The appendix has friends in the heart and mind, and if you remove the appendix those friends will also

---

[16] "The tongue is a little member, and boasteth great things. Behold, how much wood is kindled by how small a fire! And the tongue is a fire: the world of iniquity among our members is the tongue, which defileth the whole body, and setteth on fire the wheel of nature, and is set on fire by hell. The tongue can no man tame; it is a restless evil, it is full of deadly poison" (James 3:5-6, 8).

[17] "If any man thinketh himself to be religious, while he bridleth not his tongue but deceiveth his heart, this man's religion is vain" (James 1:26).

[18] Being vegetarian was, and is, an important part of discipleship. There is a story with this theme in Appendix B (p. 382).

die. This is why Christ said, "These three elements in life – the conditions, forces and laws – need to be put in their proper places." This is the meaning of Christianity, and it is the profound science of life. I do not want to give you an empty philosophy; I would like you test and verify in your own lives the things I tell you.

How will the world be set right? It will be set right once all the screws and bolts are put in their correct places. Then life will start to run like clockwork. I will give you an example of what I mean. A man buys a watch, only for it to stop working soon afterwards. He thinks to himself, "I paid so much money for this watch, and I wore it for only one week before it broke." He takes the watch to a watchmaker to have it repaired. After they agree a price for the repair work, the watchmaker blows into the watch's mechanism, a louse jumps out and the watch starts working again. "You are going to take my money just for doing that?" asks the man. "Yes," replies the watchmaker. And when the Lord comes, He will likewise simply blow and everything will start to work as it is meant to. How easy! Such insects belong elsewhere and should not remain in the watch. Christianity is a philosophy that wants to free the human soul of all parasites and to fix the screws and bolts in the tongue, the mind and the heart so that they function properly – this is how you attain salvation. When all the screws and bolts are fixed in place and the heart and mind are functioning properly, the conditions for eternal life will appear. Then resurrection will be possible.

I understand that it is long and difficult work to find all the screws and bolts and fix them into place, but when it has been done successfully humankind will celebrate its jubilee on earth.[19] On that day the children will sing the new song of life, rejoicing that their parents have fixed everything correctly and established a bright future for them. The nations will rejoice, praising and glorifying the good Lord because their spiritual leaders, teachers and political leaders found their screws

---

[19] The Teacher was making a symbolic reference to the jubilee year of Israel, a time of rest, joy and restitution, when servants were freed and land was restored to its original owner. The Lord said to Moses, "Ye shall hallow the fiftieth year, and proclaim liberty throughout the land unto all the inhabitants thereof: it shall be a jubile unto you; and ye shall return every man unto his possession, and ye shall return every man unto his family. A jubile shall that fiftieth year be unto you: ye shall not sow, neither reap that which groweth of itself in it, nor gather the grapes in it of the undressed vines. For it is a jubile; it shall be holy unto you: ye shall eat the increase thereof out of the field" (Leviticus 25:10-12).

and bolts and fitted them correctly. It will be the beginning of a bright future on earth. All people will sing a great song of life that will touch them to the depths of their hearts and souls. This song, which expresses the entire past and includes the entirety of the future, will reveal the spirit of the new life.[20]

But someone will say, "What kind of screws and bolts are these? What can they do?" The path that should be followed is described within these screws and bolts, for they connect and tighten the separate parts of life. Whoever looks and sees the threads of the screws and bolts, as well as the hand that is tightening them, will understand the profound meaning of the great laws that move everything towards an intended purpose.[21] These are the divine forces that, by the divine will, will soon appear in life and collect the disunited elements and put them in their proper places. These forces will direct the divine juices to the human soul, place the soul in its true environment, create the most appropriate conditions for the soul's development and deposit the elements of life in it. Our souls will suckle on the Divine Mother's breast, receiving pure, unpolluted milk,[22] and then the roots of divine consciousness will appear in our subconscious minds. Trunks will rise from the roots, branches will grow and the leaves of selfconsciousness

---

[20] "O sing unto the Lord a new song: Sing unto the Lord, all the earth" (Psalm 96:1). "O sing unto the Lord a new song; For he hath done marvellous things" (Psalm 98:1)

"And I saw in the right hand of him that sat on the throne a book written within and on the back, close sealed with seven seals. And I saw a strong angel proclaiming with a great voice, 'Who is worthy to open the book, and to loose the seals thereof?' And the Lamb came, and he taketh it out of the right hand of him that sat on the throne. And they sing a new song, saying, 'Worthy art thou to take the book, and to open the seals thereof: for thou wast slain, and didst purchase unto God with thy blood men of every tribe, and tongue, and people, and nation, and madest them to be unto our God a kingdom and priests; and they shall reign upon the earth.'

"And every created thing which is in the heaven, and on the earth, and under the earth, and on the sea, and all things that are in them, heard I saying, 'Unto him that sitteth on the throne, and unto the Lamb, be the blessing, and the honour, and the glory, and the dominion, for ever and ever'" (Revelation 5:1-2, 7, 9-10, 13).

[21] "I am God, and there is none like me; declaring the end from the beginning, and from ancient times things that are not yet done; saying, 'My counsel shall stand, and I will do all my pleasure'" (Isaiah 46:9-10). "My word shall not return unto me void, but it shall accomplish that which I please, and it shall prosper in the thing whereto I sent it" (Isaiah 55:11). "Behold, I create new heavens and a new earth" (Isaiah 65:17).

[22] "As newborn babes, long for the spiritual milk which is without guile, that ye may grow thereby unto salvation" (1 Peter 2:2).

273

will develop. On the twigs of consciousness the buds and blossoms of superconsciousness will appear, connecting us to the angelic world.

When this has happened it will be a sign of the spiritual spring, and the human soul will find itself in the realm of immortality, beyond the clutches of death, sin and crime. With positive faith and positive knowledge we can anticipate priceless wealth, the fruit of the tree of eternal life. The leaves of this tree will serve for the healing of human defects, and its fruit will serve for the maintenance of the immortality of the human soul and its unity with God. This great event is now on the doorstep of today's life. [23]

---

[23] Jesus said, "To him that overcometh, to him will I give to eat of the tree of life, which is in the Paradise of God" (Revelation 2:7).

"And I John saw a new heaven and a new earth: for the first heaven and the first earth are passed away. And I saw the holy city, new Jerusalem, coming down out of heaven from God, made ready as a bride adorned for her husband. And I heard a great voice out of the throne saying, 'Behold, the tabernacle of God is with men, and he shall dwell with them, and they shall be his peoples, and God himself shall be with them, and be their God: and he shall wipe away every tear from their eyes; and death shall be no more; neither shall there be mourning, nor crying, nor pain, any more: the first things are passed away.' And he that sitteth on the throne said, 'Behold, I make all things new.'

"And the angel spake with me, saying, 'Come hither, I will shew thee the bride, the wife of the Lamb.' And he carried me away in the Spirit to a mountain great and high, and shewed me the holy city Jerusalem, coming down out of heaven from God. And I saw no temple therein: for the Lord God the Almighty, and the Lamb, are the temple thereof. And he shewed me a river of water of life, bright as crystal, proceeding out of the throne of God and of the Lamb, in the midst of the street thereof. And on this side of the river and on that was the tree of life, bearing twelve manner of fruits, yielding its fruit every month: and the leaves of the tree were for the healing of the nations" (Revelation 21:1-5, 9-10, 22; 22:1-2). "And the fruit thereof shall be for meat" (Ezekiel 47:12).

Only Fear God

Jesus said,

Be not afraid of them which kill the body, but are not able to kill the soul: but rather fear him which is able to destroy both soul and body in hell.[2]

Fear is an unpleasant feeling in the soul that exists not only in people but also in animals. It is a feeling deposited in the living organism for a specific purpose. Fear indicates the presence in our natural environment, or in the other conditions in which we live, of certain elements that are in opposition to, and harmful to, our lives. Fear simply serves to protect us from anything which might damage us. When did fear first appear in human beings? The general opinion is that it originated with the Fall of Humanity. Before that time human beings did not know fear.

Fear actually has a double expression, one internal and one external. When a child makes his or her first mistake fear is instantly born in the child's soul. Whose soul can be quiet and peaceful when he or she has committed even a small sin? A feeling of fear instantly appears in that person's soul. This means some threatening elements have entered the soul. If you have a house with pine flooring, the fear will instantly be born in you that the floor might catch fire. This means there is a certain flammable element deposited in your floor that might cause the whole house to burn down.

In working in the organic world for thousands of years, fear has made human beings and animals its slaves. Fear does, however, have a positive side. The quality of vigilance was formed as a result of fear. Many animals have long legs because of fear. A long-legged animal is a fearful one. I will not tell you now the long story of the part that fear played in the history of evolution. Today well-educated people say that

[1] Three days earlier, on 16/29 October, the Ottoman Empire, Bulgaria's neighbour, entered the First World War on the side of the Central Powers: Austria-Hungary and Germany.
[2] Matthew 10:28. It is evident in the text that the Teacher actually read the whole chapter.

religion originated from fear. That is a false conception, for religion existed before fear appeared.

Christ told his disciples, "Do not fear those who can kill the body but cannot damage the soul," because he knew they feared for their homes, their bodies. Why should we not be afraid? If your house burns down and you have sufficient capital in the bank, you do not need to worry because you can build yourself a new, better house. Likewise, if the capital of your soul is deposited elsewhere, you do not need to fear for your body.

Now, let us look at the second part of the verse, about the one we should fear, the one who can destroy both the body and the soul. There have been many long arguments over the meaning of this part of the verse. Who is the one we should fear? Some people say we should fear the devil, but I say it is God whom we should fear. By this, I mean that we need to be careful not to disappoint God, or, to put it differently, we ought to be devout. Were I to interpret the divine law of life, I would not tell you whom to fear and whom not to fear; I would tell you how to obey the divine law. This is the negative form of fear. The positive form occurs when we sin. The person who fulfils God's will has nothing to fear, but there will always be fear in the heart of anyone who does not fulfil it. Such a person is never calm and free. In the chapter I read, Christ wanted to assure his disciples that there were certain laws in the world regulating human life: he told them, "Even the hairs on your head are numbered. Not one hair can fall from your head without reason."[3] If I obey God's law, I will be under God's protection, as the birds are.[4] Contemporary Christians misunderstand their relationship with God and their relationship with religion. Much suffering has been born in the human soul as a result of it. For example, some people think religion involves going to church, lighting a candle and crossing themselves – that to do these things is to be religious. Religion, however, is much more profound than that. The deepest part of religion is to love God. If we have this fundamental law inside us, we will be ready to do a thousand other things for the Lord.[5] But how do we express

[3] See Matthew 10:30

[4] Jesus said, "Are not two sparrows sold for a farthing? and not one of them shall fall on the ground without your Father" (Matthew 10:29).

[5] Jesus said, "'Thou shalt love the Lord thy God with all thy heart, and with all thy soul,

our love for the Lord whom we cannot see? Christ said, "Your Father is in heaven."[6] I look up and cannot see Him, but I tell myself that once I leave my body I will go to heaven and be with Him....

Christ said to his disciples, "Do not fear those who kill on earth." Who are these killers? As we saw in the first verse of the chapter I read, it is the evil spirits who have been given the power to kill.[7] They do not have such power over good people, however, only over bad ones. Contemporary Christians say, "I want power over my brothers." Christ, however, did not give his apostles power over other people but over evil spirits. Each one of us needs to rule over these spirits. Whoever does not understand this divine law will always make mistakes and evil spirits will set up ambushes for him or her. People have different methods of threatening such spirits, but the spirits are not afraid of them. Evil spirits are not afraid of sticks or words. To have power over evil spirits you must not have their weaknesses. If you have their weaknesses, it does not matter whether you are well educated, a philosopher or a minister, you will be their slave. These spirits can make intrigues and dethrone kings. They can do anything. But if you do not have their weaknesses, you will be their master. This is why Christ could command such spirits. He was pure, and when he said, "Come out!" they answered, "We obey you."[8]

Evil spirits not only cause illnesses but also heal them. This gives you reason to wonder, but it is the law. If you borrow money from somebody, you ought to return it, ought you not? If you hurt somebody, you ought to pay for his or her healing, ought you not? The devil causes you some harm, and you call the Lord to put things right. The Lord therefore captures the devil and says to him, "You have damaged this person's house. Go and repair it!" The devil then takes pains to fix it. Afterwards

and with all thy mind.' This is the great and first commandment. And a second like unto it is this, 'Thou shalt love thy neighbour as thyself.' On these two commandments hangeth the whole law, and the prophets" (Matthew 22:37-40).

[6] Jesus said, "Call no man your father on the earth: for one is your Father, which is in heaven" (Matthew 23:9).

[7] "Jesus called unto him his twelve disciples, and gave them authority over unclean spirits, to cast them out, and to heal all manner of disease and all manner of sickness" (Matthew 10:1).

[8] "With authority he commandeth even the unclean spirits, and they obey him" (Mark 1:27).

God says to the devil, "If you like, you may damage the house again."

Now, why does God not answer your prayers? I will tell you. It is because you are sinners. As such, when the workmen come to repair your houses, you are unable to control them and they leave. When the Lord sends workmen to repair your house, you need to have the power to command them, to stand over them with a whip, as it were. If you give them freedom, they will simply run away and your house will be left unrepaired. You should never have the weaknesses of these spirits. Some people say, "We cannot be without weaknesses." In that case your weaknesses will kill you, take your bodies and money and imprison you, and there will be no escape. Christ came and said, "I will tell you what you should fear. Fear to break God's law!" which means that you need to obey God's law for your body and soul to be free.

Each one of us should inspect his or her heart and mind, to see what weaknesses exist in them. If you like telling lies, all kinds of lying spirits will hang around you. They will be your guests whom you have attracted. If you like to gloat, all kinds of gloating spirits will hang around you. If you were clairvoyant, you would see that your homes are filled with whole armies of these spirits who do nothing but eat and drink. If you hate, all kinds of hateful spirits will eat and drink at your expense. This is why people die. When these spirits have come and stayed in your home for two or three days, you will begin to complain: "My head aches. My eyes hurt. I have pain in my hands, legs, stomach, heart and lungs." How could they not hurt you? These evil spirits draw juices from you and begin veiling your eyes; you start to become blind and deaf, your legs and arms also become unwell, and finally you are lifted up and carried to the grave. And when you go before the Lord in your rags,[9] He will ask you, "My child, did you nourish yourself with everything I gave you?" "Father, forgive me. I ate, drank and fornicated. I will not do so anymore." As God is kind, He will say, "It is sufficient that you have learnt your lesson. I will put you in credit again." This is why Christ said, "I will tell you whom to fear…." This kind of fear is kindly spiritual wisdom.

---

[9] "He shewed me Joshua the high priest standing before the angel of the Lord. Now Joshua was clothed with filthy garments, and stood before the angel. And the angel spake unto those that stood before him, saying, 'Take the filthy garments from off him.' And unto Joshua he said, 'Behold, I have caused thine iniquity to pass from thee'" (Zechariah 3:1, 3-4).

When a person has united his positive and negative feelings, as well as having united his cautiousness and his ability to think properly, kindly spiritual wisdom is born in him. Fear is the negative element of kindly spiritual wisdom. Christ therefore wanted to say, "Do not separate these elements from each other, because when you separate your mind from your feelings of fear they cannot regulate each other and you will lose both your body and soul." What is hell? It is the limited conditions of development in which one experiences a life of suffering and an empty consciousness.

Do you know the state of somebody who has died? You will experience the feeling a little more tangibly one day.... When only the deceased's bones remain, the soul circles over them and begins weeping and lamenting, saying, "How beautiful I was, and now this is all that remains of my wealth. The plaster finish has gone!" The bricks and tiles remain, however, and after a period of time these bones will restore their original temple. This is why the Lord asked the prophet, "Son of man, can these bones come to life?" The prophet answered, "Lord, You know the answer." The Lord then said, "Call the Spirit to come and bring the bones back to life."[10]

Christ said to his disciples, "Do not fear those who can kill the body." To regulate this type of fear, the way we live has to be utterly motivated by the divine law, which means for us to be aware in our inner consciousness that we are connected to God. We sometimes think to ourselves, "I want to see the Lord. I want to see Jesus Christ." But we see him everyday! Whenever the feeling of love is born in us, he is there with us and we can feel him. We only need to open our spiritual eyes to see him. You now see the external side of things, not the essential side. Whenever you suffer or you love, you are in communion with God. Someone who is suffering is like a sick person whom the Lord is healing. When the Lord bandages the wounds it causes certain pains and the patient complains. The Lord explains, "You are suffering because you did not obey My laws. Be patient and I will heal you." "But these pains are unbearable!" "True, but when I warned you not to break the law you did not listen to Me." "But it takes a long time to understand that!" "Yes, but you will learn."[11]

[10] See Ezekiel 37:1-14

[11] The Teacher also said, "Always be thankful. It is the healing process that causes suffer-

From now on you should experiment – as the early Christians did – and learn how to leave your bodies.[12] Your minds say, "It would be wonderful to be able to leave my body." Wonderful, yes, but you need certain knowledge to actually do it. First you have to free yourselves of all the weaknesses that you share with the spirits who surround you. Then, when you leave your body, you will tell them, "None of you come near my body. If you do, I will whip you!" But if the spirits know you still have weaknesses, they will take possession of your body when you leave it. This is why the Lord tightly binds contemporary people to their bodies. Were people now able to leave their bodies, it would be for the worse, for their evolution would stop. Christ paid attention to those disciples who wanted to follow him and learn these secrets of the kingdom of God, and I think this is still the method of achieving a long life.

I will tell you a fact. People who suffer and easily become angry and whose lives pass through many storms have short lives. Those who are calm, gentle and of a good disposition and who do not worry or get angry have long lives. This is why Herbert Spencer said, "When the external forces of nature are balanced with the inner processes of the human organism, we will have eternal life in the physical world." What are these external forces? They are the harmful elements. When we have balanced ourselves, when we understand what we desire and have learnt how to react against and subordinate harmful elements, we will be able to live on the earth for as long as we wish – one hundred years, five hundred years, one thousand years – and we will be able to leave whenever we want to; it will be up to us.[13] Having lived on the earth for several thousand years, we will say, "This has been enough for me. I now want to make the great journey to the other world." Our relatives and friends will accompany us to our point of departure, just

ing. The Lord pushed Jacob's hip and said, 'You can only pay for your sins with suffering'" (22 January/4 February 1915).

[12] The Apostle Paul's words, "I know a man in Christ, fourteen years ago (whether in the body, I know not; or whether out of the body, I know not; God knoweth), such a one caught up even to the third heaven" (2 Corinthians 12:2), suggest that he had had experience out of his body, and that it was a concept that would be understood by other Christians.

[13] The Teacher also said, "After resurrecting we will begin to live naturally. Up to now people have not been living; they have only been grumbling. After resurrecting we will be able to come and live on the earth when we want to, and whenever we want to leave we will only have to call Petra [St Peter] and tell him so" (21 January/3 February 1915).

as people say goodbye on a railway platform. We can buy a ticket and leave, and our friends will not walk behind our coffins lamenting: "My poor friend, taken by death." Instead, we will say, "I am going to make a journey to visit my Father's home. I might come back here some day." And our friends and relatives will wish us a good trip. Christianity is a science that should prepare us for this great journey.

Christ said to his disciples, "Do not fear." Then he looked up to heaven and continued: "Do not fear for these small houses that you have here on the earth and do not worry about petty things, because our Father has determined great things for us."[14] Look to keep your souls pure and full of light, for when you have this as your capital you will be able to travel the vast distances of Space. When the day comes for you to start for heaven, you will not take your body but will go with your soul. You will leave your body on the earth, where it was made. Your bodies are temporary vehicles made from the elements of the earth, and you will remain in them while you are in this earthly kingdom of four elements. But when you arrive at the point on the mountain where you need to walk along a goat's path, you will have to leave the vehicle and continue on foot. This is why Christ said, "Do not fear. When you arrive at the mountain path, do not lose your souls and stop your evolution."

You want to become masters, but do not become masters over your brothers and sisters. The greatest crime of people today is that they want to command others. You should not command other people. You can, and should, command evil spirits. I would like you to master and educate an evil spirit, but I do not want you to command people, which is also what Christ said.[15] Sometimes you want to know who is greater and who is lesser, who is older and who is younger. Those things do not matter, for the Lord can send you to the earth earlier or later. One day the Lord will place you at the tail, on another He will place you at the head. On one day you will be put on the spine, on another you will

---

[14] Jesus said, "Fear not therefore; ye are of more value than many sparrows. Every one therefore who shall confess me before men, him will I also confess before my Father which is in heaven" (Matthew 10:31-32).

[15] "There arose a contention among the disciples, which of them is accounted to be greatest. And Jesus said unto them, 'The kings of the Gentiles have lordship over them; and they that have authority over them are called Benefactors. But ye shall not be so: but he that is the greater among you, let him become as the younger; and he that is chief, as he that doth serve. I am in the midst of you as he that serveth'" (Luke 22:24-27).

be on the leg. These are not essential things. You will find your power in feeling yourself to be the master over evil spirits, in making them obey you. Human power is within, and this is where you need to turn your attention. Every one of you needs to begin to control these spirits. I know evil spirits torment many people. Many go to Christ for help. And how does he help them? He ties up the evil spirits. But these people then untie them! Such people cannot be helped. Will Christ occupy himself with your foxes and wolves? No, he will not, so it is you who should put them to work. Perhaps this thought has been given a little allegorically, but I give it to you as a rule. You cannot become the master of your life until you have learnt to master evil spirits.

Before you can master evil spirits, you have to have taken five of the seven steps of human spiritual development. Evil spirits are afraid of light. Therefore, the first thing you need to do is to turn to God. Why do you need to turn? Because at the moment your back is turned to God and there is darkness in your world. Turn around and face the Lord. Unless you turn to Him, nothing is possible. Turn your heart and mind inside out before His light so that you will be able to see the dust that has accumulated inside them. Then shake off the dust.

The second step is repentance, a re-examination and balancing of your accounts. Your company makes an announcement: "Trade suspended during annual accounts." You calculate your balance and discover that you are in debt. You have no choice but to go to your creditors and ask for more credit, which is repentance. You produce your accounts and say, "I am an honest person. I do not know how it happened, but I have got myself into debt. I apologise. I need more money from you." If you had not gone to them with this request, one day they would have had you imprisoned. Once they have inspected your books and accepted that you are indeed an honest person, they will say to you, "We have done good business together in the past, so we forgive you and will lend you money to put you in credit again."

The third step consists of forgiveness and salvation, which are closely connected. What Christianity calls salvation comes when you have taken the first two steps: turning to God and repenting before Christ. At this point Christ will say, "I am giving you new credit and sending you out again into the world to work." Your company then makes a new announcement: "Reopened for trade."

The fourth step is regeneration. I will explain the meaning of regeneration by describing a process in agriculture. A farmer uproots and replants his land. When the newly planted apple trees start to grow, that is the beginning of regeneration. The farmer hopes the new orchard will bear fruit. A similar process takes place in Christianity by which we are regenerated, by which we begin to grow. Regeneration is a process of growing, blossoming and beginning to bear fruit.

Turning to God, repentance, forgiveness and salvation, regeneration, and then the fifth step, rebirth. In the fifth step a human being is liberated from the karmic law of cause and effect. This means you have become a free citizen, a master, and no one can rule over you. Only when taking this fifth step can you master evil spirits. Then you will be a disciple of Christ, a high state. Christ gave his disciples power over evil spirits and sent them away to heal people and raise the dead.[16] How could such power be given to somebody who has just turned to God and has yet to look at his accounts? He has not been forgiven, nor has he been reborn, yet he wants to rule the world. That is not possible. You want to command evil spirits? It is impossible. You have to have already taken the first four steps before you can become the master of your situation.[17]

---

[16] See Matthew 10:1, 8

[17] Of the last two steps, the Teacher said, "The sixth step is enlightenment. When you are close to enlightenment, you begin a new trial greater than the last, that of rebirth. The further a human being advances, the harder the examination. When you have passed this trial, you receive enlightenment. To be enlightened means your consciousness enters a higher level and new forces are awakened within you. You now begin to communicate with perfect beings, learning their sacred language and entering their society. You are given great knowledge of the forces and laws of nature. You are entrusted with the keys to nature's laws and know the methods of working with them.

"The seventh step is resurrection. There comes a time when the enlightened person finds the light of heaven is hidden by dark clouds. He or she then passes through great darkness. This is the greatest trial, which precedes resurrection. In this trial you feel utterly alone. Even the invisible world seems to have abandoned you. It appears that all hope is lost. If you are able to endure this greatest darkness and remain faithful to the idea of God, remaining conscious that God has not really left you and that everything is happening for the good, the trial is completed and you enter the great life of freedom.

"In succeeding in this final step you are resurrected and complete your evolution on earth. That which is divine within you awakens in its great fullness. You are no longer a human being but are raised to a higher level, entering a life without any kind of suffering – as it is said in Revelation, "God will wipe away every tear from their eyes forever." When you have achieved this state, you will guide your brothers and sisters on earth to the path to freedom, the path to the light in which you live" (some time between 1927 and 1944).

You are now sitting and thinking, worrying about the extent of your virtue. There are two extremes in Christianity: some people present themselves as more humble than they really are, while others feel themselves to be more sinful than they really are. You ought to be truthful. You should not pretend to be richer or poorer than you are. We should always tell the truth as we understand it inside ourselves. You need to speak clearly, categorically and positively. Then your external relationships with others will be good. Why? Because each of us has a guiding spirit in heaven. When you settle your accounts with the spirit who guides you, it will settle your accounts with the spirits to whom you are indebted, after which they will no longer be able to hold anything against you.

You now have the method by which to rule over evil spirits, which is not having their weaknesses. If you are fearful, all kinds of fearful spirits will hang around you. This is why you need to remove all these weaknesses from yourselves. You say, "I will not smoke anymore!" but you smoke again the next day. You should have made the change without telling anyone. You say, "I have decided to plant my garden." But you have not planted anything yet. Plant your garden first and then call your friends over to see it: "Come, my friends, and see what I have done." They will enjoy themselves. At another time, you say, "I have decided to be good. Come and have a look at my plan. I will do this and I will do that." You will do nothing! I have seen millions of plans – hell is full of them. If you think of doing something, do not speak anything of it. Only say, "Lord, come and help me." When your orchards have grown and are bearing fruit, call all your friends over and say, "Eat, drink, enjoy yourselves." Do that and the Lord will bless you. This is the meaning of Christianity.

When Christ said, "Do not fear those who kill the body. Instead, fear those who kill the spirit," he meant that you do not own your earthly vehicles; you only rent them, and they will be taken from you one day. "They threw me out of my house!" Why should they not throw you out? Thank them for having been so good as to wait many years before ejecting you.

The spirits are masters of the elements that we have on the earth. These elements belong to them. This is why it is said in the Scriptures that the earth is not our native land; it does not belong to us.[18] The Lord

[18] "Beloved, I beseech you as sojourners and pilgrims, to abstain from fleshly lusts, which war against the soul" (1 Peter 2:11). "For we have not here an abiding city, but we seek

has sent us here to conquer the earth with power.[19] You want to take possession of the earth and be its masters, but to do that you first have to conquer the spirits. Only then can you conquer the outer elements, because every element has its master. You cannot master water if you have not conquered the spirits of water. You cannot master the air until you have conquered the spirits of the air. You cannot master fire unless you have conquered the spirits of fire. And so on.

Christ gave us a law by which we should act: first we need to be pure and then we should turn to him.[20] Since Christ is now coming into the world, in what state will he find you? Some of you he will find rich and others he will find poor. It is said, "If a person builds upon the foundation of Jesus Christ with gold, silver, precious stones, wood, hay or straw, it will be known to everybody, for the day will show it. Everyone's work will be tested by fire. The people whose work remains will receive payment. The people whose work is burnt up will lose something yet be saved, but only as those who have been saved from a fire."[21] Whoever does not follow spiritual wisdom and does not fear the Lord, "such a one will be given to Satan for the killing of the flesh, so that the spirit can be saved on the day of Lord Jesus".[22] If you have acquired experiences over many thousands of years, if you have suffered while holding high the banner of truth, if you have not feared those who kill the body and have sacrificed yourself for the triumph of righteousness, for the triumph of the kingdom of God, the Lord will raise you again, He will resurrect you. This is why Christ said, "Do not fear those who kill the body." If they kill your body, your soul will remain free, and that is the precious thing in life.[23]

---

after the city which is to come" (Hebrews 13:14).

[19] "God created man in his own image, in the image of God created he him; male and female created he them. And God blessed them: and God said unto them, 'Be fruitful, and multiply, and replenish the earth, and subdue it; and have dominion over the fish of the sea, and over the fowl of the air, and over every living thing that moveth upon the earth.'" (Genesis 1:27-28). "O Lord, thou madest man to have dominion over the works of thy hands; Thou hast put all things under his feet" (Psalm 8:6) "For whatsoever is begotten of God overcometh the world" (1 John 5:4).

[20] "Jesus came into Galilee, preaching the gospel of God, and saying, 'The time is fulfilled, and the kingdom of God is at hand: repent ye, and believe in the gospel'" (Mark 1:14-15).

[21] See 1 Corinthians 3:12-15

[22] See 1 Corinthians 5:5

[23] Jesus said, "He that doth not take his cross and follow after me, is not worthy of me.

Every path leading you away from the truth is deadly for both your body and soul, because fearful and faint-hearted people will not inherit the kingdom of God. In working for a just cause of the Lord, or a just cause of humanity, or a just cause of your nation, or a just cause of society, or a just cause of your home, or a just cause of an individual soul, there should be neither fear, nor hesitation, nor faint-heartedness, nor retreating from the Great Origin of Life. What is right is always right. Love and fear are incompatible in the human spirit, in the spirit of the true human being. Where there is love there is no fear. Where there is fear there is no love. Love is a sign of the wholeness and unity of all the forces, feelings and abilities of the human spirit. Fear is a sign of division in the inner harmony of the peace of the soul.[24] By that I mean what is high, noble and good in human beings. I do not mean the impudence, rudeness, cruel-heartedness and insensitivity that are often taken for bravery and fearlessness.

The ideal of heroism is this: when you are pilloried for a righteous cause and you are able to bear with magnanimity all suffering, shaming, abuse, gloating and the accusations of those around you, or even of the whole world, and you say to your Mother, "For you who gave me birth into this world of God, I sacrifice everything. In your love I find the last support of my soul. My fears in this world and my fear of those who can kill my body have outlived their time. I am not afraid because I know you. Whether you give me death or life, I will accept either with equal gratitude. With you there is meaning even in death. Without you life is purposeless. In death or in life, may you forever be the luminous crown of my spirit."[25]

He that findeth his life shall lose it; and he that loseth his life for my sake shall find it" (Matthew 10:38-39). "For what is a man profited, if he gain the whole world, and lose or forfeit his own self?" (Luke 9:25). "Or what shall a man give in exchange for his life?" (Matthew 16:26).

[24] "God is love; and he that abideth in love abideth in God, and God abideth in him. Herein is love made perfect with us, that we may have boldness in the day of judgement; because as he is, even so are we in this world. There is no fear in love: but perfect love casteth out fear, because fear hath punishment; and he that feareth is not made perfect in love" (1 John 4:16-18).

[25] "Standing by the cross of Jesus was his mother" (John 19:25). "The Jerusalem that is above is free, which is our mother" (Galatians 4:26). "Blessed is the man that endureth temptation: for when he hath been approved, he shall receive the crown of life, which the Lord promised to them that love him" (James 1:12).

The Spirit and the Flesh:
The Law of Similarity and the Law of Contrast

The Apostle Paul wrote,

> Walk by the Spirit, and ye shall not fulfil the lust of the flesh. For the flesh lusteth against the Spirit, and the Spirit against the flesh; for these are contrary the one to the other; that ye may not do the things that ye would. The fruit of the Spirit is love, joy, peace, *longpatience*, kindness, *compassion*, faithfulness, meekness, temperance.[1]

The world in which we live is governed by laws, the rules God made many years ago when creating the universe. When God placed the first human being in the world – and the Scriptures are silent on this – He taught him heavenly knowledge for a long time. God introduced the man to all the fundamental laws in the mansion He had given him to live in, and He showed him the qualities of the herbs and the elements. The Lord made the human being master of all things, and said, "If you observe My laws, which I made, you will always be happy, joyful and blissful and will succeed in every undertaking. But the day you break My command, everything will be turned against you."

The Scriptures speak of two trees, the tree of life and the tree of the knowledge of good and evil.[2] In Paradise these two trees were alive, intelligent and contained certain powers and qualities. And the Lord said to the man, "There is a great danger hidden in the tree of the knowledge of good and evil, and you will lose everything on the day you reach for it. The elements hidden in this tree are not for you, because you are not strong enough to control them. In the future you

---

[1] Galatians 5:16-17, 22-23. The original Bulgarian publication only quoted verses 17 and 22. In the Revised Version, Galatians 5:22 says "longsuffering, kindness, goodness", not "longpatience, kindness, compassion", which accords with the 1914 Constantinople Bible and better fits the lecture.

[2] See Genesis 2:8-9

may learn how, but for now you may use any tree other than the tree of the knowledge of good and evil."[3] I will not, however, be talking about the profound reasons why Adam broke the divine command.

Some people preach that we need to have faith. Actually, faith is necessary, no matter whether it be positive or negative. Faith is the foundation of life. Without it life cannot exist. Adam and Eve came to have a negative faith in God, disbelief. Lucifer entered the Garden of Paradise and seduced Adam and Eve into trusting him instead of God. They abandoned God and the result was the Fall of Humanity.[4] As the Apostle Paul said to the Romans, "You are the slave of the one you obey."[5]

This morning my lecture is on two great laws, the law of contrast and the law of similarity. These are laws we can test every day. When beside a calm and peaceful sea, suddenly you might see it become wavy, with a high tide forming. The water moves in and out, a high tide and a low tide. High and low tides also take place inside us. When the old philosophers said, "Know yourself," they meant people need to know these two laws of regular motion, high tide and low tide. Contemporary science calls it the law of rhythmic motion. In everything there is a movement from the centre to the periphery and back again to the centre. In everything there is a high tide and a low tide, a rising and falling, conception and degeneration, and so on. These tides can be for twelve seconds, twelve minutes, twelve hours, twelve days, twelve weeks, twelve months, twelve years, twelve hundred years, twelve thousand years, twelve million years and so on. The proportion always remains the same, twelve high and twelve low – thus acts this law.

The Apostle Paul spoke about the law of the flesh, which is the law of low tide. The law of the Spirit is the law of high tide. The law of contrast contains the law of low tide. The law of similarity contains the law of high tide. These two laws are great things in the world, and it is good for us to learn about them. The law of similarity is the law of heaven. The other, the law of contrast, is the law of the earth, of the organic world, of the flesh. The Apostle Paul said the flesh is opposed

---

[3] See Genesis 2:15-17; 3:2-3

[4] See Genesis 3:1-24

[5] "Know ye not, that to whom ye present yourselves as servants unto obedience, his servants ye are whom ye obey; whether of sin unto death, or of obedience unto righteousness?" (Romans 6:16).

to the Spirit, and the Spirit is opposed to the flesh. We cannot reconcile these two laws because they move in opposite directions; one moves forwards, and the other, backwards. The law of contrast is a law of destruction: it destroys harmony and happiness.

If a child is conceived and born during a condition of contrast, the child will become a criminal. If the parents live according to the law of similarity, they will give birth to a noble son or daughter who will be good and have a well-developed mind. Thus act the two great laws. The first human beings, before the Fall of Humanity, understood these laws, but after the Fall they forgot them. The Lord says, "I gave you a mind to think about how the world is ordered. I once told you about these laws, but you forgot them. And now these laws themselves will teach you...." Only when societies come to understand the deep meaning of these two laws will it be possible to set everything in good order. When we begin to act according to these laws, the world will be arranged in the same way as God set it up in the beginning. Identical causes produce identical effects; opposite causes produce opposite effects. The Hindus, who know these two laws, describe them with the word 'karma'. Karma is a law of cause and effect. Karma can be karma of the high tide or karma of the low tide, for karma can be good or bad.

Christ, who understood this law, said we should deny ourselves and become servants.[6] When you become a servant, the Lord says, "I love you." But when someone says, "I want to be a master," God replies, "It is not possible for there to be two masters; one has to be the master and the other the servant." Evil is born when two want to be the master. God says, "Two masters cannot be with Me. If they insist on being masters, they will be sent to the other side of the world."[7] What is the other end of the world? It is the earth. This is why the Lord sends people to the earth. You would like to understand the law of similarity, but the law of contrast is acting in all of you, which is why you are unhappy. You need to exit the law of contrast and enter the law of similarity. The law of similarity is self-denial. Self-denial does not mean to lose your

[6] Jesus said to his disciples, "Whosoever would become great among you shall be your minister; and whosoever would be first among you shall be your servant: even as the Son of man came not to be ministered unto, but to minister" (Matthew 20:26-28).

[7] "Brethren, through love be servants one to another. For the whole law is fulfilled in one word, even in this, 'Thou shalt love thy neighbour as thyself'" (Galatians 5:13-14).

life, but to replace one occupation with another.

The teaching of Christ belongs to the law of similarity. Christ came to the earth to establish the law of similarity. He said, "I do not want to rule over you. I want to teach you how to be happy. If you love me and obey my law, you will be very happy."[8] When you are in a bad mood, when you hate, when you gossip or when you are unhappy, you are in the law of contrast. You need to exit the law of contrast and enter the law of similarity. When you are angry or in a bad mood, it means you are on a low tide. It is necessary for high tide to come. How will it come? You need to concentrate, to direct your mind up to God, to speak to Him, and when the low tide has ended you will return to earth.

We should apply the law of similarity to produce what the Apostle Paul described as "the fruit of the Spirit", which is "love, joy, peace, longpatience, kindness, compassion, faithfulness, meekness and temperance." This fruit comes in three categories. In the first category, 'love' is the father, 'joy' is the mother, and 'peace' is their child. They form a triangle which is among those things that are divine. Whoever would like to be blessed has to possess these three things. Such a person is in heaven. In the second category, which relates to the angels, 'patience' is the father, 'kindness' is the mother, and 'compassion' is their child. When you have attained these qualities, you will be among the angels. In the third category, 'faith' is the father, 'meekness' is the mother, and 'temperance' is their child.

I say that, according to the law of similarity, first you have to have a father. Who is your father? 'Faith' is. "I have no faith." Of you, my friend, I have a bad opinion, for you have no father. You have not been born of legally recognised parents. Your mother did not give birth to you according to the divine method. A person who says, "I have faith," is blessed, because he or she has a very noble father of high birth, from a king's family. The word 'meekness' is the mother. She also comes from a king's family. If you believe in meekness, it means you have a mother. "But I do not want to be meek!" Then you are motherless. A Christian, therefore, ought to have a father and a mother, 'faith' and 'meekness', which would make him or her temperate. When we say "temperance", we mean the child of our father 'faith' and our mother 'meekness'.

[8] Jesus said, "If a man love me, he will keep my word: and my Father will love him, and we will come unto him, and make our abode with him" (John 14:23).

Some people say, "I would like to go among the angels." You may indeed go, but only if you have been born by father 'patience' and mother 'kindness'. When you have come to be born of patience and kindness, what will you be? You will be compassionate, an angel, a saint. If you are compassionate, you are an angel, and up above you have a father, patience, and a mother, kindness. This is the law which regulates human beings. It is the foundation of a philosophy that anyone may test and verify every day.

I do not lie and I do not like to be lied to. If I lie, I am a fool. If people can lie to me, I am also a fool. If I am on a low tide, I go up to God. If I am on a high tide, I come down to earth to work. If I am near God, who can lie to me? Wherever the Lord has entered, the devil cannot enter. Wherever God is not present, the devil is there. Therefore, if the Lord is in your heart, the devil cannot hurt you.[9]

According to the law of similarity, we cannot transform evil into good or good into evil. An old man visited a saint who had been living in the desert for twenty years. He told the saint, "I am a great sinner. Please pray to the Lord to forgive my sins." When the old man had left, the saint began praying to the Lord. An angel appeared and said to him, "Your prayer has not been accepted by God, because that old man is the devil. Test the truth of his words by telling him this: 'I will pray for you, but only if you make a confession to a priest, and then climb a rock and say, "Lord, have mercy on me, a great sinner," and repeat this every day for one whole year.'" Later, when the old man returned, the saint spoke to him as the angel had instructed. "What?" shouted the devil, "I cannot do that! I am the ruler of the world! I do not want to pray! You do it for me!" The saint replied, "Old evil cannot be transformed into new virtue." The people who preach the Gospel ought to know that they cannot ever transform the law of contrast into the law of similarity, which means we cannot turn anyone to the Lord if he or she constantly lives under the law of contrast. We cannot make such a person happy.[10]

[9] Jesus said, "The prince of the world hath nothing in me" (John 14:30). And the Apostle John wrote, "We know that whosoever is begotten of God sinneth not; but he that was begotten of God keepeth him, and the evil one toucheth him not" (1 John 5:18).

[10] The Teacher also said, "The disciple should not occupy himself or herself with the mistakes of others, nor with their negative qualities. If you see a mistake, correct it. If you cannot correct it, continue forwards on your path" (2 March 1922). "Never allow an impure person into your soul. Do not try to correct impure people. Let them correct

We sit around saying, "May the world be set right." But how will it be set right? A pig circles a pear tree for many many years eating the fallen pears. When there are no more pears left on the ground, it starts to dig into the tree's roots, wondering where the pears have been hidden. The pig will destroy the tree, and then how will it produce more pears? Likewise, when you do not find pears on the tree, you start digging around it, saying, "The money I seek has been buried somewhere here." You become treasure hunters. I tell you, you are in the law of contrast, and there are no pears or treasure where you are looking. You need to go elsewhere, because when the landowner sees you, he will beat you. This is what the Lord is now doing here on the earth. We are all digging for pears, and the Lord is saying, "Beat everybody with twenty-five lashes!"[11]

This is why I am telling you to apply the following law: a woman should not dig around a man's roots. If there are no pears, she needs to wait. And the same goes for men, priests, students and so on. All of you apply this law, and then you will understand life as the Lord made it. This is a philosophy which we can apply in this world. It is very simple and everyone may understand it. If you say, "I cannot do that," I will tell you that you are in a marsh, in the mud of contrast. When you say, "I can do it," you are in the law of similarity and you will make a step forwards and begin on the path of salvation. "I cannot love." Then I am sorry, I cannot help you. You are in the law of contrast. You are in the mud. "I can love." In that case you are in the law of similarity and the Lord will be with you.[12]

When you get up in the morning in a bad mood, say to yourself, "I am on a low tide. I will travel to the high tide." Do not go to the pear

themselves outside your inner garden" (19 November 1916).

[11] The story of the twenty-five lashes is given in the next lecture (see p. 302).

[12] The Teacher also said, "Divine love is a necessity that is expressed in a blessing. What is this blessing? There are about twenty thousand or thirty thousand fishing boats on the River Thames. They feed London. At low tide these boats sit in the mud. After the tide turns the boats rise on the water and the fishing starts again. The high tide is the blessing. You should seek the high tide of the Divine Spirit. If you miss such a moment of opportunity, you might have to wait for twelve hours, or twelve weeks, or twelve months, or twelve years, or twelve hundred years, and so on, before it comes again. First of all, apply divine love. It works in the heart, which is the most important organ. The heart gives the pulse. When the Divine Heart is beating inside us we are alive and on a high tide" (11/24 January 1915).

tree to look for pears when it is not the right time for them. Instead, go and pray. If you know how to pray properly, you will grow strong through the power of prayer. Prayer is the highest act we can perform in this world, a noble act. Only thus will the human heart be uplifted and ennobled. I do not speak of the external aspect of prayer, in which only the tongue participates, but of prayer that expresses the conscious aspiration of the soul towards God, the higher love. The world will remain the same while people continue only to 'pray' to others for their own material benefit, instead of praying to the Lord for the greater good. Such people live in the law of contrast. How can we human beings be good when lies accompany us on our every step? We lie to ourselves, lie to our neighbours and lie to the Lord. Let us free ourselves of fear and at least speak the truth before God. Let us say, "Today I will not speak lies before God." If we make a mistake, we ought to say, "I made a mistake." We should not blame others for our own mistakes, for when we do we are in the law of contrast. Let each of us honestly say, "I made a mistake." When we confess our mistakes, we will correct ourselves.[13]

If you want to kill somebody, you are an incarnated devil, for you are in the region of contrast and in a condition to perform any kind of evil. When you are in the region of similarity, you are an angel. Whenever you are ready to sacrifice yourself, or are ready to perform a noble deed, you are a saint, but you are unable to maintain this position for long. The human being was made in the image and likeness of God.[14] I will explain what this means. When the Lord made human beings in His image and likeness, He made them generals with epaulets. But they disobeyed the Lord's will and command, so He demoted them and removed their generals' uniforms, and that was the Fall of Humanity. If you turn to the Lord, He will say, "Right now you have the image and likeness of a general, because you are behaving according to the law of similarity, the law of being similar to God. Enter Paradise." When you stop being the

---

[13] The Teacher also said, "It is better to be aware of your sinful desire and to free yourself of it than to bury it away internally. If you do not make a mistake externally while unknowingly carrying a sin internally, you believe you are a good person. That is self-delusion, which is the path most people tread.

"The good inner work a person does to reform himself or herself, which nobody else can see, is a great thing. This is why Christ said, 'When you pray, go into your inner room, and the One who sees in secret will reward you openly'" (21 May 1933).

[14] See Genesis 1:26-27

image and likeness of God, He says, "You are behaving according to the law of contrast. As you are being dissimilar to Me, I am removing your general's uniform." If you are upright today, you are an angel in heaven. If tomorrow you lower yourself, the Lord will lower you back to earth. If you do not pray and follow the law, you are a devil.

These two laws, the law of contrast and the law of similarity, regulate the world. The spirits who live in the law of contrast do not want to return to the law of similarity. That is why the Lord cannot move these spirits from one region to another. The first thing we face as Christians is the border that exists between these two laws. When we arrive at this border, we have to leave all our baggage, our thoughts and desires which are in the law of contrast, and purify ourselves so that we may enter the law of similarity. When we live in the law of similarity, the Lord will dress us in His clothing and promote us back to generals. Humankind became naked as a result of disobeying God's command not to reach for the forbidden fruit. The Lord removed our generals' clothing and we were forced to make clothes out of leaves. The Lord then said, "Quickly, make clothes out of skin!"[15] This is why we are clothed in skin. Do you want to throw off this skin? When will you do it? When you enter the law of similarity, for then your skin will fall off you and the Lord will give you a general's uniform with epaulets of many colours. This is the Christian philosophy, a philosophy that can be applied in life. It is not a philosophy of the past but a philosophy that works in practice.[16]

You are reincarnated daily from angels to devils and vice versa. I say, "The moment you sin you are cast out of the divine church, Paradise." In one second I can be in hell. The moment I hesitate towards God and think bad thoughts about Him, I am at the bottom of hell. The moment I love God within my soul and say, "Forgive me, Lord," I am with Him – the divine right hand is stretched out, gathering me.[17] Unselfishness

[15] See Genesis 2:25–3:12, 21

[16] Jesus said, "My teaching is not mine, but his that sent me. If any man willeth to do his will, he shall know of the teaching, whether it be of God, or whether I speak from myself" (John 7:16-17).

[17] "O Lord, thou hast a mighty arm: Strong is thy hand, and high is thy right hand" (Psalm 89:13). "That thy beloved may be delivered, Save with thy right hand, and answer us" (Psalm 60:5). "Behold, the Lord's hand is not shortened, that it cannot save; neither his ear heavy, that it cannot hear: but your iniquities have separated between you and your God,

always resides in the law of similarity. To be a Christian means to make sacrifices and deny yourself for others.

and your sins have hid his face from you, that he will not hear" (Isaiah 59:1-2).

"Herein is love, not that we loved God, but that he loved us, and sent his Son to be the propitiation for our sins" (1 John 4:10). "Him did God exalt with his right hand to be a Prince and a Saviour, for to give repentance to Israel, and remission of sins" (Acts 5:31). "The Lord's right hand, and his holy arm, hath wrought salvation for him" (Psalm 98:1). And Jesus said, "I am not come to call the righteous but sinners to repentance" (Luke 5:32).

The Milk of the Word

The Apostle Peter wrote,

> As newborn babes, *desire* the *sincere* milk *of the word*, that ye
> may grow thereby unto salvation; if ye have tasted that the
> Lord is gracious. [1]

In one of the commandments of the law of Moses, it is said, "Do
not desire ..." [2] But in this letter of the Apostle Peter it is said, "Desire
..." Who was right? Both were correct from their own points of view.
If, however, Moses had been in Peter's position, he would have been
wrong, and were Peter to have been in the position of Moses, he too
would have been wrong. Moses said, "Do not desire ..." but what is
it that we must not desire: power, wealth, a woman or a man? And
Peter said, "Desire ..." But what should we desire? We ought to desire
the milk of the Word. Why? Because it is necessary for our spiritual
development.

After birth, the first thing a baby seeks is milk from the mother's
nipple, because a suckling child will grow and develop. And Peter was
saying, "Find the 'nipple' that will feed you spiritually." When a child
has grown enough to have teeth, it means his or her organism has
readied itself for solid food. And it is the same in the spiritual life: it is
not good to take in 'solid teachings' before you are ready – they could
even kill you.

It is not sufficient for a mother to give birth and breastfeed; her milk
needs to be pure. Many mothers have poisoned their babies with poor
quality milk. If a mother becomes angry several times each day, after
a few days her milk will poison the child. Similarly, priests and teach-

[1] 1 Peter 2:2-3. The Revised Version says, "As newborn babes, long for the spiritual milk
which is without guile." The alterations to the quotation in the main text have been made
to accord with the 1914 Constantinople Bible, which better suits the lecture.

[2] "Thou shalt not covet thy neighbour's house, thou shalt not covet thy neighbour's wife,
nor his manservant, nor his maidservant, nor his ox, nor his ass, nor any thing that is thy
neighbour's" (Exodus 20:17).

ers who are worried and troubled will poison their congregations and pupils. Contemporary people suffer from a great ignorance. They know many things: geometry, arithmetic, botany, physics, astronomy, how God creates human beings and how they develop. They do not, however, have the essential knowledge of the milk of the Word.

Peter spoke about the living stone.[3] We know of the dead stones from which houses are made. However, in its spiritual meaning, the word 'stone' symbolises a complete character. All forces are balanced in a living stone, and such a person's development proceeds harmoniously: the brain, the lungs, the stomach and the nervous system are healthy and function properly. This is why Christ said, "Be a stone that is able to grow and develop."[4] Elsewhere he said, "You need to build a divine home,"[5] which means a house built of living stone.

We would like to be spiritual, but what do we mean by this? Is it to be closed within ourselves, to be calm, peaceful, thoughtful and contemplative? These things do not make us spiritual. To be spiritual means to be connected to one's environment and the soil on which one lives. We also need to know how to react correctly to our soil, our environment and the conditions in it, the elements which create life. The highest position a person may reach is when his or her heart, mind and soul are at their highest level, their maximum development.

In its natural state limestone cannot accept liquid, but when it is baked it may be mixed with water and used to whitewash walls. And when the Lord wants to whitewash His home, He bakes the limestone, adds a little water to it and paints the walls white. In spiritual terms, to be whitewashed means to have been converted to the pure, good

---

[3] "Unto whom coming, a living stone, rejected indeed of men, but with God elect, precious, ye also, as living stones, are built up a spiritual house, to be a holy priesthood, to offer up spiritual sacrifices, acceptable to God through Jesus Christ. Because it is contained in scripture, 'Behold, I lay in Zion a chief corner stone, elect, precious: And he that believeth on him shall not be put to shame.' For you therefore which believe is the preciousness" (1 Peter 2:4-7).

[4] Jesus said, "Every one which heareth these words of mine, and doeth them, shall be likened unto a wise man, which built his house upon the rock: and the rain descended, and the floods came, and the winds blew, and beat upon that house; and it fell not: for it was founded upon the rock" (Matthew 7:24-25). And the Apostle Paul wrote, "Other foundation can no man lay than that which is laid, which is Jesus Christ" (1 Corinthians 3:11).

[5] Jesus said, "If a man love me, he will keep my word: and my Father will love him, and we will come unto him, and make our abode with him" (John 14:23).

life. When suffering comes to you, it means you have been put in the furnace to be converted into lime. There are some stones which are so firm that they do not bake when put in the furnace. These stones are useless; they are thrown away. When Peter said, "Desire ..." he meant that through this inner process of baking, higher forms are created in our minds that may be dissolved and diluted so that they can pass from one world to another.

Say you have two thoughts in your mind that are worrying you. Take one of them, without grieving over it, and put it in the furnace. When you have thus baked each of the thousands of burdening thoughts that come to you, it will be as if you had baked several thousand kilograms of limestone and sold it as whitewash. You will have freed yourself of a heavy burden while also making a profit from it. That which takes place in the physical world also takes place in the spiritual world. Every process in the physical world has a corresponding process in heaven, and vice versa. When you understand this correctly, you will know that when you suffer on earth there is joy in heaven, for you are being baked in the furnace. If you do not understand the deep meaning of this process, you will say, "My life is being destroyed by this fire!" In heaven, however, they say something quite different: "We are joyful that this limestone is being converted into whitewash." When you think the angels above have no compassion or sympathy for us, they answer, "We do. We see that you are becoming white and pure like us."[6] We should therefore desire not those things which can be condensed and solidified, but those things which expand our souls, minds, strengths and good qualities.

You will ask, "How can we apply these things in practical life?" "My pupils are rowdy." "My children are disobedient. How can I influence them?" "I am a priest whose congregation is uneducated, disbelieving and unable to understand the philosophy of life." "I am a trader whose partners would like to steal from me." Why do you all complain? It is because you each have a thin, weak rope, yet you want to lift a one-hundred-kilogram load with it. The rope will snap, of course, and the load will fall.

How may someone live under the Old Testament while applying

[6] "An angel of the Lord descended from heaven. His appearance was as lightning, and his raiment white as snow" (Matthew 28:2-3).

Peter's teaching? You are a follower of Moses but you also want to be a follower of Christ. A follower of Moses cannot be a follower of Christ. Moses said, "Do not desire …", but he did not say what we should do at the next stage of our development. Of course, when Moses laid down his law the conditions of life were different. The law of Moses was given to prepare humanity for Christ's teaching.[7] In today's social life our desires stem from the application of the law of Moses. People want to be rich and to receive a higher education, but under the law of Moses this opportunity is not open to everybody, which causes confrontation. In the physical realm the conditions do not exist for everybody to be rich and to have a higher education, but anybody can be good. Desire the virtue which is not of the physical world. There are people in India who understand this law and even apply it with animals. It does not matter how ferocious an animal is, you can make a connection with it and bring it to love you, to become your devoted friend. The animal will lose all desire to hurt you, and when you ask it to help you it will be ready to do whatever you want. When Christ said, "Love your enemies,"[8] he was referring to this law.

Christianity recommends suffering as a purifier. Firm stones have to pass through the furnace to become whitewash. Raw bread has to be baked so that we may eat it, and it is the same with human beings. You may only enter heaven as baked bread, for only then will you be put on the table and broken.[9] Why has the Lord given you minds, hearts, eyes, ears and tongues? You should think about the purposes they serve. You say, "I want to serve God," but you do not know how to serve. There are people who pretend to understand the spiritual laws while being unable to serve God. When they know these laws, they have to at least know

---

[7] See Galatians 3:1-29, especially 24

[8] See Luke 6:27

[9] "There shall in no wise enter into the *holy city* anything unclean" (Revelation 21:27). "But if we walk in the light, as *God* is in the light, we have fellowship one with another, and the blood of Jesus his Son cleanseth us from all sin. If we confess our sins, he is faithful and righteous to forgive us our sins, and to cleanse us from all unrighteousness" (1 John 1:7, 9). "I *John* saw, and behold, a great multitude standing before the throne of *God* and before the Lamb, arrayed in white robes. And one of the elders answered, saying unto me, 'These which are arrayed in the white robes, who are they, and whence came they?' And I say unto him, 'My Lord, thou knowest.' And he said to me, 'These are they which come out of the great tribulation, and they washed their robes, and made them white in the blood of the Lamb'" (Revelation 7:9, 13-14).

how to apply them for their own development. Some people want me to tell them many philosophical and spiritual things. I could tell you such things, but I want us to make a firm foundation on which to build, and for each stone we lay to be beautifully shaped and properly placed – cornerstones.[10] There is a great task before us, to make things better in the world. I can see that the structure of contemporary life is collapsing. One day the Lord will call us to make a new structure. But will we know how to build it? That is the question. To ready ourselves, from now on we have to feed ourselves with the milk of the Word. Let us prepare ourselves in this way, so that when God gives us new clothes, we do not stain them.[11]

Some foolish women say, "Why did the Lord make me a woman?" He did so because as a woman you study an art that you cannot learn as a man: you study the art of preparing the milk with which to feed your children. You are servants of the Lord who are raising His children. If you do not properly fulfil a mother's obligation, the Lord will say to you, "Why did I put you in such an important position? You should not give your child impure milk." "But I have already done so." "Do not do it anymore or I will dismiss you." "I want to be a man." "You will not become a man. If you continue to desire things which you have not earned, if you remain so stubborn, you will come back regressed in your next life."[12]

The contemporary Christian philosophy does not rest on a strong foundation. We say that we are 'the crowns of creation'.[13] Let us not lie

---

[10] "Thus saith the Lord God, 'Behold, I lay in Zion for a foundation a stone, a tried stone, a precious corner stone of sure foundation: he that believeth shall not make haste. And I will make judgement the *measuring* line, and righteousness the plummet'" (Isaiah 28:16-17).

[11] "As many of you as were baptized into Christ did put on Christ" (Galatians 3:27).

[12] At that time Bulgaria was a highly patriarchal society. The Teacher said, "The second greatest law, to love your neighbour, applies to the female principle and builds the social order. Consequently, the state of the present order, in all areas, is due to the humiliation of women. What should be the goal of contemporary society and government? To reinstate women to their original position. Do this and in twenty-five years the world will be improved. The salvation of the world depends on the uplifting of women.

"Today's woman is subjugated and humiliated by those in power. Unless this is corrected, all efforts to put the world right will fail. When I speak of raising the feminine principle, I want this idea to penetrate the whole of life. Not only does it need to penetrate human beings, but also the animal, plant and mineral kingdoms. The human heart needs to fully embrace the law of loving one's neighbour" (18 October 1931).

[13] "O Lord, thou hast made *man* but little lower than God, And crownest him with glory and

to ourselves and to God. We are not crowns. Only those who have completed their evolution are crowns.[14] Those of us who are willing to sell the Lord for money and houses are not the crowns of creation but the crowns of the fallen human being, the crowns of hell.

We face a dilemma. Can we ask ourselves, "Are we able to continue along this path?" We must not walk on. Contemporary humanity has reached the point at which all will be lost if it takes one more step forwards. One step back, one step forwards in the right direction and one step up and the future will be great.[15] We now need to think about where we are heading and to deny ourselves those temporary things which lead us to a fall. Christ said, "Whoever loves his or her mother and father ought to deny them and follow me."[16] It is time for people to say, "I do not want any more of today's milk." You need to deny yourselves of every tempting thing which corrupts your thoughts and desires and poisons your lives. Instead, let us seek and find the divine truth.

Women need to work harder, because the Lord has given them the key to Paradise. Women hold the key to the kingdom of God – 'Peter' is a female name.[17] Women with weak characters quickly refuse this

honour" (Psalm 8:5).

[14] Jesus said, "To him that overcometh, to him will I give to eat of the tree of life, which is in the Paradise of God. Be thou faithful unto death, and I will give thee the crown of life" (Revelation 2:7, 10).

[15] The Teacher also said, "A chemist learns about the laws which govern the elements, and he works with the elements in his laboratory according to these laws. If he sometimes breaks these laws, he might cause an explosion. He needs to be careful, just as a train driver needs to measure the pressure of the steam in the engine to drive the train safely. Contemporary people are now thoughtlessly heading along without checking the pressure of the steam. As a result of this the entire culture is approaching catastrophe. Human culture has been attuned to destruction, which has made it negative. We have a culture with negative ideas in which people create weapons and other destructive things" (10/23 January 1915).

[16] Jesus said, "He that loveth father or mother more than me is not worthy of me" (Matthew 10:37).

[17] Here the Teacher was referring to some wordplay of Jesus in the Greek Bible. In the English Bible, Jesus said to Peter, "I say unto thee, that thou art Peter, and upon this rock I will build my church; and the gates of Hades shall not prevail against it. I will give unto thee the keys of the kingdom of heaven" (Matthew 16:18-19). The name 'Peter' in Greek is Πέτρος (Pétros), which means a detached stone or rock and is a masculine noun. In contrast, the Greek for 'rock', as in fixed rock or a mass of rock, is πέτρα (pétra), which is female grammatically and the female form of the name Peter: Petra. Inserting these words into this verse as used in the Greek Bible, Jesus said to Peter, "Thou art Pétros, and upon this

assignment. Some women love a man, but then see another and say, "I will marry him. If I do not become his wife my life will be over!" And after a few years with him they are ready to marry someone else. The Lord says, "If you who hold the key to the kingdom of God do not follow My commandments, I will throw you out, so that you cry, repent and free yourselves of all your sins."

When we do not follow Christ's commandments, we deviate from him, we deny him, we think badly of him, we keep handing him to Pilate, to suffering, to be nailed to the cross daily. You ask why the world has not been set right. How will it be set right when we torment our Lord every day? Let us stop nailing his body, because the nails we hammer into his body will return to us. Do you know the story of the fisherman who wanted to give the king a valuable fish? The gatekeeper of the king's castle refused to allow the fisherman to enter unless he agreed to give him half of any reward he received from the king. When the king asked the fisherman what reward he wanted for giving him the fish, he answered, "Fifty lashes of the stick." The surprised King asked why he wanted this. "It is what I want," the man replied. After twenty-five lashes, the fisherman said, "Stop! I have a partner, your gatekeeper, who is to share my reward. Please give him the remaining twenty-five lashes." And when you hammer nails into Christ's body, he says, "You are my partner, and you will receive the remaining nails." The things which are now happening over the whole world are nothing other than the half price we demanded.

What I am preaching is, as you see, a completely practical teaching that can be applied by anyone. When a bad thought comes to you, when you desire something that is not good, put this firm stone into the furnace to be converted into the whitewash with which you can clean your soul and make it shine. If you train yourselves in this way, you will see your souls illuminated. This is a teaching that was preached by the Apostle Peter. You think that Peter was a simple fisherman, but he was a fisherman who baked his fish; he did not eat raw fish.[18] How

pétra I will build my church."

[18] "Walking by the sea of Galilee, Jesus saw two brethren, Simon who is called Peter, and Andrew his brother, casting a net into the sea; for they were fishers. And he saith unto them, 'Come ye after me, and I will make you fishers of men'" (Matthew 4:18-19).

should you bake fish? Bake it in the divine fire: love.[19] When you have baked it in this way, you may say, "What a beautiful fish."[20] If we do not become colleagues with those who live in heaven, how will we earn a place there? When the Lord tells us to deny ourselves, to lose our lives,[21] He does not mean that we should lose our lives for swine, but that we should do so for those who are at a higher level than us.[22] Only then will we gain. You will say this law is incompatible with the laws of nature. They are compatible. Those who nourish themselves with the milk of the Word will sow the new seed, and new fruit-bearing trees will be grown. Consequently, if we want to grow, we have to tread the positive, ascending path of development. When we are on this path, the angels will take part in our work. If we want their help, we have to pay them something. If we want them to sow us again in better conditions of life, we have to make payment from now until we leave the earth. If we feed ourselves with the milk of the Word, we will be close to the angels and Christ.

Bake your consciences in the divine fire like a fish you have caught. Fish have to be either baked or salted, and it is the same with us human beings. There is no middle way. Human beings have to be baked or salted, otherwise they will rot. When Christ said, "If the salt has lost its saltiness, it is no longer good for anything except to be thrown out and trodden underfoot,"[23] he meant that if you lose your saltiness, you will be thrown out. I would prefer to be baked than to be salted. Salt is for worldly people. Fire is for us. The process of burning is better, because it is a process of growth, of life. Salting is a process of preserving, to protect the seed from decaying. This means that you can be in one of two positions: either you can be in the position of growth in the divine garden or the position of a seed stored in the divine granary. Make an

[19] John the Baptist said of Jesus, "He shall baptize you with the Holy Spirit and with fire: the chaff he will burn up with unquenchable fire" (Matthew 3:11-12). "For he is like a refiner's fire, and like fullers' soap" (Malachi 3:2).

[20] The fish was an early Christian symbol for Christ.

[21] Jesus said, "If any man would come after me, let him deny himself, and take up his cross, and follow me. For whosoever would save his life shall lose it: and whosoever shall lose his life for my sake shall find it" (Matthew 16:24-25).

[22] Jesus said, "Give not that which is holy unto the dogs, neither cast your pearls before the swine, lest haply they trample them under their feet, and turn and rend you" (Matthew 7:6).

[23] See Matthew 5:13

experiment on yourselves with the verse about the milk of the Word that I read. It has a deep meaning, and volumes of books could be based on it: How to Build Life, How to Raise and Educate Children, How to Educate Men, How to Educate Women, How to Educate Students, How to Educate Society, and so on. This verse has everything, but it needs to be sown correctly. Where should it be sown? In the mind.

Boil this verse in divine water and bake it in divine fire, and this hard walnut of a verse will immediately be converted into digestible juices. If you nourish yourself with the milk of the Word of which the Apostle Peter spoke, your face and position in society will be improved. I want you to accept this divine method and prepare yourselves for the next life, for heaven. I wish you to desire the sincere milk of the Word from now on, for you to enter the positive side of life. If you do so, the Lord will provide you with everything you want.[24]

---

[24] At the Last Supper, Jesus said to his disciples, "Verily, verily, I say unto you, He that believeth on me, the works that I do shall he do also; and greater works than these shall he do; because I go unto the Father. And whatsoever ye shall ask in my name, that will I do, that the Father may be glorified in the Son. If ye shall ask me anything in my name, that will I do" (John 14:12-14). "These things saith the Amen, the faithful and true witness, the beginning of the creation of God. And he is arrayed in a garment sprinkled with blood: and his name is called The Word of God" (Revelation 3:14; 19:13).

Only God May Appoint Spiritual Teachers

In the Temple in Jerusalem, Jesus said to the crowds and to his disciples,

Be not ye called Rabbi: for one is your teacher, and all ye are brethren. [1]

There are several divine institutions in the world; for example, the father, the mother and the home. They are the first institutions on earth. There is no more noble or luminous institution than the home, and there is no higher title than that of 'father' or 'mother'. Parents have an important role: when imparting their blood to a child they also impart the qualities of their souls. After conception, a child's future upbringing is dependent upon the qualities that the mother provides during his or her early, delicate age. The nobility of the primary ingredients, the germs that the mother deposits in her child's being during pregnancy, are the valuable essence that will expand with time and, in the child's future adult life, spread out as a fragrance to other people in his or her environment. At a later date nothing more can be sown in a human being. [2] What contemporary people call education is nothing but training or taming. The education provided by the mother is a process that takes place in the child's root. It is in the root that the mind and the heart are formed and transformed. In contrast, the process of taming is only external polishing. You can tame a monkey or a pigeon, but when they are placed back in their natural environments they will return to their primary nature.

In the spiritual life, the position of the teacher to the disciple is like that of a mother to her child. To be a spiritual teacher means to give birth to someone spiritually. Christ did not say, "Do not teach others." What he said was, "Do not take the title of 'spiritual teacher'." In other words, do not take the title of 'sick mothers', because if you do you will

[1] Matthew 23:8
[2] For more on spiritually conscious pregnancy, see Appendix C (p. 384).

give birth to feeble children. If a mother has a physiological or psychological illness, her child will inherit the consequences. Is it possible for a teacher to teach his pupils how to combine oxygen with hydrogen when he does not understand their properties sufficiently to carry out the process himself? Christ said, "Do not be such teachers." To be a teacher a person requires positive knowledge and to understand things correctly. If the same tool can be used to heal or to kill, just because you work with it does not mean that you have positive knowledge. You may use a knife to operate on an ill part of the body, but it is a crime to use it to cut healthy tissue. I know of many spiritual teachers who hurt their disciples morally. The Lord did not make them spiritual teachers; they are self-appointed.

How should we understand the term 'spiritual teacher'? Spiritual teaching is an act of high selfconsciousness, a spiritual process between the teacher and the disciple. It is necessary for them both to be fully conscious of the task that they need to fulfil. A correct exchange needs to take place between them, as between a mother and her child. The spiritual teacher should impart certain truths that the disciple needs to learn to use correctly. A spiritual teacher has to be able to teach others how to develop their minds and hearts. A spiritual teacher understands the profound meaning of the renewable elements from which the spiritual body can be built.[3] The Scriptures say we will be resurrected by our spiritual bodies,[4] and the Lord is waiting for us to build them.[5]

---

[3] The Teacher also said, "What we call the building of the spiritual body means the building of the human being's causal and other higher bodies. There are three methods by which to build it. First, you need to spend at least thirty minutes each day immersed in contemplation, concentration and prayer. Second, you have to manifest love. Third, you have to serve God and serve 'the whole'" (some time between 1924 and 1944).

[4] "Some one will say, 'How are the dead raised? and with what manner of body do they come?' Thou foolish one, that which thou thyself sowest is not quickened, except it die. It is sown in corruption; it is raised in incorruption: it is sown in dishonour; it is raised in glory: it is sown in weakness; it is raised in power: it is sown a natural body; it is raised a spiritual body. If there is a natural body, there is also a spiritual body. Flesh and blood cannot inherit the kingdom of God; neither doth corruption inherit incorruption. This corruptible must put on incorruption, and this mortal must put on immortality" (1 Corinthians 15:35-36, 42-44, 50, 53).

[5] The Teacher also said, "We always need a standard by which to measure our thoughts and desires. This standard, this touchstone, is Christ. We always need to keep him before us in our minds. When we are constantly with Christ, abundant thoughts and desires and the aspiration to work are created in us. These are good signs. All thoughts, desires and

During the nine months of pregnancy, the spirit of the developing baby is not dormant but studying. It is working with the spirit of the mother to create the new body to be born. According to the same law, the disciple and the spiritual teacher have to work together with the help of the Spirit. This is why Christ said, "One is your Teacher."

Why do people love Christ? They love him because he gave something to the world: he said, "I give life to those without it, for them to have it in abundance."[6] Do you want to become a spiritual teacher? If you do, I will ask you what you are able to give your disciples. If someone becomes worse for having been taught by you, I will realise that you taught him or her nothing useful. In contemporary Christianity there is a weakness for wanting to become spiritual teachers. The aspiration is not bad in itself, but a spiritual teacher is required to know the laws of spiritual teaching. Human law requires a person to attain certain qualifications before he or she may be employed as a teacher, and it is the same in the spiritual world. To be qualified as a spiritual teacher a person has to be enlightened and guided by the Divine Spirit.[7] Those who are not enlightened by the Spirit of God have no right to be spiritual teachers, for they will break the divine law. When we understand the deep meaning of Christ's words, which have both an inner and an outer expression, we will understand what it means to be a spiritual teacher. If you would like to become a spiritual teacher, you will be asked from which school you graduated. "I have read the Bible

---

aspirations are not, however, of the same quality; we need to know which of them to choose. Thoughts and desires are stones from the same quarry, and they build the future human body, which is the spiritual body. We need to know how to choose the most suitable stones for these buildings. The building of a house requires not only stone but also iron, wood and many other materials. Spirits sell us all kinds of materials, from the expensive to the cheap. Beware of the spirits who try to sell us poor quality materials at great prices" (13/26 April 1914).

[6] See John 10:10

[7] Jesus said, "I spake not from myself; but the Father which sent me, he hath given me a commandment, what I should say, and what I should speak. And I know that his commandment is life eternal: the things therefore which I speak, even as the Father hath said unto me, so I speak" (John 12:49-50). "I will send the Spirit of truth unto you from the Father" (John 15:26). "When he, the Spirit of truth, is come, he shall guide you into all the truth: for he shall not speak from himself; but what things soever he shall hear, these shall he speak. He shall glorify me: for he shall take of mine, and shall declare it unto you. All things whatsoever the Father hath are mine: therefore said I, that he taketh of mine, and shall declare it unto you" (John 16:13-15).

and I know the Gospels." "That is not enough." "I know the Christian faith." "That is not enough." "But I belong to a church." "All right, but have you studied in heaven at the higher institution where the angels study? Do you know the inner laws of nature? Do you know the structure of the human being, of the human mind and heart, and do you understand the relationship between the soul and the spirit?" "I have read about them." Such a person thinks that he or she knows something when in fact he or she does not.

Contemporary people say that people need to be criticised in order for them to be corrected: "You are a hooligan!" "You are a thief!" and so on. Do you think you will change somebody for the better in that way? No, you will not. The spiritual law works differently. To be able to educate another person, first you have to have educated yourself. If a pregnant woman becomes irritable or says bad things about other people, I can predict the future of her child. Such a mother should not think that her child will become a saint who will also take care of her in her old age. Instead, the child will take revenge on her one day, saying, "It would have been better for you if you had never given birth to me!"

The spiritual teacher, in the full meaning of the term, is as pure as crystal water, a model example in everything and a person without doubt, hesitation or any lack of faith. Christ wanted to warn us of the great danger awaiting those who become spiritual teachers before they are ready. If a spiritual teacher damages people's souls, he or she will bear a great responsibility for it before Christ.[8] Every mother and every spiritual teacher who does not know how to educate properly will be punished for it.

Contemporary people's views of the divine laws, heaven and the angels are vague and wrong. They have no idea of the laws of heaven. Heaven is very intelligently organised and knows what it is doing. There is the same relationship between the angels and us human beings as there is between us and the plants and the animals. As we do not know how to educate properly, we hit the animals that are ploughing the field for us with sticks and think that we are acting as we ought to. The Lord says, "One day I will teach you how to rule the ox and plough the field correctly...."

Some people think that the Lord cannot regress human beings, but if

---

[8] "Be not many teachers, my brethren, knowing that we shall receive heavier judgement" (James 3:1).

He has already transformed some angels into snakes or horned animals, surely He can also grow hooves on your feet.[9] He can transform you into angels or devils. He can change your forms. Forms are important in the world, as they regulate our lives. We therefore ought to pay them special attention. If I build you unhealthy basement-houses with only north-facing windows, do you know how you will feel in six or seven years? Well, several doctors will need to visit you.... And if spiritual teachers tell you that you do not need windows facing the spiritual world, they are first-class liars, for the spiritual world is the sun of life. I also recommend that your roofs be made of glass, so that this sun shines down on you. If you have such houses with rooms bathed in light, your forms will be changed and you will become beautiful.

I could make an experiment to test what I am preaching to you, as may you, and you would see the results in four or five years' time. According to me, the world is a very good place populated with very good people. The only problem is that they all have a thorn in their heels. The Apostle Paul confirmed this and prayed to God to remove the thorn from his heel. These thorns can be in other places as well, but they are mostly in the heel, as we are mostly nailed to this world by our feet. We need to learn the scientific method of removing these thorns, because to me Christianity is a profound science.[10]

A woman knows the man she wants to marry. He is handsome, well educated and has a good income. That is all good, but those things are not essential and they alone will not make a good marriage, for the man might lose his job and income tomorrow. A wise woman discovers the condition of her loved one's mind and heart before marrying him. Like a clairvoyant, a woman needs to enter the house of the man she loves and inspect every room. It is important that she looks in his library, to see which books it contains and how well they have been arranged. She should look throughout his kitchen. She ought to walk around the garden, the garden of his love, compassion and righteousness, to see what flowers he has planted. Only once she has seen that

[9] "God spared not angels when they sinned, but cast them down to hell, and committed them to pits of darkness, to be reserved unto judgement" (2 Peter 2:4). "And the Lord God said unto the serpent, 'Because thou hast done this, upon thy belly shalt thou go, and dust shalt thou eat all the days of thy life'" (Genesis 3:14).

[10] The Teacher appears to be combining the idea of the Apostle Paul's "thorn in the flesh" (see n. 19) with part of the crucifixion process.

the entire property is well arranged can she wisely say, "I will marry this man." A man needs to make the same investigation of the woman he loves. This research will bring you to a real marriage.

Many people discuss why God made men and women different from each other and why some people have been made men and others women. In ancient times both women and men gave birth, but men lost the ability, after which only women could give birth. The Bible says, "Abraham gave birth to Isaac." It does not say that Sarah gave birth to him.[11] When men could give birth the world was in a perfect state. When men stopped giving birth the world decayed. Men need to give birth, which means they need to be good teachers. A woman may give birth and deposit every noble quality in her child's soul, but the child's next teacher needs to know how to develop these qualities. This means that it is also necessary for the teacher to give birth.

A spiritual teacher should not be like the priest who, when not in a normal state of mind, held the child he was baptising for far too long

---

[11] The Bible does in fact say that Sarah gave birth to Isaac (see Genesis 21:2-3). Rather than being literal, the Teacher's words are thought-provoking, pointing to a deeper meaning.

It is written in Genesis, "Now the Lord said unto Abram, 'I will make of thee a great nation, and I will bless thee, and make thy name great; and be thou a blessing: and I will bless them that bless thee, and him that curseth thee will I curse: and in thee shall all the families of the earth be blessed.'

"And Abram said, 'O Lord God, I go childless. Behold, to me thou hast given no seed.' And, behold, the word of the Lord came unto *Abram*, saying, 'He that shall come forth out of thine own bowels shall be thine heir.' And *the Lord* brought *Abram* forth abroad, and said, 'Look now toward heaven, and *count* the stars, if thou be able to *count* them.' And *the Lord* said unto him, 'So shall thy seed be.' And *Abram* believed in the Lord; and *the Lord* counted it to him for righteousness" (Genesis 12:1-3; 15:2-6).

"And when Abram was ninety years old and nine, the Lord appeared to Abram, and said unto him, 'I am God Almighty; walk before me, and be thou perfect. Thou shalt be the father of a multitude of nations. And I will establish my covenant between me and thee and thy seed after thee throughout their generations for an everlasting covenant, to be a God unto thee and to thy seed after thee'" (Genesis 17:1, 4, 7).

Interpreting this, the Apostle Paul wrote, "Abraham believed God, and it was reckoned unto him for righteousness. Know therefore that they which be of faith, the same are sons of Abraham. And the scripture, foreseeing that God would justify the Gentiles by faith, preached the gospel beforehand unto Abraham, saying, 'In thee shall all the nations be blessed.' So then they which be of faith are blessed with the faithful Abraham.

"Now to Abraham were the promises spoken, and to his seed. He saith not, 'And to seeds,' as of many; but as of one, 'And to thy seed,' which is Christ. As many of you as were baptized into Christ did put on Christ. And if ye are Christ's, then are ye Abraham's seed, heirs according to promise. Now we, brethren, as Isaac was, are children of promise" (Galatians 3:6-9, 16, 27, 29; 4:28).

under the water, killing the child. Oblivious to what he had done, he then said, "Bring me the next one." To baptise as a spiritual teacher you need to be in your right mind. By 'baptism' I mean the spiritual teacher depositing the Divine Spirit in the 'child' he or she is teaching. The priest, as a spiritual teacher, ought to know the divine laws. To simply wash a child in water is not a real baptism. Contemporary priests, teachers and judges are professionals working for money. According to true Christianity, they are not God's servants but only ordinary workers. The first thing a spiritual teacher should reveal to the disciple is the invisible world. This needs to be done in the same way that a mother prepares her child after conception: "Wait nine months and I will introduce you to a new world and its miracles. For now, be peaceful and still." After giving birth nine months later, the mother becomes the child's first teacher. Later other teachers will continue the child's education. The mother leaves her work when the child enters a new field of study in which a new teacher is required. This is what the Gospel means when it says that a person needs to be born again.[12]

My purpose in this lecture is to encourage you to think more about yourselves instead of thinking about becoming spiritual teachers. Why? Because people suffer from great ignorance. You say, "We believe in Christ." That is good, but do you actually know Christ? Do you know the Apostle Paul? Do you know the Apostle Peter? I know that the Christians of old directly communicated with heaven. They talked with God and the saints, which is why they readily sacrificed their lives. Christ described the lying spiritual teachers to his disciples. They dressed in robes and preached, but in reality they deceived people, and Christ rebuked them for it.[13] This is just as valid now, in our time. If Christ came now, he would say the same thing as he did back then. He has not changed his mind about it. Christ is silent at present, but when he starts talking and tells us the truth it will hurt us deeply.

You need to base your knowledge on a spiritual foundation. In the

---

[12] Jesus said, "Except a man be born anew, he cannot see the kingdom of God. Except a man be born of water and the Spirit, he cannot enter into the kingdom of God. That which is born of flesh is flesh; and that which is born of the Spirit is spirit" (John 3:3, 5-6). And John the Baptist said of Jesus, "I baptized you with water; but he shall baptize you with the Holy Spirit" (Mark 1:8). "For as many as are led by the Spirit of God, these are sons of God" (Romans 8:14).

[13] See Matthew 23:1-39

spiritual world knowledge is like steam in a steam engine: it has power. In the spiritual world knowledge is like a physical force. A tram can move when connected to the electric cable above it. A tram cannot move without this connection. Your spiritual teacher connects you to the 'electricity' above. The motor of the human tram may be excellent and in perfect operational condition, but if it is disconnected from the electric source above, it cannot move forwards. People seek the cause of their breakdowns in the wrong places. Their trams will only move again when they are reconnected to the electric source. Your thoughts are motive forces that need to be connected to the spiritual world to function properly. I understand the word 'capacity' to mean a form that contains a certain force which acts in the spiritual world. When the form disintegrates, or is destroyed, the force cannot be manifested anymore. In our central brains there are areas in which certain capacities are deposited. When these centres in our brains are connected with the forces in the spiritual world they work well; if they are disconnected they cannot work properly. Some other conditions are also required, just as a tram needs a rail to run on and a driver to control it. [14]

Christ said to his disciples, "Do not call yourselves spiritual teachers." You may say, "I turned someone to the Lord." Good. If so, the Lord will bless you. But if you damage someone's mind or heart, what will the Lord say? A judgement will be made in heaven and you will be held responsible for what you have done.

Do you know your Spiritual Teacher? Your mother and father and your ancestors for the last two thousand years were Christians, but did they know Christ? If you know him, say the password that he gave you. What is your password? What is your prayer? Well-educated people ought to have a motto by which they live. What should your motto be? It ought to be, "Serve Christ." And how will you serve him? Did you study how to do so at school? If so, where is your diploma? You do not have a diploma and yet you want to become a spiritual teacher! We want the kingdom of God to come on earth, but how will it come when we live with lies such as these? Each nation should have as much

[14] Brother Krum Vuzharov said, "According to the Teacher, when we are in contact with the spiritually wise world, everything in our lives is arranged with spiritual wisdom. How can we connect with this spiritually wise world? You may learn how from the Teacher's lectures and talks."

as it deserves, as should each human being.

Have you asked yourselves this serious question: "Do I know Christ?" I do not want the answer right now. If you can answer this question after one year, it will be a blessing for you. Perhaps you say, "I saw Christ." Paul saw Christ, and Christ asked him, "Paul, Paul, why do you persecute me?" Paul answered, "Who are you, Lord?" Paul heard the Lord. Do you likewise hear your Spiritual Teacher? When having disputes in a religious society, or in the divine temple, are you not persecuting Christ as Paul did?[15] Christ will say to you, "Paul, Paul, why do you persecute me? It is hard for you to kick against the pricks."[16] Paul realised his mistake, and the Lord told him, "As you did this unknowingly, I will send you to the Gentiles so that you learn your lesson."[17] On five occasions Paul was beaten with thirty-nine lashes,[18] and you also have to endure the same lashes so that you can become useful, like iron being hammered into a tool by the ironsmith.[19]

Before you may enter heaven you have to pass before examiners. They will put questions to you: "What are your feelings and ideas?

[15] The Teacher also said, "A public bathhouse was being constructed in a Bulgarian town. For eight years the building remained uncompleted because the town's residents argued over whether the wooden flooring should be rough or smooth. Finally they went to a respected architect to help them resolve the disagreement. He ruled that one plank of flooring should be smooth surfaced and the next one rough, and so on throughout the building. This kind of solution is relevant to dogmatic Christians who only understand the external side of things" (11/24 January 1915).

[16] See Acts 9:1-5; 26:9-15

[17] The Apostle Paul wrote, "Ye have heard of my manner of life in time past, how that beyond measure I persecuted the church of God, and made havock of it" (Galatians 1:13). "I thank Christ Jesus our Lord, for that he counted me faithful, appointing me to his service; though I was before a blasphemer, and a persecutor, and injurious: howbeit I obtained mercy, because I did it ignorantly in unbelief" (1 Timothy 1:12-13). And Jesus said of Paul, "He is a chosen vessel unto me, to bear my name before the Gentiles and kings, and the children of Israel: for I will shew him how many things he must suffer for my name's sake" (Acts 9:15-16).

[18] See 2 Corinthians 11:24

[19] The Apostle Paul wrote, "There was given to me a thorn in the flesh, a messenger of Satan to buffet me, that I should not be exalted overmuch. Concerning this thing I besought the Lord thrice, that it might depart from me. And he hath said unto me, 'My grace is sufficient for thee: for my power is made perfect in weakness.' Most gladly therefore will I rather glory in my weaknesses, that the power of Christ may rest upon me. Wherefore I take pleasure in weaknesses, in injuries, in necessities, in persecutions, in distresses, for Christ's sake: for when I am weak, then am I strong" (2 Corinthians 12:7-10).

How compassionate are you? Do you love God and your neighbour?" And it will continue on and on, with many more questions being asked. Christ is now coming and the book of life will be opened, as it is said, and people will be judged on whether they deserve to pass from one class to a higher one, or even to enter heaven. Everyone will receive according to his or her worthiness.[20] This is why Christ is turning to you and saying, "One is your Spiritual Teacher, Christ." I want you all to remember this Spiritual Teacher who came two thousand years ago to pay for your sins. You are still seeking him. Has Christ written his Name in your soul and in your heart at least once? If he has, you have been blessed; if not, you should try to meet him and ask him to write it for you. And when he does so, do not go praising yourself, saying, "Christ wrote his Name in my book!" for you do not need this blessing here but in heaven. When you are going to heaven, the angels will stop you and ask, "Show us your book." If the Lord has signed his Name in your book, they will say, "You may enter." Then Christ, the saints and your younger and older brothers will greet you, and there will be great joy that you have entered heaven.[21]

There was a rule in the Pythagorean School that every new student was to be the subject of great mockery during his first year. If he endured this test, he was accepted into the school. Likewise, Christ sends some people to the earth to mock you. This is the Pythagorean system of admission. If you endure the mockery, you know that you have passed the examination. What happens in your brain is a reflection of the divine world. Each noble thought is a form in the divine world. Thoughts have different forms and contents. When a noble thought comes to you, it will create joy and gladness inside you. Once you have uplifted your mind and heart to Christ, he will take your hand and lead you to the Divine Garden and the Spring of Love.[22] It will be the

---

[20] See Revelation 20:11-15; 21:22-27

[21] Jesus said, "He that overcometh, I will make him a pillar in the temple of my God, and he shall go out thence no more: and I will write upon him the name of my God, and the name of the city of my God, the new Jerusalem, which cometh down out of heaven from my God, and mine own new name. He that overcometh, I will give to him to sit down with me in my throne, as I also overcame, and sat down with my Father in his throne" (Revelation 3:12, 21). "And his servants shall do him service; and they shall see his face; and his name shall be on their foreheads" (Revelation 22:3-4).

[22] "The Lord God planted a garden eastward, in Eden. *And* the tree of life *was* in the midst

greatest experience of your life. The people who enter the school have to learn to be pure in their thoughts and desires, to have unshakable faith and be completely selfless and self-denying. You have to have this high level of attainment to be able to pass the exam and enter heaven.

I will now leave you with this thought: know your Spiritual Teacher, Christ. When you come to know your true Father, the angels will become your brothers.[23] Over thousands of years the angels will show you their home in heaven, and you will have many pleasant experiences: long walks, wonderful schools, new suns, meeting new beings and many more things. And when you have done all this, you will be able to say, "Now I understand the deep meaning of life and my purpose in it." This is what will happen when you have one Spiritual Teacher.

of the garden. And a river went out of Eden to water the garden" (Genesis 2:8-10). And Jesus said, "If any man thirst, let him come unto me, and drink. He that believeth on me, as the scripture hath said, out of his belly shall flow rivers of living water" (John 7:37-38). "To him that overcometh, to him will I give to eat of the tree of life, which is in the Paradise of God" (Revelation 2:7). "He that cometh to me shall not hunger, and he that believeth on me shall never thirst" (John 6:35). And God said, "I will give unto him that is athirst of the fountain of the water of life freely. He that overcometh shall inherit this; and I will be his God, and he shall be my son" (Revelation 21:6-7). "And the angel shewed me a river of water of life, bright as crystal, proceeding out of the throne of God and of the Lamb, in the midst of the street of new Jerusalem. And on this side of the river and on that was the tree of life" (Revelation 22:1-2).

[23] Jesus said, "Call no man your father on the earth: for one is your Father, which is in heaven" (Matthew 23:9).

Resurrecting Ourselves Through Christ

After his resurrection, Jesus said to his disciples,

> All authority hath been given unto me in heaven and on earth. Go ye therefore, and make disciples of all the nations, baptizing them into the name of the Father and of the Son and of the Holy Spirit: teaching them to observe all things whatsoever I commanded you: and lo, I am with you alway, even unto the end of the world. [1]

Throughout today's Christian world, preachers focus on the texts of Christ's resurrection, asking whether it was really possible. Many people consider this question from a historical and philosophical perspective. Ideologists and theologians write texts trying to explain how resurrection is possible, but they cannot prove it. I am going to focus on these words: "Go therefore and teach all nations, baptising them in the Name of the Father and of the Son and of the Holy Spirit." The teaching of the Father, the Son and the Holy Spirit is profound.

What is this science? We often speak of the Father, Son and Holy Spirit, but what do these words mean for you? They will only have a true meaning once they have affected you. When you hold a matchstick, you cannot experience its power until you light it. Once you have lit it you can feel its power. And the resurrection will remain an unknown concept for you unless you light it like a match. When you light it, it will produce light in your mind and heart. Another option is to sow the word 'resurrection' as a seed inside yourself and for it to grow until you see its fruits. Until now it has been enough for someone to understand the meaning of any one of the Trinity: the Father or the Son or the Holy Spirit. A person who understands any one of them will become a genius. If someone understands two of them, he or she will become a saint. Whoever understands all three will become one with Jesus Christ.

---

[1] Matthew 28:18-20. The original Bulgarian publication only quoted verses 19 and 20.

In every language there are words which become magical when understood. Moses raised his staff before the Red Sea and said only one word and the sea parted.[2] When Christ stood before the tomb of Lazarus, he raised his eyes and said one word: "Lazarus, come out of the tomb!"[3] In the beginning the Lord spoke only one word and the world was formed.[4] We know how to speak and write well, and we discuss many philosophical questions, but we do not know how to arrange our lives properly. We are like the philosopher who went for a trip on the sea in a small boat.

The philosopher asked the man who was rowing the boat, "Do you know anything about astronomy?" The rower answered, "No." The philosopher declared, "In that case you have lost a quarter of your life!" The philosopher then asked, "Do you know anything about geology?" "No," replied the rower. The philosopher declared, "In that case you have lost two quarters of your life!" The philosopher asked a third question: "Do you know anything about mathematics?" "No," replied the rower. The philosopher declared, "In that case you have lost three quarters of your life!" A great storm then arose, jeopardising the boat. The rower asked the philosopher, "Do you know how to swim?" "No," replied the philosopher. The rower declared, "In that case you have lost four quarters of your life!"

You are like the philosopher, asking, "How was Christ born? How did he come to the earth?" And when a storm arises in your life, some difficulties and suffering come to you, you do not know how to swim and therefore you begin to sink. Of what use are your philosophy and mathematics then? Mathematics is the science of building a spiritually wise life. Biology is the science of putting ourselves in order physically. Geology is the science of understanding our relationship with the earth. And so on.

Christ's life had three important parts: his birth, his death and his resurrection. When Christ was born, the angels in heaven proclaimed, "Peace on earth."[5] Christ's birth was triumphant, but the manner of his death was disgraceful. But then he resurrected. How did death appear in the world? We know that when Adam was in Paradise, God represented

[2] See Exodus 14:15-16, 21-22
[3] See John 11:43-44
[4] See Genesis 1:1-3
[5] See Luke 2:8-14

life and death through two fruit trees, which He called 'the tree of life' and 'the tree of the knowledge of good and evil'.[6] The occult and mystical meaning of the tree of life is the entire aspiration of nature towards the Divine, an aspiration that rises. This is the high tide that continues to rise. The tree of the knowledge of good and evil is the descending movement. How was death born? Most naturally. If two trains head towards each other on the same track, what will happen? A collision. Adam stood between two trains that were heading towards each other, and, because he did not know how to avoid the collision, he died. And any of you who eats the forbidden fruit will likewise die, because when someone does so, he or she enters the great current from above that descends to the earth. Only divine power can save a person from this current. Christ came to the earth to place people in the first current of life, the upward current from the earth to God, which we call resurrection.

To be able to understand this teaching, we have to understand the meaning of 'the Father, the Son and the Holy Spirit'. What does 'the Father' mean? It is the teaching of divine wisdom. What does 'the Son' mean? It is the teaching of divine love. What does 'the Holy Spirit' mean? It is the teaching of the uplifting of the human being, the teaching of human evolution. It is said in the Scriptures, "Whoever trusts in this teaching will be saved."[7] We need to understand the laws of this teaching. What is required of you? Every one of you is a father, but do you understand your vocation as fathers? You have also been in the position of sons, but do you know how a son should relate to his father? You are not yet like the Spirit, but you will be in the future. You are now in the process of becoming like the Spirit. It is the Spirit that uplifts people, and this Spirit will uplift Christ within us.

To understand correctly Christ's teaching we have to detach ourselves from many of the world's hooks. This does not mean to renounce the world, because that would be an incorrect understanding. The world has two faces, one divine and the other external. When speaking of denying the world, we need to understand it as the denial of its tempo-

---

[6] See Genesis 2:8-9, 15-17; 3:22-24

[7] Jesus said, "The Father hath given all judgement unto the Son. Verily, verily, I say unto you, He that heareth my word, and believeth him that sent me, hath eternal life, and cometh not into judgement, but hath passed out of death into life" (John 5:22, 24). And the Apostle Paul wrote, "The gospel is the power of God unto salvation to every one that believeth" (Romans 1:16).

rary and deceitful elements, which do not provide anything essential in our lives. We ought to keep only those things which enable us to uplift ourselves while we are on the earth.[8] As it is said in the Scriptures, "God so loved the world that He gave His only-begotten Son to help it."[9]

A man is born. He then grows up and thinks he will conquer the world and set it right. When he arrives at the age of forty-five, however, he notices a weakening of his strength, which makes him realise that he will not live forever. He therefore becomes cleverer and arranges for younger people to work for him. The man becomes softer and kinder because he is weaker and sees that he is becoming older. Today's people think that a human being cannot be resurrected and made alive again. That is the biggest delusion in contemporary life. A human being can be resurrected, just as he or she can die. When you come into contradiction with the forces acting in nature, your human form will be destroyed. When you do not understand the laws, you will be trampled upon.[10]

We need to free ourselves of certain obstacles that our souls have inherited. I will give you a story that illustrates a great law that regulates life. Some sailors on shore leave visited the town near where they were anchored and spent a drunken evening in a local tavern. Afterwards they returned to their boat to row back out to their ship. In their inebriated state, they forgot to untie the rope that secured the boat to the shore. They rowed and rowed for the rest of the night and thought they were heading towards their ship. It was not until first light that they realised they were still by the shore. One thin rope had prevented them from reaching their ship. The reason people cannot resurrect themselves is because they are tied by ropes to mooring posts on the beach.

I have seen small children catch birds and tie their feet with string. The children allow the birds to start flying while they hold the other

---

[8] The Teacher also said, "Let us dedicate our lives to the Lord. This does not mean we ought to go and live like hermits in a forest. What it means is that we should fulfil Christ's commandments in our lives and enlighten our minds, warm our hearts, rebirth our souls and make our spirits alive and fresh within us" (11/24 January 1915). "Self-denial means to rid oneself of the desire for useless things" (15/28 August 1912).

[9] "God so loved the world, that he gave his only begotten Son, that whosoever believeth on him should not perish, but have eternal life. For God sent not the Son into the world to judge the world; but that the world should be saved through him. He that believeth on him is not judged" (John 3:16-18).

[10] Jesus said, "Ye are the salt of the earth: but if the salt have lost his savour, it is thenceforth good for nothing, but to be cast out and trodden under foot of men" (Matthew 5:13).

end of the strings. When the strings become taught the birds fall to the ground. And human beings are tied to earthly things in the same way. People need to have an ideal. What ideal? The kind of ideal that will pull them towards heaven. You say, "I start flying and then I fall to the ground without knowing why." You fall because you are tied. If you have some doubt in your mind, or important questions which you have not answered, simply untie the boat from its moorings and row towards your purpose. We cannot avoid the consequences when the causes have already taken place. We think our thoughts and desires have no effects. Actually, each thought, no matter how weak it might be, has some effect. Moses said that God would avenge crimes up to the end of the fourth generation.[11] The karma of a crime has to be liquidated within one hundred years.[12]

Those who study the law notice the following rule. If a married couple come from the same race and the wife has a secret affair with a man of a different-coloured race and becomes pregnant by him, a child with his colour will be born in the first, second, third or fourth generation. If the child of a colour different from the husband's is born in the first generation it is better, because the karma of the affair is reaped by those who sowed it. If, however, the different-coloured child is born after one hundred years, the parents and their families will be astonished when the baby is delivered, wondering among themselves, "How is this possible?" It is possible because the baby's great-great-grandmother conceived a child with a man of that colour. This law also works in our feelings and thoughts. Sometimes a bad thought appears in your mind. Why? Because one hundred years ago your soul conceived a child with the devil. A bad desire is also your child. This karmic law is strict. We need to take care, because we cannot avoid the consequences of causes that have already taken place. We ought never to give room in our minds for a bad thought, because it will create its form inside us, and this form will cause us to stumble some time in the future.[13]

[11] This principle was given in the Ten Commandments (see Exodus 20:5).

[12] The Teacher also said, "God only remembers an evil act for one hundred years. During that time the perpetrator is burdened by what he or she did" (18 October 1931).

[13] The Teacher also said, "In the contemporary order, men and women hold the key to a better life in the future. Together they will build the individuals of the future society. When building a house you follow certain rules, like choosing strong materials. It is the good mothers and fathers who, with their good thoughts, will build the well-ordered fu-

The real question here is not over the skin colour of a baby and its parents but about people's vibrations. There are dark vibrations and light vibrations. People with dark vibrations aspire to the earth, not to heaven. They are people of the tree from which your first mother, Eve, ate. People with light vibrations, who are now coming into the world, are people of the tree of life. The people we become corresponds to the tree whose fruit we eat, the tree of life or the tree of the knowledge of good and evil. The tree of life is Christ.[14] There is an abstract thought that Christ sits at the right hand of the Father.[15] You, however, need to absorb the great thought that Christ is a power that penetrates the whole earth, and when this stream flows through all beings, from the smallest to the largest, salvation will take place. When Christ died, darkness came,[16] a darkness which people felt. It is said in the Scriptures that Christ then entered hell and preached there, and all who listened to him were freed from hell and came to the earth.[17] Were you not in hell when Christ was preaching there? You were, but you have forgotten it. What did Christ tell you when he descended to hell to remove you from the darkness? He said, "Go and sin no more, otherwise you will give birth to the child of darkness and more and more suffering will follow."[18]

As Christ is on the earth, he has decided to save humanity. And he will save it. Nothing has the power on earth, no matter how mighty it may be, to oppose the power of Christ. This is why he said, "Nothing can take from my hands the sheep that my Father has given me, for there is nothing greater than my Father."[19] If doubt sometimes penetrates your

---

ture conditions in which we are to live. Children's thoughts develop to become like those of their parents. If we have criminal thoughts, our children will become criminals. Our thoughts and desires will be realised in society. Our thoughts and desires will definitely be realised in one, two, three or four generations" (10/23 January 1915). "Noble parents give birth to noble children" (15/28 January 1915).

[14] The Teacher also said, "When Christ comes, people will pick their fruit only from the tree of life, from goodness. These fruits are all good thoughts, feelings and desires" (21 January/3 February 1915).

[15] "The Lord Jesus, after he had spoken unto the eleven disciples, was received up into heaven, and sat down at the right hand of God" (Mark 16:19).

[16] See Luke 23:44-46

[17] See Ephesians 4:7-10; 1 Peter 3:18-20

[18] Jesus's parting words to the woman caught in adultery whom he had saved from stoning were, "Go thy way; from henceforth sin no more" (John 8:11).

[19] See John 10:27-29

soul, it has come from your father of darkness. Cut off your connection with him. A pure soul ought never to mix itself with something impure. When a young child gets himself dirty, does his mother hug him? No, first she tells him off, and then she washes him and dresses him in clean clothes, and only then does she kiss him. That is the simple philosophy of life. Do you know why Christ suffered? The cross symbolises the human house, the body. Christ was crucified on this cross. God is now saying, "Clean your houses thoroughly and open the windows." Some people say, "Kiss this cross,"[20] but this cross first has to be purified. The cross is inside us, in the mind and in the heart. People cannot kiss this cross until they have purified their minds and hearts.[21] Each one of us is a cross – we are living crosses. We should raise the divine cross in our hearts. When we have done this we will make our crosses into circles, the symbol of eternity. In other words, we will each make the cross into a wheel or an oar with which to move ourselves.

Christ, by his teaching, wanted to show us the fundamental laws with which we can change the order of things. And we can change it. To do so, first we have to have an idea of how it can be changed and then we need to aspire to it. People cannot yet succeed in making this change for one simple reason, because great egotism exists within them. Everybody wants to be in the highest position. An artist represented this situation very well in a painting depicting a mountain with an idol on the top. A million people are portrayed looking up to the idol, but anyone actually climbing up to reach it is being pulled back by others. As everybody is constantly fighting, no one can ascend to the idol. In the Olympic Games in ancient Greece only the winner of a race took the wreath. It is different in Christianity, for everyone who follows Christ's teaching receives a crown.[22]

There are three things for us in Christ's teaching: the Father, the Son

[20] After the Orthodox Eucharist the congregants kiss a cross held by the priest while he blesses them before they leave the church.

[21] "They that are of Christ Jesus have crucified the flesh with the passions and the lusts thereof" (Galatians 5:24). "Blessed are they that wash their robes, that they may have the right to come to the tree of life, and may enter in by the gates into the holy city" (Revelation 22:14)

[22] The Apostle Paul, who described Christian life as a race (see 2 Timothy 4:6-8; Hebrews 12:1-3), contrasted the temporary crown given to the winner in human sports races and the everlasting crown awaiting Christians (see 1 Corinthians 9:24-25).

and the Holy Spirit. If you can pronounce the word 'Father' in its full meaning, you will feel the pulse of this Being who moves the world. To feel the divine thought means to know it and understand it. When you can do this, the Lord will answer your desires even before you ask for something. We ought to have perfect filial relationships with God, which means our fulfilling the obligations that we have to our Father. God did not descend to earth Himself but instead sent His Son, and we too ought to sacrifice ourselves in this world. Many people are fearful of making sacrifices, saying that there is no life in sacrifice. Many people do not understand these words of Christ: "If you do not eat my flesh and drink my blood, you will not have life eternal." [23] We eat each day to live. Do not the grains of wheat and the plants whose juices we eat sacrifice themselves for us? They say, "We die so that you will become good people." How many billions of beings serve us! But what are we now doing on the earth? We occupy ourselves with scholastic questions, like the old philosopher who conjectured about how many angels could dance on the head of a pin.

Christ's teaching contains the meaning of life. There is always a valley between two great epochs. If you examine the human brain, you will see trenches, the furrows in the surface. These furrows are necessary for the circulation of human thought. The surface of the earth is also undulated, and there are currents in its channels that are necessary to our lives. Someone says, "I do not want to live in a valley." But where would you like to live then? How many angels can live on a mountain peak? It is impossible for all human beings to live on the mountaintop. Sometimes you will be in the valley, at other times you will be on the mountaintop. You will go up and down and up and down until it has been understood that evolution is an undulating process. When humanity has learnt Christ's teaching, has learnt the circular movement of eternity, we will enter another type of evolution that is not undulating but circular. The teaching of the Spirit is real, even though contemporary people do not believe it to be so. When the Divine Spirit works within us, it simultaneously works with the principle of unity and multiplicity. The Father creates. The Spirit is the multiplicity in creation, everything from one pole to the other, all the conditions in which

[23] See John 6:53-57

we live. Christ is the juices that are constantly flowing in the tree of life.

Today's astrologers say that human beings are in communion with the whole Universe, that there exists a certain relationship between all beings. Indeed, the thoughts of the people in one nation can affect the whole world. Even Jupiter, Mars, Saturn and other planets can affect us. Someone will protest, "How can we be influenced by Mars?" We are influenced by the thoughts of the beings on Mars. Their thoughts form a current through Space, and when we pass through this current we become warlike. Everybody is now under the influence of Mars, and we will continue fighting this war until Mars's influence has fulfilled its purpose. Do not think that Christ's teaching is the teaching of peace.[24] It is the teaching of peace, but only while there is balance. When the equilibrium is lost there has to be war, because there is no other way to restore the balance.[25] We may see this law in practical life when a milk-maid churns milk to extract butter from it. War will end in the world when the butter has been extracted from the milk. Why are people fighting? It is because Christ has said, "I want butter!" People are now hard and rough, but when you have spread the butter over yourselves, you will become softer and smoother. The butter is now being churned, and when Christ has spread it you will become gentler. You need to have butter to enter the kingdom of God. This is the teaching of the Spirit. I am speaking allegorically, but when you think about it, you will understand the meaning of the forces which act to make things smooth.

The Lord created the world. Do you know why He did this? Because the first spirits in creation became crystals. It was necessary for our Earth to be created so new cells could be made that were not of a geometrically crystalline form but in the form of a circle. A crystal, a diamond, needs to become a living cell, a plant, so that it can develop itself. This plant then needs to transform itself into flesh and nerves so that it can feel and move in the way animals feel and move. Likewise, we should

[24] Jesus said, "Think not that I came to send peace on the earth: I came not to send peace, but a sword" (Matthew 10:34). "I came to cast fire upon the earth. Think ye that I am come to give peace in the earth? I tell you, Nay; but rather division" (Luke 12:49, 51).

[25] Two years before the First World War, the Teacher said, "Very important changes will take place in the world. You must not be afraid of this, because these changes are fundamental. Christ is coming to balance things, to lay a new foundation and set everything right. Once this has happened, everything will proceed and develop correctly" (15/28 August 1912).

make every necessary effort to form the cell that creates saints. At the moment we are dead, trees planted upside down in heaven. We should therefore sacrifice ourselves to become spiritually wise cells, to become one with Christ. And when we have passed through his body, his mind and his heart, and only then, we will be able to tune ourselves correctly, enabling us to understand the deep meaning of things. Of course, this is all very abstract, but if I explain these things more I will move away from the main topic of this lecture.

A primary requirement in life is obedience. In ancient Greece a disciple wanted to understand the secret science. He travelled to Egypt and studied in the school of the White Brotherhood.[26] The main hierophant of the Temple of Isis took him before a statue and said, "This is The Truth!" The disciple complained, "Why did you show me other places before bringing me here to The Truth?" The hierophant replied, "No one is permitted to come here straightaway. Do not touch or lift the veil that covers this statue. Study it externally." But a great desire was born in the disciple to see what was beneath the statue's veil. He said to himself, "When I lift the veil I will find The Truth and I will have great power when I return to Greece." One night the disciple entered the Temple and lifted the statue's veil. The next morning he was found lying dead on the floor in front of the statue.[27] So what had he learnt?

Someone says, "Lift the veil! I want to see The Truth!" It is dangerous to lift the veil. A person has to be ready for such a revelation. Christ came to the earth to prepare us to meet this moment fearlessly.[28] First

---

[26] The Teacher said that the Universal White Brotherhood had branches in other countries in earlier times (some time between 1929 and 1942).

[27] The Lord said to Moses, "Thou canst not see my face: for man shall not see me and live" (Exodus 33:20).

[28] In the Tabernacle of Moses, and later the Temple in Jerusalem, a veil separated the Holy Place from the Most Holy Place, keeping hidden the presence of the Lord and the Ark of the Covenant (see Exodus 26:31-33; 40:1-3, 18-21; 1 Kings 8:1-13; 2 Chronicles 3:14). No one but the High Priest could enter behind the veil, and he could only do so without dying on one day a year, the Day of Atonement (see Exodus 28:1-4, 43; 40:33-35; Leviticus 16:1-34; 23:26-32).

Jesus came to reconnect humanity with God, and at the moment of his death upon the cross, the veil of the Temple tore in two (see Matthew 27:50-51). The Apostle Paul wrote, "As a forerunner Jesus entered into that which is within the veil for us, having become a high priest for ever" (Hebrews 6:20). "Christ having come a high priest of the good things to come, through the greater and more perfect tabernacle, not made with hands, that is to say, not of this creation, through his own blood, entered in once for all into the holy place,

we need to learn what type of life leads to salvation. Afterwards we should pass through other processes. Christ told Nicodemus that unless he was born of water and the Spirit he would not be able to enter the kingdom of God,[29] by which he meant, "If you are not born of the higher world, you will not see the kingdom of God." To be reborn is not the same as being reincarnated.[30] Reincarnation is the process of life stopping and restarting. Reincarnation is a law of disharmony in the world. To reincarnate means to restart the work that you left unfinished the last time you were here. The law of rebirth is to fulfil the will of God. It is not difficult to fulfil God's will. The deep cause of our difficulty with it is always our incomprehension of life.

What does it mean to think? To think means to concentrate your thoughts. The world is a school. You do not want to study, to concentrate, but who forced you to enrol at this school? If you do not want to study, it is better for you to return to the plant or mineral state. Only through deep and sustained concentration can you study the teaching of the Father, Son and Holy Spirit. Through this work you will come to love the Lord. The Teacher of this teaching comes each morning and throws a thought to our souls. Despite this we become poor. Why? Because we were not able to appreciate the thoughts that Christ gave us. Instead, we think, "I want glory! I want this! I want that!" But the blessings which Christ gives are far more essential than those things. The glory of God costs far more than human glory. Christ wants to give all of you the power to become masters of life and death.[31]

Do you know who created death? It was the one thousand million spirits who constantly destroy. You want to be progressive people yet every day you fill yourselves with doubt and envy. Some spiritual people are still not free in their thoughts and do not understand life. Christ resurrected himself and thus showed the path that we should tread, the process of rebirth. Do you know what birth is? Tolstoy told of a dream

having obtained eternal redemption. For Christ entered into heaven itself, now to appear before the face of God for us" (Hebrews 9:11-12, 24). And Jesus said, "I am the way, and the truth, and the life: no one cometh unto the Father, but by me" (John 14:6).

[29] See John 3:5

[30] Jesus said, "That which is born of the flesh is flesh; and that which is born of the Spirit is spirit" (John 3:6).

[31] Jesus said, "As the Father raiseth the dead and quickeneth them, even so the Son also quickeneth whom he will" (John 5:21).

he had in which he was pregnant and experienced the pain of giving birth. In the morning he enquired of some women whether they had suffered the same pain during childbirth. When they confirmed that they had, Tolstoy said, "It is difficult to be a woman." When a thought comes to your mind, it will cause you suffering until you have given birth to it. Do not think that suffering is a bad sign. Like a mother, you need to give something of yourself to your babies – you need to give life and strength to your noble thoughts.

At last you need to have the courage to move the stones from your tombs, instead of just questioning and thinking over whether Christ was able to resurrect himself or not. There were people present at Christ's resurrection. Someone will say, "Prove it!" I can prove it, but your attitude would not change were I to try, for there is a certain law which would have to be followed. To prove this to you I would have to lead you to a certain path, to show you the way, after which you would need to test the truth for yourself. It would be proven to you only once you had verified it.... It is the final hour. We need to resurrect ourselves, and we will do so. We should not ask whether Christ resurrected himself or not, but whether the time is near for our own resurrections – that is the question. It is asked whether Christ really lay in the tomb for three days,[32] but you have been lying in the tomb for eight thousand years![33] Has this not been long enough? Yes, it has. The angel above is the call of Christ announcing the Second Coming.[34] In what condition will Christ find you when he comes? If a stone still shuts off your tomb, how will Christ be able to say, "Lazarus, come out!"? Each of you needs your neighbours and friends to do you a favour, to roll the stone away from your tomb.[35] When they have done it, Christ will say, "Stand up!"

[32] Jesus said, "The Son of man must be killed, and the third day be raised up" (Luke 9:22).

[33] According to the Teacher, that is since the Fall of Humanity. He said, "For eight thousand years women have been serving their old lover in Paradise, the handsome rascal from the Garden of Eden" (26 February 1920).

[34] "And the seventh angel sounded; and there followed great voices in heaven, and they said, 'The kingdom of the world is become the kingdom of our Lord, and of his Christ: and he shall reign for ever and ever'" (Revelation 11:15). "For the Lord himself shall descend from heaven, with a shout, with the voice of the archangel, and with the trump of God" (1 Thessalonians 4:16).

[35] "When Jesus came, he found that *Lazarus* had been in the tomb four days already. Martha therefore, when she heard that Jesus was coming, went and met him. Jesus saith unto her, 'Thy brother shall rise again.' Martha saith unto him, 'I know that he shall rise again in the

and you will be resurrected.

Whoever is listening to me this morning, I am rolling the stones away from your tombs. Christ is coming, and he will stand in front of your open tombs and say, "Come out!"

resurrection at the last day.' Jesus said unto her, 'I am the resurrection, and the life: he that believeth on me, though he die, yet shall he live: and whosoever liveth and believeth on me shall never die. Believest thou this?' She saith unto him, 'Yea, Lord: I have believed that thou art the Christ, the Son of God.'

"Jesus cometh to the tomb. Now it was a cave, and a stone lay against it. Jesus saith, 'Take ye away the stone.' Martha, the sister of him that was dead, saith unto him, 'Lord, by this time he stinketh: for he hath been dead four days.' Jesus saith unto her, 'Said I not unto thee, that, if thou believedst, thou shouldest see the glory of God?' So they took away the stone. And Jesus cried with a loud voice, 'Lazarus, come forth.' He that was dead came forth" (John 11:17, 20, 23-27, 38-41, 43-44).

Making the Precious Pearl:
The Importance of Masculinity and Femininity

Jesus said,

> The kingdom of heaven is like unto a man that is a merchant seeking goodly pearls: and having found one pearl of great price, he went and sold all that he had, and bought it. [1]

This morning I will speak about the seemingly least important verse in chapter thirteen of Matthew's Gospel, in which the merchant finds and buys the pearl of great price. It is connected to the seventh and greatest law of nature: the law of gender. Everything has a gender, male or female. There is a dispute over which is the higher gender. It is said that in the beginning, when creating the first human being, God made a man. Men support this from their point of view, claiming it proves they are higher than women. Women, defending their cause, claim they are higher than men. There are also arguments between scientists on this question. To view something objectively is the masculine way. To view something subjectively is the feminine way. The conscious realm is masculine and the subconscious is feminine. Everything needs to be considered by both the objective mind and the subjective mind, which together form a true conception of things.

You may be wondering what the connection is between this verse and men and women. There is a connection. We need to bear in mind how pearls are made. A grain of sand enters an oyster's shell. The oyster then releases a liquid that covers the sand and sculpts it into a smooth surface, turning it into a precious pearl. If the grain of sand had not entered the shell it would have remained worthless. As the grain of sand is rough, it bothers the oyster, causing it to think. It cannot eject the sand, so it comes to the idea of making it precious. It says to the sand, "You are my enemy, but I will love you and make you precious."

---

[1] Matthew 13:45-46. The original Bulgarian publication only quoted verse 46.

Christ said, "Love your enemies."[2] Whereas you would throw out this sand, the oyster turns it into a valuable pearl, a wonderful achievement for which Christ praises it. I ask you, if Christ appeared now, would he find your work to be as good as the oyster's? Would he find pearls? You protest, "We do not have the conditions in which to do such work!" You blame the fact that you do not have a house yet, that you do not have this or that, that people hinder you, that society hinders you, and so on. Unlike you, the oyster does not complain about its lack of suitable conditions. It has no legs, no tongue, no human brain, yet it creates a pearl from a grain of sand. I ask you, can you not do as much as an oyster? Surely you can do more.

But let us come to a fundamental law: the masculine and feminine external forms are the product of the internal differences between men and women. Each feature of the human face has a deep inner cause in the human soul. If only men were born, how would the world progress? God first made a man, but the man said to God, "This cannot continue! How can I do all of this work alone? How will I cultivate this enormous garden, Paradise?" God answered, "Very well, I will make you a companion similar to yourself who will help you."[3] Thus the great law of polarity entered the stage, the process that moves the world. There could be no progress, development or nobility if this law did not exist.

You only look at the external side of things, but on the inside there is a more profound meaning. You only know the female aspect of nature, for the male aspect is invisible.[4] The sun that you see is a female sun. The male sun is invisible. The female sun draws energy from the male sun. I would like every one of you to know how to give birth. The greatest blessing for a human being is to know how to create, and how to nourish his or her creation. How is it possible for a human being

[2] See Luke 6:27-28

[3] In the Bible Adam did not ask for a companion; it was God's idea (see Genesis 2:18). However, the Teacher said, "In the first human culture there were only men. Women did not exist. It was a remarkable culture, in which there was no suffering. The human being was connected with God. God was man's companion. God taught Adam great knowledge, but he became lazy and desired a companion to help him. God granted this wish and sent him a companion, woman" (24 December 1916).

[4] The Teacher also said, "By the word 'matter' we mean 'a mother that gives birth'. What we see in the visible world is a substance with which our mother, matter, has covered us" (10/23 January 1915).

not to give birth, not to create a good thought, a good desire, within himself or herself? It is a creative principle worthy of thinking beings. Of course, I am talking of the ordinary male or female human being, not the Creative Principle that can create anything from nothing, the Creator. In Christian philosophy this is Christ, the God-human being. Christ said, "The Father lives in me."[5] No one has seen God, no one has seen the Father of the world. We know the Mother. God appears to us as the Mother who creates, nourishes and educates – 'Him' we know.

It is said in the Scriptures, "Christ came to the earth to reveal the Father to us."[6] According to the same law, the human being who descended to the earth from heaven was originally like a small grain of sand. The Divine Spirit worked on this grain of sand for a long time and turned it into a pearl. You ought to be grateful to the Divine Consciousness that has worked on you for a long time to produce something of value. Sometimes the value of a thing is in its content and sometimes it is on its surface. An example of the latter is the marble that has been worked on by a great sculptor. The sculptor has expressed a wonderful idea on the surface of the stone. If a foolish person breaks the statue into pieces, only simple, valueless stones will remain. It is your noble thoughts, desires and actions that give you value. They were drawn inside you by the Divine Spirit. Only the features which God deposits in your mind, heart and soul give you value.

According to contemporary scientists, the thinking capacity of a brain corresponds to the number of furrows it has. What are these furrows? They are the features deposited in the brain, the channels of a person's thoughts. Some people want to have faces as smooth as bowls. They think a person is good-looking when his or her face is smooth. That is incorrect, for such a face is a mask. A person's face should have features which say certain things about him or her. The first thing our faces should say is that we are good people; second, that we are righteous; and third, that we are loving, wise and lovers of the truth. All these things should be manifested on the face. Each face is a book in

---

[5] See John 14:10-11

[6] "No man hath seen God at any time; the only begotten Son, which is in the bosom of the Father, he hath declared him" (John 1:18). Jesus said, "No one knoweth the Son, save the Father; neither doth any know the Father, save the Son, and he to whomsoever the Son willeth to reveal him" (Matthew 11:27).

which that person's qualities are written.

Some people ask me, "Have you listened to the Lord? Have you heard Him?" I answer, "Not only have I listened to the Lord, I see Him when He speaks to me. I am able to hear His words, and I listen to them." Human words can only be heard, but it is not only possible to hear the Word of the Lord; it can also be seen. God, who is glorious, has embodied Himself in Christ and thus become visible.[7] God's glory is embodied, expressed and visible in each human being. You ask if I have heard the Lord and spoken to Him. Yes, I have heard Him for two thousand years! Christ's teaching is an excellent philosophy. It is not a philosophy that we touch in the darkness but a philosophy that we can see, touch, smell and taste.[8]

Why is there a difference between people? There is a difference because people must not be identical. By the law, people are identical in essence but have different degrees of development. There always has to be a difference between people – it is a divine law. If you want someone to love you, there has to be a difference between you, but this difference has to combine harmoniously, in the same way as different musical tones can combine harmoniously so that we listen to them with admiration.

I will now explain the nature of the harmonious relationship that should exist between men and women. Let us apply this divine principle. Femininity is the emblem of love. Love cannot be found in masculinity. Masculinity contains another divine power, wisdom. When love marries wisdom they give birth to the truth. If you want to come to the truth, you have to find your father, wisdom, and your mother, love. Together they will give birth to and manifest the truth. The truth follows the father's line; it has a masculine nature; it is the son of love and wisdom. The father and mother, love and wisdom, also give birth to a second child, virtue, which has a feminine nature. Virtue is the sister of the truth. When virtue and truth are united, the result is righteousness.

If you want to create a pearl, it has to be cultivated by your soul. I am often asked, "Does your preaching conform to that of the church?"

---

[7] "The Son of the Father's love is the image of the invisible God" (Colossians 1:15). Jesus said, "He that beholdeth me beholdeth him that sent me" (John 12:45).

[8] The Teacher also said, "I know the Lord better than I know you. I am more closely connected to Him than I am to you" (21 January/3 February 1915).

My answer is that I preach what is consistent with the great divine law. I never tell a lie before the Lord. It does not matter to me if my teaching agrees with your views or not. The important thing to me is for my views to be in accord with the great law which says that I must not be a liar before God, before heaven and before the angels and saints. If everybody understood this teaching and thought accordingly, there would be no fear. Some people say, "You want to form a sect." According to me, only small-minded people form sects. It is easy to form a sect. For example, break a piece of wood and each piece is a sect. Break a stone and each piece is a sect. Make a quarrel among a group and split it and you have made a sect. We often forget what we are preaching and the principle that connects us. Our task is to establish the kingdom of God on earth.[9] We should therefore become conductors of the divine law, allowing it to flow through us. This law needs to conquer all minds and hearts so that all people, men, women and children, become children of the kingdom of God. When everybody is a child of God, we will live perfect lives on this earth.

When people now complain to me about the great misfortune that has come to us,[10] I tell them, "I am glad that your prisons are being destroyed, that your old views are collapsing, because if the stale, old water is not poured from the bottle, it cannot be filled with fresh water." When Christ came to the Jewish people they should have purified themselves and begun to live a new life. Instead, they said, "We know Moses but we do not know you! You want to form a sect."[11] But as you can see, Christ did not form a sect, although according to the Jews he was a heretic.[12] They said, "He wants to destroy our nation!"[13]

[9] The Teacher also said, "We ought to keep good relations with everybody. We need to avoid quarrelling among ourselves – there is quarrelling in all Christian sects. Such people preach Christianity but they do not embody it" (11/24 January 1915).

[10] This misfortune was the encroaching First World War, where a new front had opened up in eastern Thrace not far from the southeastern Bulgarian border. A week earlier, on 12/25 April 1915, Allied forces had landed on the Gallipoli Peninsula, in an attempt to take control of the Dardanelles, the sea gateway to Constantinople, the capital of the Ottoman Empire. It was hoped that a successful campaign here would lead to the swift defeat of the Ottoman Empire, persuade Bulgaria, Greece and Romania to join the Allies and be the turning point of the war.

[11] See John 9:28-29

[12] See Matthew 26:59-68, especially 63-65

[13] See Luke 23:1-2

Now, two thousand years later, we ought not to think as they did. I ask you, what did the Jews gain by crucifying Christ? Nothing. Instead of gaining something, they were dispersed all over the world.

I will tell you some more about the principle of masculinity and femininity. First, you should love the Lord with all your heart, with all your soul, with all your mind and with all your strength. Second, you should love your neighbour as yourself.[14] Third, you should love your enemies as tiny grains of sand. Christ did not come to the earth to save noble and righteous people; he came to save course grains of sand.[15] He even descended to hell to remove them from it.[16] The oyster needs to be taken and opened so that the pearl may be removed from it. By the same law, human beings are taken to heaven and opened, and the pearl in the soul is removed. When a person dies, the mourners say, "The oyster has died!" and they walk behind the oyster in tears. I say that the oyster went to heaven to present the pearl it had created and polished on earth. If the oyster had not made a pearl, it would have been worthless and it would not have gone to heaven.

I will return to some of the features of men and women. Those who study the structure of the human body say that a person's outer features are caused by his or her inner nature, the external person being an expression of the interior. I would like to give you a new direction, so that you can comprehend Christianity in its profound meaning as the science of life. Christianity is a positive science that should teach us how to live. It is a science that different people apply in different ways. Men and women cannot be the same; there needs to be a difference between them. The masculine nature is active. To be active means to work in three ways: physically, mentally and spiritually. It is not possible for all people to work simultaneously in the same way in the same place; they need to work in different fields. The differences between people can either create harmony or disharmony – it depends on them.

When two people are irritable and one of them talks, the other needs to listen. This is a law which acts on the physical level. If one person is silent in that situation, the other one will appreciate this act of patience and will repay him or her in another way. If a husband or wife does not

---

[14] Jesus said these were the first two, and greatest, commandments (see Matthew 22:35-40).

[15] Jesus said, "I am not come to call the righteous but sinners to repentance" (Luke 5:32).

[16] See Ephesians 4:7-10; 1 Peter 3:18-20

behave like this, the other will complain: "There is nobody worse than my spouse! May the Lord free us of each other!" Do not think you can be freed in that way, for if you are separated here without coming to harmony, in the next world you will chase each other. The thing which can change your lives is the divine law – when you have understood it and are applying it in your lives. You will make many mistakes. You can make thousands of them and the Lord will not judge you but forgive you. I assure you that He will forgive you, but only if you are studying the divine law and working. If, however, you have not learnt anything after making one hundred mistakes, the Lord will not continue to forgive you. Everything in the world needs to be used correctly. If some pear trees and roses have thorns, it is natural. Whoever wants to climb a thorny pear tree should not wear delicate clothing. People who do not understand the law say, "This pear tree has thorns and therefore should be cut down." It does indeed have thorns, but it also gives us nice fruit....

Women hold the keys to the kingdom of God. When Christ said to Petra, "I give you the keys to the kingdom of God,"[17] he was referring to the deep inner law that says there always needs to be a fundamental difference between men and women. This difference is the basis of the love which men have for women. The day women change position from that in which God has placed them, men's love for them will diminish.[18] A wife should see the Lord in her husband, see that the Lord lives within him. She then ought to be worthy of the Lord's love, and she will be worthy of it when she does some work for Him. As

---

[17] See Matthew 16:18-19. For the Apostle Peter as 'Petra', see n. 17, p. 301 of the present volume.

[18] The Teacher also said, "What did the Creator intend by the number 'one'? He meant there to be One Standard, One Principle, which is called God. In the physical world the number 'two' means that we need two points of support, two active forces which face each other. This polarity is why a man is attracted to a woman and a woman to a man. The number two shows the process by which nature works and that the process of polarisation is a process of evolution. A tree grows many branches, but they all come from the same source and are connected to each other. When things are branching out they have to remain connected to their foundation. All your thoughts and desires need to be connected to your souls" (10/23 January 1915). "Humanity will be saved by the uplifting of the heart. Love is only manifested in femininity. Wherever femininity is absent, love is also absent. Were people to understand the feminine principle, they would restore it to its rightful place, and then the world would be uplifted immediately. I wish the souls of all people to be filled with love" (18 October 1931).

the Lord cannot descend to the earth to work, He has given us minds, hearts and power to conquer the earth and put everything in order. In exchange for this work He will give us every blessing.

Christ told his disciples about the man who sought the precious pearl, which means he sought the preciousness of his soul. Having found it, he went and sold all his possessions to buy it.[19] If you are not ready to sacrifice everything you have in this world, you should at least sacrifice something to gain a pearl. There are people who sacrifice all their possessions but do not acquire a pearl. This is because their sacrifices were made to pay for alcoholism, or games of billiards, or gambling, or other such things. I would sacrifice anything for a pearl. This kind of sacrifice has to be carried out in a spiritually wise way, though; it is not enough simply to sell everything and give the proceeds to the poor.

I will give you another example. In ancient times there were two kingdoms separated by a mountain. It was said it would be a great blessing for both kingdoms if somebody could make a tunnel through the mountain and connect them. Only a person who never looked back could succeed in this great task.[20] Many people tried to build a tunnel, but whenever anyone came and asked them what they were doing, they turned their heads back and failed. Finally the son of the king of one of the kingdoms tried. Although many people spoke to him, he did not look back and answer them. Then a philosopher arrived and told him that he would show him an easy way to make the tunnel. The prince turned to look at the philosopher, only to see that the tunnel he had dug had filled up with earth. He restarted his work and resolved not to look back and speak to anybody again until he had completed it. He finished the tunnel, connecting the two kingdoms, and married the daughter of the king of the other kingdom. Both kingdoms then began to live happily.

This is not only an allegory; it is a great truth. The great mountain separating the two kingdoms is the human sin which separates the earth from heaven. If you were clairvoyant, you would see a dark mass

---

[19] The Teacher also said, "Christ wants us to use the touchstone, which is our divine souls. When we find it we will be free. Christ told people how to find their buried souls, their hidden wealth. Our souls are pawned, and we need to recover them. When descending from heaven to incarnate on the earth, a human being pawns his or her soul, so we have to pay the pawnbroker" (13/26 April 1914).

[20] Jesus said, "No man, having put his hand to the plough, and looking back, is fit for the kingdom of God" (Luke 9:62).

between the earth and heaven.[21] Christ descended to the earth to make a tunnel through this mountain. When Christ said, "There is only one path leading to the kingdom of heaven," he meant this tunnel, this narrow path. Although this narrow path was made two thousand years ago, few people have walked along it. There are many wide paths, but they do not lead to the same destination....[22] You can only pass through this tunnel by adhering to the law of gender, the law by which men and women, the masculine and feminine principles, should relate to each other.[23]

When we speak about rebirth, of repentance, it means we need to make harmony between God and ourselves. If the Lord does not love you, who else can? Someone says, "I have no friends. No one loves me. The Lord does not love me." That is not true. The Lord loves you, but you need to learn to love Him.[24] He is not invisible; you may see Him everywhere. This Lord of whom I speak talks to you at least ten times a day. He meets you and gives you advice. While thinking of doing something, you unexpectedly meet a friend who advises you not to do it – sometimes the Lord speaks to us through other people. While I am speaking to you now, the Lord is speaking to you through me. The words are mine, the wrapping is mine, but the content is the Lord's. Accept the gift, unwrap it and find the contents. You women and men need to be in agreement. You are wrapped up by things: you desire to be great in the world, to be rich, to own houses, to be knowledgeable, to be powerful, for everybody to love you, and for you to immediately achieve whatever you want. Very well, but you will not win those things in the lottery. You need to learn the divine law, the study of which begins from within. Were you to think about verse forty-six of

---

[21] The Teacher also said, "People's bad thoughts and desires form a dark belt around the earth" (25 January/7 February 1915).

[22] Jesus said, "Enter ye in by the narrow gate: for wide is the gate, and broad is the way, that leadeth to destruction, and many be they that enter in thereby. For narrow is the gate, and straightened the way, that leadeth unto life, and few be they that find it" (Matthew 7:13-14). "I am the way, and the truth, and the life: no one cometh unto the Father, but by me" (John 14:6).

[23] In inner spiritual terms this is the unification of the self with God through Christ, symbolised by Jesus as the bridegroom (see Matthew 9:14-15; John 3:22-30) and new Jerusalem as his bride (see Revelation 19:6-9; 21:1-2, 9-10; 22:17).

[24] "Draw nigh to God, and he will draw nigh to you" (James 4:8).

337

chapter thirteen in Matthew's Gospel for ten days in a year, or ten days in a month, do you know how many secrets you would learn?

Beauty ought to be an ideal for men and women, because all the angels, the saints and Jesus Christ are beautiful. When someone says, "My spouse does not love me," it tells me that he or she is 'ugly'. A soul in which "Virtue, Righteousness, Love, Wisdom and Truth" are inscribed is great and beautiful and can be loved by anybody. If no one loves you, it means you do not have these features. Go to the Lord and say, "Lord, work your chisel and inscribe these virtues on me." If the Lord does not work on a person with His hammer and chisel, he or she will remain an ordinary, valueless stone.

How ought a man and a woman to work? They want to have children together. Children are the carriers of the truth. They can show you the truth. If you would like to learn humility, your children will show you what it is. The children you have now were dreams in your minds to which you gave clothing. You have the pearl of which Christ spoke, but, instead of making it noble like the oyster made the sand, some of you would like to eject it. That is abortion.

Our thoughts and desires are also our children. If a good thought comes to you and you decide to eject it, you will become ill in some way. The bad thoughts that torment you are those good thoughts and desires which you aborted in the past. They interrupt your every work and make you unhappy. We should in future nourish each noble thought and each noble desire, because they will be reflected in our noses, our eyes and our eyebrows, and we will be handsome like Apollo. At present, human beings look like ogres. People are still ugly. When they go to heaven and see the beauty of the angels, they will not be able to stand it and they will run away. This is why we should pray to the Lord to become purer. It is not so difficult – even an oyster can make a pearl worthy of Christ's praise.

When you go to heaven, for what will Christ be able to praise you? Someone says, "I was the Prime Minister of Bulgaria!" To which Christ responds, "And do you have a pearl?" "No." "In that case, go back down to the earth until you have made one. I will not accept you in the kingdom of God without a pearl." A bishop comes next, and Christ asks him, "What have you done?" "I believed in you and I taught people to do good." "Did you make a pearl?" "No." "Then go away!" To those who made a pearl, Christ will say, "I rejoice, my child, that you have not made me ashamed of you. You are a worthy child."[25] When you men and women go to heaven, you will meet your children, your pearls. Your children will say, "Thank you, mother. When I was a great sinner, you took me into your womb and turned me into a good human being. I will now serve you in this world with all my soul." And that will be your joy.

All this is what Christ wanted to express in the least important verse in chapter thirteen of Matthews' Gospel. You see how much meaning it contains! Other verses are more profound, and you will learn about them one day, when you have gone to heaven, for then you will have a new understanding, new feelings and new qualities. If more were given to you now, you could not endure it. When Christ says, "You women are the emblem of divine love. God lives within you," women need to listen in silence and humility and be worthy of these words.[26] But instead you say, "Lord, You need to know that the world is no longer as it was when You made it...." It is unnecessary for us to try to teach the Lord.[27] When He speaks, we ought to be silent. When He has finished speaking, our lesson begins and we may speak: "I did one thing like this.... And I did another thing like that...." The Lord replies, "You did well with 'this thing', but you were wrong with 'that thing'." You need to listen to the Lord and apply what He teaches you in life. When Christ tells a woman, "Love your neighbour as yourself," he means that she should love her husband as herself. Likewise, when he tells a man, "Love your neighbour as yourself," he means that he should love his wife as himself. When you become living examples of this commandment, your sons and daughters will also follow it. This is what it is to create a pearl, the alchemical law applied at the physical level.

---

[25] Jesus said, "Whosoever shall be ashamed of me and of my words, of him shall the Son of man be ashamed, when he cometh in his own glory, and the glory of the Father, and of the holy angels" (Luke 9:26).

[26] "God is love; and he that abideth in love abideth in God, and God abideth in him" (1 John 4:16).

[27] "Who hath directed the spirit of the Lord, or being his counsellor hath taught him?" (Isaiah 40:13).

The New Foundation of Christ

The Apostle Paul wrote,

> Other foundation can no man lay than that which is laid, which is Jesus Christ.[2]

And Jesus said,

> I am the way, and the truth, and the life.[3]

There is a correlation between these two verses. It is said that it is impossible to lay another foundation. In other words, we cannot change the foundation of life: we cannot change human thought, human desire and human will; we cannot change their essences. We cannot make a thought anything other than a thought. You could make it good, bad or neutral, but you cannot change it further. This means you can change a thought's external form but never its essence. Consequently, I speak of a fundamental law: "No one can change the foundation laid by Christ." This means we are under the power of a great law, a foundation of good and evil. We are standing on a foundation that simultaneously creates joy and suffering, upliftment and decline, enrichment and impoverishment, health and illness. Christ descended from heaven to earth to lay this foundation, which has two supporting points.

There is a principle we need to understand: when building a bridge across a river you have to build upon two supporting points, one on each side of the river. Heaven and earth are the two supporting points upon which human life is built. Our most profound thought is the first supporting point, our desire is the second, and what we call 'will' is

---

[1] Italy entered the First World War on this day, declaring war on Austria-Hungary. The Allies now comprised Belgium, Britain, France, Italy, Japan, Montenegro, Serbia and Russia, against the Central Powers of Austria-Hungary, Germany and the Ottoman Empire.

[2] 1 Corinthians 3:11

[3] John 14:6

the process of building. When talking of human will, we should understand that it always needs two supporting points. When we begin to build on these points we will manifest our wills properly. Human will cannot be manifested without both supports. Building is the only true manifestation of the will.

We need to understand the deep meaning of Christ's teaching, instead of only thinking we have understood it, when in fact we have not. First of all, we human beings are thinking beings; second, we are beings who feel; third, we are beings who act and build. You cannot lay any foundation other than these. If you act outside these things you may degrade yourselves. You can walk in only two directions, up or down. There is no middle path in this world. Everything is moving, so you cannot stand firm on only one supporting point. Two supporting points always remain fixed, even though everything around them is moving. You need to know that the foundation is not inside you. This foundation is not in your thoughts and feelings of any particular moment. You will know that you have found this foundation, your supporting points, when you enter a state of deep peace. Many philosophers have taught the world but did not find their supporting points and therefore had no peace in themselves. When Christ said, "I am the way and the truth," he was pointing to these two supporting points. 'The life' is a process which comes from 'the way' and 'the truth'.

A spirit in space aspires to incarnate on earth. An incarnated child aspires to grow. The child grows from one supporting point, rises to a certain height and then descends, forming a curve that ends at another supporting point. Youth and old age are the two supporting points of human life. When you have passed from childhood to old age, you will see the two supporting points of your life. When you return to the earth next time, you will build on the two supporting points of your previous incarnation, unless you have forgotten it. If you forget it, you will have to start again from the beginning. There are people who cross from point to point without ever building anything. An arching line should connect the two supporting points – this is the law of movement.

The law of movement is expressed in human thought. It is a law of laying a foundation and building upon it. We should build according to a certain plan. For example, while the human body is being built in the womb, the limbs are formed first and the lungs last. The moment the respiratory system is formed the baby should be born. The arms are connected to the human will. The face, nose, mouth, lungs and stomach are connected to human desire. The human brain is an organ of human thought. Some people say the brain itself creates thoughts, but they are wrong. The human brain is similar to the Earth, which does not itself give birth; the creative force comes from Space, from the Sun. The creative force of the Sun acts on the surface of the Earth. The Earth is the foundation on which the Sun builds and creates. The human spirit is the human 'sun' that shines on the human brain and creates thoughts. All beings think: oxen, snakes, lizards, flies and so on. They create their bodies, their houses to live in, according to their way of thinking. The present human organism is the fruit of our thoughts. If the human spirit were to make sufficient effort, it could make bigger lungs, bigger heads and so on. The size of the head is not as important as how well it has been cultivated – after all, you see how large the earth is....

When the Lord sent human beings to the earth, He told them, "Go and master the earth and the elements."[4] As we could not master the earth, God gave us a small 'earth' in our heads, our brains. Once we have learnt to master our brains, we will discover the laws by which we will also master the earth. If you cannot control the centres of your brain and master your emotions, and if you cannot direct your will, how will you master anything outside yourself? This means we cannot lay another foundation, for there is a law which restricts our activities. We can only build within the limits prescribed by this law. Our happiness or unhappiness hinges on this great thought: "Am I walking on the right path?"

I would like to give you a thought: begin building your lives. I will tell you a story. A man was hiking in the east. One day a wild buffalo charged at him, and the man jumped into an empty well to save himself, only to find that there was a snake at the bottom.... The buffalo symbolises destiny, which pushes people. The snake symbolises death. Why is the buffalo chasing you? So that you work. You are lazy, but the buffalo wants to get you running. What is suffering on the earth? It is this buffalo that is charging at the world. Kings, generals and judges are all running from the buffalo while preaching freedom to the

[4] See Genesis 1:27-28

people. They are all clever philosophers who think that the world has been made badly. But how can they think properly when they have no foundation? Can a person who is running from his or her destiny think properly? If we are strong enough, it is not bad to be chased by a buffalo, for we can turn around, grab it by the horns and stop it. Our fear of the buffalo is caused by our not finding our two supporting points. "No one can lay another foundation except that which Christ laid." What foundation did Christ lay while he was on the earth? In the Beatitudes, Christ gave the nine rules by which we have to live to attain the nine types of bliss, the nine blessings.[5] He also gave us two great laws: first, to love God, and second, to love our neighbours.[6] These are the two supporting points upon which you ought to build your lives. Contemporary social life and the family also need to be built upon them.

We need to learn to think correctly. When you meet people, you need to form a correct conception about them and behave towards them as you would wish to be treated were you in their place. We ought to behave well, because whatever we do to others will be done to us in return one day.[7] In Ottoman Bulgaria there was an arrogant and proud music teacher who lost his job at a school because of his quarrelsomeness. After spending his savings, he went three days without food and became desperately hungry. He then came across a priest he knew, who invited him to his home and fed him. After the meal, the priest gave the man some money and said, "Come back when the money has run out. I will help you until you find a job." After a couple of months, the man found work as clerk to a Turkish court, because he

---

[5] The Beatitudes: "Blessed are the poor in spirit: for theirs is the kingdom of heaven. Blessed are they that mourn: for they shall be comforted. Blessed are the meek: for they shall inherit the earth. Blessed are they that hunger and thirst after righteousness: for they shall be filled. Blessed are the merciful: for they shall obtain mercy. Blessed are the pure in heart: for they shall see God. Blessed are the peacemakers: for they shall be called sons of God. Blessed are they that have been persecuted for righteousness' sake: for theirs is the kingdom of heaven. Blessed are ye when men shall reproach you, and persecute you, and say all manner of evil against you falsely, for my sake. Rejoice, and be exceeding glad: for great is your reward in heaven: for so persecuted they the prophets which were before you" (Matthew 5:3-12).

[6] See Matthew 22:35-40

[7] Jesus said, "As ye would that men should do to you, do ye also to them likewise" (Luke 6:31). And the Apostle Paul wrote, "Whatsoever a man soweth, that shall he also reap" (Galatians 6:7).

knew the language. At some later date the priest was accused of being a revolutionary against Turkey. The documentary evidence to be used in the prosecution was given to the clerk of the court for safekeeping. The man looked through the papers and removed everything which incriminated the priest, who was subsequently acquitted. The clerk later told him, "The help you gave me when I was hungry saved your neck." Had the clerk known how to behave properly, he would not have lost his job as a teacher. Had the priest not helped him when he was unemployed, the clerk would have allowed the court to hang him. We need to think about the consequences of our every thought and action.

When we are unhappy, we ought to think about the causes of our unhappiness and misfortunes. What caused our pride? What caused our cruelty? What caused our greed? We need to start thinking.[8] "You are cruel." This cruelty is not really yours, however; it is some fake capital that you inherited from your ancestors. I will explain this with an example. One man showed another man a diamond and offered to sell him many more like it at a very good price. The man therefore paid for a bag full of diamonds. When he arrived home and examined them closely, he realised he had been cheated. Only the diamond he had been shown was real; the rest were fakes. You may likewise be carrying a bag, thinking that you are rich, but when you open it you will see that it is full of fake diamonds. According to the law of inheritance, our ancestors left us wealth. Part of this wealth is virtue, which is gold; the other part is only fake diamonds. This is why we can have a false conception of life. We think that we are good, but we are not. We think we have some capital, but we do not. Instead, we have a false foundation of life.

The Apostle Paul said to the early Christians, "No one can lay a foundation other than that which Christ laid." And Christ said, "I have not come to do my will but the will of God,"[9] which is the first supporting point. He also said, "I did not come to take people's lives but to give my life to them,"[10] which is the second supporting point. I speak the truth, Christ came to give us life. He manifested and preached love towards

---

[8] The Teacher also said, "Happy are they who can benefit from their unhappiness by learning its lesson and becoming happy" (15/28 January 1915).

[9] See John 6:38

[10] See John 10:10-11

one's neighbour, because Christianity means loving one's neighbour.[11] It is a science of love, and whoever learns this science can build.

This science is not found in sweet words, kisses and gifts. I will use a story to explain what I mean. A fly landed near a spider. The spider began to praise the fly: "You are beautiful. What lovely eyes you have. Your wings are finely decorated. I have never seen such a beautiful creature as you." "Really?" asked the fly. "Yes," replied the spider, "there is no other creature as beautiful as you are. I have a mirror in my house. Please come in and look at yourself in it." The fly followed the spider into the house, and never left it....

When someone tells you, "How beautiful you are. Come with me and I will give you many things," like the fly, you will be led to a place you will never leave. It is depraved to give that type of gift. I am not saying you should not give or accept gifts, but that a gift should have human knowledge, wisdom and love deposited in it and needs to be given with the right thoughts, feelings and words. I know many women who were lowered because of the gifts of men. They received beautiful gifts but lost their purity and good reputations. I also know many people who were put in positions of power and then lost their virtue and purity. Society prizes such people: "That man is famous." Yes, he is famous, but he used to be a diamond and now he is mud. Do not take a position of power and rule over others if it will cause you to sell and disgrace yourself.[12]

You need to do everything unselfishly, as Christ did. Someone says,

---

[11] At the Last Supper, Jesus said, "A new commandment I give unto you, that ye love one another; even as I have loved you, that ye also love one another. By this shall all men know that ye are my disciples, if ye have love one to another" (John 13:34-35). And the Apostle John wrote, "Beloved, let us love one another: for love is of God; and every one that loveth is begotten of God, and knoweth God. If we love one another, God abideth in us, and his love is perfected in us: hereby know we that we abide in him, and he in us, because he hath given us of his Spirit. And this commandment have we from him, that he who loveth God love his brother also" (1 John 4:7, 12-13, 21).

[12] The Teacher also said, "People's honesty may be measured by the amount of money it takes to corrupt them. And we ask ourselves, 'Why am I unhappy?' Whoever sells himself or herself will be yoked and worked like an ox – this misery is self-inflicted. Those who make a habit of stealing degenerate and become foolish and the world treads on them. As Christ said, 'When the salt has lost its saltiness, ...' but it will not lose its saltiness as long as divine love is present. A person who is 'golden' cannot be bought, for he or she has true wisdom and knowledge. A person who has a price will degenerate in one lifetime" (15/28 January 1915).

"I cannot do that." Why not? You can gossip, you can hate. A person who cannot hate cannot love. When you have only one supporting point, find the other one. When hate and love are united they will provide you with what you need in life. Together they will give you the right direction. A saint is a person who has mastered the two principles of life and used them to uplift himself or herself. Just as you can tame a lion or a snake, you can also tame the devil. He cannot be made good, but he can be made harmless. Start with your thoughts. A thought that bothers you is a lion or a snake. Do not eject it or kill it but tame it – be victorious. Be courageous like those Africans who understand the psychology of lions. When an African man comes across a lion on his path he does not alter his course, because the lion would attack him were he to make the slightest deviation or to turn back. Instead, the man heads straight at the lion. When the man is a few steps away, the lion will step aside and allow him to pass. And you need to do the same with those thoughts that bother you. [13]

Were we to be faithful and the earth to be destroyed, we would rise to heaven, which is the other supporting point, the other end of the bridge. If there is danger at one end of the bridge, we will cross over to the other end and defend ourselves from there. When you have this bridge the enemy can never harm you, because you will have the strength to lift the bridge from your end, making a gap between yourself and the enemy. Only an enemy with great knowledge of the laws could attack you then. Good people are unconquerable because they have two supporting points. When in great danger at one supporting point, a good person can move to the other point and guard his or her position from there. This is the foundation that we need to lay. 'Jesus' and 'Christ' are the two supporting points. Jesus is the human being who suffers on earth, the suffering human soul building its salvation. Christ is the human being who has conquered, who serves God, who is ready to sacrifice himself. You should become Jesus and Christ. [14]

[13] "Be sober, be watchful: your adversary the devil, as a roaring lion, walketh about, seeking whom he may devour" (1 Peter 5:8). The Teacher said, "A Christian's power is expressed in fighting the devil. The devil is a big coward: when a Christian raises his or her net to catch him out, he runs away. The devil is the father of the lie, which is why he runs away from the truth and the light" (11/24 January 1915).

[14] In the non-canonical Acts of John, just before his passion, Jesus said to his disciples, "If thou hadst known how to suffer, thou wouldest have been able not to suffer. Learn thou

When you men and women can co-operate you will have completed one of the great tasks in life, but if you cannot co-operate you will
not be able to cope with anything in the world. Some people ask, "Why
do people get married?" They do so to learn how to co-operate. The
male and female principles are the two supporting points upon which
life builds. Why did Adam need a woman who was to get him into so
much trouble? God did not make the woman to get Adam into trouble
but to give him some work. Eve was intelligent and had initiative. She
was more intelligent than all of you here, who think you are so clever.
Contemporary culture and knowledge are due to her. She committed
a sin but later corrected her mistake, saying to her husband, "I have
lowered you and I will raise you. I will now save you by helping you
to develop a good mind, because had you been intelligent you would
not have wanted me to come to the earth."[15] Were you women to have
understood this law as your old mother, Eve, did, you would be most
intelligent. But you do not understand it and instead are only quarrel-
some. You are bad daughters. Your mother is much more intelligent
than you. She has been working hard these last eight thousand years.[16]
Do not think that Eve does not work. Our present civilisation is due to
her. Adam only follows her orders. He only knows how to fight. When
he returns to his wife, she asks him, "Did you finish your enemy?"
"Yes." "Well done."[17]

We need to lay a new foundation. We need to discard our illusion
that we can wait until we go to heaven to be taught how to do it. If you
want to be taught in heaven, you have to go there carrying rare, not
dense, material. I would like to take you to heaven, but for how many
days would you be able to stay there? A great price is required to stay.
Some of you would have enough money to stay for one or two days,

to suffer, and thou shalt be able not to suffer. What thou knowest not, I myself will teach
thee."

[15] In the previous lecture, the Teacher said that God made woman because man, the original human being, asked Him for a helper in life (see p. 330).

[16] That is, since the Fall (see n. 33, p. 327 of the present volume).

[17] The Teacher also said, "I understand the word 'man' to mean 'a being that thinks'. When
Eve met the serpent, the black adept, the second human culture began, the culture of the
knowledge of good and evil. In this culture, man, the being that thinks with God, has
no voice. The new culture is coming, in which the principles of thought and life will be
united" (24 December 1916).

and others would last for ten days. Then you would have to say, "I must return to earth to earn some more money."

When we have understood the deep meaning of Christian life, we should use it to lay a foundation. I will not talk to you about salvation and other such things in the simple way that others have spoken to you about them. A spiritually wise structure needs to be built on our contemporary social order. We ought to ask ourselves how we should educate the present and future generations. What kind of people should be our judges, teachers, priests, fathers, mothers, brothers, sisters, friends, traders, engineers and so on? The right people will be created with time. Time will not, however, ask you what you want it to create for you....

The serpent came to Eve and said, "Why do you not eat the fruit of the tree of the knowledge of good and evil?"[18] Christ is now asking her, "Why have you not eaten the fruit of the tree of life for thousands of years?" Eve replies, "Because we have been forbidden from doing so." Christ asks, "Why is it forbidden?" At first Eve wants to lie, but she decides to tell the truth: "Because we sinned." "That is right," says Christ. "And when you have corrected your sin, when you have cast it from you, you will be allowed to eat from the tree of life again. When you eat the fruit of the tree of the knowledge of good and evil, you feel as though you have contracted an infection. When you eat the fruit of the tree of life, another science and a new social order, the opposite of the present one, will come to you." These things may seem allegorical to you, but for me they are reality. These two trees are in our brains. The tree of the knowledge of good and evil is located in the back of the brain. The tree of life is at the front. Christ is asking us, "Are you ready to think correctly and no longer live from the back of the brain, to stop tasting the forbidden fruit and instead think and build in the way that I will tell you to?" We answer, "We have tasted the fruit of the tree of the knowledge of good and evil, and we have seen what evil it has brought us." We therefore need to consider whether the same evil will come to us if we taste the fruit of the tree of life.

Our Prime Minister has said that Bulgaria should be neutral in this war.[19] Neutrality is only one supporting point, though. We need to

---

[18] See Genesis 3:1-4

[19] The Tsar and Prime Minister had declared Bulgaria to be neutral from the outbreak of the war, while allowing themselves to be courted by both sides. Unlike the Central Powers,

find another supporting point to be able to weave. Bulgaria will not be alone in deciding whether or not it will fight; heaven will make the decision with us.[20] Christ has put a question to us: "Are you for us or against us?"[21] We have to make the decision to be with Christ or against Christ. Neutrality is not possible now. There is great competition in the world. All people are fighting and everybody has to go on one side or the other. A great problem will be solved. What happens in the world simultaneously happens inside us. We must not think that we can gain something without great loss. Joy always comes after great suffering. A woman cannot have children without sacrificing some of her beauty. If a woman does not lose her virginity, she will not become a mother. This is a great law in nature.

We need to learn how to digest our thoughts properly, how to think. Say the thought comes to you to commit a crime, to steal, free yourself of it by redirecting your mind. Turn your eyes to the soul of the person you want to wrong. Love him and say to yourself, "If I were in his place, would I want someone to steal from me?" When the thought comes to you to commit an evil act against somebody, stop and say to yourself, "If I were in her place, would I want someone to do this to me?" When a husband and wife quarrel, they both need to put themselves in the position of the other one and ask themselves the same question. This foundation needs to be laid in life, and it is not difficult to do it. When the thought comes to you to do something bad, tell yourself, "I am a servant of the Son of the Lord, who sent me from heaven to earth. My Master, my Father, is watching me." If you do this, the bad thought will immediately change, because you know your Father will not praise you otherwise. The fundamental thing in Christ's teaching is not to bite or

the Allies could not offer the Macedonian land that Bulgaria wanted, owing to Serbian unwillingness to surrender it, which put them at a great disadvantage in bidding for the country's military commitment.

[20] Within five months Bulgaria would enter the war on the side of the Central Powers. Earlier in the year, the Teacher said, "I could tell you about the whole plan for the present war, but there are spirits around you who would spread this information. The war will soon come to us in Bulgaria. Many things will be solved before 1919. You need to be stable enough to withstand it to the end. Were I to tell you everything that will happen, you would not be able to sleep for a week. The war is now entering a new phase; it is a matter of life and death. One aspect of the war will be capitulation. Romania, Italy and Greece will also become involved in the war" (21 January/3 February 1915).

[21] Jesus said, "He that is not with me is against me" (Matthew 12:30).

kick others, but to think as a human being and to fulfil your duties on the earth, to bring joy and gladness wherever you go and to comfort somebody who is sad and enlighten his or her mind. Knowledge is required to do these things. You may get a true idea about a person when you shake his or her hand: you may learn of that person's character, heart and mood. Sensitive people have nodes on their hands with which to sense such things. Foolish people and bad people have few of these sensory nodes. Why do they not have more of them? Because they do not need them; all they want is to eat and drink.

People want culture, and Christ laid the foundation of the culture that people want: "I am the way, the truth and the life," and, "Love God and love your neighbour." If you can apply these two laws, there will be no power that can oppose you and you will have no thoughts which are not under your authority and do not serve your ideal. Only the divine law can regulate and ennoble human love, because without it we might deplete those we love by sucking out all their emotions and stealing their hearts. To do that is parasitical, and it is not love but ignorance. Christ said, "I came to give life, not to take life from others." Are you women able to give life to your husbands, to help them learn to think for themselves without telling them that you are doing so? You may turn your husband into the man you want him to be, but to do so you need to put him on an anvil between these two forces, these two laws, which will heat him up and transform him.[22] A person's beauty depends on this heat. The further you move away from the centre of these two laws, the more ugly you become. You can only become beautiful, intelligent and luminous to the extent that these two laws act within you. Unite the back and front parts of your brain and make them each do their correct portion of work in life. Do this and you will be able to achieve whatever you want, to have the best children and the best friends, to have anything in the world.

You need to begin working within yourselves, applying the law of Jesus Christ, which is to love God and to love your neighbour, and experimenting with it. When you would like to do something good, the word 'cannot' should be replaced with the word 'can'. When you

---

[22] The Teacher also said, "There is an important law which states that when a woman loves a man, she has the power to uplift him, but if she comes to hate him, she will be the end of him" (18 October 1931).

are going to sin, stop and say, "I cannot do it." When a good thought comes to you, say, "I can do it." When a bad thought comes to you, say, "I cannot do it."[23] As a woman weaves cloth, moving the shuttle from one end of the loom to the other, let her also weave her thoughts, her desires and her character. When she weaves her character, Christ will send her a master tailor to make her a uniform with everything in its place, and then everyone will love her. The new foundation that Christ wants to lay is for us to know how to work properly. You are the first supporting point. The second supporting point is Christ. Unite them in the way a man and a woman unite, as brother and sister unite, because "Unity Is Strength". Where there is unity there is work, building, thought, feeling, aspiration and civilisation.

I leave you this thought: "No one can lay a foundation other than that which Christ laid." Our present lives are the best possible lives we could have to build upon. The Lord could not have given us better lives. This life is perfect, full of many blessings with which we can perform miracles. You do not suspect the great wealth that has been invested in your lives. You do not suspect the power that lies in your future, what you can become and what you can achieve.[24] At first an unborn child is of microscopic size in its mother's womb, but after nine months he or she becomes an independent organism. A mother gives birth and provides her child with the conditions for his or her development and

---

[23] The Teacher also said, "When God speaks to our souls, we should say, 'I can do it.' When the devil speaks to our souls, we should say, 'I cannot do it.' We ought to respond to each divine impulse by saying, 'I can do it.' If we have, or if anyone wants us to carry out, an intention that is not divine, we ought to say, 'I cannot do it.' Whenever we say, 'I can do it,' to a divine impulse, God comes to help us with the most difficult things, but then we absolutely must do what we said we could do.

"The devil is powerful because we say, 'I can do it,' when he tells us to lie or to commit many other kinds of sins. Christ wants us to say, 'I can …' and 'I cannot …': 'I can love,' and, 'I cannot hate,' and, 'I can tell the truth,' and, 'I cannot lie.' These two spirits appear to us every day. A good spirit tells us something and we reject it, but that does not make us free, because an evil spirit awaits us with its suggestion…. Christ is now coming to teach us to recognise what is good and what is evil, so that we will say, 'I can do it,' when we should do something, and, 'I cannot do it,' when we ought not to do something" (6/19 April 1914).

[24] "Beloved, now are we children of God, and it is not yet made manifest what we shall be. We know that, if he shall be manifested, we shall be like him; for we shall see him even as he is" (1 John 3:2). Jesus said to his disciples, "Verily, verily, I say unto you, He that believeth on me, the works that I do shall he do also; and greater works than these shall he do; because I go unto the Father" (John 14:12).

351

growth, and after twenty years her child becomes an adult who begins to think maturely. By the same law, contemporary human beings are microscopic beings in comparison with God. But one day, when we have developed and been born again, when we have uplifted ourselves, we will understand great things. To uplift ourselves, we have to change the form of our heads, change the nature of our minds, our hearts and our characters, and feel the great harmony of life in our spirits. When we have achieved this, we will enter the ranks of the angels and come closer to heaven. This is the new foundation of humanity.

Divine Providence

Jesus said,

> Are not five sparrows sold for two farthings? and not one of
> them is forgotten in the sight of God. But the very hairs of
> your head are all numbered. Fear not: ye are of more value
> than many sparrows.[1]

Today people want many arguments, facts and logical conclusions
to convince them of the existence of the divine providence that guides
human life through certain laws. Sometimes when something strange
happens in life we interpret it incorrectly. Such misinterpretations have
created a strange philosophy for many generations. This philosophy
states that everything in life happens by chance. According to this philosophy, there is no divine law and order, and therefore human laws are
constructed to benefit those who are powerful, or clever, or cunning
and so on. Do I need to prove that this is a great delusion?

Christ always attended to small things. He said to his disciples, "Do
not be fearful, for your lives are under divine providence," using the
example of how God does not even forget about five sparrows, how not
one of them can fall dead to the ground without the Father's willing it.
Why did Christ not use the example of one sparrow but instead spoke
of five? He did so because no one who lives by the law of the number
'five' can fall dead to the ground without God willing it. Jesus also said,
"Your lives are under divine providence, for even all the hairs on your
heads have been counted." We might ask, "How can it be important
that our hairs are counted?" It is important. If the Lord keeps count
of the hairs on our heads, there has to be a good reason for it. Do you
know how many hairs you have on your head? You may pull one out
and throw it away, but even this single hair served a purpose on your
head. I will not talk more about hair now but will return to my topic.

[1] Luke 12:6-7. The original Bulgarian publication only quoted verse 7.

What Christ said about the sparrows means that our spiritual lives are under the protection of divine providence. What he said about the hairs on our heads means that our physical lives are also under the protection of the same divine providence. It is necessary for us to build our faith in this providence, because we can only develop ourselves correctly once we have faith in it. If any doubt about the existence of divine providence penetrates our minds and hearts, it pulls us away from understanding the true order of things, and we then form a different law and order according to our own views.

A good marriage is not made on earth. There are three kinds of marriage: first, those made in heaven; second, those made on earth; third, those made in hell. God makes the first kind of marriage, human beings make the second kind, and the third kind is made by the devil. A marriage established by God will make for a loving, peaceful and joyful home. In such a marriage there will always be agreement between husband and wife, they will not speak bad words to each other and they will live blissfully together. A marriage established by human beings is a process by which the couple evolve towards perfection. There will be friction in such a marriage, which is necessary for the polishing of the characters of the husband and wife. When the devil establishes a marriage, there will be discord and depravity in the home – everything that is bad. Learn to discern between divine actions, human actions and the devil's actions, so that you do not mix them.

There are three types of person: first, those who perceive things in a divine way; second, those who perceive things in a human way; and third, those who perceive things in a devilish way. The first type of person perceives things as the Lord ordered them in the beginning. The second type of person thinks that the Lord does not participate in everything, and therefore he or she unwittingly interferes with the Lord's work. For example, when the Lord is making something, such a person says, "The Lord's work is unfinished. It is up to me to complete it." The third type of person wants to be the Lord.... Thousands of years ago people perceived things in a divine way. After the Fall of Humanity they lost this ability. When you are in a good mood you believe in God in your soul. When your affairs are going well, you say, "Glory to God! The Lord is taking care of me." But when unhappiness comes to you, you claim that the Lord has forgotten you and that He is the cause of your suffering. In reality, the Lord said, "As you have forgotten Me, I will also forget you." If you go away from the Lord, He will also go away from you.[2] God is unchangeable.[3] He is constant in His love, yet when some people distance themselves from God, they think He ought to follow them like a mother following her young child, calling out, "Wait, My child! Do not go far from Me!" When you say that the Lord has moved away from you, you are wrong. The Lord actually remained stationary; it was you who moved away from Him. And when you come back closer to the Lord, He will 'remain' with you again.[4]

All of you are moving along your own paths, which means you cannot understand me equally. Why is that so? It is because you are on different orbits. I do not judge you. I look on things objectively and philosophically. You, however, will complain, saying, "But this is my path!" The question is whether the path you are on is the one you have been given or the path you have made yourself. I tell you, you are not on your path. There is a railroad between Sofia and Varna that is always breaking and costing a great deal of money to repair. Did the Lord make this railroad? No. Had the Lord made it, He would have made it most intelligently. It was people alone who made it, which is why it is not as good as it should be. Were you to build a railroad according to the laws of divine providence, there would not be any misfortunes on it. Mechanical engineers have a better understanding of how to build a railroad than Christians have of how to build their lives. The mechanical engineer says, "We need to make careful calculations for how the train will run on the bends and the slopes of the railroad. If we do not, there will be a catastrophe." Christians say, "The Lord is good. He is thinking about us. It does not matter what kind of slope we go on." But when their train carriages turn over, they say, "Our work is not going well!" "Of course your work is not going well. Your carriages have turned over because you have been foolish and did not bear in mind the laws of divine providence." Spiritual people sometimes need to learn from worldly people, to become their pupils. There is

[2] "The Lord is with you, while ye be with him; and if ye seek him, he will be found of you; but if ye forsake him, he will forsake you" (2 Chronicles 15:2).

[3] "I the Lord change not" (Malachi 3:6).

[4] "'Return unto me,' saith the Lord of hosts, 'and I will return unto you,' saith the Lord of hosts" (Zechariah 1:3).

nothing shameful in this. But when it comes to spiritual matters that are unknown to worldly people, they need to become your pupils. You cannot be teachers all the time. Sometimes you will be teachers, sometimes you will be students.

Divine providence exactly determines everything; nothing happens by chance. All phenomena, no matter of what nature, be they physical, psychological or social, are directed by a High Being who always observes their progress. The lives of the passengers of a train are dependent on the train driver. Our planet, the Earth, also has its train driver, a driver who sometimes makes more fire in the engine and sometimes less. The path of the Earth has some turns and curves, and it sometimes comes closer to larger planets that influence it. These things seem distant now, but you will study and understand them in the future.

I will tell you a story about the divine providence you need. In ancient times there was a learned, intelligent king who understood the language of animals. Every year he held a gathering of animals, during which he would teach them. He always closed the gatherings with a speech, which he ended with same words: "That which the Lord has made no one can destroy."[5] One year, two giant eagles attended the gathering. When the king finished his closing speech, one of the eagles declared, "I can destroy something made by the Lord!" The king replied, "Very well, prove it," and then ended the gathering. That same year another king's daughter married a prince. When the wedding guests were leaving the temple, one of the giant eagles swooped down, seized the princess and carried her to a distant island. There it kept her prisoner in its nest high in a tall tree. Her husband took a ship and travelled in search of her. The ship sank, and the waves carried the shipwrecked prince to the very island on which his wife was held captive. The prince complained to the Lord: "Why have I been stranded on this unpopulated island? Was it not enough for me to lose my wife? It would have been better had I never been born!" Hearing these lamentations, the princess climbed down from the nest to find that they were coming from none other than her husband. After they had reunited, she hid him in the nest. When the time came, the two

[5] This is a paraphrasing of Jesus's words on marriage and divorce, "What God hath joined together, let not man put asunder" (Matthew 19:6).

giant eagles took their nest and flew with it to the annual gathering. The king finished his closing talk in the usual way: "What the Lord has made no one can destroy." The giant eagle then said, "I have destroyed something made by the Lord." "Prove it," said the king. The eagle told the story of what it had done, after which the king demanded to see the young woman. The eagle ordered the princess to come out of the nest, and she did – but with her husband. When the eagle saw that it had not been able to destroy that which the Lord had made, it exploded with anger and died. The eagle symbolises the human mind. We sometimes say we can destroy the things that God has made, to destroy their forms, but in the end they remain just as God made them. And we, as proud eagles, are also exploding with anger.

There are no cleverer spirits in the world than devils. Have you entered their kingdom to see how they live? They know about physics, chemistry, psychology and other such things. They know how to lie and deceive. But their knowledge does not enable them to make law and order in the world, because it is based on elements which cannot cement life. Knowledge has to be cemented by divine love. Therefore, when someone speaks of knowledge and facts, I ask, "Do you have the cement to bind your facts and knowledge?" If you have this cement, you have divine knowledge. If you do not, you have only bare facts, which are useless. Were you to have two hundred thousand, or a million, loose woollen fibres without knowing how to connect them, what use could you make of them? Only when you have spun and woven the wool correctly may you make clothes with which to dress yourself. By the same law, only when we are able to bind our thoughts and desires inside us with the cement of divine providence may we make clothing for our inner nakedness. We need this providence to be able to live well and develop.[6]

Christ said, "Do not fear," and then asked, "Why did the five sparrows not fall to the ground?" There were five sparrows, just as there are five senses and five fingers on each hand. 'Five' is the emblem of the human being on the earth. The number five symbolises a wise and intelligent person. It is said that such a person will not fall down until he or she sins. So long as you are wise and fulfil the will of God you

[6] Jesus said, "I counsel thee to buy of me white garments, that thou mayest clothe thyself, and that the shame of thy nakedness be not made manifest" (Revelation 3:18).

will not fall down, but the day you sin will be the day God allows one of the sparrows to fall to the ground. And when the sparrow falls, so will the hair on your head, which is a sign of the beginning of the destruction of your life. So remember that divine providence watches over you as long as you unhesitatingly follow God's laws, but if you distance yourself from God your life will start to disintegrate. Turn again to the sun of divine providence so that you can start to grow again.

The New Wineskins:
Those Who Are Ready for the Teaching of Christ

Jesus said,

> No man putteth new wine into old wine-skins; else the
> new wine will burst the skins, and itself will be spilled, and
> the skins will perish. But new wine must be put into fresh
> wine-skins. [1]

The parable of the wineskins is classic in its expression and content.
In it, Christ made a great generalisation of certain ideas. He said that no
one should pour new wine into old wineskins, because the wine would
cause them to burst. Christ was making an analogy between the new
teaching, the new wine, and the people who can only understand the
old teaching, who are like old wineskins. Wine that has ceased fermenting can be kept inside old wineskins. New wine, which is still in the
process of fermentation, would burst old wineskins were it to be stored
inside them. This parable contains a hidden thought, a great law, that
the divine ideas deposited in this world require new wineskins, which
have enough elasticity to withstand the pressure of the wine's fermentation. New wineskins symbolise the people whose minds and hearts
are capable of accepting the new truth. If the mind is engaged with the
old ideas, thoughts and feelings, the new teaching cannot enter it.

Wine symbolises power, and we need power to provide the impe-
tus for human evolution. This power is nothing other than the human
spirit, which works and builds according to divine laws. God wants
everything to grow and develop, hence He does not love old wineskins.
When you accept the new teaching, do not think that it will not ferment within you. It will not be possible for you to remain unchanged,
just as it is not possible for a sculptor to chisel a statue out of marble
without breaking any pieces of the stone. Many pieces are broken off.

[1] Luke 5:37-38

The old type of people, who are worried about the chipped pieces falling on their heads, should stay away. If they do not, they are responsible for the consequences, not the sculptor. "I am making a statue for future generations," says the sculptor, "and everybody needs to protect themselves while I am working on it." It does not matter whether an artist works with a paintbrush, a violin bow or a chisel, the important thing is to work according to the divine order. When obstacles begin to crop up in our work, we should not explode with anger. Whoever wants to walk forwards, whoever aspires to God, whoever wants to grow in the divine life, has to work and struggle. Eternal rest only exists in cemeteries. These aspirations are good for the individual, for society and for all humankind. Those who want to rest may keep their old understanding of life. They do not comprehend the active life of the new ideas expressed in the parable of the new wine.

Do you know how long a vine takes to grow and produce wine? Do you know the power of wine? At first it is sweet and later it becomes sharp. After the sharp stage it becomes stronger, and if you drink too much of it then you will lose your normal state of mind. Those who would like to accept the new teaching have to rid themselves of their old wineskins. If you do not have a new wineskin, it is better to stay away from this teaching. Others, the new type of people, will come along into whom the new teaching will be poured. If you have an old wineskin now, it will only be possible to pour the teaching into you after you have rid yourself of it, which means only after you have freed yourself of the desires and vices that interfere with the acceptance of the new teaching.

There was a man in India who caught and trained snakes and sent them to Europe. He would keep the snakes in a large pot overnight, securing them with a lid. One evening the lid was not closed properly. The snakes escaped during the night and coiled themselves around the sleeping snake-catcher. Waking up to this predicament in the morning, the man knew that were he to move, his life would be over. He had the self-control to remain calm and still. Later in the morning his servant wondered why his master had not left his bedroom. He went to investigate and found his master covered in snakes. The servant went away and brought back a pot of boiled milk and put it on the bedroom floor. The snakes smelled the milk and went over to the pot. The snake-catcher carefully stood up and put the snakes back into the large pot and shut them inside. He said to himself, "From now on I will always make sure that the lid has been closed properly." Sometimes you will find your-selves in the predicament of the Indian snake-catcher, so you need to have self-control and milk. By 'milk' I mean the spiritually wise life.

Christ said, "Do not pour new wine into old wineskins," because it will destroy you if you do. Two ideas on a collision course cannot be reconciled. The law of Moses says, "An eye for an eye and tooth for a tooth."[2] According to Christ, the law is the exact opposite of that. He said, "Love your enemies. If they slap you on one side of the face, turn and offer them the other cheek."[3] This is the new teaching. Were you to hold on to the old teaching, how could you reconcile it with the new one? The law of Moses is for old skins. The teaching of Christ requires new skins. It says, "You can turn your enemies into friends. You can disarm them and even make them serve you."[4]

Let us come to the inner psychological meaning of Christ's words. We ought never to think that we understand the complete truth and have nothing left to learn in life. Whoever thinks that is among the old wineskins, who have stopped their development on earth. They say, "We are well educated." What does that mean? "We have read many books by many authors." So what? What we need is a profound under-standing of the philosophy which can correct our lives and give us the happiness we seek. To be happy, we need properly functioning arms, strength, good minds and good hearts and an uplifting purpose.

Women who would like to have good children have to absorb the new ideas. If you have the old ideas, I recommend that you do not give birth, for what kind of children would you have? They would not be good people, and there are already enough like that. The Holy Scrip-tures say, "Go forth and multiply."[5] It does not say we should give birth to bad people, but to people who have the image and likeness of God.[6]

---

[2] See Exodus 21:23-25; Leviticus 24:19-20

[3] See Matthew 5:38-39, 43-44

[4] Jesus said, "Do good to them that hate you" (Luke 6:27).

[5] See Genesis 1:28

[6] "God said, 'Let us make man in our image, after our likeness.' And God created man in his own image, in the image of God created he him; male and female created he them" (Genesis 1:26-27).

This is the new teaching that Christ preached, and when it is properly understood it will correct the world. The vine and the juices are within us.[7] One day, when our vines produce grapes, the grapes' juices will begin to ferment – this is a law in the world. Those who think they can live without fermentation do not understand life.

Christ said, "Whoever wants to follow me, let him take up his cross."[8] The new wine is the cross. The cross is a source of power for those with the right understanding. You say, "Once I have all my affairs as I want them, my wife, our children and I will begin on the new path, and then the new wine will ferment." If you think you can first arrange your life and then follow the Lord, you are deceiving yourself. Education is a continuous, simultaneous process for the entire family. While the parents are educating themselves, their children learn from their example.

Christ said, "New wineskins are needed." People with new wineskins should not try to give the new wine to people with old wineskins. The new wine should only enter the arteries and veins of the new people. Today there is much conflict and complaint because the new wine and old wine are fighting each other. To this, Christ would like to say, "Do not put new wine in yourself unless you are ready for it." That is why it is said, "First purify yourselves."[9] Each teaching and each philosophy can be useful for us when we are pure. The new teaching requires flexibility in the process of progression and spiritual upliftment. Were we able to perceive the consciousness of an old person, we would see dim candlelight. Were we to perceive the consciousness of a young person, we would see bright candlelight. An old person is like the earth when it is lit by moonlight. A young person is like the earth

---

[7] Jesus said, "I am the true vine, and my Father is the husbandman. I am the vine, ye are the branches: He that abideth in me, and I in him, the same beareth much fruit: for apart from me ye can do nothing. Herein is my Father glorified, that ye bear much fruit; and so shall ye be my disciples" (John 15:1, 5, 8).

[8] See Luke 14:27

[9] "John came, who baptized in the wilderness and preached the baptism of repentance unto remission of sins. And he preached, saying, 'There cometh after me he that is mightier than I, the latchet of whose shoes I am not worthy to stoop down and unloose. I baptized you with water; but he shall baptize you with the Holy Spirit.'

"After John was delivered up, Jesus came into Galilee, preaching the gospel of God, and saying, 'The time is fulfilled, and the kingdom of God is at hand: repent ye, and believe in the gospel'" (Mark 1:4, 7-8, 14-15).

when it is lit by sunlight. Spiritual development requires the new wine.

Those who have only drunk the old wine, having never tasted the new, say, "The old wine is better."[10] The old wine can only anaesthetise people and make them merry; it will never make them work and progress. If we are unhappy, it is because our lives are fermenting, making the wine sharp; it is no longer sweet. When people quarrel, the wine begins to ferment. New wineskins are needed for the new wine, which will give us a new life. It will teach us how to live and work and how to develop strong relationships between ourselves. This is the teaching of Christ. It is said that Christ's teaching cannot be applied in real life. Actually, you can apply it. Read this parable, focus your mind and think about the new wine for five minutes every day and observe the results. Stop for five minutes and think about God, about the good people on the earth who work unceasingly, about the good mothers who patiently raise their children, and the good fathers who take care of their families, and you will see the effect of the new wine.

You need to say, "Lord, I understand You, and now I would like to work for You with youthful vigour." Free yourselves of your lower passions, put away your old wineskins. Put them far away from you. People with old wineskins and old wine are not for the kingdom of God. I do not want them to pour out their old wine; I want them to put new wine in new wineskins. When they understand this divine thought, it will uplift them with its power. They wonder how to educate people. The method is very easy. When a boat at sea is holed below the waterline, patch the hole and you will be saved. Some days you are dissatisfied, which means you have a hole in your boat. Nothing good will happen to you until you patch the hole.

There are moments when a human being should be very obedient. The child of a train driver was playing on the railway track when a train was fast approaching. Seeing that the child would be hit in a moment, some people nearby shouted, "Lie Down!" The child immediately obeyed, and the train passed by safely above and to the sides of the child's body. You are sometimes told, "Lie down!" and you answer, "But why?" "Lie down now without asking why! You will understand once the train has passed over you." There are dangerous moments when we

---

[10] Jesus said, "No man having drunk old wine desireth new: for he saith, 'The old is good'" (Luke 5:39).

need to kneel, and when the danger has passed we should thank God for having saved us.

Someone says, "I do not want to adapt myself to the new conditions. I do not want to be flexible." You will have to adapt yourself, because the conditions of life are going to change no matter what you want. The rain never takes into consideration whether you are appropriately dressed or not, nor does the sun consider whether or not you can endure the power of its light. You have to adapt yourselves to changing conditions so that you can withstand them. The Lord has decided to burst old wineskins and to pour new wine into new skins. If people with the old ideas and thinking believe they can live in the new conditions, they are deceiving themselves. This is our destiny, in accordance with the divine law. [11]

The Lord wants you to rejuvenate yourselves, to rebirth yourselves. [12] Some people ask, "How will we rebirth ourselves?" You will rebirth yourselves and new forms will be made into which you will deposit your lives. These forms will be real, not dreams. Were you to understand the law that governs your lives, you would be able to rejuvenate yourselves. When you learn this law, you will renovate your interiors, your souls. When talking about resurrection, I am referring to the process of resurrecting the forms that God uses to work inside us. [13] We need to prepare new wineskins for ourselves. When somebody has done it, the Lord will say, "Bring your new wineskin to Me so I can pour new wine

[11] The Teacher also said, "The entire physical world is entering a new phase, even though all beings are not at one and the same level of development. The new wave that is coming will not leave you in the same old condition. This transformation will not only take place on Earth, but throughout the entire Cosmos. Those who do not accept the divine wave will experience a great sorrow similar to hell. The more you consciously or unconsciously resist this wave, the more you will suffer. If you experience this suffering, you will know that you are opposing this wave and need to harmonise yourself with it. To do so, say to yourself, 'I should be in agreement with the great divine love and act as the divine world is acting'" (3 February 1924).

[12] Jesus said, "Except a man be born anew, he cannot see the kingdom of God. Except a man be born of water and the Spirit, he cannot enter into the kingdom of God" (John 3:3, 5). And the Apostle Paul wrote, "According to his mercy God saved us, through the washing of regeneration and renewing of the Holy Spirit, which he poured out upon us richly, through Jesus Christ our Saviour" (Titus 3:5-6).

[13] God said, "My people have committed two evils; they have forsaken me the fountain of living waters, and hewed them out cisterns, broken cisterns, that can hold no water" (Jeremiah 2:13).

into it." Some people ask, "What is the Lord doing right now with the world?" He is preparing new wineskins and new wine. This is why Christ said, "My Father is working, and I am working for you."[14] We should prepare ourselves so that we do not destroy the new wineskins, for it is easy to destroy the human mind and heart but very difficult to correct them. Let the Lord see that you are working and that you have earned something.

You ask yourselves, "Why is life not different?" I see in the eyes of many people that they are drunk on the old wine. They need to recover from their hangovers. Joy should fill your hearts, because this world has been created for you with all the necessary conditions for your development. "But there is war and great misfortune in the world." That does not matter. Nothing has been lost. Probably thousands and thousands of houses will be destroyed, the old wineskins, but new ones will be created. The Lord is now pouring the new wine into new wineskins. Only people who are drunk with the old wine fight. The men and women who are quarrelling are drunken. Where there is new wine there is music and singing, there is harmony. This is Christ's teaching. Read the Gospels and deposit this new teaching in yourselves. Each day, spend five minutes thinking about eternal life, God, good people, good mothers and fathers, good friends and noble things. This will uplift you, and then you will be able to understand more profound things. You have to have prepared yourself before you can have such understanding.

How will life be in the future? It will be perfect, beyond anything we have seen, heard or dreamed. How can a person see the beauty in the world if he or she is sleeping? Your sleeping souls must wake up. You need to put the pot of milk on the floor and catch the snakes. Be carriers of the new wine, carriers of the new teaching. Preach joy and gladness in the world. And when you suffer, say, "I am suffering because I did not obey God's law." We often say that the conditions of life in which we find ourselves determine our lives, but we also create the conditions of our lives. If you know how to apply the divine laws, you will master the conditions of life. If you do not know, you will be the slave to the conditions of your life. Whoever wants to become a master has to be penetrated by the new teaching. This teaching contains

[14] See John 5:17

the answers to the riddles of life. If you are put in an unfortunate situation in life, somebody may become your master. If you learn how to serve well in such a desolate situation, the Lord will remove you from it. Thank providence for sometimes giving you difficult conditions so that you learn something important.

You have not yet learnt how to cultivate your minds and hearts, which is why you feel empty and dissatisfied. You eat four or five times a day to fill your emptiness and have become obese. Your minds are also obese. Physical and mental obesity need to be transformed into energy. Have you noticed that people who work hard spiritually and mentally are never obese?[15] When you have excess fat, use it as fuel in the car of life and go forwards and realise your noble dreams. This will be your blessing.

[15] The Teacher also said, "In the spiritual world the beings are fed with nectar that is a millionth of the quantity of what we eat here. People who eat too much while on the earth suffer when they pass into the spiritual world" (9/22 April 1914).

The Freedom of the Spirit

The Apostle Paul wrote,

> **The Lord is the Spirit: and where the Spirit of the Lord is, there is liberty.**[2]

The condition of freedom comes from the Spirit. We understand freedom to mean a free life. It is also to have inner freedom, which comes from having the correct relationship between our thoughts and desires and the motives driving what we manifest in the world with our wills. Wherever there is a living soul, there is movement. This movement is a result of the will.[3] This movement can be in one direction or several. It is said in the New Testament, "Wherever the Spirit of the Lord is, there is freedom," and also, "The Son of God will set you free."[4] There is no difference between the Son and the Spirit.[5] The son is the intelligent expression of the intelligence of the father and mother,

---

[1] This was the Teacher's last recorded lecture before Bulgaria entered the First World War. On the day after this talk Bulgaria signed a secret agreement to fight with the Central Powers. Not only was Bulgaria being offered Serbian Macedonia for its involvement, but also, crucially, the war now appeared to be going the Central Powers' way, with the Russians in retreat on the Eastern Front and the Allies having failed to achieve victory in the Gallipoli Peninsula. In five weeks' time, on 1/14 October, Bulgaria would declare war on Serbia, intent on vengeance for its having not honoured its treaty obligations over the division of Macedonian lands after the First Balkan War and for Bulgaria's humiliating defeat in the Second.

[2] 2 Corinthians 3:17

[3] The Teacher also said, "When you lose the conditions you need for your development, it means your freedom has been limited. The freedom of the Spirit can only be restored with the truth. There are three kinds of freedom: first, the freedom of the body; second, the freedom of the will; and third, the freedom of the heart in the manifestation of one's feelings and thoughts. Christ said, 'The truth will set you free.' The truth shows us the path to freedom" (13/26 April 1914).

[4] See John 8:31-36

[5] Jesus said, "The Spirit of truth shall guide you into all the truth: for he shall not speak from himself; but what things soever he shall hear, these shall he speak. He shall glorify me: for he shall take of mine, and shall declare it unto you. All things whatsoever the Father hath are mine: therefore said I, that he taketh of mine, and shall declare it unto you" (John 16:13-15).

just as sunlight is the expression of the inner condition of the sun. We know the sun by its light. How can we know a human being? We can know a person by the light of his or her thoughts, desires and acts.[6]

I am speaking about the freedom of the Spirit because there is a danger in becoming religious. When some people become religious they become twice as bad as worldly people, because they become restricted in some way, tied to something like a horse or a cow tied to a pole in a field. People can be tied to anything. They can be tied to material things, or tied to a particular philosophy, or tied to their religious understanding, and so on. If you are tied to something which lowers you and takes away your freedom, it is lifeless, it is an old wineskin.

Freedom is called 'the meaning of life' by contemporary philosophers and 'citizenship' by politicians. Whoever seeks the freedom of the Spirit has inner spiritual wisdom. How will you recognise whether or not you have the Spirit inside you? You will know that you have it if you are a spiritually wise person whose thoughts, desires and actions have the power of freedom, and you extend the blessing of this freedom to others wherever you go. Freedom can be understood as light. When you travel at night you have less freedom than when you travel by day, for the simple reason that you are unable to see as well.[7] You do not know what God is, you do not know what the Lord is, but you do know earthly kings and rulers. They have the power to punish people, as does the Lord, and this has brought the results that we now see in the world....

We need to free ourselves of this inner slavery. How will we do it? By a profound transformation of the structure of the brain. You have not yet studied this structure. Each morning you pray to find the Lord, but sometimes you think He is not listening to you. The Lord only listens to those whose ears are also open to Him. He does not listen to those who are deaf to Him, nor does He talk to them.[8] You need to have a very sensitive ear so that you can perceive even the smallest things the Lord says to you. He likes to see and listen to people who do useful work. He does

[6] "The fruit of the light is in all goodness and righteousness and truth" (Ephesians 5:9).

[7] Jesus said, "If a man walk in the day, he stumbleth not, because he seeth the light of this world. But if a man walk in the night, he stumbleth, because the light is not in him" (John 11:9-10).

[8] "The Lord's ear is not heavy, that it cannot hear: but your iniquities have separated between you and your God, and your sins have hid his face from you, that he will not hear" (Isaiah 59:1-2).

not want to occupy Himself with people who do meaningless work. He does not occupy Himself with foolish things.

Christ provided a definition of freedom: "Do not behave towards others in a way you would not like them to behave towards you."[9] This rule ought to be our inner law. We should speak and act in a manner that gives others freedom.[10] A few days ago, a woman came to me and told me that, nowadays, religious people astonished her. She had recently been to a gathering in which the group prayed perfectly, but after the prayers they began gossiping. They did not give other people freedom. She told me, "I want us to have the freedom to serve the Lord, not their lord." I advised her that whenever she found herself among those kinds of people, she should tell them what she had just told me. You have not understood Christ's teaching if you are intolerant of others and restrict their freedom, for that is to have only an imaginary caricature of it. Rid yourselves of this caricature. Do not imagine God in that way.

What does religion mean? Religion is simultaneously the science of forms and the science of divine love. If you study an outer form but not its inner content, you will deceive yourself and change the form. For example, a woman changes her clothes every day. Just as the clothes are not the woman, the form of a religion is not the religion itself. When someone you know dies, you think that you have to wear black clothing and cannot wear white. Actually, you may wear any kind of clothes, black, white, red, green, blue and so on – it is not a sin. We ought to judge each teaching by its results. When a spiritual teaching can be applied in social life with good results, it is good. If it cannot, it is not good.

We should apply the freedom of the Spirit in our lives. We need to ask ourselves, "Am I free? Is the Spirit within me?" You will recognise the arrival of the Spirit because you will sense the light it produces in your mind and heart. Whenever you restrict the Spirit in another person, restricting how he or she thinks, feels or acts, the Spirit leaves you. When the pupils disrupt the lesson and do not listen, the teacher leaves

[9] See Luke 6:31

[10] The Teacher also said, "Everyone aspires to freedom in this world. By the word 'freedom' we understand the breadth of the actions, thoughts and desires that are hidden within us and the elimination of all limiting conditions. Freedom is a quality of the Spirit. To deprive someone of his or her freedom is to fall down" (13/26 April 1914). "Everyone is free to test the karmic law in the world, but I would like you to live according to the law of Christ" (15/28 August 1912).

the classroom. Their fathers will punish them for not having listened to their teacher. Moses, who was the guardian of the Jewish people, punished them and asked, "Did you listen to your Teacher?"[11] And when you ask why you are being punished, I will tell you, "Because you did not listen to the Spirit. You ought to listen to it."

Let me explain the word 'freedom'. You come across somebody whose hands and legs are tied with rope, and you begin to comfort him, saying, "The Lord is good. He will untie you." Are you really only talking to the man about freedom when you could actually untie him yourself and set him free? That is wrong. Take out your knife and cut the rope! Instead of freeing him, you are binding him more.[12] People need to be untied. When Christ said, "Go and preach,"[13] he meant, "Go and untie people." This freedom is internal. All quarrels and misunderstanding between people are caused by a lack of freedom.

Talking about irritability, how irritated must the Lord be when He sees what the world He created is doing? If the Lord is angry, it is good, but if I am angry, how will I benefit from it? I will not. Does the Lord become angry? No, He does not. The Old Testament truthfully speaks of the 'wrath of God', but this wrath needs to be understood in its inner meaning. Christ said, "Why do you call me 'good'? Only God is good."[14] God cannot be angered, because whoever is good cannot be angered. It is right to say, "Wherever the Spirit of the Lord is, there is freedom," because God really said this.

Love cannot be awakened without freedom. People do not love a person who torments them. That which brings destruction cannot bring freedom. When we pray to the Lord in a group, and someone makes a mistake in the payer and is corrected by others, that is not giving freedom. You behave like actors — take off your masks! When you

[11] During Moses's absence at the top of Mount Sinai, the Israelites disobeyed God's commandments by making an idol, the golden calf, and worshipping it. When Moses returned and saw what they had done, he punished them with an enormous slaughtering (see Exodus 20:1-5, 22-23; 32:1-35).

[12] "Faith, if it have not works, is dead in itself" (James 2:17). The Teacher said, "If someone says, 'God is good,' he or she should prove the truth of those words" (1 November 1931).

[13] Jesus said to his eleven disciples, "Go ye into all the world, and preach the gospel to the whole creation" (Mark 16:15).

[14] See Mark 10:17-18

stand before the Lord and correct each other's prayers, it is not giving freedom. When praying, we should forget about the external environment and enter our secret rooms, our souls, where nothing external should disturb us.[15] None of you listening to me here today is free. I see that some of you are tied to a pole, while others are tied to two, three or ten poles. You are now preparing yourselves for the kingdom of Christ and the kingdom of God, the kingdom of freedom. You cannot enter this kingdom with the old form, your old wineskins. I am not here to judge you for your delusions; I am here to show you the right path, because you are seeking freedom. Your slavery stems from Adam and Eve eating the fruit of depravity. If we want to understand Christ, the Spirit has to be free inside us.

How can we attain this inner freedom? There can be good and bad sides to common prayer and spiritual gatherings. When two or more people gather together for prayer or spiritual work, they need to be at sufficiently compatible spiritual levels to facilitate the correct exchange of magnetic energies. If there is too much difference in the spiritual levels of the group members, there will be misunderstandings and arguments.[16] This is why Christianity recommends self-purification before praying to the Lord with others.[17] Before praying with others, each person should pray alone as a preparation. First learn to pray alone, then with someone else, then in a group of three, and so on. When the Divine Spirit appears and enters two souls, it will establish peace and understanding within them and between them. When one is speaking, the other will be pleased to listen. If he or she takes no pleasure in listening to the other person, it means the devil is present, not the Spirit. Spiritual gatherings and common prayers should not be run to strict routine but according to the guidance of the Spirit. On one occasion the Spirit might desire prayers, and another time it might desire silence. It is of fundamental importance for us to give the Spirit

[15] Jesus said, "When thou prayest, enter into thine inner chamber, and having shut thy door, pray to thy Father which is in secret, and thy Father which seeth in secret shall recompense thee" (Matthew 6:6).

[16] The Teacher also said, "Group prayer has power when there is harmony among the participants" (5 March 1920).

[17] The Apostle Peter said, "Repent ye, and be baptized every one of you in the name of Jesus Christ unto the remission of your sins; and ye shall receive the gift of the Holy Spirit" (Acts 2:38).

this freedom. It is also of fundamental importance to have the patience to listen when another person speaks, to listen to him or her as if the Lord Himself is speaking to you.[18]

If you enter a religious society and become irritable, you have gained nothing. Many doctors and other people have perfect knowledge of the structure and physiology of the human being. They know which foods are good and which are bad, but they live their lives in the old way. They say smoking is unhealthy, but they themselves smoke. They say drinking is unhealthy, but they themselves drink. They say meat is unhealthy, but they eat meat. They have knowledge but they do not apply it themselves. They do not do as they preach. Where is the freedom of the Spirit in them? Christ wants us to have this freedom.

Some people want freedom only for their individual selves, wanting others to be subordinate to them. People might subordinate themselves to them out of fear, but they will not do it out of love. Mutual respect is a primary requirement in your relationships. When somebody provokes us, we should not embitter God by disturbing the freedom of His Spirit. I can see your thoughts – you transmit them like telegrams. Many 'telegrams' are written which show just how free you are.... One day these telegrams will be presented to the Lord, when you go to the next world. Nothing escapes the eye of the Lord. We cannot hide anything from Him.[19] I am not saying this to frighten you. God in His genesis is a Spirit who only wants to teach and correct us; He neither wants to punish nor to avenge. When we see punishment and suffering in the world, they relate only to external forms. When it seems that we are being punished, God is actually trying to free us from our slavery. If you want to free a sheep from the mouth of a wolf, is it possible not to hurt the sheep while pulling it from the wolf's jaws? Freedom and inner peace will make us calm and joyful and will much uplift the Spirit inside us.

I will talk again about the religion with which we ought to serve God. Christ said, "When I was hungry you did not feed me. When I was thirsty you gave me nothing to drink. When I was a stranger you did

[18] The Teacher also said, "You should not interrupt a person who is speaking. If you do not want to hear what someone is saying, go away from him or her. A talking person is a flowing spring. If you would like to say something, allow the spring to flow until it finishes, and then you may speak" (19 November 1916).
[19] "'Can any hide himself in secret places that I shall not see him?' saith the Lord. 'Do not I fill heaven and earth?' saith the Lord" (Jeremiah 23:24).

not invite me into your home. When I was naked you did not dress me. When I was ill and imprisoned you did not visit me."[20] The Lord will judge the world for such things,[21] and it will make no difference if you pray in the street ten times daily like the Pharisees of old.[22]

Do you know what 'psychological drinking' is? It is not religious behaviour. A young woman often liked to meet a certain bachelor. She took pleasure in these meetings but did not gain anything else from them. This pleasure, this tickling, did not mean that her mood was divine. She spent her energy on nothing lasting. In contrast, when God comes close to us, we not only feel His presence momentarily but also for a long time afterwards, secretly feeling it in our souls.

When people are quarrelling, I go towards them but do not tell them to stop. First I should stop myself. When two people are quarrelling, I should not tell them to be silent. First I should be silent. When two people are quarrelling, I should not preach morality to them, but should instead stop and pray to the Lord for them. A priest in Varna saw a man hitting his wife. Wanting to protect the woman, he took a stick and began to hit her husband. Both husband and wife then turned on the priest, and the woman said, "What right do you have to attack my husband? Our relationship is our business, not yours!" The priest went away wondering why he had interfered. And you also should not come between people and try to mediate when uninvited. You can only help in such circumstances when the couple asks you to. Show people the law of freedom, and thus show them how they should set their relationships right.

Religion should bring people freedom, peace and joy. If the old persecutions arise again, the world will not be set right. How many doubters will rise because of the external forms of religion? People will begin to shout, "Your teaching is from Satan!" Whoever is not of Satan has to serve humanity selflessly out of love. It is even more to sacrifice oneself for humanity. Whoever seeks to be praised, or to have the first place, or to put

---

[20] See Matthew 25:42-43

[21] Jesus said, "When the Son of man shall come in his glory, and all the angels with him, then shall he sit on the throne of his glory. Then shall he say unto the unrighteous, 'Depart from me, ye cursed, into the eternal fire which is prepared for the devil and his angels'" (Matthew 25:31, 41).

[22] See Matthew 6:5

the world to rights, cannot keep to the law of freedom. The Spirit is not in such people. To be first before God you have to be last in the world. If you are first in the world, you are last before God.[23] I do not seek human glory. I prefer that God thinks well of me. While I have been saying these things, some of you have been thinking, "I am not that kind of person. But he and she are!" Such thoughts come from the devil. Everyone needs to go deep inside himself or herself and forget about other people's wrongs and instead consider his or her own sins. I do not judge you for being in the condition of thinking yourselves higher or lower than others, but I would like to show you how to remove yourselves from it.

Follow the Spirit within you. If you want freedom, give freedom to others. If you want love, give love to others. If you want to be treated justly, be just to others. Like attracts like – this is the law of similarity. If you sincerely and pure-heartedly love other people, they will love you in return. Do not tell someone that you love him or her. Do not speak about love. If you do, your love will vanish. The people who talk the most about love have only a small amount of it inside themselves. Those who talk the most about freedom are the same: they only possess a little freedom inside themselves and therefore cannot give it to others. If my relationship with you is not as it should be, my sweet preaching will only sound like beautiful music while giving you nothing. The music which creates noble impulses is beneficial. The music which gives only short-term pleasure is of no more benefit than a tickle.

Let the friction between you stop right now. I will give a white stone to those of you who have the Spirit of freedom. I will write my name on this stone, and when the Lord comes to you He will see what has been written.[24] I know whether or not the Spirit is inside a person just by looking in his or her eyes. When the Spirit enters someone, his or her eyes are neither very dark nor very light. Sometimes human eyes shine like snake's eyes, which shows that a person has a desire to eat someone. Have you ever seen how a cat's eyes shine in the dark when it is trying to catch a mouse? There are different kinds of light. There

[23] Jesus said, "He that is greatest among you shall be your servant. And whosoever shall exalt himself shall be humbled; and whosoever shall humble himself shall be exalted" (Matthew 23:11-12).

[24] Jesus said, "To him that overcometh, I will give a white stone, and upon the stone a new name written, which no one knoweth but he that receiveth it. I will write upon him mine own new name" (Revelation 2:17; 3:12).

is the light which grabs, which kills, and there is the light which gives life. The Spirit senses people's weaknesses and will only enter those who are on the right path.

When you next gather together, the telegrams you send out will say whether there is still friction between you or not. The Lord does not want fractious prayer gatherings. I will give you some methods of ensuring that all your prayers are acceptable to the Lord. If you meet a soul in need of comfort, a weary soul, either pray to God for that person or pray with him. If you meet a poor person, help her. The Lord does not want gatherings that are exclusively for rich people. The Lord wants common gatherings attended by the rich and the poor and the intelligent and the ignorant.

The woman I spoke about earlier told me that thirty minutes after the gathering had finished praying, the women began gossiping. When she noticed that her presence disturbed them, she left. We talk about how people do not pray correctly in church, but do we pray correctly ourselves? Throw out the old devil. Give others freedom and respect. Pray secretly in your souls and do not gossip. Those who gossip cannot develop properly psychologically. If you have this weakness, you need to free yourself of it. If the thought comes to you to gossip, do not allow the devil to enter you and use you as his town crier. Instead, put down the telephone and do not pass on his opinion.

The devil never says good things. He tells people, "You are a hooligan!" "You are a thief!" "You are promiscuous!" He deceives people into helping him to do his work. When you arrive at suffering for having followed the devil, the Lord tells you, "Next time, do not listen to him." Anger, jealousy, hatred, mistrust, lying and all the negativity in the world are the qualities of the devil. Throw out this old father and you will be free and you will be with the Lord, who is all wise, good, righteous, alert, quick-thinking, considerate, loving and forgiving, and who helps the poor and those who suffer. If you make a hundred mistakes and turn to the Lord, He will forgive you. The Lord only punishes devils. He damns them and makes a great fire for them.[25] Those who do

---

[25] Jesus said, "The Son of man shall send forth his angels *at the end of the world*, and they shall gather out of his kingdom all things that cause stumbling, and them that do iniquity, and shall cast them into the furnace of fire: there shall be the weeping and gnashing of teeth" (Matthew 13:41-42).

not want to be connected with these devils have to be merciful, alert, quick-thinking and considerate.[26]

From now on let us apply Christ's teaching without showing the world that we are religious. Let us keep our religion hidden within. Hide your beauty inside yourself; do not parade it externally. Do not say how good you are, what a great soul you are, how ready to be charitable you are and that you pray three times a day. If you do, you will become the world's laughing stock. Christ said, "Out in the world you need to be as clever as snakes and as harmless as doves."[27] Worldly people are not foolish; they are clever. They are not as good as we are at relating to the higher life, but they apply their intelligence better than us in worldly matters. Nowadays it is said that we should be focussed on our personal directions without getting sidetracked into being generous to others. But how will we improve things in the world if everybody behaves like that? When someone gives us a bad look, we become angry. But how many times have we given others bad looks? We have not counted them, of course. The Lord did not create us with bad eyes but with good eyes. The religious life involves having freedom oneself and giving freedom to others, of excusing people their mistakes and seeking every opportunity to unite in spirit with others. Let us apply this teaching and preach it to others.

From now on do not gossip! Try not to gossip for one year. Keep a record of how you are doing in a notebook. If you did not gossip all day, say, "Today, for the glory of God, I did not gossip," then mark a '7' in your notebook. If you gossiped that day, mark a '1' in the notebook.

---

[26] The Teacher gave the following guidance on how to develop freedom.

"Follow these rules of life.

"When your heart is becoming cold and cannot embrace the freedom of others, enlarge the radius of your heart to embrace people's weaknesses, and continue on the sacred path of your heart towards the God of Love through the greatest difficulties.

"When your mind is beginning to darken and cannot understand and accept some truth, extend the radius of your mind and think that everything is as it should be and find God in everything, so that the God of Eternity may be manifested in His entire diversity, and continue the great path of your mind towards the truth through the greatest contradictions.

"When your will is becoming self-will and has stopped doing good, double the radius of your will and accept your will as a gift from God and dedicate it to Him, and continue the powerful path of the will in the manifestation of divine kindness in the face of the greatest evils."

[27] Jesus said to his twelve disciples, "Behold, I send you forth as sheep in the midst of wolves: be ye therefore wise as serpents, and harmless as doves" (Matthew 10:16).

At the end of the year add up how many ones and sevens there are and see how well you succeeded.

When a young bachelor is ready to marry, some young women fall in love with him and start praising him. After he chooses to marry one of them, the others begin to say bad things about him. Instead, they should have said, "We are pleased he chose a wife from among us." A European prince visited a large town. The twelve most beautiful women in the town were chosen to greet him when he arrived. They were asked to select one of themselves to present the prince with a bouquet of flowers, but each woman voted for herself.... Likewise, you who are now in this teaching are not yet ready to present a bouquet to Christ. Everyone says, "I will do it!" Do not vote for yourselves. Without your voting on it, Christ already knows who deserves to be honoured.

It is Christ's teaching to be alert, quick-thinking and considerate and not to discuss what we know about other people. Occultists say, "If you want to be strong, do not speak about others, because the moment you do, you connect with their spirits and are infected with bad thoughts." It is better to think good of people than bad, for you will damage yourself if you think badly of others. A person of whom you speak ill will benefit psychologically as a result of your gossip. If you speak well of someone else, you gain; if you speak ill of another, he or she gains at your expense – this is the law. If you consciously want to say bad things about others so that they will gain something, I will be glad of your sacrifice, but then do not complain about the consequences. You are great spirits, after all, are you not?[28]

Remove the devil of gossip from yourselves! This year the Lord has decided to tie up devils. None of you should protest if you are bound, for you will have been yoked for work. Just as a farmer uses an ox to plough the field, either you will yoke the devils to work for you or the devils will yoke you to work for them. If you want to succeed in yoking devils, you have to have the Spirit within you, for it will make you strong and mighty.[29]

[28] The Teacher also said, "Not all thoughts and desires and the things we work towards bring us freedom. Each word is like a cannonball. A bad word or thought can take away our freedom. When we utter an offensive word, it has an effect" (13/26 April 1914).

[29] "Be strong in the Lord, and in the strength of his might. Put on the whole armour of God, that ye may be able to stand against the wiles of the devil. And take the helmet of salvation, and the sword of the Spirit, which is the word of God" (Ephesians 6:10-11, 17).

Religious freedom needs to be absolute, for God is a God of love and freedom. Only in this way will everyone find his or her correct place in life. It does not matter what work a person does, ploughing or digging, it should be done with gratitude.[30] Life on earth needs to be run according to the freedom of the Spirit, the freedom which distinguished Socrates, who lived as the last of men. Many kings have been forgotten, but his name lives on. A person may have a very high position in life without being noble. The Spirit requires each of us to be equally free, no matter whether we are kings or the last of people.

I am preaching the teaching of Christ: to have freedom and to give freedom, to have freedom and to give freedom, and again, to have freedom and to give freedom; intellectual freedom, freedom of the heart, religious freedom, social freedom, freedom in the home.

Freedom everywhere.

[30] The Teacher also said, "To obtain freedom we must be thankful for everything that happens to us, good or bad, for then Christ will live within us. When Christ lives within us, all positions in life and all forms of employment will be considered important and worthy of respect. We will not be given a higher position until we have fulfilled the task of the position below it. We should always begin with the smaller things and proceed towards the greater ones" (13/26 April 1914).

Appendices

Appendix A

Many years after the Teacher had passed away, the Bulgarian translator, Maria Mitovska, had the following experience when a young woman.

Maria was staying at the disciples' secret summer camp high in the Rila Mountains, not far from the foot of Musala, the tallest peak in the Balkans. One morning, as usual, the disciples woke early and climbed a nearby top known as the Sphinx to meet the sunrise. Once there, they stood in a line facing east. When the sun had cleared the horizon, Brother Krum Vuzharov began to lead the morning prayers. To Maria's astonishment, she saw the spiritual form of the Teacher appear to the front and side of Krum, who then followed the prayers and songs as led by the Teacher. The atmosphere was heavenly, and it seemed to Maria that she was in another world. At the end the Teacher turned towards Krum and greeted him. With his spiritual body, Krum bent and kissed the Teacher's hand, after which the Teacher disappeared. Thinking that she must have been fantasising, Maria took courage and decided to speak to Krum about it.

Later, when she could take him aside for a quiet word, Maria told Krum what she had seen.

"Yes," said Krum, "that is exactly what happened."

Over time Maria observed that a few others among the Teacher's closest disciples had the same invisible connection with him, although none of them ever spoke about it or gave any indication of its existence.

Appendix B

Snezhka Mihaleva, a Bulgarian disciple known to the translators of this volume, related the following story to them.

When a young man, Snezhka's paternal grandfather, Iliya, was a soldier for a period around the early 1920s. While on duty one day, he was working on something on Vitosha Mountain when he and his fellow soldiers saw an old man speaking to a crowd of people in a nearby clearing known as the Bivouac (it was the Teacher giving a lecture to his disciples). Several of the soldiers, including Iliya, were curious and went over to listen.

When he had finished speaking, the Teacher came over to Iliya and asked if he could help him by taking his suit jacket to his home. He gave Iliya the house-key and told him the address: 66 Opulchenska Street.

Iliya obtained permission to travel to Sofia and found a truck driver who was willing to take him to the house. The man drove straight to Opulchenska Street and dropped Iliya off. The Teacher's housekeeper, Vasilka, who also lived at number 66, happened to be walking home at the same time as Iliya was approaching the house. Recognising the jacket that the stranger was carrying, Vasilka confronted him, asking what he was doing with the clothing of someone she knew.

Iliya replied, "A nice old man gave me this jacket and his house-key and asked me to bring it here to his home for him."

"He gave you his key!" said Vasilka. "But I have the only other key to the house...."

The two of them walked to the house door, unlocked it and went inside. There, to Iliya's astonishment, they found the Teacher sitting behind a desk working. Not only did he wonder how the old man had got in, Iliya also could not understand how he had arrived here before him, as he had still been at the Bivouac when Iliya had set off in the truck. Iliya realised that this was a very special person before him.

The man spoke to Iliya: "I have been waiting a long time for you to become my disciple, but to do so you must give up eating meat."

"But I have a pig that I have been saving to eat at Christmas," said Iliya. "What should I do with it?"

"Set the pig free in the woods and stop eating meat," advised the Teacher.

Iliya thought to himself, "I will eat the pig at Christmas and then stop eating meat."

On his next leave, Iliya travelled to his home in a small village in Strandzha Mountain, in the southeast corner of Bulgaria, near the border with Turkey. When he arrived, he told his wife, Katina, the story about the old man who had told him to stop eating meat. He then showed her a photograph of the Teacher.

"That is the man who taught me how to read and write in my dreams!" said his wife (for Katina had become literate without any schooling or tutoring).

From that moment on Katina became a vegetarian. Her husband did not.

Christmas came and Iliya slaughtered the pig and ate it. Immediately after his feasting, Iliya became terribly fevered and a doctor was called for. After examining Iliya, the doctor gave Katina grave news: "Your husband is near to death and there is nothing I can do for him."

Remorseful and feeling himself to be dying, Iliya asked his brother to send a telegram to the Teacher, to say that he was sorry he had not listened to him. Once his brother had left for the post office to send the telegram, Iliya's temperature began to drop. By the time his brother had returned, Iliya was well again.

Now Iliya did give up eating meat. He and his wife became disciples and both lived to be one hundred years old.

Appendix C

The Teacher said the following about the ideal conditions for pregnancy.

Conception and pregnancy are important processes. A woman needs to be given the most favourable conditions during pregnancy. She should eat correctly while in a good mood, never eating before sunrise or after sunset. She should breathe deeply and think and feel correctly. As a pregnant woman is very sensitive, perceptive and imaginative, those close to her, and she herself, should provide her with the highest occupations and pleasures for her time, and the most sublime views for her to behold.

Her morning walks should begin before sunrise, so she can take in the splendour of the rising sun. Afterwards she should stroll through gardens with fragrant, blossoming flowers and beautiful fruit trees, for the meaning of life is found where it grows and develops.

Physical and spiritual purity is necessary for the pregnant woman, and where can she find purity greater than that of nature? She should therefore visit pure springs and rivers, whose waters will act as mirrors of her life. Peaceful, pleasant nights under skies filled with countless stars form pictures of unsurpassable beauty for the future mother.

I say that a mother begins educating her baby during pregnancy, not after the birth. A child's most receptive state is when in the womb. Once born, the child requires the conditions to cultivate that which was sown in the womb. This is why the mental life of the pregnant woman should not be neglected. The finest, most elegant literature should nourish her mind. The lives of saints and great people should drive her thoughts.

Calm and quietude are necessary for the pregnant woman and for nature itself, for together they are performing a great creative act, the making of a human being. The silence of her life should occasionally be interrupted by beautiful, sublime poetry and beautiful music and songs.

If you want good fruit, give the tree the right conditions and allow nature to do its work. The same applies to the creation of a human being. The good, spiritually wise person is conceived and developed in special conditions. Everything you need for this can be found in spiritually wise nature, which itself is health, beauty and purity. Birth is not a lottery. The world is in need of new people to uplift it and set it right. It is up to women to produce them.

(1 November 1931)

References

Epigraph

v   My words have been recorded very well and understandably on paper, ...
„Правила на разумния живот," Разумния живот, Печатница: Малджиев, Русе,
c. 63–64
"The Rules of the Spiritually Wise Life," *The Spiritually Wise Life*, Printing House:
Maldzhiev, Ruse, pp. 63–64
(The Teacher said this on 31 August 1924.)

Translators' Note

xi   [1]Written use of 'Учителят' ... can be found as early as January 1915.
Виж „Бележки измежду разговорите с приятелите, казани от Учителя на 5
януари 1915," Искайте сила, имайте вяра, Всемир, София, 1994, с. 27
See "Notes of What the Teacher Said During Conversations with Some Friends on
5 January 1915," *Desire Strength, Have Faith*, Vsemir (Universe), Sofia, 1994, p. 27

Peter Deunov spent eleven years ... studying the character of the people
Виж Точността (Общ окултен клас, 08 април 1923), Печатница: Малджиев,
Русе, 1923, с. 13
See *Exactitude* (General Occult Class, 08 April 1923), Printing House: Maldzhiev,
Ruse, 1923, p. 13

My task is to give you the divine teaching....
Разговорите при Седемте рилски езера, София, 1948, с. 171
Conversations at the Seven Lakes, Sofia, 1948, p. 171

xii   After 1950 even the secret printing of lectures ... came to a halt.
Виж Словото на Учителя: Каталог, Всемир, София, 1998
See *The Word of the Teacher: Catalogue*, Vsemir (Universe), Sofia, 1998
(In this catalogue of the lectures, which includes their publishing details, it can be
seen that no lectures were published in Bulgaria during the communist time
after 1950.)

was begun by Boyan Boev, ... and completed by Lalka Krusteva.
Виж пак там, с. 3
See *ibid.*, p. 3

the Teacher recommended her ... in the documentation of his word.
Виж пак там
See *ibid.*

xiii   he told Krum Vuzharov ... he would reduce it to its essence.
Krum Vuzharov said this to Maria Mitovska, the Bulgarian translator.

xiv   [4] To make shorter versions of the lectures ... parts of the country or abroad.
The Bulgarian translator, Maria Mitovska, learnt this from older disicples.

387

xv   [5] "Over thirty years ago I foretold there would be a war in 1914 ..."

Изворът на доброто, Последно Слово на Учителя, Мърчаево – 1944 година,
Рояал – 77, Варна, 1992, с. 218

The Wellspring of Good: The Last Word of the Teacher, in Murchaevo in 1944, Royal 77, Varna,
1992, p. 218

Introduction

xvii   On 7/19 March 1897, Peter Deunov ... for the development of the Slavic people.

Виж Акордиране на човешката душа, I Том, Бяло Братство, 1999, София, с. 339

See *The Tuning of the Human Soul, Volume One*, Byalo Bratstvo (White Brotherhood), Sofia,
1999, p. 339

"There is something sublime in the Slavic consciousness: love for God."

Изворът на доброто, с. 318

The Wellspring of Good, p. 318

I am Elohim, the Angel of the Lord's Testament....

„Призив към народа ми, Български синове на семейството славянско," Ходете
във виделината, Всемир, София, 1994, с. 3–11

"A Call to My People, Bulgarian Sons of the Slavic Family," *Walk While You Have the
Light*, Vsemir (Universe), Sofia, 1994, pp. 3–11

xviii   which is headed by Christ.

Виж Вяра и съмнение (Общ окултен клас, 17 юни 1923), Печатница: Малджиев,
Русе, 1923, с. 39

See *Faith and Doubt* (General Occult Class, 17 June 1923), Printing House:
Maldzhiev, Ruse, 1923, p. 39

"The White Brotherhood is a great society in the divine world ..."

Разговорите при Седемте рилски езера, с. 121

Conversations at the Seven Lakes, p. 121

xix   "The beings of the White Brotherhood have completed their evolution ..."

Съмнение и воля! (Общ окултен клас, 11 февруари 1923), с. 14

Doubt and Willpower! (General Occult Class, 11 February 1923), p. 14

"The White Brothers are servants of God. They are angels."

Вяра и съмнение (Общ окултен клас, 17 юни 1923), с. 40–41

Faith and Doubt (General Occult Class, 17 June 1923), pp. 40–41

This Universal Brotherhood works with love, wisdom and truth.

Виж пак там, с. 40

See ibid., p. 40

In July 1900, he ... presented the ideas of the new teaching.

Учителят, Печатница: Изгрев, София, 1947, с. 11, 18

The Teacher, Printing House: Izgrev, Sofia, 1947, pp. 11, 18

One day in September, when he was climbing ... I am ready."

Акордиране на човешката душа, I Том, с. 339

The Tuning of the Human Soul, Volume One, p. 339

Lectures

1   **Christ as a Best Friend**
     „Поздрав на всички,“ Ходете във виделината, с. 19–20
     "Greetings to You All," *Walk While You Have the Light*, pp. 19–20

4   **The Kingdom of God Is Near**
     „Мир да бъде на всички ви,“ пак там, с. 12–13
     "Peace Be with You All," *ibid.*, pp. 12–13

8   **The Word of Jesus Christ**
     „Слово,“ пак там, с. 14–18
     "The Word," *ibid.*, pp. 14–18

12   [21] "The future belongs to the meek...."
     Разговорите при Седемте рилски езера, с. 159
     Conversations at the Seven Lakes, p. 159

15   **Hope, Faith and Love**
     „Любовта,“ Ходете във виделината, с. 21–22
     "Love," *Walk While You Have the Light*, pp. 21–22

17   **The Coming Epoch**
     „Бележки от едно тефтерче на Д. Голов,“ пак там, с. 23–24
     "Notes from a Diary of Dimitar Golov," *ibid.*, pp. 23–24

     [2] "The present war is a misery, but it will bring much good to humanity...."
     „Но Син Человечески, кога дойде, дали ще намери вяра на земята,“ Искайте
        сила, имайте вяра, с. 42
     "When the Son of Man Comes, Will He Find Faith on the Earth?" *Desire Strength, Have
        Faith*, p. 42

     [3] "Number 'thirteen' is the number of the spiritual world...."
     „Искайте сила, имайте вяра,“ пак там, с. 56
     "Desire Strength, Have Faith," ibid., p. 56

     [3] "At present all kings think they are Christ, ..."
     „Христос ще дойде и ще се прояви,“ пак там, с. 51
     "Christ Will Come and Manifest Himself," *ibid.*, p. 51

18   [6] "The sixth race is coming. It is a shining race, called 'the Children of God'...."
     „8000 години,“ пак там, с. 59
     "Eight Thousand Years," *ibid.*, p. 59

19   [6] "In the future, relations between all nations will be fraternal...."
     Новият ден, София, 1940, с. 46
     The New Day, Sofia, 1940, p. 46

     [6] "The sixth race is a race of justice and of the kingdom of God...."
     Изворът на доброто, с. 307
     The Wellspring of Good, p. 307

² "All nations are called to fulfil the will of God...."
Разговорите при Седемте рилски езера, с. 274
Conversations at the Seven Lakes, p. 274

31 **Good and Evil**
„Защо Бог не премахне злото завинаги," Ходете във виделината, с. 31
"Why God Does Not Eliminate Evil Forever," *Walk While You Have the Light*, p. 31

¹ "The present war was created by people constantly talking about it...."
„Но Син Человечески, кога дойде, дали ще намери вяра на земята," Искайте
   сила, имайте вяра, с. 38
"When the Son of Man Comes, Will He Find Faith on the Earth?" *Desire Strength, Have
   Faith*, p. 38

32 **Rely on the Lord**
„Упование на Господа," Ходете във виделината, с. 32
"Rely on the Lord," *Walk While You Have the Light*, p. 32

33 **Entering the Kingdom of God**
„Събрание, водено от г-н П. Дънов," пак там, с. 33
"A Meeting Chaired by Mr P. Deunov," *ibid.*, p. 33

³ "We ought not to talk to the devil, ..."
„Ако Ме любите, ще опазите Моите заповеди," Разсмотрете криновете в
   полето как растат, с. 3
"If You Love Me, You Will Keep My Commandments," *Consider the Lilies of the Field,
   How They Grow*, p. 3

⁴ "We should help each other with our thoughts, ..."
„Христос ще дойде и ще се прояви," Искайте сила, имайте вяра, с. 52
"Christ Will Come and Manifest Himself," *Desire Strength, Have Faith*, p. 52

34 **Love, Unity and Service**
„Любов и единство," Ходете във виделината, с. 33
"Love and Unity," *Walk While You Have the Light*, p. 33

36 **Mastering Destiny**
„Що значи съдба?" пак там, с. 34
"What Does Destiny Mean?" *ibid.*, p. 34

38 **Resurrection**
„За да възкръснеш," пак там, с. 35
"To Be Resurrected," *ibid.*, p. 35

39 ⁴ "Prayer is a necessity...."
„Но Син Человечески, кога дойде, дали ще намери вяра на земята," Искайте
   сила, имайте вяра, с. 41
"When the Son of Man Comes, Will He Find Faith on the Earth?" *Desire Strength, Have
   Faith*, p. 41

[1] "Once the last trumpet sounds, from then on you will quickly perceive …"
Explanations and Directions for the Use of the Book The Testament of the Colour Rays of Light, Vsemir (Universe), Sofia, 1995, p. 15

50 **Give Ten Percent to the Lord**
„Подквасата," Ходете във виделината, с. 44
"Leaven," *Walk While You Have the Light*, p. 44

51 **Christ Will Come Back as Light**
„Ще дойде като светлина," пак там, с. 46–49
"He Will Come as Light," *ibid.*, pp. 46–49

[4] "It needs to be known that, when you speak in a bad way …"
„За слава Божия," Устойчиви величини, Литопечат, София, 1943, с. 290
"The Glory of God," *Stable Quantities*, Lithoprint, Sofia 1943, p. 290

52 [10] "Christ is coming! …"
Explanations and Directions for the Use of the Book The Testament of the Colour Rays of Light, p. 14

53 [11] "Christ spoke about one eye, which is located in the centre of the brain, …"
„Светило на тялото," Сила и живот, Трета серия, Солта, Второ издание, Печатница: Гужгулов и Котев, София, 1920, с. 89
"The Light of the Body," *Power and Life, Volume Three: The Salt*, Second Edition, Printing House: Guzhgulov and Kotev, Sofia, 1920, p. 89

[11] "People are too concerned with the physical aspect of Christ, …"
„Изгряващото слънце," пак там, с. 85
"The Rising Sun," *ibid.*, pp. 85

55 **The Testament of the Colour Rays of Light**
[1] The disciples as a collective … became known as the White Brotherhood.
Виж „Пояснения относно беседите на Учителя, Лалка Кръстева," Ходете във виделината, с.107
See "Explanations of the Teacher's Lectures, by Lalka Krusteva," *Walk While You Have the Light*, p. 107

the Teacher presented a new book, *The Testament of the Colour Rays of Light*
Завета на цветните лъчи на светлината, София, 1912
The Testament of the Colour Rays of Light, Sofia, 1912

it was written under the guidance of Christ.
See *Explanations and Directions for the Use of the Book The Testament of the Colour Rays of Light*, p. 4

[3] "This book is the first lesson that Christ is giving you…."
Ibid., p. 8

I will tell you the colour corresponding to … Sunday, amethyst.
Ibid., p. 12
(The Teacher said this on 18/31 August 1912.)

When we combine the verses ... humanity will return to its original state.
Ibid., p. 5
(The Teacher said this on 15/28 August 1912.)

56   [4] "Upon a *white* stone shall be seven eyes."
The Testament of the Colour Rays of Light, Vsemir (Universe), Sofia, 1995, p. 59

The Sacred Command of the Teacher ...
Завета на цветните лъчи на светлината, 1912, с. 61
The Testament of the Colour Rays of Light, 1912, p. 61

57   **Gossip**
„Вие сте поканени да работите,“ Ходете във виделината, с. 56–59
"You Are Invited to Work," *Walk While You Have the Light*, pp. 56–59

[2] "On the days when the devil takes hold of you, you are sour, ..."
„Христос ще дойде и ще се прояви,“ Искайте сила, имайте вяра, с. 52
"Christ Will Come and Manifest Himself," *Desire Strength, Have Faith*, p. 52

59   [5] Arbanasi, which is where he wrote ... in the summer of 1912.
Виж Боян Боев, „Как да се употребява книгата на Учителя ‘Завета на цветните
лъчи на светлината,’“ Ходете във виделината, с. 52
See Boyan Boev, "How to Use the Book *The Testament of the Colour Rays of Light*," *Walk
While You Have the Light, p.* 52

60   **Unblocking the Path for Future Disciples**
„Защо ви помагам?“ пак там, с. 60–61
"Why Do I Help You?" *ibid.*, pp. 60–61

[4] "In cases of disputes within the Chain [the Brotherhood], use the yellow ..."
Explanations and Directions for the Use of the Book The Testament of the Colour Rays of Light, pp. 12–13

62   **Correct Thought and Prayer**
„Въжето на дявола,“ Ходете във виделината, с. 62
"The Rope of the Devil," *Walk While You Have the Light*, p. 62

[1] "If we bear the brunt of our mistakes and do not deliberately repeat those ..."
„Равновесие между Мъдрост и Любов,“ Искайте сила, имайте вяра, с. 58
"The Balance Between Wisdom and Love," *Desire Strength, Have Faith*, p. 58

63   **Carry the Cross with Gratitude**
„Преходната граница,“ Ходете във виделината, с. 63–65
"The Border of Transition," *Walk While You Have the Light*, pp. 63–65

66   **Moral Character**
„Обсадно положение,“ пак там, с. 66–67
"A State of Siege," *ibid.*, pp. 66–67

[4] "This war was delayed for two years; it should have begun in 1912"
„Искайте сила, имайте вяра,“ Искайте сила, имайте вяра, с. 56
"Desire Strength, Have Faith," Desire Strength, Have Faith, p. 56

67   [7] "You must restore your inner peace, ..."
      Explanations and Directions for the Use of the Book The Testament of the Colour Rays of Light, p. 13

      [7] "When we were in the Teacher's aura, we were transformed...."
      Живата връзка, Спомени за Учителя Беинса Дуно от Крум Въжаров, Всемир,
         София, 2013, с. 92
      The Living Connection: Reminiscences of the Teacher Beinsa Douno by Krum Vuzharov, Vsemir
         (Universe), Sofia, 2013, p. 92

68   **Monotony and Diversity**
      „Елохим," Ходете във виделината, с. 68–69
      "Elohim," *Walk While You Have the Light*, pp. 68–69

70   **The Dawning Epoch**
      „Същественото за днес," пак там, с. 70–71
      "That Which Is Essential for Today," *ibid.*, pp. 70–71

71   [5] "Animals suffer at the hands of human beings ..."
      „Въжето на дявола," пак там, с. 62
      "The Rope of the Devil," *ibid.*, p. 62

      [5] "In the beginning the human being was a master, ..."
      „Но Син Человечески, кога дойде, дали ще намери вяра на земята," Искайте
         сила, имайте вяра, с. 40
      "When the Son of Man Comes, Will He Find Faith on the Earth?" *Desire Strength, Have
         Faith*, p. 40

      [9] "The invisible world is now using fire as the most efficient way ..."
      Разговорите при Седемте рилски езера, с. 284
      Conversations at the Seven Lakes, p. 284

72   [10] "Archangel Michael is fighting above and will bring down the bad spirits...."
      „Разговор за Откровението," Искайте сила, имайте вяра, с. 28–29
      "A Conversation About the Book of Revelation," *Desire Strength, Have Faith*, pp. 28–29

73   **The Religion of Life**
      „Събрание, водено от г-н П. Дънов," Ходете във виделината, с. 72
      "A Meeting Chaired by Mr P. Deunov," *Walk While You Have the Light*, p. 72

75   **The Name of God**
      „Името Господне," пак там, с. 72–73
      "The Name of the Lord," *ibid.*, pp. 72–73

      [4] "The Spirit gives birth to love, because love is the fruit of this Spirit"
      „Гърбавата жена," Сила и живот, Трета серия, с. 162
      "The Hunchbacked Woman," *Power and Life, Volume Three*, p. 162

      [5] "Christ said that the spiritual eye corresponds with the human heart...."
      „Светило на тялото," пак там, с. 90
      "The Light of the Body," *ibid.*, p. 90

96 [14] "When we pray, we should feel warmth in the place where the soul resides...."
„Равновесие между Мъдрост и Любов," Искайте сила, имайте вяра, с. 58
"The Balance Between Wisdom and Love," *Desire Strength, Have Faith*, p. 58

[14] "The soul is in the whole chest, but it also abides in the pit of the stomach, ..."
„Мисли от г-н Дънов," пак там, с. 17
"Thoughts of Mr Deunov," *ibid.*, p. 17

[16] "A field cannot belong to two masters; it either belongs to good or to evil, ..."
„Четирите основни елемента," пак там, с. 16
"Four Fundamental Elements," *ibid.*, p. 16

98 **From Children of Lucifer to Children of God**
„Като младенци," Ходете във виделината, с. 98–99
"As a Child," *Walk While You Have the Light*, pp. 98–99

99 [7] "There is great meaning in carrying out a good deed in the right way...."
„Отношение на два закона," Новата Ева, Издигнете жената! Печатница:
Венера, София, 1931, с. 22–23
"The Relationship Between Two Laws," *The New Eve: The Upliftment of Women!* Printing
House: Venus, Sofia, 1931, pp. 22–23

102 **A Division in Love Causes Evil**
„Делението," Ходете във виделината, с. 90–91
"Division," *Walk While You Have the Light*, pp. 90–91

103 **The Narrow Path of Development**
„Смел и решителен," пак там, с. 92–94
"Courage and Resolve," *ibid.*, pp. 92–94

105 [11] "Our thoughts and feelings should be in solidarity, ..."
„Равновесие между Мъдрост и Любов," Искайте сила, имайте вяра, с. 58
"The Balance Between Wisdom and Love," *Desire Strength, Have Faith*, p. 58

106 **The Right Desire in Life**
„Ще се приравнят всички по закона на Любовта и Мъдростта," Ходете във
виделината, с. 95–97
"Everybody Will Become Equal Through the Law of Love and Wisdom," *Walk While
You Have the Light*, pp. 95–97

[1] "When people ask what it is to live correctly, the idea of brotherhood ..."
„Но Син Человечески, кога дойде, дали ще намери вяра на земята," Искайте
сила, имайте вяра, с. 40
"When the Son of Man Comes, Will He Find Faith on the Earth?" *Desire Strength, Have
Faith*, p. 40

[1] "The meaning of the new culture is for everybody to have the right ..."
Разговорите при Седемте рилски езера, с. 181
Conversations at the Seven Lakes, p. 181

[1] "The Slavic people now hold the power of the soul, which is love...."
Изворът на доброто, с. 318

The Wellspring of Good, p. 318

108 ⁷ "Our planet is leaving the Thirteenth Sphere. We are passing into new regions …"
„Нова земя,“ Заветът на любовта, III Том, София, 1944, с. 112
"The New Earth," *The Testament of Love, Volume Three*, Sofia, 1944, p. 112

⁷ "The divine fire has two qualities: …"
Разговорите при Седемте рилски езера, с. 202
Conversations at the Seven Lakes, p. 202

109 **Constancy in Life**
„Постоянството. Благословение от Бога,“ Ходете във виделината, с. 100–103
"Constancy: The Blessing of God," *Walk While You Have the Light*, pp. 100–103

² "It is necessary to learn to be exact in everything you do…."
Точността (Общ окултен клас, 8 Април 1923), с. 15
Exactitude (General Occult Class, 8 April 1923), p. 15

³ "The earth is a school …"
„Мисли от г-н Дънов,“ Искайте сила, имайте вяра, с. 17
"Thoughts of Mr Deunov," *Desire Strength, Have Faith*, p. 17

110 ⁴ "When people offend us they are deluded in some way, …"
„Мисли от г-н Дънов,“ пак там, с. 17
"Thoughts of Mr Deunov," *ibid.*, p. 17

114 **Spiritual Light, the Nourishment of the Soul**
„Поздрав за Новата 1914 година. Към всички,“ пак там, с. 3–8
"Greetings to All for the New Year of 1914," *ibid.*, pp. 3–8

115 ⁴ "Why do branches grow up and roots grow down? …"
„Но Син Человечески, кога дойде, дали ще намери вяра на земята,“ пак там, с. 40
"When the Son of Man Comes, Will He Find Faith on the Earth?" *ibid.*, p. 40

119 **The Beginning of the New Epoch**
„Беседа за празника на пролетта,“ пак там, с. 9–13
"Lecture for the Spring Feast," *ibid.*, pp. 9–13

¹ "We are at the boundary of two epochs…."
Разговорите при Седемте рилски езера, с. 283
Conversations at the Seven Lakes, p. 283

¹ "Our Solar System is leaving the Thirteenth Sphere, which has condensed …"
Пак там, с. 86
Ibid., p. 86

¹ "The Earth is still passing through a dark zone, but the future will be bright…."
Новият ден, с. 46
The New Day, p. 46

120 ³ "In the spiritual life we must constantly be sowing if we want to harvest later on"
Explanations and Directions for the Use of the Book The Testament of the Colour Rays of Light, p. 6

[6] "The physical body is given to us as rough material …"
„Мисли от г-н Дънов,“ Искайте сила, имайте вяра, с. 19
"Thoughts of Mr Deunov," *Desire Strength, Have Faith*, p. 19

121   [10] "The human soul has none of the qualities of the fallen souls, …"
„Равновесие между Мъдрост и Любов,“ пак там, с. 58
"The Balance Between Wisdom and Love," *ibid.*, p. 58

123   **Behold the Man! The True Human Being**
„„Ето човекът!““ Сила и живот, Първа серия, Второ издание, Печатница:
     Гутенберг, Казанлък, 1924, с. 3–14
"'Behold the Man!'" *Power and Life, Volume One*, Second edition, Printing House:
     Gutenberg, Kazanluk, 1924, pp. 3–14

124   [5] "The sun shines every day…."
„Четирите основни елемента,“ Искайте сила, имайте вяра, с. 15
"Four Fundamental Elements," *Desire Strength, Have Faith*, p. 15

127   [11] "The people of the sixth race will have correct features…."
Изворът на доброто, с. 309
The Wellspring of Good, p. 309

129   [14] "The meaning of love is to keep Christ's commandments, …"
„Ако ме любите ще опазите моите заповеди,“ Разсмотрете криновете в полето
     как растат, с. 4
"If You Love Me, You Will Keep My Commandments," *Consider the Lilies of the Field, How
     They Grow*, p. 4

130   [20] "When Christ comes to someone, he or she will feel …"
„Христос ще дойде и ще се прояви,“ Искайте сила, имайте вяра, с. 50
"Christ Will Come and Manifest Himself," *Desire Strength, Have Faith*, p. 50

131   [22] "A town gave some of its population the task of finding out why …"
„Докато фарисеят не стане митар, не може да бъде християнин,“ пак там, с. 31
"A Pharisee Cannot Become a Christian Until He Becomes a Publican," *ibid.*, p. 31

136   [39] "We seek Christ and we find him, but when he appears inside us …"
„Ако ме любите ще опазите моите заповеди,“ Разсмотрете криновете в полето
     как растат, с. 5
"If You Love Me, You Will Keep My Commandments," *Consider the Lilies of the Field,
     How They Grow*, p. 5

137   **The Grain of Wheat, the Emblem of the Human Soul**
„Житното зърно,“ Сила и живот, Първа серия, с. 15–28
"The Grain of Wheat," *Power and Life, Volume One*, pp. 15–28

139   [5] "We love someone very much because he or she gives something to us…."
„Четирите основни елемента,“ Искайте сила, имайте вяра, с. 14–15
"Four Fundamental Elements," *Desire Strength, Have Faith*, pp. 14–15

144   [23] "The existence of everything in our lives comes from Christ, …"
„Познайте истината и истината ще ви направи свободни," пак там, с. 21
"Know the Truth and the Truth Will Set You Free," *ibid.*, p. 21

147   [27] "It is impossible for everyone to become spiritual; …"
„Докато фарисеят не стане митар, не може да бъде християнин," пак там, с. 31
"A Pharisee Cannot Become a Christian Until He Becomes a Publican," *ibid.*, p. 31

    [28] "We ask, 'Why does the Lord keep us in this suffering?' …"
„Но Син Человечески, кога дойде, дали ще намери вяра на земята," пак там, с. 37, 43
"When the Son of Man Comes, Will He Find Faith on the Earth?" *ibid.*, pp. 37, 43

150   **The Spirit Manifests Itself to Every Soul**
„Явлението на Духа," Сила и живот, Първа серия, с. 29–43
"The Manifestation of the Spirit," *Power and Life, Volume One*, pp. 29–43

151   [5] "We are bound with thousands of obligations in life: …"
„Познайте истината и истината ще ви направи свободни," Искайте сила, имайте вяра, с. 20–21
"Know the Truth and the Truth Will Set You Free," *Desire Strength, Have Faith*, pp. 20–21

152   [6] "The human being is a tripartite being, …"
„Разговор за Откровението," пак там, с. 29
"The Book of Revelation," *ibid.*, p. 29

    [6] "Contemporary science has studied the human body in detail, …"
„Ако солта обезсолее, с какво ще се осоли?" пак там, с. 44
"If the Salt Has Lost Its Saltiness, with What Will It Be Salted?" *ibid.*, p. 44

    [7] "From a religious point of view there needs to be layers…."
„Докато фарисеят не стане митар, не може да бъде християнин," пак там, с. 31
"A Pharisee Cannot Become a Christian Until He Becomes a Publican," *ibid.*, p. 31

153   [9] "Each thought, feeling and deed that we understand is a great blessing …"
„Реалността на живота," Езикът на Любовта, с. 53
"The Reality in Life," *The Language of Love*, p. 53

156   [12] "Our ideal should be to love God, who has given us life…."
„Ако солта обезсолее, с какво ще се осоли?" Искайте сила, имайте вяра, с. 48
"If the Salt Has Lost Its Saltiness, with What Will It Be Salted?" *Desire Strength, Have Faith*, p. 48

160   **Divine Gifts: The Parable of the Talents**
„Талантите," Сила и живот, Първа серия, с. 45–55
"Talents," *Power and Life, Volume One*, pp. 45–55

161   [3] "You need to follow the law of rhythm…."
„Христос ще дойде и ще се прояви," Искайте сила, имайте вяра, с. 55
"Christ Will Come and Manifest Himself," *Desire Strength, Have Faith*, p. 55

168   [8] "Thank the Lord when you eat, ..."
„Мисли от г-н Дънов," пак там, с. 18
"Thoughts of Mr Deunov," *ibid.*, p. 18

170   **Love, Patience and Benevolence**
„Любовта," Сила и живот, Първа серия, с. 57–72
"Love," *Power and Life, Volume One*, pp. 57–72

    [2] "Human life is made of two substances: acid and alkali...."
„Ако солта обезсолее, с какво ще се осоли?" Искайте сила, имайте вяра, с. 44–45
"If the Salt Has Lost Its Saltiness, with What Will It Be Salted?" *Desire Strength, Have Faith*, pp. 44–45

    [2] "A person needs to be ever young of heart and mature of mind"
„Деца по сърце," Ходете във виделината, с. 45
"Children in Their Heart," *Walk While You Have the Light*, p. 45

171   [3] "There are three things which can deceive us ..."
„Ако солта обезсолее, с какво ще се осоли?" Искайте сила, имайте вяра, с. 46
"If the Salt Has Lost Its Saltiness, with What Will It Be Salted?" *Desire Strength, Have Faith*, p. 46

173   [10] "A primary quality of a saint is patience"
„Разговор за Откровението," пак там, с. 28
"The Book of Revelation," *ibid.*, p. 28

178   [16] "Gratitude is a medicine which frees human beings from all difficulties ..."
„За Слава Божия," Устойчиви величини, с. 296
"The Glory of God," *Stable Quantities*, p. 296

182   [24] "The Bulgarians are saying, 'We have been beaten ... "
„Разговор за Откровението," Искайте сила, имайте вяра, с. 29–30
"The Book of Revelation," *Desire Strength, Have Faith*, pp. 29–30

183   **Nobility of Character: The Example of Joseph**
„Сънищата на Йосифа," Сила и живот, Първа серия, с. 73–85
"The Dreams of Joseph," *Power and Life, Volume One*, pp. 73–85

187   [11] "You should avoid sexual intimacy with promiscuous people, ..."
Акордиране на човешката душа, I Том, с. 190
The Tuning of the Human Soul, Volume One, p. 190

    [13] "It was not long before Eve became dissatisfied with Adam...."
„Ще бъдат научени," Да възлюбиш Господа, Печатница: Житно зърно, София, 1946, с. 53
"They Will Be Taught," *You Will Love the Lord*, Printing House: Grain of Wheat, Sofia, 1946, p. 53

195   **The Law of Service**
„Законът на служенето," Сила и живот, Първа серия, с. 87–99
"The Law of Service," *Power and Life, Volume One*, pp. 87–99

212 [11] "Everyone should follow the teachings of Christ, …"
„Ако ме любите ще опазите моите заповеди," Разсмотрете криновете в полето как растат, с. 5
"If You Love Me, You Will Keep My Commandments," *Consider the Lilies of the Field, How They Grow*, p. 5

[13] "In the future people will cast out the nets of their personal occupations …"
„Христос ще дойде и ще се прояви," Искайте сила, имайте вяра, с. 55
"Christ Will Come and Manifest Himself," *Desire Strength, Have Faith*, p. 55

214 **Immortality: Attuning Ourselves to the Lord**
„„Мир вам!"" Сила и живот, Първа серия, с. 109–117
"Peace Be with You," *Power and Life, Volume One*, pp. 109–117

[3] "Death is just decayed matter.…"
„Ако солта обезсолее, с какво ще се осоли?" Искайте сила, имайте вяра, с. 46–47
"If the Salt Has Lost Its Saltiness, with What Will It Be Salted?" *Desire Strength, Have Faith*, pp. 46–47

217 [10] "When you do not understand a feeling, it causes a depression in your heart.…"
„Реалността на живота," Езикът на Любовта, с. 43
"The Reality in Life," *The Language of Love*, p. 43

222 **Knowing God Is Eternal Life**
„Необходимостта да познаваме Бога," Сила и живот, Първа серия, с. 119–134
"The Necessity of Knowing God," *Power and Life, Volume One*, pp. 119–134

227 [13] "The people of the sixth race will not die.…"
Изворът на доброто, с. 308–309
The Wellspring of Good, pp. 308–309

236 **The Value of Human Life**
„Колко по-горе стои човек от овца!" Сила и живот, Първа серия, с. 135–147
"How Much More Valuable Is a Human Being than a Sheep!" *Power and Life, Volume One*, pp. 135–147

239 [6] "To kill someone is not a manifestation of will.…"
„Но Син Человечески, кога дойде, дали ще намери вяра на земята," Искайте сила, имайте вяра, с. 38
"When the Son of Man Comes, Will He Find Faith on the Earth?" *Desire Strength, Have Faith*, p. 38

242 [17] "There are three laws in our society which connect us.…"
Explanations and Directions for the Use of the Book The Testament of the Colour Rays of Light, pp. 10–11

[17] "To 'Be perfect as our heavenly Father is perfect' means …"
Ibid., p. 14

247 **The Pharisee and the Publican: The Basis of All Human Types**
„Фарисей и Митар," Сила и живот, Първа серия, с. 149–167

291 [10] "The disciple should not occupy himself or herself with the mistakes ..."
„Важни правила," Трите живота, Второ издание, Литопечат, София, 1942, с. 49
"Important Rules," *Three Lives*, Second Edition, Lithoprint, Sofia, 1942, p. 49

[10] "Never allow an impure person into your soul...."
„Разсмотрете криновете в полето как растат," Разсмотрете криновете в полето
как растат, с. 8
"Consider the Lilies of the Field, How They Grow," *Consider the Lilies of the Field, How They Grow*, p. 8

292 [12] "Divine love is a necessity that is expressed in a blessing...."
„Ако ме любите ще опазите моите заповеди," пак там, с. 3
"If You Love Me, You Will Keep My Commandments," *ibid.*, p. 3

293 [13] "It is better to be aware of your sinful desire and to free yourself of it ..."
„Вяра, надежда и любов," Дреха на живота, Печатница: Житно зърно, София,
1950, с. 58–59
"Faith, Hope and Love," *The Clothing of Life*, Printing House: Grain of Wheat, Sofia,
1950, pp. 58–59

296 **The Milk of the Word**
„Словесното мляко," Сила и живот, Втора серия, с. 129–141
"The Milk of the Word," *Power and Life, Volume Two*, pp. 129–141

300 [12] "The second greatest law, to love your neighbour, applies to the female ..."
„Отношение на два закона," Новата Ева, с. 35–36
"The Relationship Between Two Laws," *The New Eve*, pp. 35–36

301 [15] "A chemist learns about the laws which govern the elements, ..."
„Но Син Человечески, кога дойде, дали ще намери вяра на земята," Искайте
сила, имайте вяра, с. 38
"When the Son of Man Comes, Will He Find Faith on the Earth?" *Desire Strength, Have Faith*, p. 38

305 **Only God May Appoint Spiritual Teachers**
„Учителите," Сила и живот, Втора серия, с. 99–127
"Teachers," *Power and Life, Volume Two*, pp. 99–127

306 [3] "What we call the building of the spiritual body means ..."
Акордиране на човешката душа, I Том, с. 191
The Tuning of the Human Soul, Volume One, p. 191

[5] "We always need a standard by which to measure our thoughts and desires...."
„Познайте истината и истината ще ви направи свободни," Искайте сила,
имайте вяра, с. 20
"Know the Truth and the Truth Will Set You Free," *Desire Strength, Have Faith*, p. 20

312 [14] "According to the Teacher, when we are in contact with the spiritually wise ..."
Живата връзка, с. 63
The Living Connection, p. 63

330 ³ "In the first human culture there were only men. Women did not exist...."
„Ще бъдат научени," Да възлюбиш Господа, с. 52–53
"They Will Be Taught," *You Will Love the Lord*, pp. 52–53

⁴ "By the word 'matter' we mean 'a mother that gives birth'...."
„Но Син Човечески, кога дойде, дали ще намери вяра на земята," Искайте
    сила, имайте вяра, с. 40
"When the Son of Man Comes, Will He Find Faith on the Earth?" *Desire Strength, Have
    Faith*, p. 40

332 ⁸ "I know the Lord better than I know you...."
„Христос ще дойде и ще се прояви," пак там, с. 53
"Christ Will Come and Manifest Himself," *ibid.*, p. 53

333 ⁹ "We ought to keep good relations with everybody...."
„Ако ме любите ще опазите моите заповеди," Разсмотрете криновете в полето
    как растат, с. 4
"If You Love Me, You Will Keep My Commandments," *Consider the Lilies of the Field,
    How They Grow*, p. 4

335 ¹⁸ "What did the Creator intend by the number 'one'? ..."
„Но Син Човечески, кога дойде, дали ще намери вяра на земята," Искайте
    сила, имайте вяра, с. 39–40
"When the Son of Man Comes, Will He Find Faith on the Earth?" *Desire Strength, Have
    Faith*, pp. 39–40

¹⁸ "Humanity will be saved by the uplifting of the heart...."
„Отношение на два закона," Новата Ева, с. 36, 39–40
"The Relationship Between Two Laws," *The New Eve*, pp. 36, 39–40

336 ¹⁹ "Christ wants us to use the touchstone, which is our divine souls...."
„Познайте истината и истината ще ви направи свободни," Искайте сила,
    имайте вяра, с. 21–22
"Know the Truth and the Truth Will Set You Free," *Desire Strength, Have Faith*, pp. 21–22

337 ²¹ "People's bad thoughts and desires form a dark belt around the earth"
„8000 години," пак там, с. 59
"Eight Thousand Years", *ibid.*, p. 59

340 **The New Foundation of Christ**
„Новото основание," Сила и живот, Втора серия, с. 27–54
"The New Foundation," *Power and Life, Volume Two*, pp. 27–54

344 ⁸ "Happy are they who can benefit from their unhappiness by learning ..."
„Но Син Човечески, кога дойде, дали ще намери вяра на земята," Искайте
    сила, имайте вяра, с. 42
"When the Son of Man Comes, Will He Find Faith on the Earth?" *Desire Strength, have
    Faith*, p. 42

345 ¹² "People's honesty may be measured by the amount of money it takes ..."
„Ако солта обезсолее, с какво ще се осоли?" пак там, с. 47

"If the Salt Has Lost Its Saltiness, with What Will It Be Salted?" *ibid.*, p. 47

346 [13] "A Christian's power is expressed in fighting the devil...."
„Ако ме любите ще опазите моите заповеди," Разсмотрете криновете в полето как растат, с. 4
"If You Love Me, You Will Keep My Commandments," *Consider the Lilies of the Field, How They Grow*, p. 4

[14] "If thou hadst known how to suffer, thou wouldest have been able ..."
The Apocryphal New Testament: Being the Apocryphal Gospels, Acts, Epistles, and Apocalypses, with Other Narratives and Fragments Newly Translated, The Clarendon Press, Oxford, 1960, p. 254

347 [17] "I understand the word 'man' to mean 'a being that thinks'...."
„Ще бъдат научени," Да възлюбиш Господа, с. 52–53
"They Will Be Taught," *You Will Love the Lord*, pp. 52–53

349 [20] "I could tell you about the whole plan for the present war, ..."
„Христос ще дойде и ще се прояви," Искайте сила, имайте вяра, с. 54
"Christ Will Come and Manifest Himself," *Desire Strength, Have Faith*, p. 54

350 [22] "There is an important law which states that when a woman loves a man, ..."
„Отношение на два закона," Новата Ева, с. 35
"The Relationship Between Two Laws," *The New Eve*, p. 35

351 [23] "When God speaks to our souls, we should say, 'I can do it.' ..."
„Четирите основни елемента," Искайте сила, имайте вяра, с. 15–16
"Four Fundamental Elements," *Desire Strength, Have Faith*, pp. 15–16

353 **Divine Providence**
„Божественият промисъл," Сила и живот, Втора серия, с. 179–188
"Divine Providence," *Power and Life, Volume Two*, pp. 179–188

359 **The New Wineskins: Those Who Are Ready for the Teaching of Christ**
„Стари и нови мехове," пак там, с. 143–157
"Old and New Wineskins," *ibid.*, pp. 143–157

364 [11] "The entire physical world is entering a new phase, ..."
„Плодовете на Духа," Сила и живот, Шеста серия, с. 401–2
"Fruits of the Spirit," *Power and Life, Volume Six*, pp. 401–2

366 [15] "In the spiritual world the beings are fed with nectar ..."
„Мисли от г-н Дънов," Искайте сила, имайте вяра, с. 17
"Thoughts of Mr Deunov," *Desire Strength, Have Faith*, p. 17

367 **The Freedom of the Spirit**
„Свобода на Духа," Сила и живот, Втора серия, с. 159–177
"The Freedom of the Spirit," *Power and Life, Volume Two*, pp. 159–177

[3] "When you lose the conditions you need for your development, ..."
„Познайте истината и истината ще ви направи свободни," Искайте сила, имайте вяра, с. 20
"Know the Truth and the Truth Will Set You Free," *Desire Strength, Have Faith*, p. 20

369 [10] "Everyone aspires to freedom in this world...."
Пак там
Ibid.

[10] "Everyone is free to test the karmic law in the world, ..."
Explanations and Directions for the Use of the Book The Testament of the Colour Rays of Light, p. 4

370 [12] "If someone says, 'God is good,' he or she should prove the truth ..."
„Изново," Новата Ева, с. 96
"Starting Again," *The New Eve*, p. 96

371 [16] "Group prayer has power when there is harmony among the participants"
„Вяра," Аз ви избрах, Всемир, София, 1995, с. 51
"Faith," *I Choose You*," Vsemir (Universe), Sofia, 1995, p. 51

372 [18] "You should not interrupt a person who is speaking...."
„Разсмотрете криновете в полето как растат" Разсмотрете криновете в полето
как растат, с. 8
"Consider the Lilies of the Field, How They Grow," *Consider the Lilies of the Field, How
They Grow*, p. 8

376 [26] "Follow these rules of life...."
Живата връзка, с. 242
The Living Connection, p. 242

377 [28] "Not all thoughts and desires and the things we work towards bring us freedom...."
„Познайте истината и истината ще ви направи свободни," Искайте сила,
имайте вяра, с. 20
"Know the Truth and the Truth Will Set You Free," *Desire Strength, Have Faith*, p. 20

378 [30] "To obtain freedom we must be thankful for everything that happens to us, ..."
„Познайте истината и истината ще ви направи свободни," пак там, с. 22
"Know the Truth and the Truth Will Set You Free," ibid., p. 22

Appendices

Appendix C
384 Conception and pregnancy are important processes....
Изново," Новата Ева, с. 123–125
"Starting Again," *The New Eve*, pp. 123–125

Bibliography

Published Lectures
In chronological order of content, according to the first lecture of each book

Петър Дънов, Ходете във виделината, Всемир, София, 1994
Peter Deunov, *Walk While You Have the Light*, Vsemir (Universe), Sofia, 1994

Beinsa Douno, *Explanations and Directions for the Use of the Book The Testament of the Colour Rays of Light*, Vsemir (Universe), Sofia, 1995[1]

Петър Дънов, Искайте сила, имайте вяра, Всемир, София, 1994
Peter Deunov, *Desire Strength, Have Faith*, Vsemir (Universe), Sofia, 1994

Петър Дънов, Сила и живот, Първа серия, Второ издание, Печатница: Гутенберг, Казанлък, 1924
Peter Deunov, *Power and Life, Volume One*, Second Edition, Printing House: Gutenberg, Kazanluk, 1924

Петър Дънов, Разсмотрете криновете в полето как растат, Всемир, София, 1997
Peter Deunov, *Consider the Lilies of the Field, How They Grow*, Vsemir (Universe), Sofia, 1997

Петър Дънов, Сила и живот, Втора серия, Второ издание, Печатница: Малджиев, Русе, 1927
Peter Deunov, *Power and Life, Volume Two*, Second Edition, Printing House: Maldzhiev, Ruse, 1927

Учителят, Да възлюбиш Господа, Печатница: Житно зърно, София, 1946
The Teacher, *You Will Love the Lord*, Printing House: Grain of Wheat, Sofia, 1946

Петър Дънов, Сила и живот, Трета серия, Солта, Второ издание, Печатница: Гужгулов и Котев, София, 1920
Peter Deunov, *Power and Life, Volume Three: The Salt*, Second Edition, Printing House: Guzhgulov and Kotev, Sofia, 1920

Петър Дънов, Аз ви избрах, Всемир, София, 1995
Peter Deunov, *I Choose You*, Vsemir (Universe), Sofia, 1995

Учителят, Трите живота, Второ издание, Литопечат, София, 1942
The Teacher, *Three Lives*, Second Edition, Lithoprint, Sofia, 1942

Учителят, Устойчиви величини, Литопечат, София, 1943
The Teacher, *Stable Quantities*, Lithoprint, Sofia 1943

Учителят, Съмнение и воля! (Общ окултен клас, 11 февруари 1923)
The Teacher, *Doubt and Willpower!* (General Occult Class, 11 February 1923)

---

[1] Extracts from this book may have undergone some reworking to improve the translation or to match the style of the present volume. Therefore, none should be assumed to be pure quotation.

Учителят, Точността (Общ окултен клас, 8 април 1923), Печатница: Малджиев,
    Русе, 1923
The Teacher, *Exactitude* (General Occult Class, 8 April 1923), Printing House: Maldzhiev,
    Ruse, 1923

Учителят, Вяра и съмнение (Общ окултен клас, 17 юни 1923), Печатница:
    Малджиев, Русе, 1923
The Teacher, *Faith and Doubt* (General Occult Class, 17 June 1923), Printing House:
    Maldzhiev, Ruse, 1923

Петър Дънов, Сила и живот, Шеста серия, Двата природни метода, Печатница:
    Фотинов, София
Peter Deunov, *Power and Life, Volume Six: Two Natural Methods*, Printing House: Fotinov, Sofia

Учителят, Разумния живот, Печатница: Малджиев, Русе
The Teacher, *The Spiritually Wise Life*, Printing House: Maldzhiev, Ruse

Учителят, Новият ден, София, 1940
The Teacher, *The New Day*, Sofia, 1940

Учителят, Новата Ева, Издигнете жената! Печатница: Венера, София, 1931
The Teacher, *The New Eve: The Upliftment of Women!* Printing House: Venus, Sofia, 1931

Учителят, Дреха на живота, Печатница: Житно зърно, София, 1950
The Teacher, *The Clothing of Life*, Printing House: Grain of Wheat, Sofia, 1950

Учителят, Езикът на Любовта, Литопечат, София, 1939
The Teacher, *The Language of Love*, Lithoprint, Sofia, 1939

Учителят, Заветът на любовта, III Том, София, 1944
The Teacher, *The Testament of Love, Volume Three*, Sofia, 1944

Book by the Teacher

Беинса Дуно, Завета на цветните лъчи на светлината, София, 1912
Beinsa Douno, *The Testament of the Colour Rays of Light*, Sofia, 1912

Beinsa Douno (Peter Deunov), *The Testament of the Colour Rays of Light*, Vsemir (Universe),
    Sofia, 1995

Books by Disciples

Учителят, Съставители: Методи Константинов, Боян Боев, Мария Тодорова, Борис
    Николов, Печатница: Изгрев, София, 1947
The Teacher, Compiled by Metodi Konstantinov, Boyan Boev, Maria Todorova and Boris
    Nikolov, Printing House: Izgrev, Sofia, 1947

411

Учителят, Разговорите при Седемте рилски езера, Представят: Методи
Константинов, Боян Боев, Мария Тодорова, Борис Николов, София, 1948
The Teacher, *Conversations at the Seven Lakes*, Presented by Metodi Konstantinov, Boyan Boev,
Maria Todorova and Boris Nikolov, Sofia, 1948[2]

Петър Дънов, Изворът на доброто, Последно Слово на Учителя, Мърчаево – 1944
година, Записал словото Боян Боев, Съставитекство Борис Николов, Редактирано
от Мария Кисова, Роял – 77, Варна, 1992
Peter Deunov, *The Wellspring of Good: The Last Word of the Teacher*, in Murchaevo in 1944, Recorded
by Boyan Boev, Compiled by Boris Nikolov, Edited by Maria Kisova, Royal 77, Varna,
1992[3]

Словото на Учителя: Каталог, Съставител Лалка Кръстева, Всемир, София, 1998
The Word of the Teacher: Catalogue, Compiled by Lalka Krusteva, Vsemir (Universe), Sofia, 1998

Учителя Беинса Дуно, Акордиране на човешката душа, I Том, Архив на Боян Боев,
Бяло Братство, 1999, София
The Teacher Beinsa Douno, *The Tuning of the Human Soul*, Volume One, Recorded by Boyan Boev,
Byalo Bratstvo (White Brotherhood), Sofia, 1999[4]

Живата връзка, Спомени за Учителя Беинса Дуно от Крум Въжаров, Съставител
Мария Митовска, Всемир, София, 2013
The Living Connection: Reminiscences of the Teacher Beinsa Douno by Krum Vuzharov, Compiled by Maria
Mitovska, Vsemir (Universe), Sofia, 2013

Scripture

The Holy Bible (Revised Version, 1885), Oxford, 1921

Библия, Печатница: Х. Матеосян, Цариград, 1914
The Bulgarian Bible (Revision of 1871 Constantinople Edition), Printing House:
H. Mateosyan, Constantinople, 1914

Montague Rhodes James, *The Apocryphal New Testament: Being the Apocryphal Gospels, Acts, Epistles, and
Apocalypses, with Other Narratives and Fragments Newly Translated*, The Clarendon Press, Oxford,
1960 (first published in 1924; reprinted with appendices by J. W. B. Barns in 1953)

---

[2] Although not credited in the publication, it was openly known among the disciples that it was Boyan Boev who had noted down these words of the Teacher. The book consists of undated conversations during the Brotherhood's annual summer camps in the Seven Lakes region of the Rila Mountains. On page 7, it says the first of these recorded talks was in 1929 and the last in 1942, hence quotations from this book are dated "some time between 1929 and 1942".

[3] From January to October 1944 the Teacher stayed in the village of Murchaevo, in the foot of the western part of Vitosha Mountain, and his words in this book were said there during that time but not specifically dated. Quotations from it are therefore dated simply "1944".

[4] On page 5, it says that Boyan Boev began taking shorthand notes of the Teacher's conversations in 1924. None of the conversations that have been used from this book were dated, and therefore they are given as "some time between 1924 and 1944".